PIMLICO

33

THE EDWARDIAN
TURN OF MIND

Samuel Hynes was born in Chicago in 1924 and was educated at the University of Minnesota and Columbia University. He has taught at Swarthmore College, Northwestern University and Princeton University. From 1943 to 1946, and again in 1952-3, he served as a pilot in the United States Marine Corps. His books include *The Pattern of Hardy's Poetry*, *Edwardian Occasions* and *Flights of Passage: Reflections of a World War II Aviator*.

The Edwardian Turn of Mind is the first volume of Samuel Hynes's trilogy of cultural histories covering the relationship between literature, theatre and public events during the first decades of the twentieth century. The others – *A War Imagined* and *The Auden Generation* – are also published by Pimlico.

Edwardian London, by Alvin Langdon Coburn

THE EDWARDIAN
TURN OF MIND

———

SAMUEL HYNES

PIMLICO

PIMLICO

20 Vauxhall Bridge Road, London SW1V 2SA

London Melbourne Sydney Auckland Johannesburg
and agencies throughout the world

First published by Princeton University Press 1968
Pimlico edition 1991

Printed and bound in Great Britain by
Mackays of Chatham PLC, Chatham, Kent

ISBN 0-7126-5028-8

Preface

This is a book about England in the years just before the First World War—the period we call Edwardian, though its roots are in the 1890's and its end is August 1914. That time stands in an odd pivotal position between the nineteenth century and the twentieth: it was not quite Victorian, though conservatives tried to make it so, nor was it altogether modern, though it contained the beginnings of many ideas that we recognize as our own. It was a brief stretch of history, but a troubled and dramatic one—like the English Channel, a narrow place made turbulent by the thrust and tumble of two powerful opposing tides. That turbulent meeting of old and new makes the Edwardian period both interesting and important, for out of the turmoil contemporary England was made.

In this Edwardian conflict of old and new, "old" is, generally speaking, a Victorian inheritance. In some cases the ideas and attitudes it identifies were advanced in their time —as in the case of Victorian science, of literary conventions, and of Liberal political principles—but by 1900 these ideas had begun to seem inadequate, limited, and restrictive. "New" means all those movements of the early twentieth century that aimed at liberating English society from the stiff limitations of its immediate past.

The meeting of old and new in Edwardian England was complex and cannot be described simply in terms of generations, or of classes, or of political parties. The sides were not clearly drawn, loyalties were shifting and uncertain, and even within single groups or movements there were curious anomalies (how was it, for example, that so many Edwardian Socialists admired Nietzsche?). The extraordinary crudity and violence with which many Edwardians faced the issues of their time may in part be explained by the circumstance that they were often uncertain of where they stood and of who stood with them.

Some of these conflicts, the fighting of them, and the consequences, are the subject of this book. I have selected the areas of conflict that seem to me most crucial—politics, science, the arts, the relations between men and women—and within those areas I have selected the examples and the individuals that have interested me most. No doubt the fact that I came to the period as a student of literature has influenced my decisions: certainly I have found the literary forms of the conflicts both entertaining and useful to an understanding of the literary history of the time. The object of my study, however, is not literary history but the intellectual climate of Edwardian England.

Like many American scholars I have been aided in this work in the most essential way by foundations. The John Simon Guggenheim Memorial Foundation supported a year of research in London in 1959-60, and the Bollingen Foundation made a second year of research and writing possible in 1964-65. Swarthmore College has also been generous in granting leave and research funds.

I wish also to acknowledge the other kind of scholar's debt —to the people who helped me to gather the materials on which this book is built. The late Alvin Langdon Coburn, greatest of Edwardian photographers, shared his recollections with me and allowed me access to his file of pictures of the period, some of which are published here for the first time. Mr. Arthur Crook, of the *Times Literary Supplement*, provided information about the early days of that journal and published a version of my Chapter I. Mr. Jonathan Sofer patiently guided me through the intricacies of English law and legal records. Mrs. C.F.G. Masterman advised me on the genealogy of her family, the Lytteltons, which appears here as Appendix B. Mr. F. Seymour Smith, of W. H. Smith & Sons, opened the firm's archives to me. Mr. C.S.A. Dobson,

Librarian of the House of Lords, showed me the Gosse materials there. Mr. G. Woledge, Librarian of the British Library of Political and Economic Science, London School of Economics, allowed me to examine the Passfield papers. I also received generous assistance from the staffs of the Fabian Society, the Society of Authors, the Society for Psychical Research, the Tate Gallery, and the Theosophical Society in England. Mr. Howard Williams, Reference Librarian of the Swarthmore College Library, came to my aid many times. Miss Catherine Crowther, of Lady Margaret Hall, Oxford, helped in last-minute research and in the selection of illustrations.

I have been encouraged, advised, and instructed in the writing of history by generous colleagues, of whom I should like particularly to thank Professor Jean Herskovits, of the History Department, City College, City University of New York. Whatever errors of fact or judgment remain are, of course, my own, but there are fewer of them because I have historical friends.

Swarthmore, Pennsylvania

Acknowledgments

....

Mrs. George Bambridge, the Macmillan Company of Canada, and Methuen & Co., Ltd., for lines from "The Islanders," copyright 1902, from *Five Nations*; Mrs. Bambridge, Macmillan, Methuen, and Doubleday & Co., Inc., for lines from "For all we have and are," copyright 1914, from *The Years Between*.

Mrs. Dorothy Cheston Bennett and Methuen & Co., Ltd., for Arnold Bennett's *Whom God Hath Joined*.

Victor Bonham Carter, and the Society of Authors, for the minutes of the Council of the Society.

The Trustees of the Galsworthy Estate, England, for the extracts on pp. 85-86 and 128-29.

William Heinemann, Ltd., for two cartoons by Max Beerbohm: "Mr. John Galsworthy envisaging Life," from H. V. Marrot's *Life and Letters of John Galsworthy*, and "Mr. Asquith in Office," from Beerbohm's *Fifty Caricatures*.

Mrs. Eva Reichmann, for Max Beerbohm's "C. F. Masterman preserving his ideals."

The Fabian Society, for H. G. Wells' *The Faults of the Fabian*.

Field, Roscoe & Co., Ltd., for a letter by Harley Granville Barker.

The Illustrated London News, for pictures of the trial of Lord Russell and the King's garden party.

The Raymond Mander and Joe Mitchenson Theatre Collection, for a photograph of Nijinsky's *Le Sacre du Printemps*.

The Mansell Collection, for a photograph of the funeral of King Edward VII.

Mr. Beaumont Newhall, Director, George Eastman House, for four photographs by Alvin Langdon Coburn.

ACKNOWLEDGMENTS

The Honorable John Parker, Secretary of the Beatrice Webb Trust, for the Fabian Window.

The Trustees of the Passfield Trust, for Beatrice Webb's *Our Partnership*, and for quotations from the Passfield Papers.

The Victoria and Albert Museum, for photographs of *An Englishman's Home* and *Votes for Women!*

The Executors of the Estate of H. G. Wells, for quotations from his letters and books.

J. B. Lippincott Company, Collins-Knowlton-Wing, Inc., and the copyright (renewed 1962) owners, George Philip Wells and Francis Richard Wells, for quotations from H. G. Wells' *Experiment in Autobiography*.

The Public Trustee and the Society of Authors, for an unpublished letter of George Bernard Shaw.

Contents

....

ILLUSTRATIONS

THE EDWARDIAN

TURN OF MIND

Chapter I

....

THE EDWARDIAN GARDEN PARTY

....

In a familiar portrait photograph, King Edward VII and Queen Alexandra sit, posed stiffly on straight-backed chairs, in a garden. They are dressed in the formally elegant manner of their age and class: the King wears a light-colored top hat and a frock coat with an enormous carnation in the buttonhole and holds a stick; the Queen's hat is veiled and plumed, a parasol rests against her knee, and a feather boa droops from her chair. Behind them stretches an avenue of trees, orderly and straight and striped with sun, reaching far back to a spot of light. Although we can see far behind the two figures, we cannot see what it is that they face with such stiff composure.

This picture may stand as an emblem of the Edwardian Age: a present, dominated by King and Queen, symbols of the established order—rich, punctilious, and unoccupied— and behind them the past, a corridor of peace, sunlit and pastoral. But in the scene there is some incongruity. Why are the drawing-room chairs on the lawn? Are topper and boa quite right for this occasion? And what are the royal subjects watching? The scene is a highly artificial one, held together, one feels, by the will of the watchful King. Somewhere just out of camera range are elements of disorder that will soon make this scene anachronistic. Still, for the moment how opulent, how stable, how peaceful it all seems.

This is scarcely a complete picture of Edwardian England, but it is the first picture that the word "Edwardian" calls up, because it has the King himself at its center. As English reigns go, Edward's was a short one; but few monarchs have so precisely embodied the spirit of their time. Edward VII was a man who cared, as his time cared, for material things and fleshly pleasures; he was overweight and overdressed, and his appetites were of a sort that, though in a king they may be called convivial, would be called gross in a common man. He was sociable and popular with all classes, and he valued his popularity more highly than the more traditional kingly virtues of dignity and respect; the *Times* rightly observed that, had he been born to a humbler station, he would have made a successful business man. His habits were the easy, extravagant habits of the Edwardian rich: racing, gambling, shooting, and sailing; journeys to continental spas filled much of his time; and though he realized the responsibilities of his crown, he did not consider that such responsibilities conflicted with the fashionable pastimes of a wealthy man. His moral views, too, were those of his time and company, a contradictory mixture of public propriety and private indulgence: he opposed putting women on a Royal Commission on Divorce because the subject might be indelicate, but he made little effort to conceal his own affairs from other members of his class. The conception of royalty that Edward's life expressed—luxury, ostentation, and diplomacy-by-kinship—was just possible in the first decade of this century; if he had lived for another ten years he would have been as obsolete as mounted cavalry.

It is easy to feel nostalgia for that leisurely time, when women wore picture hats and did not vote, when the rich were not ashamed to live conspicuously, and the sun really never set on the British flag. Writers on Edwardian England are inclined to call the time "golden"—"a golden afternoon" or "a golden security"—or to describe it, as a BBC program of Edwardiana did, as a "long garden party." And certainly it must have seemed like a long garden party on a golden afternoon—to those who were inside the garden. But a great deal that was important was going on outside the garden: it was out there that the twentieth-century world was being made. Nostalgia is a pleasing emotion, but it is also a simplifying one; to think of Edwardian England as a peaceful, opulent world before the flood is to misread the age and to misunderstand the changes that were dramatized by the First World War.

For though the war dramatized and speeded the changes from Victorian to modern England, it did not make them. Virtually everything that is thought of as characteristically modern already existed in England by 1914: aircraft, radio-telegraphy, psychoanalysis, Post-Impressionism, motion picture palaces, the Labour party were all Edwardian additions to the English scene. The first books of Ezra Pound, D. H. Lawrence, James Joyce, and Virginia Woolf and all but one of E. M. Forster's novels are Edwardian; so are the early poems of Eliot, the first sculptures of Epstein, and Rutherford's Nobel Prize work in radiation. The mention of Rutherford reminds us that the Edwardians also had most of the modern world's problems: if the physicists had not yet produced an explosive weapon, the trade unions had, and there were also armament races, a popular press, class conflict, and women to worry about. This side of the period, if dwelt on too exclusively, produces curious distortions, but it cannot be ignored. In the years before the war the two worlds—they could be called the Garden Party World and the Labour Party World—were both true; it was a time of transition, like the corresponding decade of the previous century, when old and new ideas dwelt uneasily together.

But Edwardian England was transitional with a difference. The old order had been in power, in much the same forms, for a very long time—at least for the length of the old Queen's reign. The result of this lengthy tenure was an ossification of authority that encased and cramped the new: the *forms* of values had become the values; institutions had become more important than the ideas they embodied. If propriety expresses the forms of morality without the convictions, then the Edwardian period was an Age of Propriety, of propriety carried to absurd extremes. Conventional standards of behavior which had developed from the evangelical ethics of a century earlier had become rigid and empty gestures of decorum, important not because they implied moral rightness, but because they seemed to protect social stability, public morals, religion, and the British Empire against the threat of change. One can see this kind of rigidity all through official Edwardian England: it is nicely exemplified in the King's obsessive concern with the minutiae of dress, as when he chastised his grandson for wearing the uniform of one regiment of Foot Guards with the spurs of another.

This process of ossification was, of course, a gradual thing; in the middle of the nineteenth century the established code of values and behavior did not seem oppressive or arbitrary to most Englishmen, and many artists and thinkers of stature were able to accommodate themselves to it, but by the end of the century code and current thought had parted, and the relation between the established order and the intelligentsia was one of antagonism and suspicion. Consider, as a demonstration of this point, the two laureates, Victorian Tennyson, the best poet of his time, and Edwardian Alfred Austin, a poet so bad that even the King, who seems never to have opened a book, thought his poems trash. When Tennyson died there was no poet at hand who was both gifted and acceptable; the Prime Minister, Lord Salisbury, sadly explained that no one but Austin had applied for the job.

The Edwardian Age may be described as a time of calm, then, only if one is conscious of how insecure and fragile the calm was. H. G. Wells, looking back from 1914, described that troubled time:

At no time was it a perfectly easy task to pretend that the crazy makeshifts of our legal and political systems, the staggering accidents of economic relationship, the festering disorder of contemporary philosophy and religious teaching, the cruel and stupid bed of King Og that is our last word in sexual adjustment, really constituted a noble and enduring sanity, and it became less and less so with the acute disillusionments that arose out of the Boer War. The first decade of the twentieth century was for the English a decade of badly strained optimism. Our Empire was nearly beaten by a handful of farmers amidst the jeering contempt of the whole world—and we felt it acutely for several years. . . . And close upon the South African trouble came that extraordinary new discontent of women with a woman's lot.[1]

This is Wells the Polymath, handing out judgments with both hands, but the problems that he mentions—politics, economics, philosophy and religion, sex, the Empire, women's rights—are the sources of Edwardian anxieties, as they are the subjects of Wells' Edwardian novels. Wells was peculiarly qualified by his lowest-middle-class birth and his scientific (and therefore unfashionable) education to witness the social conflicts of his time, and his novels of 1900-1914 offer an excellent New Man's Guide to Edwardian life. But the social concerns are not peculiarly his—they were the preoccupations of the time.

On most of these troublesome issues, and on many others, the Edwardian tension took the form of a conflict between old and new ideas. In Parliament, the Liberal party fought the House of Lords over Lloyd George's "People's Budget" and the Parliament Bill; in the Army, Haldane struggled to make a modern army from the inefficient force that had nearly lost the Boer War; in the Navy, Sir John Fisher imposed reforms that scrapped both obsolete capital ships and obsolete officers and was nearly sunk by his opponents. The

[1] *The Wife of Sir Isaac Harman* (London: Macmillan, 1914), pp. 258-259.

list could be continued to include the Home Rule fight, the conflicts between unions and employers, the battles of suffragette against anti-suffragette and of men against women. Wherever the new appeared, it seemed to confront and confound the old: sometimes grotesquely, as with jam in pillarboxes; sometimes comically, as when Bernard Shaw and the Bishop of Kensington debated the morality of Gaby Deslys in the columns of the *Times*. In all these confrontations, the pattern was the same: the New behaved brashly, insolently, or violently, and the Old responded with an arthritic resistance. Taff Vale, the Cat-and-Mouse Act, and the revolt of the backwoods peers have this in common— all were rigid, unreasoning ways of dealing with new problems.[2]

But while it is important to recognize the conflicts between the established, conservative elements of Edwardian society and the proponents of radical new ideas, it is equally important to avoid over-simplifying the elements of the conflict. Neither political nor social categories describe the situation quite accurately: it was not simply the Upper Classes vs. the Middle and Lower Classes. Neither side of the opposition was homogeneous enough to make the usual easy metaphors appropriate—they were not camps, or armies, or even wings, but simply two large categories of people, both composed of heterogeneous elements that were quite distinct and often incompatible with each other.

The supporters of the new ideas were against Victorian rationalism, positivism, and materialism (in both senses of the word) on the one hand, and against evangelism and

[2] Taff Vale: in the suit of the Taff Vale Railway Company against the Amalgamated Society of the Railway Servants (1901), the court found the union liable for damages done by its agents, and subject to injunction. Cat-and-Mouse Act: an act passed by Parliament in 1913 enabling the Home Secretary to release hunger-striking suffragettes from prison, in order that they should not die in government custody, but to re-arrest them later. Revolt of the backwoods peers: resistance in the House of Lords to the 1909 Budget and to the Parliament Bill of 1911.

prudery on the other. They saw these aspects of the Victorian period as limitations on human freedom and fulfillment, and they regarded their own activities and ideas as means of liberating modern men from those Victorian bonds. This sense of the time as one of liberation from the Victorian past was very strong among advanced groups, and it must be understood if one is properly to understand the Edwardian period. But it is also necessary to note that liberation was often the only thing that these liberating movements had in common; together they did not add up to a coherent system of beliefs or define a large common goal.

When, for example, Edward Carpenter, the poet-prophet, listed the major advanced movements at the end of the nineteenth century, he included socialism, trade unionism, feminism, and theosophy. Each of these can properly be described as anti-Victorian and liberating, but one can hardly imagine a meeting of minds among Beatrice Webb, John Burns, and Madame Blavatsky. The Edwardian period was a time of undifferentiated rebellion, when many rebellious minds seem to have regarded all new ideas as adaptable if only they were contrary to the old order; one finds individuals who thought it possible to be both Nietzschean and Socialist, fin-de-siècle and Fabian, Bergsonian and Post-Impressionist, and Carpenter himself had no difficulty in being at once a Socialist, a mystic, a scientist, a spiritualist, and an anti-theist.

On the other hand, it was also possible to take up one liberating cause while remaining in other respects conservative. Beatrice Webb is an example: with her husband, Sidney, she dominated English socialism during the Edwardian years, yet her personal life and tastes would have suited an archdeacon (she described herself as "conservative by temperament and anti-democratic through social environment"[3]). The point is simply that one cannot talk precisely

[3] Beatrice Webb, *Our Partnership* (London: Longmans, Green, 1948), p. 361.

about an Edwardian avant-garde: the advance was being carried out in too many different directions.

The conservative elements of society seem somewhat more integrated, simply because they constituted an already existing order. One can point to close relations and common values among members of the Established Church, the Tory party, the peerage, and the Royal Household: bishops were members of the House of Lords; headmasters of public schools were often clergymen who taught the sons of peers; officials of the Household were Army officers. Certainly these more or less institutionalized forms of conservatism exercised considerable power to preserve the social and political structure of England as it had existed at the turn of the century and to oppose and suppress ideas that were regarded as radical and socially dangerous.

It is tempting to follow current practice and call these groups collectively the "Establishment," but to do so is to fall into misleading simplification. To talk about the Establishment is to reduce a complex of individuals to a single conscious agent of conservatism; in fact resistance to change during Edward's reign (and surely this is true of any other time as well) was not unified, but represented rather the individual actions of many separate people with separate, often very different, motives. Furthermore, though the Established Church, the peerage, and the other categories mentioned above were on the whole conservative, not all members of any category were: some members of the Christian Social Union, for instance, were mildly socialist Anglican clergymen, and the Countess of Warwick appeared on the speaker's platform at Socialist meetings. Finally the royal set itself, though it revolved around a king who was conservative in politics, included elements that were a radical departure from the preceding court: Jewish financiers, for example, and actresses.

But though the "Establishment" is not a satisfactory term, there is nevertheless some justice in the implied analogy between the Established Church and certain powerful conservative groups. In both cases members thought of themselves as possessed of a special, sanctified authority beyond democratic mandates, an authority that carried with it the responsibility to guide and direct society for its better welfare. Members of secure, conservative, socially dominant groups in Edward's time certainly believed that they composed an established ruling class, and their behavior is often comprehensible only if one sees behind each action the assumption of the right to rule. This right to rule, whether as a cabinet minister or a bishop or a headmaster, or simply as a Leader of Society, was taken as extending in a generous, undefined way from one established position to cover all society, so that bishops acted freely as literary censors and peeresses expressed their views on birth control with an air of fulfilling a social responsibility. Perhaps the best way to identify such conservative attitudes, while disallowing the existence of a single Establishment, is simply to refer to "established orders," meaning by that plural phrase those members of the Church, the peerage, the Tory party, and Society, who styled themselves the ruling class of England.

This is not to say that they *were* the ruling class—certainly they were not after the Liberal victory of 1906—but members of that order were clearly not aware of the fact that their rule had ended. The election, which put 377 Liberals into Parliament against only 157 Conservatives and Unionists, had been something like a public gesture of dismissal, but old orders are not clever at interpreting such gestures, and Tories in and out of government seem to have taken the election as at most a sinister and shocking threat to their established rights, to be met with shocking tactics. But though the election was clearly anti-Tory, it was less clear what the vote was a mandate *for*—the enemies of the established order were too heterogeneous to compose a party; the Liberals, as Wells put it in 1911, were not so much a party as a "multitudinous assemblage."

For multitudinousness has always been the Liberal characteristic. Liberalism never has been nor ever can be anything but a diversified crowd. Liberalism has to voice everything that is left out by these other parties. It is the party against the predominating interests. It is at once the party of the failing and of the untried; it is the party of decadence and hope. From its nature it must be a vague and planless association in comparison with its antagonist, neither so constructive on the one hand, nor on the other so competent to hinder the inevitable constructions of the civilized state. . . . The Liberal Party is the party against "class privilege" because it represents no class advantages, but it is also the party that is on the whole most set against Collective control because it represents no established responsibility. It is constructive only so far as its antagonism to the great owner is more powerful than its jealousy of the state. It organizes only because organization is forced upon it by the organization of its adversaries.[4]

This Liberal assemblage represented in politics the ideas and desires of most of the heterogeneous new elements in Edwardian society, and its assumption of power in the General Election of 1906 was a turning point of the period. During the preceding years—the last years of Salisbury's ministry and the three years of Balfour's—the Tories had accomplished a good deal. They had passed the Education Act and the Licencing Act, they had established the Entente Cordiale, and they had created the Committee of Imperial Defence and the Poor Law Commission. These measures did much to define the Edwardian period and gave direction to coming social and political changes. But they did not create the mood of optimism and anticipation that one might have expected. Those last years of Tory government were rather a time of uncertainty and caution, of declining

4 *The New Machiavelli* (London: John Lane, 1911), pp. 325-26.

public confidence in Tory leadership, and of unadventurous conservatism in British art and thought. The end was an overwhelming defeat of the party.

The time that followed, from the 1906 election until the death of the King in 1910, was a brief but brilliant period of Liberal optimism, when Edwardian creativity flowered, and the liberation of England from the repressions of the past seemed possible. That optimism died in the troubles of the pre-war years—it was buried under crises in Ireland and in the House of Lords, crises abroad at Agadir and Constantinople, and crises at home in the mines, on the docks, and on the railroads. The party that had to deal with these crises expressed, in its disorganized multitudinousness, the disorderly state of progressive thought during those troubled years; the opposing party expressed, in its fierce and mindless hostility to change, the ossification of conservatism at the time. And it was in part, at least, because at this crucial time Liberal disorder faced Conservative rigidity that England drifted so helplessly toward the explosion of 1914.

Perhaps, as some historians have suggested, there would have been a social explosion if the war had not come. Perhaps the war can be seen as the old order's last effort to retain control of society. But it seems more likely that without the shock of war the old ruling class ideas would simply have withered away in a slower if no more seemly fashion. As it was, the trauma of 1914-1918 ended the garden party as swiftly and rudely as a shower of hail or a four-letter word. It did so most dramatically within the fighting forces, though only after a good deal of bloody fumbling; but it also ended the more gracious aspects of the age. After the war there was never again so much money in the hands of the wellborn. (Nor were there so many wellborn—the best of them were dead in France.) But though the financial and social changes were great, they do not in themselves explain the completeness with which Edwardian England was

destroyed. The conclusive factor was the attitude of the soldiers themselves toward their elders, the Old Men in Whitehall who had sent them into battle. The mood of bitterness
that emerged from the First World War has no like in any
other war that England has fought; no other British army
felt itself so betrayed, or so scorned the causes for which it
had fought. In that mood the post-war generation rejected
altogether the world-before-the-war—its propriety, its over-
stuffed luxury, its conceptions of society and manners, its
confidence in England and in Progress.

The end of the Edwardian Age is as certain as it was sudden—August 4, 1914; the beginning is less precise, varying
according to the terms of definition, but belongs roughly to
the turn of the century. The fourteen years between make
a brief age, but they compose a time of definite, definable
qualities. "Expectancy and surprise are the notes of the age,"
the Liberal politician, C.F.G. Masterman wrote in 1905:

> Expectancy belongs by nature to a time balanced un-
> easily between two great periods of change. On the one
> hand is a past still showing faint survivals of vitality; on
> the other is the future but hardly coming to birth. The
> years as they pass still appear as years of preparation, a
> time of waiting rather than a time of action.[5]

It is to that time of waiting, waiting for the death of the old
world and the birth of the new, that this book directs itself.

[5] *In Peril of Change* (London: Fisher, Unwin, 1905) , p. xii.

Chapter II

··

THE DECLINE AND FALL
OF TORY ENGLAND

··

The mood of England at the beginning of the present century was in some ways very like the mood of the early seven-
teenth century. In both cases the century began with the
death of a great queen after a long and successful reign—a
queen who had given her name to a period when England
had increased in power and possessions and in national assurance. At the end of such a reign, and at the beginning
of a century, men expect great changes—liberating, perhaps,
but with unknown consequences and therefore disturbing;
an old familiar world has passed, and the future is empty
and uncertain. Edwardian responses to Victoria's death
were a mixture of feelings: nostalgia for the order, confidence, and material well-being of the Victorian Golden Age;
grief for the queen who had become a symbol of security;[1]
hope for the New Age to come; anxiety and apprehen-

[1] Some 3,000 elegies were published in the press of the United Kingdom and the colonies within a month of Queen Victoria's death. A
selection of these can be found in *The Passing of Victoria*, ed. J. A.
Hammerton (London: Horace Marshall & Son, 1901).

The poems in this volume are without exception bad, but one cannot question the genuineness of the feelings they express. The most
striking thing about them is the frequency with which they apostro-
phize the old queen as Mother. Her maternal role is so repeatedly mentioned as to suggest that it was a commonplace of her reign; the
queen-as-mother of her people is not treated poetically as an extravagant figure of speech but as an accepted truth. Occasionally this trope
is carried one step farther, into a kind of Victoriolatry, and the Queen-
Mother becomes the Queen of Heaven (see A. C. Benson's "To Our
Mother").

sion for what that New Age might bring; deep depression at the late decline of High Victorian idealism.

To Victoria's last Prime Minister, Lord Salisbury, her reign seemed a fortunate transition from an English past to an Imperial present:

> . . . above all things [he said in a funeral address to the House of Lords], I think, we owe her gratitude for this, that by a happy dispensation her reign has coincided with that great change which has come over the political structure of this country and the political instincts of its people. She has bridged over that great interval which separates old England from new England. Other nations may have had to pass through similar trials, but have seldom passed through them so peaceably, so easily, and with so much prosperity and success as we have. I think that future historians will look to the Queen's reign as the boundary which separates the two states of England— England which has changed so much—and recognise that we have undergone the change with constant increase of public prosperity, without any friction to endanger the peace or stability of our civil life, and at the same time with a constant expansion of an Empire which every year grows more and more powerful. We owe all these blessings to the tact, the wisdom, the passionate patriotism, and the incomparable judgment of the Sovereign whom we deplore.[2]

But in the Commons Arthur Balfour probably came closer to the general feeling when he said that "grief affects us not merely because we have lost a great personality, but because we feel that the end of a great epoch has come upon us."[3]

This sense of the end of an epoch gives to the Edwardian Age a touch of melancholy, and a touch of apprehension. In

[2] Great Britain, Parliament [*Hansard's*] *Parliamentary Debates: Official Report*, vol. 89 (Jan. 25, 1901) , col. 10. Hereafter cited as *Hansard*.
[3] *Hansard*, vol. 89, cols. 19-20.

retrospect it may seem a *belle époque*, but no *époque* is altogether *belle* to those who are living through it, and ·the Edwardian period shares our century's right to appropriate Auden's phrase, "The Age of Anxiety." This mood was caught by a shrewd observer of Edwardian society, Elinor Glyn, in her comment on the Queen's funeral procession:

> It was impossible not to sense, in that stately procession, the passing of an epoch, and a great one; a period in which England had been supreme, and had attained to the height of her material wealth and power. There were many who wondered, doubted perhaps, whether that greatness could continue; who read in the failures of the early part of the Boer War a sign of decadence, and, influenced perhaps unduly by Gibbon's *Decline and Fall* and by my French upbringing, I felt that I was witnessing the funeral procession of England's greatness and glory.[4]

Mrs. Glyn was not the only Edwardian to think of Gibbon; the idea of imperial decline and fall haunted imaginations of the time. Nor was she alone in finding about her the evidences of national decadence.

The most obvious sign was the one Mrs. Glyn mentioned: the slow, humiliating effort of the Boer War, begun jingoistically in one reign and ended without glory in another— a cruel, expensive struggle between the world's strongest nation and one of the weakest. In the course of the war Britain's "splendid isolation" had come to seem less splendid and more lonely; she had lost military prestige; and she had lost confidence in her own military superiority and in her military leaders. Most disturbing, she had lost the wholehearted support of her own people: for the first time in a century an English war had been fought in the face of serious and outspoken opposition at home. The new century found England isolated from other western powers,

[4] Elinor Glyn, *Romantic Adventure* (New York: E. P. Dutton, 1937), pp. 97-98.

demonstrably weak in her imperial defenses, and with a divided people. And so, at a time when the British Empire was more widespread and more imperial than it would ever be again, Englishmen worried about its decline and fall.

We can see the changes of mood that the imperialist cause underwent in Edward's reign recorded in the career of Rudyard Kipling. Kipling was an imperialist by birth and by inclination; he believed with evangelical intensity in the virtues that built empires, and he celebrated those virtues in his writings. He was a close friend of Cecil Rhodes and lived for a time on Rhodes' estate in South Africa. He knew and admired Dr. Jameson, whose abortive raid on Johannesburg precipitated the Boer War, and he drew upon Jameson's character, it is said, for the stoic virtues of "If." When the war in South Africa began he was on the scene to observe and report it, and to support belligerently the British cause. In the last years of Victoria's reign, he was the acknowledged Voice of the Empire.

But the century turned, and a new, less confident mood appeared, which Kipling could not understand and did not admire. The principal political and social developments of the Edwardian period seemed to him willful diminishments of British greatness, and he turned in his writings from the celebration of English virtues to the damnation of England's enemies. As G. K. Chesterton observed, Kipling loved England not because she was English but because she was great, and when that greatness seemed to falter his love turned rancorous.[5] His topical writings became increasingly uncontrolled and crude and touched with a kind of Tory paranoia: a few examples are "The City of Brass," his poem against Lloyd George's "People's Budget" (1909); "The Female of the Species," his poem against women's suffrage (1911); and "Ulster," his poem against Home Rule (1911). All these were published in daily newspapers, as acts of

[5] "On Mr. Rudyard Kipling and Making the World Small," in *Heretics* (London: John Lane, 1905), p. 47.

aggressive political propaganda. In the years just before the war his public statements on the Irish Question were so inflammatory that the question was raised in the House of Commons whether Kipling should be prosecuted for sedition.[6] By this time Kipling was no longer the Voice of Empire but the snapping and snarling voice of an old Tory dog that grew more ill-tempered as it lost its teeth.

No more vivid and regrettable example of Edwardian change exists than this history of a potentially great artist's disintegration. But the point is that Kipling's decline was parallel to the decline of the cause and the values that he believed in: class and conquest, self-abnegation and stoicism, practical science, the values that would lead to a Kipling world, a world governed by white men with machines. No doubt in 1900 Kipling's faith still served to govern the colonies, for obsolete values die slowest at the edge of empire; but it was Kipling's unfortunate destiny to live at the center of the empire with the values of the perimeter.

To see the fundamental change in Kipling's tone of voice and in the attitude of his readers, it is only necessary to consider two notable poems that he published in the *Times*: "Recessional," in 1897, and "The Islanders," in 1902. "Recessional" appeared as a slightly tardy contribution to the Diamond Jubilee of Victoria's succession to the throne; it was printed in the July 17 issue, weeks after the actual celebration, and on the same page as the Queen's statement of gratitude to her subjects. It was a complex poem, an unusual poem for Kipling, that said a good deal more about imperialism than he usually did. It said, for example, that all empires were transitory, that imperialists were foolishly boastful, and that it was vain to put one's trust in force. But it also proposed that the British Empire was held in dominion by God's will, and that the dominated peoples were "lesser breeds without the law." It was a poem that an emperor might find disturbing (the old Queen could

<hr>

[6] *Hansard*, vol. 37 (Apr. 15, 1912) , col. 17.

scarcely have been comforted by the reminder that "the cap-
tains and the kings depart"), but that an imperialist might
find bracing if he read it selectively. It is a measure of the
mood of the moment that the *Times'* leader writer of the
day did read the poem in that selective way:

> The most dangerous and demoralising temper into which
> a State can fall [he wrote] is one of boastful pride. To be
> humble in our strength, to avoid the excesses of an over-
> confident vanity, to be as regardful of the rights of others
> as if we were neither powerful nor wealthy, to shun "Such
> boasting as the Gentiles use, or lesser breeds without the
> Law,"—these are the conditions upon which our domin-
> ion by sea and land is based even more than on fleets and
> armies. At this moment of Imperial exaltation, Mr. Kip-
> ling does well to remind his countrymen that we have
> something more to do than to build battleships and mul-
> tiply guns. All that is, of course, a matter of duty, and,
> indeed, of necessity; but our immense Imperial power
> depends for its effectiveness on the spirit that is behind
> it, not only on the courage and firmness of our people,
> not only on their patience and reasonableness, but
> on their strong and sincere conviction of moral re-
> sponsibility. Among all the splendors of the Jubilee,
> among the justifiable expressions of national pride and
> of personal devotion to the Sovereign, this last feeling
> was, we rejoice to believe, a dominant note. It rings out
> as clearly in the simple grandeur of the Queen's message
> as in Mr. Kipling's soul-stirring verses.[7]

The poem that Kipling published five years later revealed
a dramatic change of mood. In the interval he had seen the
war in South Africa drag on and had been by when his
friend Rhodes died, and it must have seemed to him that
Rhodes' dreams of Empire were near dying too. In 1902
Kipling was still an imperialist, but he was an embittered

[7] *Times*, July 17, 1897, p. 13.

one. "The Islanders" is a fierce denunciation of the English people for becoming soft and prosperous and dependent on colonial troops for victory; the English had let the Empire down. The poem contains many of the Tory concerns of the decade: it urges national military service, for example, and warns of the threat of invasion. It is violent and abusive throughout, but one passage in particular penetrated English complacency with notable effect:

> And ye vaunted your fathomless power and ye flaunted
>   your iron pride
> Ere—ye fawned on the Younger Nations for the men
>   who could shoot and ride!
> Then ye returned to your trinkets; then ye contented
>   your souls
> With the flannelled fools at the wicket or the muddied
>   oafs at the goals.[8]

The sentiment struck even the *Times'* editors as a bit strong: a leader noted the poem's "rhetorical exaggeration," but added that it had "a kernel of grave reproof and of indignant protest which none of us can afford to disregard."[9] Nor were readers inclined to disregard it; letters began to appear in the *Times* immediately, and a controversy developed that continued for several weeks. One would expect that Kipling's attack on team sports would have upset his English readers, and to be sure there were plenty of furious letters from athletes and headmasters. But the striking thing about the "Islanders" controversy is that more than two-thirds of the letters printed in the *Times* supported Kipling. In the last months of the South African war the British people were demoralized and looking for explanations of the military inadequacies, and though cricket and football could not be seriously blamed for failures on the veldt, they seemed to symbolize a civilian soft-

8 "The Islanders," *Times*, Jan. 4, 1902, p. 9.
9 *Times*, Jan. 4, 1902, p. 9.

ness and idleness that was a more palatable explanation of British failures than some alternatives.

A more serious and disturbing explanation came from the Army: sixty percent of Englishmen were physically unfit for service. The figure was first cited by General Sir Frederick Maurice in an article in the *Contemporary Review* in January 1902.[10] A few months later the sociologist B. S. Rowntree picked up Maurice's figure and asked British doctors

> is it, or is it not true that the whole labouring population of the land are at present living under conditions which make it impossible that they should rear the next generation to be sufficiently virile to supply more than two out of five men effective for the purposes of either peace or war?[11]

The sixty-percent figure was quoted again in the following year, in a memorandum on the causes of rejection of recruits, written by Sir William Taylor, Director-General of the Army Medical Service. General Taylor reported that in fact only thirty-seven percent of applicants examined were rejected as unfit, but he concluded that if the number of men too obviously unfit even to be considered was added, the total would be close to Maurice's estimate.[12]

Faced with this testimony to British frailty, the government formed an Inter-Departmental Committee on Physical Deterioration, with the following terms of reference:

[10] "Miles" [Major-General Sir Frederick Maurice], "Where to Get Men," *Contemporary Review*, vol. 81 (Jan. 1902), 78-86. See also his elaboration of the argument in "National Health: A Soldier's Reply," *Contemporary Review*, vol. 83 (Jan. 1903), 41-56. Maurice, a veteran of several African campaigns, was the son of F. D. Maurice, the Victorian Christian Socialist.

[11] Quoted in Appendix I, "Report of the Inter-Departmental Committee on Physical Deterioration," *Reports from Commissioners* (1904), vol. 32, p. 103.

[12] Appendix I, "Report of the Inter-Departmental Committee," p. 95 (quoted from the *British Medical Journal* [Aug. 16, 1902], where it first appeared).

To make a preliminary enquiry into the allegations concerning the deterioration of certain classes of the population, as shown by the large percentage of rejections for physical causes of recruits for the Army and by other evidence. . . .[13]

The terms of reference frame, in a careful circumlocution, the true nature of the problem. "Certain classes of the population" meant in fact the urban poor, and the committee properly directed most of its attentions to conditions of life in city slums: the overcrowding, the polluted air, the sub-standard working conditions, the high infant mortality. The report submitted in August 1904 shows that though the urban population of England and Wales had increased over the latter half of the nineteenth century from fifty percent of the population to seventy-seven percent, there had been no corresponding increase in public attention to urban problems, and that consequently the English poor were worse off than they had ever been (infant mortality, for example, had increased between 1850 and 1900). But it also shows that the government was anxious to contradict the idea, which must have been widely held, that the English race was deteriorating. The conclusion of the report reads

The Committee hope that the facts and opinions they have collected will have some effect in allaying the apprehensions of those who, as it appears on insufficient grounds, have made up their minds that progressive deterioration is to be found among the people generally.[14]

If the intention of this report was to allay apprehensions, it was a failure. The very fact that a report on "Physical Deterioration" existed was enough to make the idea current; and deterioration quickly became interchangeable with degeneracy or decadence, thus adding an implication of moral

[13] "Report of the Inter-Departmental Committee," p. v.
[14] "Report of the Inter-Departmental Committee," p. 92.

decline to the idea of physical worsening which the report was in fact intended to refute. A week after the report was tabled in Parliament, Sir John Gorst, M.P. for Cambridge University, was referring to it in debate as the "recent report upon the degeneracy of our race,"[15] and it was as such that it reached those inclined to feel alarm for the condition of England.

The currency of the idea of national decadence made it inevitable that analogies should be drawn to the fall of the Roman Empire. The analogy was first developed in print in 1905, in an anonymous pamphlet entitled *The Decline and Fall of the British Empire,* "A brief account," as the title-page describes it, "of those causes which resulted in the destruction of our late Ally, together with a comparison between the British and Roman Empires. Appointed for use in the National Schools of Japan. Tokio, 2005." The author was a young Tory pamphleteer named Elliott Mills, just down from Oxford, where he had prepared himself by taking a fourth-class degree in history; his account of the Fall of Britain is dull reading as satire, but it is useful as a summary of Tory anxieties in the middle of the Edwardian period. Mills lists eight causes of British decline:

    I. The prevalence of Town over Country Life, and its disastrous effect upon the health and faith of English People.

    II. Growing tendency of the English throughout the Twentieth Century to forsake the sea except as a health resort.

    III. The Growth of Refinement and Luxury.

    IV. The Decline of Literary and Dramatic Taste.

    V. Gradual Decline of the Physique and Health of the English People.

    VI. The Decline of intellectual and religious life among the English.

[15] *Hansard,* vol. 140 (Aug. 10, 1904), col. 47.

VII. Excessive Taxation and Municipal Extravagance.

VIII. Inability of the British to defend themselves and
their Empire.[16]

Mills' list is typically Tory in its general assumption that
all change is decline, in its moral attitude toward social
processes that are beyond the reach of individual moral
choice, and in the image of an English Golden Age that it
implies—a time when Englishmen were agrarian, seafaring,
frugal, and pious. Some of the evidences of decadence that
Mills discovered seem a bit quaint now, though they were
serious enough to Edwardian Tories: the newly organized
professional football leagues, for example, which under-
mined the public health by encouraging city dwellers to
substitute spectator-sports for participation, and the
"strange creeds" of the time, by which Mills meant Christian Science, palmistry, positivism, and determinism. One
creed that Mills did not dismiss was Darwinism; the idea of
natural selection inevitably turns up whenever Edwardians
discuss the physical condition of the people, for it seemed
possible (and if possible, then frightening) that what was
observed as physical deterioration was in fact a biological
adjustment of the species to the new and degrading conditions of urban life. Tories and Liberals alike were appalled
at the thought that perhaps the creatures of the slums might
be fittest to survive in the new world. And as with people, so with nations: Social Darwinism might promise the
progressive evolution of nations, but it also held the possibility of decline. Mills, mixing biology and theology,
warned that "God's unalterable law concerning the survival
of the fittest is just as applicable to the life of the Nation as
it is to the briefer existence of an animal or a human
being."[17]

16 Anon. [Elliott E. Mills], *The Decline and Fall of the British Empire* (Oxford: Alden & Co., n.d. [1905]) ; my list is the subtitles of the
book's sections.

17 *Decline and Fall*, p. 22.

The most important fact about *The Decline and Fall of the British Empire* is not its content, however, but its enormous success. It was favorably reviewed in the *Times*, the *Standard*, and the *Spectator* (all Conservative papers); and more important, it was seized upon by General Baden-Powell, at that time still Inspector-General of Cavalry but already preparing for the Boy Scout movement. In a speech early in 1906, Baden-Powell told his audience,

> If you care to show your patriotism to the extent of expending sixpence, I hope each one of you will go tomorrow morning and buy a copy of the pamphlet called *"The Decline and Fall of the British Empire."* If you will carefully study it personally, each one of you, no matter what his line of life may be, will see what should be his share in saving his country from the possibility of disaster.[18]

A number of people seem to have taken Baden-Powell's advice; the pamphlet sold 12,000 copies in six months.

The most direct effect of Mills' pamphlet was on Baden-Powell himself. The idea of a British decline-and-fall made a deep impression on his imperialist sensibility, and when he began to organize the Boy Scouts two years later, a considerable motive was his desire to save Britain from the fate of Rome. Rome appears several times in the first edition of *Scouting for Boys*, and always in relation to the present threat to Britain:

> Our great Empire is to-day to the rest of the world very much what the Roman Empire was two thousand years ago. But the Roman Empire, great as it was, fell.
>
> "The same causes which brought about the fall of the great Roman Empire are working to-day in Great Britain."

[18] Quoted in back matter of "Vivian Grey" [a pseudonym of Mills], *The Further Surprising Adventures of Lemuel Gulliver* (Oxford: Alden & Co., 1906) .

These words were lately spoken by one of our best known democratic politicians. . . . That they are true is practically admitted by those who have studied and compared the general conditions of both countries.[19]

In another passage he made an important connection clear between the threat of imperial decline and his intentions for the Scouts:

Recent reports on the deterioration of our race ought to act as a warning to be taken in time before it goes too far.

One cause which contributed to the downfall of the Roman Empire was the fact that the soldiers fell away from the standard of their forefathers in bodily strength.[20]

This was the Tory response to the Physical Deterioration Report—it assumed that the primary importance was in what it implied about the British common soldier and about imperial defense. When Baden-Powell organized his scouting movement he did so with one clear motive—to prepare the next generation of British soldiers.

The book that he wrote for his Scouts is in many ways like the current *Boy Scout Handbook,* and it is easy to see why it quickly became popular. It is full of the kinds of information and advice that boys want, interspersed with anecdotes of heroism and adventure, many from Baden-Powell's own adventurous career in India and South Africa, each making a clear moral point. The writing is direct, vigorous, and monosyllabic; short sentences are organized in short paragraphs in a way that anticipates the techniques of modern high-readability experts. But the book is also a crude and insistent expression of the Tory imperialism that provided the motivation for the movement. Baden-Powell saw his movement as a preparation for war and the defense of the Empire. He also saw it as a campaign against

19 *Scouting for Boys* (London: Horace Cox, 1908) , pp. 335-336.
20 *Scouting for Boys,* p. 208.

radicalism and socialism. Take, for example, the following passage from one of the "Camp Fire Yarns" in the "Patriotism" section:

> There are always members of Parliament who try to make the Navy and Army smaller, so as to save money. They only want to be popular with the voters in England so that they and the party to which they belong may get into power. These men are called "politicians." They do not look to the good of the country. Most of them know and care very little about our Colonies. If they had had their way before, we should by this time have been talking French; and if they are allowed to have their way in the future we may as well learn German or Japanese, for we shall be conquered by these.
>
> But fortunately there are other better men in Parliament who are called "statesmen"; these are men who look out for the welfare of the country, and do not mind about being popular or not so long as they keep the country safe.[21]

The voters and the working classes are generally denigrated in the book; the labor movement because it is unpatriotic, and paupers because they lack will power.

The scout movement was immediately successful, and not only with the boys. By 1909, 6,000 girls had joined Boy Scout troops and were participating in scouting activities. This seemingly harmless enthusiasm caused great distress among parents and youth-movement leaders, and strong letters of protest were written to the papers. One such letter, in the *Spectator*, complained that "these mixed corps on returning from country expeditions are dismissed when the town is reached, girls and boys finding their way home often in a state of very undesirable excitement," and added, "scouting for girls leads nowhere from the national point

21 *Scouting for Boys*, p. 328.

of view. . . ."[22] The *Spectator*'s editor, St. Loe Strachey, supported the correspondent and urged Baden-Powell not to jeopardize the cause of the Boy Scouts "by setting public opinion against them, as he most certainly will by insisting on this mad scheme of military coeducation."

Baden-Powell, with his sister Agnes, promptly organized the Girl Guides to solve this problem; and in their first prospectus for the new movement they attacked the question of "the national point of view." "Decadence is threatening the nation," the pamphlet begins, and it goes on to define the anti-decadent aims of the movement. Girls can help the nation and the empire by learning

1. To make themselves of practical use in case of invasion. . . .
2. To prepare themselves for a Colonial life in case their destiny should lead them to such. . . .
3. To make themselves more useful to others and to themselves by learning useful occupations and handiwork and yet retaining their womanliness.[23]

Three years later, when the *Handbook for Girl Guides* was published, it bore the subtitle, "or How Girls can Help Build the Empire."

The Boy Scouts and Girl Guides constituted an important effort to reverse national decadence in the next generation —decadence, that is, in the two matters that most bothered conservatives: the physical deterioration of the race and the deterioration of imperialistic enthusiasms in the people. But the Boy Scouts did not solve the immediate problem; the decline and fall of the British Empire might not wait for the next generation. To many Englishmen the immediate prospects were gloomy, and it was to these pessimists that

[22] Letter from Violet R. Markham to the *Spectator*, no. 4,249 (Dec. 4, 1909), 942.
[23] Baden-Powell, *Girl-Guides. A Suggestion for Character Training for Girls* (London: no publisher, n.d. [1909]), p. 7.

Balfour, the leader of the Tory party, addressed himself in January 1908 when he spoke at Cambridge on the subject of "Decadence." The lecture is a characteristically Balfourian performance—a tentative, questioning, philosophical circling around the problem of whether there is in nations a process corresponding to senescence in men. He chose as his case the obvious one, the decadence of the late Roman Empire; but it soon becomes clear, as one reads the text, that Balfour had constructed out of Roman history what amounts almost to a parable of the contemporary state of affairs in the British Empire. He first described Rome before its fall—an empire in a strong military position, with a tolerable tax burden, high income, and happily integrated constituent nations. It had some weaknesses: the population was diminishing, and some historians thought the native stock had decayed; there was also a general mood of discouragement among Romans, "the sense of impending doom, by which men's spirits were oppressed long before the Imperial power began visibly to wane. . . ."[24] And there was a growing bureaucracy, a "crude experiment in Socialism" that weakened the government. But none of these points accounted for the decline of Rome, and Balfour concluded that one could only postulate a failure of national energy, which could not be explained, but could be recognized and called "decadence."

But though Balfour accepted decadence as a stage in the pathology of empires, he could not, as Leader of the Opposition, suggest that Britain had reached this stage. His argument for the possibility of further progress was an ingeniously Tory one. One could not look for progress through political action, he argued, because Democracy is not progressive. "If in the last hundred years the whole material setting of civilized life has altered, we owe it neither to politicians nor to political institutions. We owe it to the combined efforts of those who have advanced science and

[24] Balfour, *Decadence* (Cambridge: University Press, 1908) , p. 24.

those who have applied it."[25] Science was the great instrument of social change, but it might be more than that; it might be the source of inspiration, the positive variable in modern society that religion had been in the past, and through faith in and use of this variable the British Empire might continue to progress. Thus Balfour at one stroke spiritualized the conservative, essentially Victorian view of science and material advancement as the measure of progress, and at the same time dismissed the idea of progress through progressive politics.

In his concluding remarks, Balfour added one more Tory argument—he made the Empire itself an instrument in its own collective progress:

The conclusions at which I provisionally arrive are that we cannot regard decadence and arrested development as less normal in human communities than progress; though the point at which the energy of advance is exhausted (if, and when it is reached) varies in different races and civilisations: that the internal causes by which progress is encouraged, hindered, or reversed, lie to a great extent beyond the field of ordinary political discussion, and are not easily expressed in current political terminology: that the influence which a superior civilisation, whether acting by example or imposed by force, may have in advancing an inferior one, though often beneficent, is not likely to be self-supporting; its withdrawal will be followed by decadence, unless the character of the civilisation be in harmony both with the acquired temperament and the innate capacities of those who have been induced to accept it: that as regards those nations which still advance in virtue of their own inherent energies, though time has brought perhaps new causes for disquiet, it has brought also new grounds for hope; and that whatever be the perils in front of us, there are, so far, no symptoms either

[25] *Decadence*, p. 55.

of pause or of regression in the onward movement which for more than a thousand years has been characteristic of Western civilisation.[26]

A more sophisticated version of the White Man's Burden can scarcely be imagined. Nevertheless the speech, like the Physical Deterioration Report, was taken as evidence of the arguments that it sought to refute and helped to convince less philosophical minds that more direct action, on a wider front, was necessary.

More alarming evidence came later in the same year, when the Report of the Royal Commission on Care and Control of the Feeble-Minded was published. This commission had been appointed in September 1904, a month after publication of the Physical Deterioration Report; hearings were held through the winter and all the following summer—in all, fifty-one days of testimony, during which 35,000 questions were asked of 200 witnesses. Publication was delayed, however, until by 1908 M.P.s were asking impatient questions about the report. It finally appeared in July, in four large volumes.

A substantial part of the report is concerned with the contemporary administration of public facilities for the mentally ill and with statistical records, which could only interest persons professionally involved in the matter. But two points were of more general interest. One was the evident increase in the number of mentally defective persons in Britain; census reports quoted showed an increase of 21.44 percent in the decade from 1891 to 1901, as compared with a 3.23 percent increase in the preceding decade, and a 7.04 increase from 1871 to 1881. This startling and sudden increase was probably due at least in part to a change in the language of the census form and perhaps in part to an extension of public aid to the mentally defective, but to a public already anxious about decline-and-fall it seemed

26 *Decadence*, pp. 58-59.

another evidence of the general decadence of the nation. The other point of interest was the report's answer to the question: What causes mental defectiveness? Virtually all the witnesses answered "Heredity"; as one witness put it, "The thing can only be bred out." Testimony of witnesses who argued for environmental causes was dismissed as unsound. This is a crucial point, since the answer given to the question of causes will determine the line of action taken. If one argues for heredity, one worries about the race and tries to improve it genetically by segregating and in effect sterilizing the subnormal. If one argues for environmental causes, one worries about the physical circumstances of existence and tries to improve them by legislation and social action. The former, conservative view carried the day and stimulated Tory reformers to wage war, not against poverty, but against *fertile* poverty. The mentally defective were poor because they lacked the moral fiber that goes with intelligence, so the argument ran, and they were prolific for the same reason: there was, said Baden-Powell, "much pauper over-population due to want of self-restraint on the part of men and women."[27] If the feebleminded could be segregated by sex, feeblemindedness would inevitably diminish, and radical social reforms would be unnecessary. When the National Social Purity Crusade, an organization of conservative reformers, launched a new "forward movement" in 1908, a movement aimed at raising the standard of social and personal purity, it included among its proposals for moral improvement the genetic isolation of the mentally defective; to these conservative minds, feeblemindedness was a moral issue.[28]

For Tories and imperialists—which is to say for most Englishmen at the turn of the century—the core of anxiety about national decadence was the question of national and

[27] *Scouting for Boys*, p. 209.
[28] For a detailed account of the Crusade's activities see below, Ch. VIII.

imperial defense. This anxiety is written in the history of the time in many ways; it is most evident in public and official reactions to the Boer War and to the Royal Commissions that subsequently investigated it, and in the legislation that was passed to reform the administration of the Army and Navy. But it was also apparent in the flourishing of an odd sub-category of popular literature—the literature of invasion.

Invasion stories had appeared in considerable numbers at two times of national anxiety during the last thirty years of Victoria's reign: in the early 1870's, just after the surprising Prussian defeat of the French, and in the early 'eighties, during the Channel Tunnel scare. The books and pamphlets that appeared made a number of common points: the British were unprepared to defend themselves; the Volunteers were badly trained; the national economy would be destroyed by an invasion.[29] The anxieties reflected in these books are of two kinds: a growing awareness of England's isolation from continental alliances and a conservative fear that radicals, by transferring power from the traditional ruling classes to the lower classes, would weaken England's will to defend herself. The external threat was not identified with any single enemy; among the invaders Germany and France are about equally represented, and there are also literary invasions by the Russians, and even the Chinese.

Over the years from 1900 to the war, the publication of invasion literature increased markedly; there were as many books and pamphlets published during these fourteen years as during the preceding thirty.[30] But numbers alone do not tell the whole story; one must add three points. First, the

[29] See, for example, anon [G. T. Chesney], *The Battle of Dorking* (Edinburgh & London: Blackwood & Sons, 1871), a pamphlet which may be considered the beginning of the late-Victorian and Edwardian vogue for tales of invasion.

[30] For a bibliography of these works see I. F. Clarke, *The Tale of the Future* (London: The Library Association, 1961).

circulation of this Edwardian invasion literature was vastly increased, partly through publication in mass-circulation newspapers like the *Daily Mail*; second, the flow of books was not steady through the period—it hit a peak in the years 1906-1909; and third, it concentrated on one enemy— Germany.

The best of the lot is Erskine Childers' *The Riddle of the Sands*, the only novel by a strange man who served his country in two wars and died before an Irish firing squad as a traitor. Childers was a House of Commons clerk who served with the artillery in the South African war (and wrote a good book about it) ; he was an aerial observer and intelligence officer in the First World War. He was also a daring yachtsman and a Home Ruler of such conviction that he quit his job as clerk in the House in 1910 to devote himself to work for the Irish cause. Yachting and Home Rule met in 1914, when he commanded the first vessel to smuggle arms to the I.R.A. He suspended his political activities to fight in the war, but returned to Ireland after demobilization, joined the Irish Republican Army, and was captured and executed by the Irish Free State in 1922.

Although Childers was always a good writer, he was not concerned with the art of fiction; he wrote his novel to advance a specific military point—that England could be invaded by Germany. *The Riddle of the Sands* is nevertheless an exceptional adventure story—gripping in its action, more subtle in psychology than most such books are, and written in a clean and supple prose. It is now relegated to the dreary category of children's classics, along with Stevenson and Jules Verne, but in fact it is an entirely readable adult novel. It is above all a sailor's book, full of real feeling for the sea and for small boats; Childers makes the technical problems of sailing as exciting as any land-based cloak-and-dagger plot, and a good deal more credible.

The Riddle of the Sands is a spy story. Two Englishmen in a small yacht sail the sand banks and estuaries of the

German North Sea coast (as Childers often did), discover a plan for the invasion of England, and after many adventures report it to the British authorities. To make sure that his readers did not miss his didactic intention, Childers framed his tale with a preface and epilogue which assert that the story was factual and that the two principals had been persuaded to publish their story as "a drastic cure for what had come to be nothing less than a national disease":

> some poisonous influence, whose origin still baffles all but a very few, was persistently at work to drive back our diplomacy into paths which even without this clarion warning they would be wise on principle to shun.[31]

Childers is never specific about the identity of this "poisonous influence," but it becomes clear, as his story develops, that his views are not far from those of Mills' *Decline and Fall*. He skillfully sets up a contrast between his two spies —Carruthers, a snobbish Whitehall fop who represents English luxury and decadence, and Davies, a patriotic and able sailor who has been turned down by the Navy. Like many other like-minded men, Childers took good seamanship to be the fundamental English virtue and set Carruthers' expectations of a luxurious cruise against Davies' plain but efficient realities to make his point. On the first night of their cruise, Carruthers thinks:

> Hazily there floated through my mind my last embarkation on a yacht: my faultless attire, the trim gig and obsequious sailors, the accommodation ladder flashing with varnish and brass in the August sun; the orderly snowy decks and basket chairs under the awning aft. What a contrast with this sordid midnight scramble over damp meat and littered packing-cases! The bitterest touch of all

[31] Erskine Childers, *The Riddle of the Sands* (London: Smith, Elder, 1903), p. vi. The title page of the first edition reads: "The Riddle of the Sands. A Record of Secret Service Recently Achieved. Edited by Erskine Childers."

was a growing sense of inferiority and ignorance, which I had never before been allowed to feel in my experience of yachts.[32]

By the end of the cruise, Carruthers has learned how to do his own sailing, and England has been temporarily saved from invasion. The two points are obviously connected.

Through the book runs the theme of "the German threat." Davies, the perceptive, sea-going patriot, lectures Carruthers on German intentions and necessities; they must have colonies, he says, and therefore they must have naval strength and command of the seas. War with England therefore seems inevitable. Davies nevertheless admires the German Emperor: "He's a splendid chap, and anyone can see he's right." "By Jove," he exclaims, "we want a man like this Kaiser, who doesn't wait to be kicked, but works like a nigger for his country and sees ahead." England, on the other hand, is asleep in the arms of officialdom. "We're a maritime nation," Davies tells Carruthers:

> We've grown by the sea and live by it; if we lose command of it we starve. We're unique in that way, just as our huge Empire, only linked by the sea, is unique. And yet, my God! read Brassey, Dilke, and those "Naval Annuals," and see what mountains of apathy and conceit have had to be tackled. It's not the people's fault. We've been safe so long, and grown so rich, that we've forgotten what we owe it to. But there's no excuse for those blockheads of statesmen, as they call themselves, who are paid to see things as they are.[33]

There are a number of ways in which Childers' book obviously belongs to an early stage in the German Invasion scare. The Germans are treated with respect and even affection: they represent a competitor rather than an enemy.

[32] *Riddle of the Sands*, p. 18.
[33] *Riddle of the Sands*, p. 104.

The English principals, on the other hand, are strong and capable men; they may have their English shortcomings (Davies is no good at languages, and Carruthers is a snob), but they also have the virtues that the English have always admired in themselves—courage, resourcefulness, endurance, patriotism, good humor, reticence. The action takes place on German soil and in German waters, and the invasion scheme is frustrated before it can be put into effect. Nevertheless, an invasion plan has been made, and Childers pressed on his readers the possibility that such a plan might exist in actuality, and the likelihood, given England's state of military preparedness, that it would be successful. A postscript, dated March 1903, ends with this passage:

> It so happens that while this book was in the press a number of measures have been taken by the Government to counteract some of the very weaknesses and dangers which are alluded to above. A Committee of National Defence has been set up, and the welcome given to it was a truly extraordinary comment on the apathy and confusion which it is designed to supplant. A site on the Forth has been selected for a new North Sea naval base— an excellent if tardy decision; for ten years or so must elapse before the existing anchorage becomes in any sense a "base." A North Sea fleet has also been created: another good measure; but it should be remembered that its ships are not modern, or in the least capable of meeting the principal German squadrons under the circumstances supposed above. . . . Is it not becoming patent that the time has come for training all Englishmen systematically either for the sea or for the rifle?[34]

Childers' final question was one that many Englishmen were asking during the Edwardian years; the question of national defense was inevitably tied to the question of national service, and the most persistent campaigns for greater

[34] *Riddle of the Sands*, pp. 335-336.

military preparedness were conducted by the supporters of compulsory military training for all men. The loudest and longest warning voice was that of Lord Roberts, the field marshal who had commanded British troops in South Africa in 1900 and served as Commander-in-Chief of the army from 1901 to 1904. Roberts was nearly seventy when the Boer War ended, but he was still a vigorous, strong-minded soldier, with more than a decade still to live—a decade that he devoted to warning the British of the inadequacies of their defenses and fighting with the War Office about policies and tactics. In the years between 1900 and 1914, Roberts wrote continuously on military subjects: books of his own, as well as prefaces to thirty other books, most of them on matters of defense (one of these was Childers' *War and the Arme Blanche*, an attack on the obsolete armament and tactics of British cavalry, who still carried lances and swords into battle). Of all British soldiers, Roberts was the one most likely to reach the people; he was the greatest living military hero, a wearer of the Victoria Cross, a defender of the Empire in India and South Africa, and the most experienced commander in the Army. His popularity is suggested by the fact that nineteen books were written about him between 1900 and 1914. Many of these were for boys; like Baden-Powell, Roberts was concerned with the military training of the young, and he supported his own quasi-military youth group, the Lads' Rifle Brigade.

In 1904 Roberts resigned from active duty to devote himself to the cause of national preparedness. Once freed from the restraints of Army discipline he became more and more outspokenly the opponent of the government's military policies. In 1905 he assumed the presidency of the National Service League, a militant organization for universal military training, and began to speak at public meetings and in the House of Lords. When Balfour, in a speech to the Commons in May 1905, assured the members that invasion was "not an eventuality which we need seriously consider,"

Roberts was one of the speakers who rose in the Lords to oppose the Prime Minister's complacency: "I have no hesitation," he said, "in stating that our armed forces, as a body, are as absolutely unfitted and unprepared for war as they were in 1899-1900." The Minister for War, Arnold-Foster, replied to Roberts three days later in the Commons, but it was Roberts' dramatic remark that got the publicity.

At about the same time, Roberts was engaged in another, less public activity—he was helping a hack writer to write a novel. The book was called *The Invasion of 1910*; the author was a popular writer of thrillers and an amateur spy, William Le Queux. *The Invasion* is essentially a fictional projection of Roberts' warnings, an account of a weak and complacent England invaded by a well-trained German army. Le Queux's qualifications for the job were his connections with men like Northcliffe and the fact that in 1894 he had written another invasion novel, *The Great War in England in 1897*; his principal disqualifications were his prose style, which was crude even for a hack, and his ignorance of the problem at hand. It was to this ignorance that Northcliffe and Roberts addressed themselves. Northcliffe financed three months of travelling the east coast of England (a trip which, according to Le Queux, cost the *Daily Mail* £3,000) ; Roberts planned the invasion and checked the book in proof. There was one snag in the operation; the towns through which Roberts had planned to move his German invaders were not towns that bought the *Daily Mail*, and in the end strategy had to be sacrificed to sales. But Roberts was apparently satisfied, he wrote an introductory letter which was reproduced in facsimile and tipped into the book, as though the very handwriting of a hero were an argument for his cause. In the letter Roberts wrote,

The catastrophe that may happen if we still remain in our present state of unpreparedness is vividly and forcibly illustrated in Mr. Le Queux's new book which I recommend to the perusal of every one who has the welfare of the British Empire at heart.[35]

In Le Queux's 1894 novel the invaders had been Russian and French; in 1906 they were Germans. To men like Le Queux and Roberts, Germany was the only possible enemy, and it seemed monstrous to them that the British government (the Liberals) was not more actively anti-German. On the day of invasion, two of Le Queux's Tory patriots discuss the situation:

"Well, if what you say is the actual truth," exclaimed Sir James, "to-day is surely the blackest day that England has ever known."

"Yes, thanks to the pro-German policy of the Government and the false assurances of the Blue Water School. They should have listened to Lord Roberts," snapped his lordship.[36]

This passage is typical both of Le Queux's style and of the role played by Roberts in the novel that he helped to write.

Like most other invasion novels, *The Invasion of 1910* ends in a British victory, but in this case it is a cheerless one. The people rise against their German conquerors, drive them from London, and regain command of their country; but a feeble government fails to prosecute the victory, and a compromise peace is made by which Germany annexes Denmark and Holland, and Britain gets nothing but the bill. The cause of the collapse Le Queux found in the condition of England:

The whole character of the nation and the Government had changed since the great days when, in the face of famine and immense peril, the country had fought Na-

[35] In William Le Queux, *The Invasion of 1910.* With a Full Account of the Siege of London. Naval Chapters by H. W. Wilson. Introductory Letter by Field-Marshal Earl Roberts (London: Eveleigh Nash, 1906).
[36] *Invasion of 1910,* p. 17.

poleon to the last and overthrown him. The strong aristocratic Government had been replaced by a weak administration, swayed by every breath of popular impulse. The peasantry who were the backbone of the nation had vanished, and been replaced by the weak, excitable populations of the towns.

Socialism, with its creed of "Thou shalt have no other God but thyself," and its doctrine, "Let us eat and drink, for to-morrow we die," had replaced the religious beliefs of a generation of Englishmen taught to suffer and to die sooner than surrender to wrong. In the hour of trial, amidst smoking ruins, among the holocausts of dead which marked the prolonged, bloody, and terrible battles on land and sea, the spirit of the nation quailed, and there was really no great leader to recall it to ways of honour and duty.[37]

The book was first published in the *Daily Mail* and was widely publicized. On the day before publication full-page advertisements with invasion maps appeared in the principal daily papers, and sandwich-men in German uniforms marched the pavements of Piccadilly. All this publicity may have pleased Roberts and Northcliffe, but it upset the Liberals; on March 13, 1906, the member for Harborough, R. C. Lehmann, asked "whether the Government can take any steps or express any opinion which will discourage the publication of matter of this sort, calculated to prejudice our relations with other Powers."[38] The Prime Minister, Campbell-Bannerman, replied with evident regret that the government could do nothing; he advised leaving the book "to be judged by the good sense and good taste of the British people." The British people responded by buying up edition after edition; the book was also translated into twenty-seven languages, including German. (Le Queux was

37 *Invasion of 1910*, p. 542.
38 *Hansard*, vol. 153 (March 13, 1906), col. 1120.

upset to discover that the German translator had given the book a German happy ending, with German troops in London, and that the revised version had been made a prize book in German schools.) [39]

Compared to *The Riddle of the Sands, The Invasion of 1910* is amateurish and crude; Childers was a far better writer in his first and only novel than Le Queux ever became (though he wrote 200 books). But the crudeness may be more than a matter of talent; Le Queux's book is also more violent, more melodramatic, and far more bloodthirsty than Childers', and this seems to suggest a change in the mood of the English audience. Le Queux's Germans are inhuman brutes who massacre and burn, destroy whole towns, murder children, and force their victims to dig their own graves; they are, in fact, the Huns of 1914. Even the Londoners who rise against them kill with a savage relish that has nothing of English virtue about it. That the book should have received Lord Roberts' imprimatur is a sign of the deterioration of good sense and decency under the pressure of national anxiety.

The Edwardian invasion scare was primarily a Tory creation, and most of the literary treatments of the theme carry obvious Tory political sentiments; but there is one important exception. In 1908 H. G. Wells wrote *The War in the Air* and gave invasion his own peculiar Socialist slant. Wells had been invading England off and on for years, but previously he had brought his invaders from outer space; *The War in the Air* used terrestrial invaders, and, like the other writers in this Edwardian tradition, Wells made the invaders Germans. The novel also resembles others of this class in two other ways: his British are unprepared and they are physically deficient. Bert Smallways, his hero, is "a vulgar little creature, the sort of pert, limited soul that the old civilisation of the early twentieth century produced by

[39] William Le Queux, *Things I Know About Kings, Celebrities, and Crooks* (London: Eveleigh Nash, 1923) , p. 250.

the million in every country in the world."[40] But that last phrase indicates one important way in which Wells' book is different from the others—it is essentially international, not imperial; it is in fact anti-imperial, and treats the Empire as a clumsy and archaic obstacle to peace and freedom. Similarly, Wells' conception of the war itself was international. Of Edwardian writers he was the only one who saw that warfare had ceased to be a conflict between two sets of national interests and that the next war could involve the world. Consequently, his image of war was prophetic in a way that no other invasion novel was; the others generally modelled their actions on Franco-Prussian or even Napoleonic strategy, but Wells imagined the techniques and problems of aerial bombardment as they appeared in 1939-1945. Six years later, in *The World Set Free*, he visualized atomic bombs and the Third World War. No one imagined a war that was anything like 1914-1918; it was then, as it is now, unimaginable.

All Edwardian invasion novels were polemical, and all were concerned to answer the question, what is the matter with England? But whereas Tory writers found their answers in the state of military preparedness, Wells proposed larger and more radical answers. The troubles with England, he said, were that it had retained its empire, that it had vulgarized democracy by giving it into the hands of the untrained and ignorant, that it had not planned its society, that it had succumbed to racism, nationalism, and a yellow press, that it was complacent and unprepared for social change and challenge. But while the context of these remarks is a radical one, not all would have been offensive to Lord Roberts' followers—the view of Liberal Democracy, for example, echoes passages from many Tory invasion stories, from *The Battle of Dorking* to *The Invasion of 1910*. And there is another point that Wells might well have

[40] H. G. Wells, *The War in the Air* (London: George Bell & Sons, 1908), p. 67.

borrowed from Kipling—that civilization had declined because mankind had suffered a failure of will. This is scarcely an argument at all, and certainly not one that can be supported or refuted; it is characteristic of Wells, and of much radical thought of his time, that in the end his analysis of the condition of England was based not on a theory, but on a melancholy mood.

> Could mankind have prevented this disaster of the War in the Air? An idle question that, as idle as to ask could mankind have prevented the decay that turned Assyria and Babylon to empty deserts or the slow decline and fall, the gradual social disorganization, phase by phase, that closed the chapter of the Empire of the West! They could not, because they did not, they had not the will to arrest it. What mankind could achieve with a different will is a speculation as idle as it is magnificent. And this was no slow decadence that came to the Europeanized world; those other civilizations rotted and crumbled down, the Europeanized civilization was, as it were, blown up.[41]

The phrases in this closing passage suggest how much Wells shared the Edwardian mood: "decay," "decline and fall," "decadence" are the language of the time and not of a party. In his shaping of the novel's conclusion Wells also showed himself to be in the spirit of the age. After 1906 the invasion novels tended toward bleaker ends—the invasions were more often successful, the British were defeated, and civilization suffered. Wells' is the extreme example of this tendency: at the end of *The War in the Air* the modern world has been destroyed, and mankind—those fragments that have survived—has reverted to a primitive existence that will be nasty, British, and short. The novel proposes no alternative to this disaster, beyond the idle speculations of a "different will."

In 1908 and 1909, imperial defense became a still more

[41] *War in the Air*, p. 349.

inflammatory issue with the publication of the German naval estimates and the subsequent cabinet debates over the building of dreadnoughts to meet the German challenge. In January 1909, in the midst of the cabinet discussions, a clumsy melodrama of invasion, written by an unknown author who called himself simply "A Patriot," opened in London and was an immediate hit. The play was *An Englishman's Home*, and the author was Major Guy du Maurier, an officer in the Royal Fusiliers stationed in South Africa. Major du Maurier had never before written a play—or anything else, for that matter—but the sense of impending national disaster was apparently great enough to turn even regular officers into playwrights. This new author had one unusual advantage, though; his brother Gerald was a prominent actor-manager in London. It was Gerald who read the play while Guy was in South Africa, recognized it as "the real stuff," gave it a title, and produced it. The success of the play surprised everyone except Gerald; the *Times'* critic concluded that it was

> startling testimony to the hold which the great National Defence question has taken of the thoughts and imagination of the English public. The thing itself is crude enough, and indeed somewhat amateurishly done; what is significant is that the thing should have been done at all.[42]

The plot of the play is the barest invasion story; enemy troops in a surprise attack occupy an Englishman's home; the Volunteers try unsuccessfully to expel the invaders; finally British regulars approach and will presumably defeat the enemy. The invaders are troops of "Her Imperial Majesty the Empress of the North," from a country called "Nearland." (The Lord Chamberlain's office was inclined to be touchy about plays that might offend other governments, and to avoid being refused a license the producers made some effort to avoid identifying the enemy as Ger-

[42] *Times*, Jan. 28, 1909, p. 10.

man.) They were dressed in uniforms of a vaguely Franz Leharish style, and given non-German names, though they were allowed enough Prussian mannerisms to keep the point sufficiently clear. Their actions are civil and retain some of a professional soldier's ideals of military behavior (they pay for what they take), though they are also ruthless. Above all, they are efficient, trained soldiers.

The English, on the other hand, exemplify the worst aspects of the Physical Deterioration Report and Lord Roberts' warnings. The principal civilian characters, members of a lower-middle class family called Brown and their friends, are a catalogue of physical deficiencies: Mr. Brown is overweight, his son Syd is thin and spotty, and his daughter's suitor is "short, thin, narrow-chested, sloping shouldered, knock-kneed, and lark-heeled," and has bad teeth. They are an idle and stupid lot who are whiling away a foggy Boxing Day with diabolo, football scores, sporting papers, and newspaper competitions when the Nearland troops appear. They are untrained to defend themselves— Mr. Brown cannot fire a gun, and the women don't know how to tend the wounded—and they laugh at the one character who has joined the Volunteers. They have, in fact, only one virtue: they are English. When Mr. Brown is told that he has no right to fight because he is a civilian, he replies: "Bah! What does that matter? I'm an Englishman." And there is no evident irony in the speech. He dies in the last act because he has fought back and has been captured, but his only error lies in the fact that he seized a gun too late; his mood as he is led off to execution is one of fierce patriotism, which du Maurier apparently expected his audience to admire and emulate.

In this expectation he seems to have been correct. *An Englishman's Home* was a success not only at the box office but at the recruiting office. Two weeks after the opening, the *Times* reported that "the fortunate increase in the number of recruits . . . [in the London Territorials] would not have been recorded had it not been for the production of a play at Wyndham's Theatre. . . ."[43] The government was understandably pleased and gave the play an unusual degree of official protection. When the director of a revue theater announced a satiric skit based on the play, he received a prompt telegram from the Lord Chamberlain's office informing him that no skit of *An Englishman's Home* would be allowed.[44]

The play was performed around the world, with predictable political results. It was a great success in Pietermaritzburg, Natal, where the author attended the opening, and in Sydney; but it was so unkindly received in Berlin that the first performance had to be stopped; in Dublin it had to be done largely in dumb show because dialogue was not audible above the shouts of "Sinn Fein" and the singing of "God Save Ireland."[45]

The extreme badness of this successful play seems to have brought some Englishmen, at least, to their senses. The forbidden satiric skit was in fact played, and *Punch* began to parody du Maurier and the military mood; a few months later a very funny burlesque of the whole invasion scare appeared, the first and indeed the only comic contribution to Edwardian invasion literature. The book was called *The Swoop! or How Clarence Saved England: A Tale of the Great Invasion*, and the author was the young P. G. Wodehouse. The immediate target of Wodehouse's ridicule was a recent novel called *The Swoop of the Vulture*, in which a German fleet raided England and began a war. In Wodehouse's novel, England is invaded simultaneously by the Germans in Essex, the Russians at Yarmouth, the Mad

[43] *Times*, Feb. 15, 1909, p. 6.

[44] *Times*, Feb. 25, 1909, p. 13.

[45] Du Maurier was not the only recruiting playwright. Henry Arthur Jones wrote a one-act propaganda play called *Fall In, Rookies*, which was produced on Oct. 24, 1910. Before the play opened Jones read it to Lord Roberts; Roberts approved of it and attended the first night performance.

Mullah at Portsmouth, the Swiss Navy at Lyme Regis, China at Llgxtpll, Wales, Monaco at Auchtermuchty, Moroccan brigands at Brighton, and Bollygolla at Margate. The nation is saved by the single-handed and ingenious heroism of a Boy Scout called Clarence. Wodehouse thus managed to include in his satire not only the fiction of invasion but also the related activities of Baden-Powell, and to be both funny and sensible about the mood of the time.

Humor and good sense may have had a temporary effect; at any rate the number of invasion stories declined sharply after 1909. But the mood of melancholy, anxiety, and depression did not die away; it is evident, more strongly than ever, in the last of the pre-war invasion stories, two books published in 1914. *War,* by W. Douglas Newton, attempts a realistic description of an invasion as it would appear to an ordinary civilian observer. Newton avoided the spectacular elements of maneuvers and communiques and conferences in high places that lend an air of unreal romance to books like *The Invasion of 1910* and confined himself to the probable local experiences of war—civilian casualties, panic, hunger and disease, looting, rape, and executions. The scene is not identified, nor are the combatants, but the place is obviously the south of England, and by 1914 no English reader would have identified the enemy as any nation but Germany.

Though *War* is not a didactic novel, it does contain a few passages condemning English unpreparedness, both material and psychological: the English, Newton said, were not ready either to fight a war or to experience war. Father Hugh Benson, who wrote a preface, took Newton's point to be a pacifist one, an argument for alternative solutions. Kipling, on the other hand, gave permission for the use of a militant passage from his writings, as a kind of epigraph, and must have assumed that Newton was writing another "Wake Up, England" book. But in fact the book is neither pro- nor anti-war; it is simply anti-delusion. Newton thought, with considerable reason, that the English people were talking themselves into a national disaster without realizing what war would mean. His book must have shocked his readers—Father Benson found it necessary to apologize for Newton's bloodiness—but, by comparison with the actual war that came so soon after, it seems a mild narrative of small-scale horror. But the point of the book, coming when it did, is in what it does not include. It contains no mention of national honor, of victory, of conquest, or of glory. It has no heroes and no heroism—in fact it mentions none of the splendid abstractions that had fed the war fever. Instead, it offers suffering, helplessness, destruction, and meaningless death. It does not even follow the war to its conclusion; the book ends with the observer's death before a firing squad (where he is not even allowed the romantic firing-squad scene, but is simply shot). There are only two emotions in the book, the two true emotions of the experience of war—fear and confusion.

Newton's novel has no particular literary merit, and author and book are alike forgotten. The last Edwardian invasion novel has survived, though, not because it is better written, but because it was written by Saki. *When William Came* appeared on the very eve of war, and appropriately enough it took the invasion theme up at the latest possible point—the point at which England has lost its war with Germany and London is ruled by the Hohenzollerns (so that technically it is not an invasion novel, but an occupation novel). The book is not a warning—Saki assumed that it was too late for England to wake up—but a bleak prophecy; the decline of the old virtues had gone too far, and the fall of England was inevitable.

It is an unpleasant book, full of Saki's most unattractive qualities: his inhumanity, his bitter contempt for human affections, his pleasure in degradation, his preference for predatory animals and predatory people, his sick sentimentality. But the unpleasantness is not, perhaps, entirely of

Saki's doing; it is at least in part an expression, in an extreme form, of moods of the time: anxiety and fear of the future and rage at the passing of an English dream of glory and stability. The values that the book proposed as good are essentially those of du Maurier, Childers, and Lord Roberts—Duty, Self-Sacrifice, The Empire, The English Earth. Saki celebrated them all in the peculiarly overripe prose that he reserved for the description of emotions about abstractions or about scenes without human figures. These are the values that in their more attractive forms we call patriotic; but as Saki represented them they emerge more often as militaristic, arrogant, and xenophobic—the values that made the Empire and at the same time made England's enemies.

The values are in the Tory tradition, but Saki was different in that he could find scarcely anyone in England worthy of his ideals and so wrote a book in which disgust is the principal emotion and action seems nearly impossible. His two principal spokesmen for the Old English virtues are a broken-spirited invalid who withdraws from German London to a self-indulgent foxhunting life, and a broken-hearted old countess living in retirement at her country house (Saki calls the house Torywood). London and its society have been left to foreigners, Jews, and social climbers —representatives of that "Cosmopolitianism" which for Saki, and so many conservatives like him, was the antithesis of English values.

In his account of the causes of decline and fall, Saki showed the same Bourbon-like consistency, and resistance to changing ideas, that is the mark of his Tory literary line. He noted national unpreparedness, complacency, luxury, and moral softness; he regretted equally the passing of the old religious faith and of the old insular suspicion of foreigners. This Tory continuity is nowhere more apparent than in the last scene of this last Edwardian example of the genre. The German conquerors have decided to concentrate on winning the loyalties of the young; to this end they have scheduled a review of the Boy Scouts by the Emperor in Hyde Park. The Scouts refuse to parade, and Yeovil, Saki's principal character, watching the collapse of the Imperial triumph, thinks with a flush of pride and shame,

> *He* had laid down his arms—there were others who had never hoisted the flag of surrender. He had given up the fight and joined the ranks of the hopelessly subservient; in thousands of English homes throughout the land there were young hearts that had not forgotten, had not compounded, would not yield.[46]

How Baden-Powell must have loved that brave conclusion. And would not Kipling have seen, in that beaten but still patriotic figure under the trees, an echo of the blind hero of *The Light That Failed*, cheering on British troops with "Give 'em hell, men, Oh, give 'em hell"? Kipling had written that episode before the Boer War, and some Liberal critics had hoped that the actual experience of war would modify the English taste for such dreams of blood and glory. But in Saki, writing just before another and more terrible war, the same dreams reappear; his Germans have prohibited their English captives from bearing arms, and Saki regrets that English lads will be deprived of this rich experience:

> The martial trappings, the swaggering joy of life, the comradeship of camp and barracks, the hard discipline of drill yard and fatigue duty, the long sentry watches, the trench digging, forced marches, wounds, cold, hunger, makeshift hospitals, and the blood-wet laurels—these were not for them.[47]

[46] Saki [H. H. Munro], *When William Came* (London: John Lane, 1914), p. 322.
[47] *When William Came*, pp. 190-191.

But they were, ironically, for Saki; he found his blood-wet-laurels two years later in France, during the attack on Beaumont Hamel.

Looking back over the invasion literature of the Edwardian period, one can discern what seems to be a progressive pattern: from invasion anticipated and foiled, to invasion easily defeated, to invasion defeated with difficulty and at political expense, to defeat and occupation. Such a sketch is obviously too simple to represent anything so complex as national attitudes, but it does suggest changes in the Edwardian frame of mind that are demonstrable in other terms and that can perhaps be best described as a loss of national self-confidence. The fact that the literature is concentrated in the years from 1906 to 1909 suggests that the change of mood had political origins, and certainly it is obvious that the militaristic group around Roberts and Northcliffe worked to induce anxiety in the English people for political reasons. Conjectural explanations may be offered for the decline of invasion writing after 1909: the Tories were preoccupied with the fight against the Parliament Bill; or they had decided to play the "Ulster card"; or they felt that the Naval Estimates of 1909 showed that the cause had been won. But whatever the causes of the invasion writing, the mood that it expressed became a reality that was more than political; anxiety and the expectation of war were a part of the Edwardian consciousness.

Chapter III

The social conditions that Tories took as signs of decadence, more liberal-minded men saw as indictments of Edwardian society, matters for compassion rather than condemnation, for reform rather than retrenchment. The spirit of the great Victorian reformers—men like Ruskin and Morris, Kingsley and Maurice—was alive in young Liberals at the century's turn, and their responses to the social problems of their time were strenuous and indignant and seemed to promise that a Liberal government, when it came, would be a reforming government. But though the Liberals came to power in 1906 with an overwhelming majority and remained in power until the war came, they did not significantly alter the social conditions that they deplored. The question of why the Liberals, possessed of such unusual power, and with such clear occasions for the beneficent use of it, did not act to correct flagrant social wrongs is one of the crucial questions of the Edwardian era.

That the condition of England required radical reforms no one could have denied. The poor were more wretched and more numerous than at any other time in English history, and the rich were richer and more conspicuous in their luxuries. The extreme gap between penury and ostentation, between the East End of London and the West End, was an unavoidable social fact. To Edwardians of social conscience it was a crime that the world's richest nation could not neglect. The "crime of poverty" (a phrase that recurs in writings of the time) had been made more visible in the years around the turn of the century by the development of English sociology, which began to put before the public studies of contemporary poverty that were at once irrefutable and intolerable. Charles Booth's *Life and Labour of the People of London*, the first systematic and comprehensive study of the poor, was begun in 1889 and completed in 1903; it ran to seventeen volumes, of which four were devoted to poverty. In 1901 Seebohm Rowntree published his study of the slums of York in *Poverty: A Study of Town Life*. These two writers agreed on one statistical conclusion, so appalling that it needed no emotional ambience, only the statement itself: nearly a third of the people of England at the beginning of the twentieth century were living in conditions that would not support life at the lowest level of human tolerance. And the cause of this circumstance, Rowntree said flatly, was not drink or idleness or the irresponsibility of the poor; it was simply that "the wages paid for unskilled labour in York are insufficient to provide food, shelter, and clothing adequate to maintain a family of moderate size in a state of bare physical efficiency."[1] One third of the nation, it appeared, was being starved by the other two-thirds.

These first studies were followed by others, in which sociology and economics combined to analyze the condition of England: L. G. Chiozza Money's *Riches and Poverty* (1905), Will Reason's *Poverty* (1909), Philip Snowden's *The Living Wage* (1912), and, the most impressive of them all, Sidney and Beatrice Webb's *Minority Report of the Poor Law Commission* (1909). The effect of such studies was to make poverty in England actual, a matter of facts and figures that demanded public action. The Liberal response was the controversial People's Budget of 1909. It was an important bill, the most important single piece of legislation of the Edwardian period: first, because it declared, for the first time in British history, a government's

[1] Rowntree, *Poverty: a Study of Town Life* (London: Macmillan, 1901), p. 133.

willingness to use taxation as a means of redistributing wealth, and second, because it roused the Tories to enraged resistance and led to the struggle with the House of Lords and to the Parliament Bill, which stripped the Lords of their veto and reorganized the balance of power in English politics. But one thing it did not do: it did not alter the condition of the poor, and the Edwardian Age ended with little social improvement accomplished. It had been more an Age of Reformers than an Age of Reform.

The failure of the Liberals to put reforms into practice is one aspect of that larger failure of action that characterized the party during the Edwardian years. Over the eight years between the 1906 election and the war, the party was amply provided with legislative suggestions—from Royal Commissions and parliamentary committees, from outside groups like the Fabian Society and the Women's Social and Political Union, and from its own back-benchers; yet in that time it achieved very little toward altering social conditions. A standard explanation of the Liberals' failure to seize the day is that they were hampered by their own traditions. Their inheritance of nineteenth-century laissez-faire individualism made the idea of strong government control seem anti-Liberal, and their traditional constituency, the commercial middle class, was hostile to government interference and to high taxes. Furthermore, as the period progressed the Liberals came increasingly under pressure both from the outraged Right and from the growing Labour party on the Left. If the Liberals wooed the workers with social reforms, they lost their middle-class constituents to the Tories; if they wooed the middle classes, they lost the workers. Caught in the middle of a classic three-party squeeze, the Liberals procrastinated, and let Labour take over the role of the progressive party in English politics.

This political account of the collapse of liberalism is a credible one, but it seems possible to describe the process in another, non-political way, as the failure of the Liberal imagination, squeezed, one might say, as the political party was squeezed, between the Tory imagination of traditional English virtues, on the one hand, and the Socialist imagination of a planned and just society, on the other. Just as the center of progressive legislation moved during the Edwardian decade from the Liberals to the Socialists, so the intellectual center of progressive thought and imagination went over to the Fabians.

This chapter is a study of two Liberal imaginations that failed. Neither C.F.G. Masterman nor John Galsworthy was a great man or even (to reduce the scale) a great Edwardian; they are the more representative of the Liberal failure for that reason. Their careers show how in the Edwardian years the faiths of liberalism failed to provide sustenance for men of imagination, and how that failure was manifested in imaginative terms.

Masterman was one of those young Liberals who carried the Victorian radical tradition into the twentieth century. He was both a writer on social questions and an active politician, a Liberal M.P. from 1906 until the war, and a member of Asquith's cabinet in 1914. His career is worth pausing over as an example of how nineteenth-century liberalism lived on into the Edwardian years and died there.

Masterman was a man who seemed to have all the necessary gifts and all the appropriate convictions for a great career in his party; his family background was middle class, evangelical, and philanthropic (there were Buxtons and Frys among his connections); his university record was impressive (a double first at Cambridge, president of the Union, editor of *Granta*) ; his wife was a Lyttelton (daughter of the Chief of the Army General Staff, granddaughter of an earl, and niece of a bishop, of a headmaster of Eton, and of Mrs. Gladstone [see Appendix B]). He had spent his first years out of Cambridge in social work in South London, he had edited the journal of the Christian Social Union, and he had written a book on the religious meaning of Tennyson's poetry which had won him a fellowship at Christ's College. He was a man of quick intelligence and wit, an excellent speaker, a fluent writer, a clever parliamentarian; and he was a man of strong social and religious convictions, which is evident in the emotional tone of his writings and is also apparently characteristic of his public speeches.[2]

Masterman entered Parliament in the Liberal sweep of 1906 and for nearly ten years advanced steadily in the party; in 1908 he was made Parliamentary Secretary of the Local Government Board; in 1909 he became Under-Secretary of State in the Home Department under Winston Churchill; he went in 1912 to the Treasury as Financial Secretary; and in 1914 he was appointed Chancellor of the Duchy of Lancaster and a Cabinet Minister. But here, at the end of the Edwardian afternoon, Masterman's ascent ended too. On being appointed to the Cabinet, he resigned his seat, as was customary, and ran for re-election; he was defeated, tried again and lost, and was nearly ten years in getting back into Parliament. He died in 1927 without again holding high political office. So absolute and dramatic was Masterman's fall that when in 1926 Lord Beaverbrook hit on the idea of a newspaper series titled "Splendid Failures," he chose Masterman as his first subject.

Masterman's failure had its personal elements, but it can also be read as a model of the larger failure of the liberalism that he represented. His writings record, often very movingly, the faiths and aspirations of an Edwardian Liberal; they also record the weaknesses and eventual defeat of those high motives before the problems that they were inadequate to solve. His compassionate concern for the condition of England was evident in all his words and acts, but as the

[2] According to Lucy Masterman her husband was the model for Langham in H. M. Tomlinson's *All Our Yesterdays*, and for Raeburn, the supremely untidy politician in Wells' *Mr. Britling Sees it Through*. He is also described by G. K. Chesterton in his *Autobiography* and by Ford Madox Ford in *Return to Yesterday*.

Edwardian decade passed his words lost urgency, and he seemed to lose confidence in the power of reform. Like his party, he simply lost momentum.

The sense of social urgency is most apparent in his first writings on social questions, his contributions to *The Heart of the Empire* (1901). This book, which Masterman edited (and very considerably rewrote), is a collection of essays by young Liberals on problems of modern city life. The general argument is that the city is the heart of the Empire and the source of its life, and that the attentions of Englishmen should therefore be turned toward the city's social problems and not toward the imperial extremities. Coming as it did during the Boer War, the book must have displeased imperialists, but it pleased enough anti-imperialists to sell out the first edition in a month.

The Heart of the Empire is very much a book by young men—idealistic, impatient of the past, optimistic for the future. Masterman's preface begins,

> The Victorian Era has definitely closed. For many years it was manifest that the forces characteristic of that period had become expended, and that new problems were arising with a new age. But during the latter years of the nineteenth century men were content to confront the evils of national life with the old remedies. There had indeed been some modification in the general tendency of opinion, but this had by no means kept pace with the altered conditions of the world. The rapidity of social and economic change will perhaps be more easily realised now that the death of the Queen and of the century have reminded us all that nature and time spare nothing, however customary, honoured and secure. The present can never take refuge behind the past.[3]

A new century, a new monarch, new problems, new remedies: these are the positive aspects of the Edwardian sense

[3] *The Heart of the Empire* (London: Fisher Unwin, 1901), p. v.

of change. The book that follows this brave preface is somewhat less positive, however; the contributors were alert to the new problems created by the growth of the cities; they rightly emphasized the increasing gap between rich and poor, the artificial conditions of life and work, the ugliness and dreariness of slum existence. But their discussions of these problems show how much they were the heirs of Victorian reformers: almost without exception they treated social problems as moral problems, and they were inclined, having passed their moral judgments, to stop short of making proposals and to rest on piety. For example, Masterman, discussing the problem of the unjust distribution of wealth, said this of the rich:

> At the one end of the scale the lives of a large proportion of the rich are far from satisfactory. Separated from many of the realities of life, they are unable to find natural ways of expending their money, and, in consequence, are driven to indulge in sumptuous living or vulgar display. Thousands of pounds representing the toil of years in the cultivation of choice flowers or rare wines are dissipated for the gratification of a few guests at an evening party. Nor do the owners of this wealth really profit by their indulgence. Tyrannised over by their own conventions, slaves to their servants, frequently devoid of any real appreciation of the beautiful, their lives are spent without knowledge of the highest forms of happiness, with disastrous loss of energy, and opportunity—a loss that falls on all.[4]

This portrayal of the rich is a very Edwardian one—it continues through the decade, both in essays like these and in literature: one finds it in the novels of Galsworthy and Wells, the plays of Shaw and Barker, and in a mass of popular romances by writers like E. Philips Oppenheim and

4 *Heart of the Empire*, p. vi.

Ethel M. Dell. It is not anti-aristocratic, nor does it imply opposition to the idea of individual wealth in itself; it is simply a moral judgment of the misuse of wealth. This anti-plutocratic attitude was almost inevitable in a period during which the gross value of unearned income increased by half, but it is not essentially a political attitude: many a Tory gentleman would have heartily endorsed Masterman's statement.[5] Conservative and Liberal could agree that if England was suffering social decay, one cause was the separation of wealth from breeding and the creation of a new kind of rich man.

There was also, said Masterman, a new kind of poor, a New Town type:

> . . . its development is too recent to enable its characteristics to be fully apprehended. Briefly, however, we may say that it is physically, mentally, and spiritually different from the type characteristic of Englishmen during the past two hundred years. The physical change is the result of the city up-bringing in twice-breathed air in the crowded quarters of the labouring classes. This is a substitute for the spacious places of the old, silent life of England; close to the ground, vibrating to the lengthy, unhurried processes of Nature. The result is the production of a characteristic *physical* type of town dweller: stunted, narrow-chested, easily wearied; yet voluble, excitable,

[5] Lord Charles Beresford, for example, wrote: "The Plutocrat is gaining power each day on both sides of the Atlantic, and the Democrat is likely to be crushed under the heel of a worse tyrant than a King who wore the purple, or any Ecclesiastical Dignitary, who set up claims to temporal power.

"British society has been eaten into by the canker of money. From the top downwards, the tree is rotten. The most immoral pose before the public as the most philanthropic, and as doers of all good works. Beauty is the slave of gold, and Intellect, led by Beauty, unknowingly dances to the strings which are pulled by Plutocracy." "The Future of the Anglo-Saxon Race," *North American Review*, vol. 171 (Dec. 1900), p. 807.

with little ballast, stamina, or endurance—seeking stimulus in drink, in betting, in any unaccustomed conflicts at home or abroad.[6]

This passage derives from the same Edwardian concern that produced the Physical Deterioration Report and the Boy Scout movement. It shows how social anxieties had been affected by the spread of a kind of popular Darwinism, which one might compare to the popular Freudianism of the 1920's. Simplified versions of the theory of natural selection crept into discussions of many kinds of change, as a vague fear that irrational natural forces might usurp men's rational control of human society. In the quotation from Masterman the implication is that the human characteristics of highest survival value in a city slum might be, from society's point of view, the most undesirable ones—that down there in the abyss, south of Waterloo and east of Liverpool Street, a new and frightening race was evolving.

It is one of the curious aspects of the Edwardian period that this concern for the poor did not find expression in fiction, as one might have expected it would. Although the Edwardians produced the first important sociological studies of urban poverty in England, they did not write novels about it. The writers who had brought realism to England in the preceding decades—notably George Moore and George Gissing—turned to other subjects (and Gissing died early in the period, in 1903). The best of the novelists who followed them, like Bennett and Wells, raised their sights slightly and dealt with the lower fringes of the middle classes, or still higher, like Forster, and wrote about the middle-class intelligentsia, but for nearly twenty years, from Maugham's *Liza of Lambeth* to Frank Swinnerton's *Nocturne*, there was no important realistic novel published. One might propose various explanations for this fact: that Booth and Rowntree had made realistic fiction unnecessary or that the realities of Edwardian poverty were beyond

[6] "Realities at Home," in *Heart of the Empire*, pp. 7-8.

realism. But the real key may be in the mood of Masterman's description of the poor—a mood of uncertainty and apprehension. The poor were no longer simple, dependent inferiors to be dealt with in a district-visitor manner; they were a mysterious and frightening new force. The best representation of them in fiction is not, therefore, realistic: it is Wells' description of the Morlocks, the evolved underworld creatures of *The Time Machine*.[7]

The effect of these changing conceptions of classes was to create a mood of estrangement and anxious uncertainty. A new, irresponsible rich, living in a new vulgarity, and a strange new poor, living in new ugliness, were replacing the old class division of gentry and peasantry. Those rooted connections with the English land that men had trusted to preserve the native English breed were passing; three-quarters of the population lived in towns and cities, and the land was becoming the playground of the rich. The problem was not simply to see and solve the issues; it was also, for men like Masterman, an emotional problem—the problem of accepting the idea of a twentieth-century, urban, industrial England. Men who could not manage this adjustment—Masterman was one in politics, and John Galsworthy is an obvious example in literature—ran down in the end as their generous sympathies became sentimental and nostalgic. Both men survived into the post-war years, but they survived like mastodons in ice, two curious examples of extinct Edwardian attitudes.

The reforming proposals that *The Heart of the Empire* made were reasonable enough, in a general way: return to the land, housing reform, temperance reform, education, improvement of the conditions of female labor. One contributor, G. M. Trevelyan, argued for greater control of the economy, but on the whole the essays were not strongly

[7] *The Time Machine* (London: Heinemann, 1895). The evolution of a new urban type is also discussed by Ford Madox Hueffer [Ford] in *The Soul of London* (London, Alston Rivers, 1905), Ch. V.

in favor of collective, centralized governmental action. The strongest reforming statement in Masterman's essay is one that is not social at all:

> At the commencement of the twentieth century of the Christian era, in a world-wide disenchantment, the most progressive races of our western civilisation stand as if paralysed before a problem apparently beyond human solution—seeing human action vanishing in a kind of wide and barren marshland through which pulsate no tides of the Infinite sea. But if the cry of "Back to the Christ," which so many observers note as a manifest sign of the coming years, be but the herald of a deep and earnest attempt of the Churches to realise once again the life and the teaching of their Master, then to the anxious watcher the night may indeed be far spent—the dawn be nigh at hand.[8]

Here already the mood of the later Masterman is evident: modern life posed an apparently insoluble problem, and the best solution that he could offer was a conditional hope of religious revival. The state of mind was a common enough one in the early years of this century, but it is not a state of mind that could lead to significant reforms. The condition of Edwardian England could not wait upon a change of heart.

In the decade that followed, Masterman published three other books on social questions. *From the Abyss* (1902) is a collection of impressionistic essays about slum life, based on his experience in South London. As impressionism, the book is very good; Masterman was a skillful writer of a rather poetical, decorated prose, though his prose style, like his social ideals, shows that his natural ties were with the nineteenth century—with writers like Ruskin and Carlyle. As a testimony to his sympathies with the poor, the essays are effective. But as sociological or political writing they

[8] *Heart of the Empire,* pp. 51-52.

are negligible; they contain no ideas and no proposals—only feelings.

Three years after *From the Abyss* Masterman collected a group of literary and social studies from his prolific writings for periodicals and published them as *In Peril of Change* ("Damn the feller," Campbell-Bannerman grumbled when he saw the book, "I thought he *wanted* change.")[9] The title is certainly ambiguous, but no more so than the book, for though Masterman was sensitive to the changes in his world, he was not at all sure that he wanted them. The tone of the book is sombre and elegiac, as Masterman, like some minor prophet from the Old Testament, recorded the decline of England.

Expectancy and surprise [he wrote] are the notes of the age. Expectancy belongs by nature to a time balanced uneasily between two great periods of change. On the one hand is a past still showing faint survivals of vitality; on the other is the future but hardly coming to birth. The years as they pass still appear as years of preparation, a time of waiting rather than a time of action. Surprise, again, is probably the first impression of all who look on, detached from the eager traffic of man. The spectator sees him performing the same antics in the same grave fashion as in all the past: heaping up wealth which another shall inherit, following pleasure which turns to dust in the mouth, and the end weariness: thinking, as always, that he will endure for ever, and calling after his own name the place which shall know him no more. But surprise passes into astonishment in confronting the particular and special features of the age. Here is a civilisation becoming ever more divorced from Nature and its ancient sanities, protesting through its literature a kind of cosmic weariness. Society which had started on its mechanical advance and the aggrandisement of material goods with

[9] Lucy Masterman, *C.F.G. Masterman* (London: Nicholson and Watson, 1939), p. 56.

the buoyancy of an impetuous life confronts a poverty which it can neither ameliorate nor destroy, and an organised discontent which may yet prove the end of Western civilisation. Faith in the invisible seems dying, and faith in the visible is proving inadequate to the hunger of the soul. The city state, concentrated in such a centre as London, remains as meaningless and as impossible to co-ordinate with any theory of spiritual purposes as the law of gravitation itself.[10]

There is much in this passage that is typical of Masterman's party and of his age, as well as of his own melancholy nature: the attitude of the present toward the Victorian past—like that of a weak son toward a bullying parent; the sense of the present as a "time of waiting"; the regret for the passing of a civilization intimately in touch with nature. The book has many admirable qualities: the critical judgments are often very perceptive (Masterman is good on Gissing's slum novels, for instance); the analyses of the social crisis are intelligent; the prose style is easy and graceful. But the book has one profound flaw: it lacks vitality. For a Liberal writing in 1905, when it must have been apparent to the dullest prophet that the Tory government was dying, the tone of *In Peril of Change* seems inexplicable. The party of reform was about to return to power, after ten years in opposition; there were changes to be made, problems to be solved, the nation to be restored to progressive life. But this is Masterman's version of the coming political change:

> There is opportunity for a statesman who would rightly apprehend the situation, and definitely interpret to the nation the danger of the collapse of ruins. Yet, confronting present affairs and the temper of the people, one can but emphasise something of the almost forlorn heroism of the enterprise.[11]

10 *In Peril of Change* (London: Fisher Unwin, 1905) , pp. xii-xiii.
11 *In Peril of Change*, p. 327.

Masterman entered the government as a man might enter a fever hospital or a leper colony, determined to do his best, but without hope that the sickness of England could be cured.

The last and most important of Masterman's Edwardian books was written during the first months of 1909. The Liberals had then been in power for three years, with the largest Parliamentary majority in the party's history; the Cabinet was fighting the battle of the dreadnoughts, and Lloyd George was at work on his "People's Budget." At this turbulent and critical time, Masterman wrote a book that reveals a sensitive awareness of turbulence and crisis, but reveals more clearly a passive mood of bafflement and regret; his reforming spirit had lost what direction it had, and he had become a prophet without a prophecy. *The Condition of England* is in two parts: an analysis of "some, at least, of the characteristics of the various classes of Society to-day in England," and a diagnosis of the social maladies of the country. Masterman's treatment of the classes is what one might expect of an Edwardian Liberal: he found the plutocrats idle and vulgar, the middle-class suburbanites vacuous, and the workers miserable (though such a bare summary does not do justice to Masterman's sympathetic accounts of the lives of the oppressed). But it is in his analysis of the causes of social disintegration that Masterman most revealed himself. In three chapters entitled "Science and Progress," "Literature and Progress," and "Religion and Progress," he dealt with the possible sources of faith in modern society and found them all lacking: science was not equipped to offer spiritual values, religion had failed to do so, and literature had been made an instrument of escape. England, Masterman concluded, had lost contact with the traditional sources of altruism and had found no new sources. He looked at the leaders from whom inspiration should have come (including presumably the leaders of his own party), and saw only "a strange mediocrity, a strange sterility of characters of supreme power in Church and State." And he saw, in the structure of English society, a disastrous fissure that separated the summit from the base of society.

The most striking thing about this Liberal's description of the condition of England is its close resemblance to the Tory version. Masterman's account of the loss of national altruism would have pleased Baden-Powell, and his description of suburban idleness and vacuity could have come from any pamphlet of the National Service League (much of it in fact did come from the opening scene of *An Englishman's Home*). His predictions of increasing lawlessness, his fears of government by violence, and his mood of irresolution and discouragement are all echoed in Tory writings of the time. And so is the note of nostalgia that he struck again and again—nostalgia for a simpler and better past, when life was decent because men were decent, and men were decent because they were in touch with the English earth. This note one expects from Conservatives, but in a Liberal it suggests a facing in the wrong direction. Masterman could write movingly about the things that moved him, and his deep sympathies for the poor sometimes made him sound like a radical reformer; but his emotions were not directed toward action; they were, apparently, sufficient in themselves. If he wrote feelingly about the urban poor, he wrote in the same mood about the decline of the rural peasantry, and in each case the burden of his argument was not reform but decent feelings.

Masterman once shrewdly remarked of H. G. Wells that his appeal was "not so much against conditions of modern civilization as against life itself." Masterman certainly saw himself as the opposite of Wells in this—as a man who *did* appeal against conditions. But though he could be ardent about the things that he was against—about poverty and urban ugliness and hopelessness—he had little to appeal *for*; he was unlike Wells, also, in that he had no vision of an earthly paradise. He shared with other Edwardians the vague, anxious mood of the time—a mood of nostalgia for the past, regret for the present, and apprehension for the future.

But if his anxiety was of his time, the forms it took were dictated by his party inheritance. Masterman was a Liberal, and heir to the party's nineteenth-century traditions of evangelism and reform. When he looked to the conditions of modern civilization, it was with the evangelical rather than the reforming eye; he looked, that is, not *at* the social problems but *behind* them, and there he found spiritual causes of the condition of England. His essays return again and again to the loss of faith and the need for religious revival, and it is clear that this spiritual impoverishment of the people caused him more profound distress than their material sufferings did; like other religious men, he could more readily endure a world without bread than a world without belief. When he thought of reform, he thought of it as fundamentally a moral action—a change of heart from which material changes would somehow follow—and the prospect of social improvements without spiritual renewal filled him with vague fears. "It is rather in the region of the spirit that the doubts are still disturbing," he wrote at the end of *The Condition of England*:

> Fulness of bread in the past has been accompanied with leanness of soul. And the modern prophet is still undecided whether this enormous increase of life's comforts and material satisfactions has revealed an equal and parallel advance in courage and compassion and kindly understandings. The nations, equipped with ever more complicated instruments of warfare, face each other as armed camps across frontiers mined and tortured with the apparatus of destruction. A scared wealthy and middle class confronts a cosmopolitan uprising of the "proletariat," whose discontent it can neither appease nor forget. The industrious populations which have been swept into masses and congestions by the new industry have not

yet found an existence serene, and intelligible, and human. No one, to-day, looking out upon a disturbed and sullen Europe, a disturbed and confident America, but is conscious of a world in motion: whither, no man knows.[12]

Masterman was the "undecided prophet" that he describes here, but if he is important in the history of Edwardian England it is because there were so many men like him—men of liberal good will who felt keenly about social injustices but who failed to translate feeling into decision. Chesterton shrewdly analyzed the sources of Masterman's failure when he wrote of him

> What was blamable, as distinct from what was blamed, in him was due to two things; he was a pessimistic official. He had had a dark Puritan upbringing and retained a sort of feeling of the perversity of the gods; he said to me, "I am the sort of man who goes under a hedge to eat an apple." But he was also an organiser and liked governing; only his pessimism made him think that government had always been bad, and was now no worse than usual. Therefore, to men on fire for reform, he came to seem an obstacle and an official apologist; but the last thing he really wanted was to apologize for anything.[13]

Chesterton was describing the man; but the traits that he found in the man were also in the party, and with the same paralyzing consequences—the same heritage of evangelicalism and the same disbelief in the power of political action to make men good or happy. The man and the party failed to act because they did not believe in action.

Part of Masterman's failure, then, was the failure of liberal evangelism as a reforming force; another part seems best described as a failure of intellectualism, a surrender to

[12] *Condition of England* (London: Methuen, 1909) , p. 208.
[13] G. K. Chesterton, *Autobiography* (London: Hutchinson, 1936) , p. 124.

the temptation to substitute rhetoric for action. Masterman was by nature as much a man of letters as he was a man
of religion—a point that his first book, *Tennyson as a Religious Teacher*, makes clear. He wrote easily and well, and
about all he wrote belletristically. He was for many years
dependent on his income from writing and from his work
as literary editor of a daily paper. He wrote as often and as
well about literature as about politics and included many
writers among his friends—men like Bennett and Wells and
Ford Madox Ford.

When Masterman wrote about social problems, therefore,
he turned naturally to imaginative literature for his examples, where a less literary man would have turned to sociology and economics. His literary editing had made him
aware that a good deal of Edwardian literature was, as he
put it, "at war with civilisation," and he drew upon this
kind of writing for support. The examples he chose are revealing of the extent to which Masterman's own state of
mind was shared by other writers of his time: writers, that
is, who regretted the most characteristic features of the present and shared nostalgic feelings for unattainable past sim-
plicities, writers of the kind of social criticism that moves
in the wake of the time, deploring faded injustices and
admiring archaic virtues. Masterman was a connoisseur of
Edwardian literature of right feelings, a class of writing that
was sufficiently large and sufficiently popular to earn a place
in the history of the period.

For literary examples of poverty, Masterman drew upon
two Edwardian autobiographies: W. H. Davies' *Autobiography of a Super-Tramp* (1908) and Stephen Reynolds'
A Poor Man's House (1909). Reynolds' book is an account
of life among Devon fishermen; it is a romanticized version
of the working class, close to nature and far from cities, and,
whatever its literary virtues, it has little to do with the realities of Edwardian working-class problems. Indeed, insofar as the book celebrates the rewards and virtues of the

simple life and suggests that class is a wall built by the poor to keep out the rich, it is directly counter to the spirit of social reform. Davies' book is a better, more permanently interesting book, but it has some of the limitations of Reynolds'. Davies was a sentimental anarchist by nature, and his descriptions of urban poverty, though often touching, imply no solutions beyond endurance and a free heart. Both books have considerable literary merit—Davies' is a minor classic—but neither is a book that a Liberal politician, analyzing the condition of Edwardian England, could choose to represent the condition of the poor without seriously deviating from reality; fishermen and super-tramps do not compose a significant segment of the poor, and the Wordsworthian ideal of independent poverty that both books celebrate is a literary rather than a social concept. Masterman could have drawn on any of the Edwardian sociologists; the Webbs' Minority Report had just appeared, for example, and Masterman had recognized it as "an historic document." But when he wrote about poverty he preferred to use materials that were more literary and less urgent.

For an account of the upper classes Masterman turned to John Galsworthy's *The Island Pharisees*, "an impeachment," as he thought, "of the country house and conventional life of successful England." Galsworthy's later reputation as a novelist has depended almost entirely on the Forsyte series, and those novels are probably read more as bland social history than anything else; but his Edwardian reputation was rather different, and Masterman was simply repeating the common judgment of his contemporaries when he took Galsworthy seriously as a social critic and satirist. In the decade before the First World War, Galsworthy wrote in a variety of forms about a variety of injustices; during those years he must have been England's second most productive social critic (no one, of course, could match Shaw). The five novels that he wrote between 1904 and 1911 were all, in his own phrase, *"class* novels," and all were critical of established aspects of English society; most of them also contain episodes—often quite extraneous to plot and theme—illustrating particular social ills that troubled Galsworthy: blood sports, prison conditions, laws of marriage and divorce, poorhouses.[14] At the same time that he was writing these novels he was also criticizing society in his plays, in satirical sketches, and in pamphlets and letters to editors. In all these activities he was taken very seriously by his contemporaries, both by admirers like Masterman and by Tory opponents.

The novel that Masterman so admired, *The Island Pharisees*, is early, clumsy Galsworthy, and because it is so obviously done it shows clearly his characteristics as a social critic. The theme of the book is a young man's discovery of social inequalities and injustices, and the action is a journey—a sort of tour of privilege and poverty. The hero, an upper-middle-class young man called Shelton, is engaged to marry Antonia, the conventional daughter of a country gentleman. He meets a penniless vagabond, Ferrand, and through Ferrand is introduced to the world of the slums, where he learns that the poor are wretched and cynical, and the rich unsympathetic. From this beginning he goes on to question the institutions that support his own stable, middle-class world: the clubs and universities, the clergy, country-house society, the prison system, marriage. His journey through injustice leads him at last to his fiancée's country house, where he tries to communicate his new

[14] Among Galsworthy's papers his biographer found a list of 25 causes to which he had at one time or another given active support: abolition of the censorship of plays, sweated industries, minimum wages, labor unrest, labor exchanges, woman's suffrage, ponies in mines, divorce law reform, prison reform, airplanes in war, docking of horses' tails, for love of beasts, slaughterhouse reform, plumage bill, caging of wild birds, worn-out horse traffic, performing animals, vivisection of dogs, dental experiment on dogs, pigeon shooting, slum clearance, zoos, Cecil houses, children on the stage, three year average income tax. (H. V. Marrot, *Life and Letters of John Galsworthy* [London: Heinemann, 1935], pp. 215-216.)

doubts to Antonia. At the end he returns to London and breaks his engagement.

The Island Pharisees is a very bad novel, but it is bad in ways that reveal permanent qualities of Galsworthy's mind and imagination. It is loosely constructed, because Galsworthy's desire to get all his feelings about social injustices into one book was stronger than his artistic impulses—right feelings were more important to him than right forms. It is thematically unresolved, because, like Masterman, Galsworthy was unable to go beyond feelings to questions of causes and remedies. Shelton is instructed in poverty, hypocrisy, phariseeism, and snobbery, and he reacts to his new knowledge with the right emotions, but the results in terms of his thoughts and behavior are vague and negative; he breaks with his fiancée, but not with her class, and he breaks with Ferrand—the symbol of everything that is the opposite of country-house propriety—at the same time and with equally mixed feelings. The final episode is an inconclusive, almost meaningless withdrawal from the scene and terms of the conflict and suggests an ambivalence that marks all of Galsworthy's social criticism—he was attracted by the authority and stability of the upper-class world that he attacked, and he mistrusted the emotionalism and freedom of the world that he admired. But in fact the entire book has been a long withdrawal from action. Shelton is given many opportunities to comment on social evils, but the conclusions that he reaches are condemnations of human nature rather than of human institutions:

Mean is the word, darling [he writes to Antonia]; we are mean, that's what's the matter with us, dukes and dustmen, the whole human species—as mean as caterpillars. To secure our own property and our own comfort, to dole out our sympathy according to rule just so that it won't really hurt us, is what we're all after. There's something about human nature that is awfully repulsive, and the healthier people are, the more repulsive they seem to me to be. . . .[15]

A statement like this—and it is entirely characteristic of Shelton's judgments—is not in any reasonable sense social criticism; Shelton speaks with the voice of doom, not with the voice of reform.

Oddly, the novel that followed the clumsy *Island Pharisees* is Galsworthy's best-made and most trenchant book of social criticism. The explanations commonly proposed for the excellence of *The Man of Property* are that Galsworthy was moved by his deep personal involvement in his themes to give them a focus and definition lacking in his other books. He was at the time involved in a love affair with his cousin's wife, Ada Galsworthy, and believed that she was suffering acutely and unjustly because of society's attitudes toward marriage and divorce. At the same time he was living on an unearned income provided by his middle-class, commercial family. And so marriage and property became the joint objects of his passionate attack. But even in this novel Galsworthy's ambivalent social attitudes are apparent; he obviously knew which side he *ought* to be on, but he wasn't altogether there. The *Spectator*'s reviewer was not being stupid when he wrote of *The Man of Property* that "many people will regard it as a vindication of the laws of conventional morality"; this is not the point that Galsworthy intended to make, but there was enough of Soames Forsyte in his nature to make the point in spite of his intentions.

The year after *The Man of Property* was published, Galsworthy began to write a series of satirical sketches for the *Nation*. The sketches are brief vignettes, each aimed at an aspect of the lives and values of the rich or the poor; as lit-

[15] *The Island Pharisees*, revised edition (London: Heinemann, 1908), p. 33.

erature they have no value, but as evidences of Galsworthy's attitudes they are direct enough to be interesting. The rich characters in the sketches are all Forsytes—cautious, avaricious, complacent, lifeless, secure; the poor, who are carefully arranged in juxtaposition to the rich, are brutal and brutalized, miserable, and hopeless. The whole treatment is heavy, humorless, and grotesquely over-simplified, and this is in part a function of the mode of observation; the observer is a consistent, though uninvolved, character who sees everything from an upper-class, sympathetic, but detached point of view. He sees feelingly, but he never enters the human situations, except occasionally to ask a question; he is separated from the rich by their callous indifference and from the poor by their brutality. There is one particularly revealing feature of his treatment of the poor: again and again he describes them as animals —as cats, rats, and especially as dogs. In a sketch called "Demos," for example, a lower-class wife-beater (all Galsworthy's lower-class husbands beat their wives) exclaims: "I'm 'er 'usband, an' I mean to 'ave 'er, alive or dead." The observer comments:

> I saw that this was not a man who spoke, but the very self of the brute beast that lurks beneath the surface of our State; the very self of the chained monster whom Nature tortures with the instinct for possession, and man with whips drives from attainment.[16]

There is both revulsion and fear in this passage, and these feelings toward the lower classes emerge in other works by Galsworthy too—sometimes as the responses of the fastidious upper classes, but often with a hint that these emotions are also the author's.

The sketches were collected in 1908 as *A Commentary* and received the unfavorable notices they deserved. One review in particular is notable for the force of its attack.

[16] *A Commentary* (London: Grant Richards, 1908), p. 214.

Lord Alfred Douglas, who was then editing the *Academy* in a fiercely pugnacious fashion, selected *A Commentary* for an attack on Liberal attitudes.

> Mr. Galsworthy [Douglas wrote] has for some time been supplying *The Nation*, which is a six-penny weekly Liberal review, with brief fictional sketches of a character presumed to be acceptable to the Liberal mind. When one looks closely into these sketches as reprinted in the volume before us one is appalled. For Mr. Galsworthy's book makes it quite plain that the Liberal mind is a sour, dour, superior affair, full of kinks and ill-disposed to mankind at large. We find Mr. Galsworthy writing here in the harshest, most strident, and most exaggerated manner about matters which he himself admits that he does not understand. We find him posing as a helper of the poor and as a sympathizer with the pains of life. Yet all the time one feels that his sentiments are of a bitter and almost brutal kind, and that if the saviours of the poor are to come out of the ranks of the John Galsworthys of this world, heaven must help the poor.[17]

Douglas was an habitual and sometimes slightly hysterical controversialist, but he was a clever critic, and his judgment of Galsworthy's attitudes is a shrewd one. There is in fact no human warmth in *A Commentary* and no suggestion that observer and poor might belong to one human community. It is interesting that Douglas could suggest that such a "sour, dour" book was a characteristic expression of the Liberal mind. In the year of the Poor Law Report and the Report on the Feeble-minded, the proposition has some validity; Galsworthy's *Commentary* shared with those documents certain attitudes which one must assume were Liberal—a removed superiority of attitude and an inability to reach conclusions.

[17] "Reprint from 'The Nation,'" by "X," *Academy*, vol. 74 (June 20, 1908), 906-907.

The technique of juxtaposing rich and poor, used in *A Commentary*, provided the structural principle for Galsworthy's next novel, *Fraternity* (1909). Galsworthy had first intended to call the book *Shadows*, and throughout it he repeated, in many variations, the idea that the poor are the shadows of the rich: "Each of us," says an old philosopher, "has a shadow in those places—in those streets,"[18] and by this Galsworthy seems to mean two things: that the poor are inseparable from the rich and that they are indistinct and unknowable. The rich in this novel are Pateresque intellectuals who live comfortable lives in comfortable Kensington houses, who support charities, but cannot imagine what it is like to be poor. When a poor model does penetrate this world, disorder and unhappiness follow, in forms appropriate to the classes concerned: a poor husband attacks his wife with a bayonet and goes to prison; an upper-middle-class husband leaves his wife without a word. At the end of the story the two worlds are as separate, and as unhappy in their own ways, as at the beginning. If the book has a moral, it is that each class is condemned to its own conventions and that no member of one class can know a member of another. It is mildly satiric of artists and intellectuals (Galsworthy was always an anti-intellectual at heart) and aloofly sympathetic toward the poor, but the idea that it attacks most bitterly is the idea of the title—the old philosopher's dream of universal brotherhood.

It is surprising to find that this dim, discouraged book moved some readers to extreme rage. The *Times Literary Supplement* thought it was not a sane book and compared it to a symptom of disease; the *Saturday Review* called it "a very dangerous and revolutionary book."

"Fraternity" [the review continued] is nothing more or less than an insidious and embittered attack on our social system. It is calculated to bring the official governing class

[18] *Fraternity* (London: Heinemann, 1909), p. 29.

into contempt and to import prejudice into the consideration of many important problems. . . . It is class hatred gone mad, and it is class hatred not of the noisy mob kind but of the quiet, dangerous sort of man who has felt and suffered and come to the conclusion that all is for the worst in the worst of all possible worlds. What Mr. Galsworthy has attacked and what we have called the upper middle class is the class from whose ranks are drawn most of our naval and military officers, Civil servants, judges and clergy—in short the official class. To this class the chief characters in the story belong, and every one of them is unsatisfactory. They have either got so much sense of what they ought not to do that they do nothing, or so much consciousness of what they ought to do that they never do anything. In every case they are poor specimens, self-conscious to a degree, morbid, restless, dangerous to the community. Such is the author's resentment against these people that he cannot give them a redeeming feature. His book in fact in its unrelieved gloom comes perilously near caricature. He turns and twists and writhes around his subject, and even if he does not scream it is impossible not to be always conscious of his pain. Moreover, he has introduced into his novel several unnecessarily unsavoury incidents and descriptions. Throughout he seems to have deliberately rejected and refused to see any light in the dark places of the world. Some of his similes and allusions are gratuitously coarse and indelicate. The book is quite unworthy of the author of "The Country House" and "A Man of Property." It is closely written and laborious—entirely lacking in spontaneity. In manner it lacks grace or charm. It is a book that gets upon the nerves.[19]

It seems clear that what got upon the nerves of this reviewer was the fact that Galsworthy had chosen to criticize the offi-

[19] *Saturday Review*, vol. 107 (March 13, 1909), 341-342.

cial governing class, and perhaps especially because that class was Galsworthy's own. At a time when the governing class felt itself under heavy and undeserved attack from many quarters—from the Socialists, from the suffragettes, from the unions—Galsworthy's novel must have seemed an act of class treason.

But the reviewer need not have worried: Galsworthy's days as a writer of social criticism in fiction were over. Perhaps because Ada Galsworthy's divorce had made it possible for him to marry her, and to rejoin polite society; perhaps because he had established himself as a fashionable writer; perhaps because liberalism had lost momentum and no longer offered inspiration; whatever the reason, Galsworthy abandoned his critical position on the outside of English society and assumed a familiar and on the whole admiring position within it. This change was so evident in his next novel that the *Spectator* could not resist gloating: *The Patrician*, it said, was "quite the most remarkable act of literary homage to the hereditary system which has been paid in the realms of fiction for a long time."[20] And though it was perhaps unkind to gloat, the *Spectator* was right—Galsworthy had switched loyalties.

However, if one reconsiders the arguments of Galsworthy's "*class* novels," his conversion becomes less surprising. He may have seemed a "rather fierce" social critic to Masterman, "the Conscience of the Age" to Conrad, "dangerous and revolutionary" to the *Saturday Review*, but none of these opinions is really supported by the novels. Nor did Galsworthy himself take any such positive view; from his own accounts of his motives and intentions he emerges a less certain, more ambiguous critic. In the preface to the Manaton Edition of *The Country House*, he explained himself in this way:

A temperamental dislike, not to say horror, of complacency, conscious or unconscious, undoubtedly played a

[20] *Spectator*, 4,316 (March 18, 1911), 408.

part in the writing of "The Country House," "The Patrician," and "The Freelands," as indeed in the writing of "The Island Pharisees," and to some extent of the "Forsyte" Series, which all deal with sections of "Society." To think that birth, property, position—general "superiority," in sum, is anything but a piece of good luck is, of course, ridiculous. But to see this too keenly, too introspectively, is to risk making a pet of self-distrust (another kind of complacency), and becoming a Hamlet. . . .[21]

This suggests that Galsworthy's hostility was directed not against privilege but against an attitude toward privilege; it does not suggest that a redistribution of the good luck would be desirable or possible. On this point the quotation is a fair judgment of the social attitudes of the novels: Galsworthy would have been content with the existing arrangements of society if only men and women had been kinder to one another. The last sentence of the quotation adds another, very English touch; Masterman once complained that in Europe introspection was regarded as a duty but that in England it was regarded as a disease, and Galsworthy supports this point.

However, though this passage reveals some of Galsworthy's attitudes, it has the limitations of a retrospective self-judgment made in public. An earlier remark, made in a letter to Edward Garnett, adds other elements. Galsworthy had just finished *The Patrician* when he wrote,

The *critical* essence of the book . . . consists in an opposition of authority and dry high-caste life with the lyrical point of view, with the emotionalism and dislike of barriers inherent in one half of my temperament. In other words this book, like *The M. of P., The C. H.* and *Fraternity*, is simply the criticism of one half of myself by the other, the halves being differently divided according

[21] Preface to *The Country House*, Manaton Edition, vol. 6 (London: Heinemann, 1923), p. xi.

to the subject. It is not a piece of social criticism—they none of them are. If it's anything it's a bit of spiritual examination.[22]

This statement has a certain circumstantial authority: it is a contemporary evaluation, it was made privately, and it was addressed to the man who was Galsworthy's principal literary adviser. It shows that, at that turning point in his career, Galsworthy was aware of the ambivalence that had marked his earlier work. Looking back at those *"class novels,"* he saw that what he had in fact been writing about was the tension, within himself, between security and freedom, order and emotion: between Soames Forsyte and his wife, Irene. It suggests, in that odd last phrase, that he saw the unlikelihood of that tension's ever finding a resolution; each novel would be only a bit of a long examination.

In his social novels, Galsworthy was not a recorder of life, like Arnold Bennett, nor a reformer of life, like Wells (both of whom were Fabian Socialists). When he brought injustice into a story, he did so in a way that was neither objective nor didactic but simply emotional; and his motive in doing so was not the alleviation of injustice but the alleviation of emotion. "When the miserable inequality of things strikes an observer with its naked edge," he wrote,

> he will—given the power of expression—avenge the blow, though he may know well enough that his riposte will spend itself in air, and even that no remedy exists. The cancer in human society is like cancer in the human body; we may palliate, but we cannot, it seems, cure.[23]

That is what Galsworthy's class novels are about—the miserable inequality of things or, more precisely, his reactions to that inequality. He brought in his victims of injustice—the

[22] Edward Garnett, ed., *Letters from John Galsworthy, 1900-1932* (London: Cape, 1934), p. 199.

[23] Preface to *A Commentary and other Essays*, Manaton Edition, vol. 17, pp. ix-x.

pauper, the beaten wife, the snubbed divorcee, or it might be a convict or a dead rabbit—rather as tests of right feeling than as soluble problems, and the episode was completed to Galsworthy's apparent satisfaction when the appropriate emotional response had been recorded. For example, the hero of *The Island Pharisees* finds himself, for no reason that the plot reveals, looking down at Princetown Prison, and it is "suddenly borne in on him that all the ideas and maxims which his Christian countrymen believed themselves to be fulfilling daily were stultified in every cellule of the social honeycomb."[24] Having had this feeling, he goes on his way; nothing more is said of the problem of the just punishment of crime: in fact justice is never mentioned. But justice is not what the episode is about; it is about Shelton's feelings, and he has passed the test by responding properly in the presence of imprisonment. In giving Shelton the right emotions, Galsworthy himself had passed another bit of his spiritual examination, though in a few pages he would have to set and pass a new test.

Much the same thing may be said of Galsworthy's Edwardian plays, though at first glance they appear somewhat more insistent in their reforming intentions. *The Silver Box*, *Strife*, *Justice*, and *The Eldest Son* are all concerned with injustices, with the ways in which those made strong by money or by class or by position impose upon the weak: employers bully servants, magistrates invoke one law for the rich and another for the poor, husbands abandon wives, gentlemen seduce servants, adults starve children. In one case a play by Galsworthy did have a direct reforming effect; Winston Churchill, then Home Secretary, and Ruggles-Brise, head of the Prison Commission, saw *Justice* and were moved by it (or by the publicity it was given) to modify the rules for solitary confinement in British prisons. But this is rather a special case: Galsworthy had a peculiar obsession with solitary confinement; it was, he said, his night-

24 *Island Pharisees*, p. 129.

mare and his sworn foe,[25] and he managed to get some of
his horror into the play, though solitary confinement is not
really what the play is about. In general it may be said that
the injustices in these plays are unresolved injustices, built
into the nature of things, for which the appropriate response is pity, not action. Like the novels, the plays offer
tests for right feelings.

These tests were necessary for Galsworthy because right
feelings were, as near as one can tell from his writings, the
only basis of standards and values that he had. He was
aware of a surge of social change, as any thinking man must
have been during those years, but he was uncertain and divided in his social values and unsure of the direction and
validity of action. Looking back in later years, he saw in
the Edwardian period two principal elements: it was "a
period of depression," and it was a period of revolt. When
he wrote his new preface to *A Commentary* in 1923, he tried
to explain what the revolt had meant:

Early Victorian personages, and novelists (even the three
Charleses—Dickens, Reade, and Kingsley—for all their
generous revolts against particular evils) solidly accepted
the conventions, morals, standards, ideals, and enterprises of their day; believed with all their hearts that life
was worth while; regarded values as absolute, lacked
ironic misgivings, and all sense that existence was a funny
business. They had no appreciation of any grin on the
face of Fate. In a word, they were almost majestically un-
self-conscious. This attitude to life was being broken-up
from 1885 onwards, about the time that discovery of our
simian origin began to be accepted; but the break was
not fully manifested in literature till somewhat later,
though by 1906 practically all the values were being challenged, and the literary pioneers of the change—Ruskin,

25 Letter to Beatrice Webb, May 21, 1909, in Passfield Papers, London
School of Economics.

Morris, Swinburne, Pater, Matthew Arnold, and Samuel Butler—had become almost old-fashioned.

Nowadays, we who were the later and ironic extremists of that challenge, are challenged in our turn, because we hold by our child the social conscience, which is now voted a bore. The revolt of 1885 to 1910 turned on a passionate or ironic perception of inequalities, injustice, call them what you will, on the emergence of the introspective social conscience, and the sympathies and compassions which belong thereto.[26]

This is scarcely an adequate account of the period, but it is a revealing description of Galsworthy's own idea of it. The time, for him, was made of revolt—a revolt against certainties that expressed itself in irony and compassion—and of depression that the loss of certainties inevitably brought. The irony, the compassion, and the depression are in Galsworthy's works, as they were in his mind, and one can define the man and the work in terms of those feelings. Galsworthy believed in the social conscience, he said, but he believed in it only as an emotion; he thought sentiment could be a civilizing force—perhaps the only civilizing force. If this was so, then a feeling perception of social evils was a necessary, and a sufficient, response to those evils; surely he saw no other answer. If Galsworthy was, like Soames Forsyte, a Man of Property (and he was), he was also a Man of Feeling, a sentimentalist.

It is in this fundamental sentimentality that Galsworthy resembles Masterman, and it is not surprising that Masterman should have admired so feeble a novel as *The Island Pharisees*. For that novel has essential qualities in common with *The Condition of England*: it dwells on feelings, treats poverty as an emotional experience, condemns the upper classes in sweeping criticisms; and over it all hangs the cloud

[26] Preface to *A Commentary*, Manaton Edition, vol. 17, pp. xii-xiii.

of an anxious, unresolvable depression, the feeling that for these problems there is no present answer. That mood, which is the defining mood of these two writers, is a common and a significant one among Edwardian Liberals; it is the mood of a time and a party that look nostalgically back to certainty, and apprehensively forward to uncertainty, a time that had found its new problems but not the answers.

The Condition of England and *Fraternity* were both events of 1909. They shared that year with a number of other events of political and social importance: the People's Budget and the Lords' veto of it; the Minority Report; suffragette hunger strikes; the panic over German naval superiority. These events define immediate and future problems that faced the Liberal party; all required swift and imaginative treatment, and none was handled altogether satisfactorily. There is a connection to be made, I think, between the limp, depressed, and passive tone of the books by Masterman and Galsworthy and the Liberals' inadequate response to the challenges of the day. The connection is in a common failure of imagination, the inability of intelligent men to conceive of new modes of action for new and challenging circumstances. The Liberal party needed vision to meet the great occasion, but the prophets who rose to prophecy were sad and undecided, and the occasion passed.

Chapter IV

....

THE FABIANS:
MRS. WEBB AND MR. WELLS

....

In politics and in social theory the liberating movement of the Edwardian period was socialism. As liberalism, tangled in its conflicts and indecisions, grew less and less capable of action, socialism assumed the progressive role in English political life. It did so the more readily because it had one significant advantage over both liberalism and conservatism— it was not a political party and thus was not bound by either traditions or expedients. What it was was a vital but unchanneled movement, and indeed it was the only political view to which movement could accurately be attributed during those years.

Because socialism was a range of ideas rather than an organization, it could assimilate a variety of groups within it: the Marxist Social Democratic Federation, the Independent Labour party, some trade unions, and the Fabian Society were all Socialist, but they were very different in their principles and intentions, and it was just this variousness that gave Edwardian socialism its flexibility and its momentum. The dogmas of the militant action groups did not govern, or even inhibit, the discussions of the Fabian intellectuals, nor did Fabian theorizing determine direct political action. If Sir William Harcourt was right when he said, "We're all Socialists now," it is because at the turn of the century socialism in England was an open movement, an energy rather than a policy.

But if at the beginning of Edward's reign socialism was an undefined energy, by the end of his reign it was a channeled force, represented in parliament, with a growing political party and a highly organized research and propaganda system. The principal instrument of this extraordinary growth and definition was the Fabian Society and, within the Society, two curious and forceful intelligences—Beatrice and Sidney Webb. The Webbs defined English socialism in *their* way, as practical and unvisionary, emphasizing efficiency rather than equality, and taking the state itself as a useful tool rather than as an enemy of freedom; to do so they fought off men of imagination and vision who would have made socialism a revolutionary, not an evolutionary, creed. During the Edwardian years they met one threat of particular force and attractiveness, the revolt of H. G. Wells. The outcome of that battle determined the future shape of Fabianism and thus of modern England. But to understand what the battle was about, one must go back to the beginnings of the Fabian Society.

The Society began in the 1880's as The Fellowship of the New Life, a front-parlor discussion group that aspired to reform society in spiritual and moral as well as material ways. The Fellowship was, like many of the radical groups of its time, a mixture of heterodoxies: its members included communists, spiritualists, psychic researchers, and single-taxers, held together (though only briefly) by a common desire to lead the Higher Life. But they could not agree on what the Higher Life should be, and after a few meetings the less spiritual members broke away to form the Fabian Society. The new organization was somewhat more unified than the Fellowship had been—the members agreed, at least, that society should be reconstituted on Socialist principles—but in other respects was still extremely eclectic. H. G. Wells' account of those early Fabians is colored, no doubt, by his later quarrels with them, but it seems nevertheless a fairly accurate description. Wells recalled that when he came to London in the late 1880's,

London Fabianism was Socialism, so far as the exposition

of views and policy went. There was no other Socialist propaganda in England worth considering. But the Fabian Society had gathered together some very angular and incompatible fragments to secure its predominant position, and at every meeting it stirred with mutterings beneath its compromises. Some members denounced machinery as the source of all our social discomfort, while others built their hopes on mechanisation as the emancipator of labour, some were nationalist and others cosmopolitan, some were anti-Malthusian and others—with Annie Besant—neo-Malthusian, some Christian and some Atheist (denouncing religion as the opium of the people), some proposing to build up a society out of happy families as units and some wanting to break up the family as completely as did Plato. Many were believers in the capacity of Everyman to control his affairs by universal suffrage, while others had an acuter sense of the difficulties of the task and talked of oligarchies, toryisms and benevolent autocrats.[1]

This patchwork membership was held together partly by the forcefulness of the Society's leaders—G. B. Shaw and Sidney Webb in particular—and partly by the Society's policy of avoiding direct action, party alliances, and unnecessary political controversy. "The Fabian Society," Shaw wrote in the 'nineties,

> endeavours to pursue its Socialist and Democratic objects with complete singleness of aim. For example:
> It has no distinctive opinions on the Marriage Question, Religion, Art, abstract Economics, historic Evolution, Currency, or any other subject than its own special business of practical Democracy and Socialism.[2]

[1] Wells, *Experiment in Autobiography* (New York: Macmillan, 1934), p. 201.
[2] *Report on Fabian Policy* (Fabian Tract No. 70) (London: Fabian Society, 1896), p. 3. Unsigned, but identified as Shaw's.

In turn-of-the-century England this stance of high-minded disengagement must have been hard to sustain, but in fact the Society managed to enter the twentieth century without taking any position on the Boer War, Home Rule, Church disestablishment, or women's suffrage. These vast exclusions cost the Fabians some members—Ramsay Macdonald and Mrs. Pankhurst were among those who resigned over the Boer War issue—but those who remained were those content with a doctrine of gradualism and a discipline of research and propaganda.

The aims of the Fabians substantially defined the kind of person likely to be attracted to the Society: at the turn of the century the Fabian atmosphere was civil-service, academic, middle-class, and exclusive. The Fabians thought of themselves as scientific Socialists, and their society as an elite; they did not seek out new members—rather they made membership complicated and difficult—nor did they attempt to make the membership representative (there was only one worker on the rolls in 1884, and the number does not seem to have increased much in the years that followed). They were by intention undemocratic, exclusive, and scholarly. "The Fabian Society," said Shaw, "does not aim to be the people of England, or even the Socialist party." The general spirit of the Society at the century's end was perhaps best defined by Beatrice Webb when she described herself and her husband as belonging to "the B's of the world—bourgeois, bureaucratic, and benevolent."[3] It was from the "B's" of England that the Fabian Society drew its members, and it was the "B's" that the Fabians desired to influence.

Between 1900 and 1914 the Fabian Society underwent a remarkable change in both the numbers and the nature of its members. In 1900 it had scarcely 800 members, and over the next four years that number declined slightly; by 1907, however, membership had risen dramatically—to 1,267 by

[3] Margaret Cole, *Beatrice Webb* (London: Longmans, Green, 1945), pp. 65-66.

Edward Pease's count, to 2,000 according to Margaret Cole —and by 1914 was nearly 4,000. Many of these new members were or were to become well-known public figures: Granville Barker, Arnold Bennett, Rupert Brooke, Cecil Chesterton, Edward Garnett, Holbrook Jackson, G. M. Trevelyan, H. G. Wells all joined, and none could quite be described as "bourgeois, bureaucratic, and benevolent."

The causes of this wave of recruits are several. One cause is surely the increasing renown of the star Fabian, Bernard Shaw. By the early years of this century Shaw had achieved a reputation such as few literary men have known. He had the kind of public identity that is usually accorded only to practitioners of the less cerebral arts—matinee idols, fan dancers, monarchs, and politicians. He had established this identity, over many years, by extraordinary endeavors in many fields; he had been a novelist, a journalistic critic of the arts, a public speaker and campaigner for Socialists, a writer of political pamphlets; he had held political office— as a member of the St. Pancras Borough Council—and had been defeated for the London County Council. He had also written a number of plays, and by 1905, when both *Man and Superman* and *Major Barbara* opened in London, he was England's best-known, as well as England's best, playwright. He was also, as he had been for twenty years, a member of the Fabian Society's Executive Committee, and his presence there must have attracted men like himself, men more imaginative than academic, who added to the vitality of the Society, but also increased its volatility.

It is also evident from membership records that the most sudden increase in members came after the General Election of 1906. In this election 53 Labour members were elected to Parliament, and Labour for the first time sat as an independent Parliamentary party; many socialist-minded people must have become Fabians then under the impression that the Society would now become a political party. Certainly there was a powerful thrust toward political action in these years, which it required all the Fabian skills of Shaw and the Webbs to resist.

But an explanation of the appeal of the Fabian Society to Edwardian intellectuals cannot rest on personalities and political events alone. For quite apart from such considerations, the Fabians offered intellectuals a vision of extreme seductiveness—of a world run by the intelligent: not philosopher-kings but philosopher-experts. The clever people who came around to the meetings must have imagined themselves governing, by their new expertise, the inexpert masses of society, whose cause they had advanced, not by action but by diplomacy, the intriguing art of the clever. Even Beatrice Webb was shocked, in looking back over her Edwardian activities, at the intrigues: "not so much the intrigues themselves as our evident pleasure in them!"[4] It was surely in part that evident pleasure that drew Edwardian intellectuals to the Fabian cause.

Furthermore, because the Society was not a political party, it could be heterodox and receptive to extreme, eccentric ideas. The Fabians prided themselves on requiring of each other only a minimal confession of faith, the brief "Basis" which committed the signer only to work for the extinction of private property by the spread of Socialist opinions. The Society was therefore designed to avoid that crisis at which political intellectuals falter—the point at which party loyalty must be put before intellectual conviction. Ironically, it was its very heterodoxy that caused the Fabians their greatest troubles during the Edwardian years; for the heterodox, having been accommodated into the Society, turned and demanded a new orthodoxy. The old guard—the academic gradualists like the Webbs—were challenged by the new men—the imaginative activists like Wells and A. R. Orage.

Wells had known of the Fabians from his early days in Lon-

[4] Webb, *Our Partnership* (London: Longmans, Green, 1948), p. vi. (The diary entry is dated May 1922.)

don in the 1880's, but the Fabians didn't notice him until after the turn of the century. By 1902, however, his existence had to be noticed; in that year the *Fabian News* carried three admiring reviews of Wells books, all by members of the old guard: *Anticipations* reviewed by Haden Guest in March, *The Discovery of the Future* by Edward Pease in June, and *Mankind in the Making* reviewed by Hubert Bland in December. Pease was Secretary of the Society, and he and Bland were long-time members of the Executive Committee. *Anticipations* was Wells' eighteenth published book, and it seems at first odd that he had not reached the Fabians sooner; but it is not so odd when one considers what he had been writing, for Wells had changed with the century, and the writer of the 'nineties had become a New Man. The seventeen earlier books consisted of three works in the physical sciences, seven scientific romances, four volumes of short stories, two novels, and a book of essays and sketches. Of the next seventeen—those from *Anticipations* in 1901 to *Ann Veronica* in 1909—more than half could be classified in a general way as political-sociological. Wells brought the same vivid imagination to his new interests, but in shifting from scientific romance to the prediction of the actual future he was assuming a task for which imagination was not enough.

Anticipations—or, to give it its full title, *Anticipations of the Reaction of Mechanical and Scientific Progress Upon Human Life and Thought*—was the first of Wells' prophetic tracts, and it seems to have reached a wide and varied audience at once (Wells said that it sold as well as a novel) ; there were at least seven editions in the first year after publication. The reasons for its success are obvious enough. Coming as it did just after the turn of a new century, it appealed to a natural popular curiosity about what this twentieth century was going to be like. Wells offered a vivid, simplified, credible image of the future, based apparently on the firm authority of scientific principles, but thoughtfully sparing readers the dull details of science—the evidence, the logic, and the proofs.

The tone of the book is the confident, categorical tone of a classroom lecturer, enlivened with imagined scenes of future wars in the style of Wells' romances. The confident tone and the forceful style would surely convince the general reader that Wells' imaginings were facts, and his large generalizations natural laws. In fact, it is entirely a work of the imagination, and though some of his guesses were right—he anticipated trench warfare, tanks, and machine guns—others, and particularly the political guesses, were altogether wrong. This is not surprising, since Wells wrote as a trained scientist but was an amateur at political thinking.

At this pre-Fabian stage in his career Wells seems to have considered himself a Socialist, but the socialism of *Anticipations* is of an aggressively anti-democratic kind. What Wells imagined as the government of the future was a kind of technocracy, socialistic in its economy, but politically authoritarian—a world-state ruled by a scientist-elite of "functional men" who would seize power during a crisis and maintain it by their obvious efficiency. (Shaw parodied these New Men in his cockney engineer, Enry Straker, of *Man and Superman*, and Beatrice Webb made the same point about class when she wrote of Wells' "crude gospel" that it was "the idealisation of the scientifically educated materialist lower middle class man":[5] that is to say it is the idealization of *Wells*, though neither Shaw nor Mrs. Webb quite made the identification.) Wells treated the process by which the Enry Strakers took control in two conflicting ways: the general process of political change he described as evolutionary, but the scenes he invented to describe the actual assumption of power by the scientists read like an account of the establishment of any twentieth-century dictatorship. In his evolutionary determinism Wells is not unlike Marx; but in his taste for authoritarianism he is anticipating not

[5] B. Webb, Diaries, August 22, 1909. Passfield Papers, London School of Economics.

the British Labour government so much as National Socialism.

Anticipations is obviously not in any sense a reformer's book: it does not argue from humanitarian principles, nor does it treat reform as a moral imperative. On the other hand, it is not really a scientist's book either. It is rather a work of prophecy that *uses* science as authority for social and political predictions. Since Wells came to social theory by way of biological theory, it is not surprising that he used nineteenth-century biology's greatest advance—the theory of natural selection—as his authority for predicting the necessary failure of democracy and the rise of a new order.

> It has become apparent that whole masses of human population are, as a whole, inferior in their claim upon the future, to other masses, that they cannot be given opportunities or trusted with power as the superior people are trusted, that their characteristic weaknesses are contagious and detrimental in the civilising fabric, and that their range of incapacity tempts and demoralises the strong. To give them equality is to sink to their level, to protect and cherish them is to be swamped in their fecundity. The confident and optimistic Radicalism of the earlier nineteenth century, and the humanitarian philanthropic type of Liberalism, have bogged themselves beyond hope in these realisations. The Socialist has shirked them as he has shirked the older crux of Malthus. Liberalism is a thing of the past, it is no longer a doctrine, but a faction. There must follow some newborn thing.[6]

There is nothing in this passage that Lord Roberts or Baden-Powell would have boggled at—and nothing that a modern Socialist would be likely to accept. It is a familiar kind of turn-of-the-century radicalism, mixing Darwin and Nietzsche and the idea of efficiency to compose a society that would be, in effect, an inhuman machine.

[6] Wells, *Anticipations* (London: Chapman & Hall, 1902) , pp. 289-290.

It is curious that this book should have impressed the Fabian leaders and have persuaded them that Wells' socialism could make common cause with theirs; but so it did. Beatrice Webb read the book in December 1901 and wrote in her diary that it was

> the most remarkable book of the year: a powerful imagination furnished with the data and methods of physical science, working on social problems. The weak part of Wells' outfit is his lack of any detailed knowledge of social organisations—and this, I think, vitiates his capacity for foreseeing the future machinery of government and the relation of classes. But his work is full of luminous hypotheses and worth careful study by those who are trying to look forward.[7]

It is characteristic of Mrs. Webb that she did not become aware of Wells as a social thinker until he wrote a book of sociology. Yet she could have observed the same gift for "luminous hypotheses" in several of his earlier scientific romances. *The Time Machine*, for example, is an allegory of the class war, *The First Men in the Moon* of the specialization of social functions. Wells' knowledge of scientific possibilities provided him with parables for the forces that he saw at work in his world. It is generally true of these romances that they are not, strictly speaking, *about* science; they use science to make admonitory statements about social forces. But Mrs. Webb did not read science fiction and had to be reached on her home grounds, sociology.

Having discovered Wells, and deciding that he would be useful, Mrs. Webb set out with her husband—on bicycles, according to Wells—to bag him for the Fabians. Wells' first response to their advances was somewhat ambivalent: "The Webbs are wonderful people," he wrote in a letter in January 1902, "and they leave me ashamed of my indolence and

[7] *Our Partnership*, p. 226.

mental dissipation and abjectly afraid of Mrs. Webb."[8] This was the sort of effect that the Webbs had on many people— their unending industry in the cause of socialism made even so energetic a man as Wells feel slothful. The surprising thing is that Wells thought them wonderful. Mrs. Webb in particular was in many ways exactly the sort of woman that he disliked most. She was a lady by birth, and a patrician by instinct.[9] She certainly endeavored to pursue her Socialist objectives with complete singleness of aim, but her attitudes in matters not directly touching her socialism were more likely to be determined by her class than by her cause: she signed an anti-suffrage manifesto in 1889 and did not support the women's cause until 1906; in 1911 she signed a manifesto of the National Council of Public Morals deploring the degradation of the racial instinct, thus allying herself with Tory peers and bishops in a fundamentally Tory cause. Her tastes in the arts were proper and genteel: she disliked the plays of her fellow Fabians Shaw and Barker when they dealt too frankly with sexual matters, and she did not like poetry at all. Her standards of personal behavior were conventional and severe, and she was coldly and unforgivingly censorious of moral lapses. She regarded High Society as corrupting, and the lower classes as especially corruptible; she explained Wells' fall to her own satisfaction as the effects of the Elchos and the Desboroughs—the titled Smart Set of the day—upon a "growing bourgeois morality." When Edward Carpenter remarked at a meeting that "the great danger was prigs and priests," Mrs. Webb replied that "all the good in the world had been done by either priests or prigs,"

[8] In the files of the Fabian Society.

[9] When Bertrand Russell asked Mrs. Webb whether in her youth she had ever had any feelings of shyness, she replied, "Oh no. If I ever felt inclined to be timid as I was going into a room full of people, I would say to myself, 'You're the cleverest member of one of the cleverest families in the cleverest class of the cleverest nation in the world, why should you be frightened?'" Bertrand Russell, *Autobiography* (Boston: Little, Brown, 1967), p. 107.

adding with evident satisfaction that the Fabians were all prigs and that her husband was perhaps the best prig of the lot.[10]

Whether he was the best prig or not, Sidney Webb was a good deal less terrifying than his wife; but he was also considerably less charming. Even his wife described him as "undistinguished and unimpressive in appearance," and the phrase, if unwifely, is accurate. He was a man who had no intimate friends, was bored by women and disliked casual conversation, and lived a life of extraordinary remoteness from ordinary existence. There are many stories demonstrating his total ignorance of nature—of how, for example, he asked at a dinner party whether peas came from sweet pea vines—and his habitual state of abstraction. "I sometimes ask myself," Shaw once wrote to him, "what would become of you if I were to die, and leave you without any point of contact with the real world."[11]

It is hard at first to see how a Society dominated by such diligences could have commanded the loyalties of men like Wells. Neither of the Webbs ever gave evidence of appreciating any of the arts; they seemed to reserve for statistics those warm enthusiasms that less bureaucratic souls attach to poetry and music. And Wells in particular, with his scratchy lower-class distrust of persons of position and breeding—one can scarcely imagine him sitting down to chat with Mrs. Webb. But Beatrice Webb could and did offer Wells one thing that he wanted—the flattering companionship of the powerful and great. In the autumn of 1902 the Webbs hit upon the idea of a small dining club, composed of selected experts from many fields and of many political views who were to meet regularly to discuss problems and formulate policy. The idea is very typical of the Webbs—assuming as

[10] "First Public Conference on Mr. H. G. Wells' 'Samurai,'" *New Age*, n.s. 1 (May 2, 1907), 11.

[11] Letter dated Jan. 19, 1907. In Passfield Papers, London School of Economics.

it does that discussion by experts holds the solution to all problems and that uniformity of attitude is not important. The club, called The Coefficients, existed for some six years and included at various times a most heterogeneous collection of members: Liberal Imperialists like Sir Edward Grey and Haldane, Fabians like Sidney Webb and Pember Reeves, Conservatives like Lord Milner and L. S. Amery, Josiah Wedgwood the single-taxer, Bertrand Russell, the poet Henry Newbolt, the *Times'* military critic, the head of the London School of Economics, and the editor of the Tory journal the *National Review*. Wells was a member from the start, and an appreciative one; the meetings, he said, played an important part in his education: "I had much more to learn than anyone from those conversations," he later wrote, "and less tradition and political entanglement to hamper my learning."[12] But though he was pleased and flattered to be a member of the Coefficients, he would not have been pleased to know Mrs. Webb's motives for taking him up: "He is a romancer spoilt by romancing," she wrote of Wells early in their relationship, "but, in the present stage of sociology, he is useful to gradgrinds like ourselves in supplying us with loose generalisations which we can use as instruments of research."[13]

If Beatrice Webb had genius, it lay in this ability to see all experience in terms of its usefulness to Fabianism and to treat it all with the same cold analytical eye. Her analysis of Wells, written in her diary in the first months of their acquaintance, is a good example of this gift; she saw at once his limitations and his talents and weighed his utility as though he were not a man but a bundle of potential pamphlets.

We have seen something lately of H. G. Wells and his wife [the diary reads]. Wells is an interesting though somewhat unattractive personality except for his agreeable disposi-

[12] *Experiment in Autobiography*, pp. 651-652.
[13] *Our Partnership*, p. 289.

tion and intellectual vivacity. His mother was the house-keeper to a great establishment of 40 servants, his father the professional cricketer attached to the place. The early associations with the menial side of a great man's establishment has left Wells with a hatred of that class and of its attitude towards the lower orders. His apprenticeship to a draper, his subsequent career as an assistant master at a private venture school, as a state student at South Kensington living on £1 a week, as an army crammer, as a journalist and, in these last years, as a most successful writer of fiction, has given him a great knowledge of the lower middle-class and their habits and thoughts, and an immense respect for science and its methods. But he is totally ignorant of the manual worker, on the one hand, and of the big administrator and aristocrat on the other. This ignorance is betrayed in certain crudities of criticism in his *Anticipations*: he ignores the necessity for maintaining the standard of life of the manual working population; he does not appreciate the need for a wide experience of men and affairs in administration. A world run by the physical science man straight from his laboratory is his ideal: he does not see that specialised faculty and knowledge are needed for administration exactly as they are needed for the manipulation of machinery or forces. But he is extraordinarily quick in his apprehensions, and took in all the points we gave him in our 48 hours' talk with him, first at his own house and then here. He is a good instrument for popularising ideas, and he gives as many ideas as he receives. His notion of modern society as "the grey," not because it is made of uniform atoms of that shade, but because of the very variety of its colours, all mixed together and in formless mass; his forecast of the segregation of like to like, until the community will become extraordinarily variegated and diverse in its component parts, seems to us a brilliant and true conception. Again, democracy as a method of dealing with men in a wholesale way—every man treated in the bulk and not in detail, the probability that we shall become more *detailed* and less *wholesale* in our provision for men's needs—that again is a clever illumination. Altogether, it is refreshing to talk to a man who has shaken himself loose from so many of the current assumptions, and is looking at life as an explorer of a new world. He has no great faith in government by the "man in the street" and, I think, has hardly realised the function of the representative as a "foolometer" for the expert.[14]

The surprising thing is that Mrs. Webb could analyze Wells' character and work so perceptively and yet could not see that he would be a disastrous disturbance in the Fabian Society. For all the personal qualities that Wells brought into play in the subsequent row were precisely observed back there in 1902: his hatred for the aristocracy, his contempt for the masses, his ignorance of the complexity of political administration, his total faith in the "physical science man," his extraordinary talent for communicating ideas to a popular audience, his quick and restless intelligence all caused Mrs. Webb trouble before the decade was out.

Mrs. Webb's earlier note on *Anticipations* shows the same mixture of brilliance and blindness. She shrewdly analyzed the book's qualities, pointing directly and precisely to its most fundamental weakness; but she avoided the evident conclusion—that the man who had written *Anticipations* could not be useful and might be dangerously disruptive to an intellectual society of gradual Socialists. The Wells that she sketched in her diary—a physical scientist, politically ignorant and socially difficult, with a wide-ranging but undisciplined power of invention and a gift for clever phrases—this man is the antithesis of the Fabian "scientific socialist." But he had two striking qualities of mind which must have dazzled Mrs. Webb because she had neither—he had a

14 *Our Partnership*, pp. 230-231.

trained command of the mysteries of physical science, and he had a novelist's imagination. These qualities, in combination, hardly existed in any mind that Mrs. Webb might have come across, and it was no doubt the oddness of the combination that made her consider Wells more remarkable in his social and political thinking than in fact he was. Because she could see some resemblances between his views and her own —they shared a regard for "scientific" methods, a preference for government-by-experts, an indifference to the common people, and a certain vague religiosity—she took Wells to be a valuable ally; and because he seemed valuable, she saw— or at least acknowledged—only those characteristics in him that she saw to be useful. A Fabian utilitarianism filtered her human judgments.

The second passage quoted from Mrs. Webb's diary above suggests another kind of insensitivity on her part that led to troubles with Wells. Her analysis of Wells' character implies —though she never made the point overtly—a causal connection between Wells' humble origins and his ignorance and crudity, and between these qualities and his value as "a good instrument for popularising ideas." The connection may very well have been there, but to a man as socially difficult and insecure as Wells the patronizing implied in these remarks, when it became evident, would surely be infuriating. And so it was. As the difficulties between Wells and the Webbs became more open, so also did their social differences. Mrs. Webb noted witheringly in her diary that Wells' behavior was "a case of 'Kipps' in matters more important than table manners," and Wells, in a parting shot at the Webbs, described them as like the Bourbons, incapable of either learning or forgetting anything. The war between them became, before it was over, a kind of class war.

Wells became a Fabian shortly after *Anticipations* was published, and he demonstrated his new involvement by writing, over the next five years, a number of sociological-prophetic books and pamphlets: *The Discovery of the Fu-*

ture (1902), *Mankind in the Making* (1903), *A Modern Utopia* (1905), *Socialism and the Family* and *The Future of America* (1906), *This Misery of Boots* (1907), *New Worlds for Old* (1908). His production of fiction during the period, though prolific by anyone else's standards, was less than during the preceding years and was on the whole of poorer quality; of the fiction written between 1901 and 1908, only *Kipps* has any real merit.

In this new career as a social thinker Wells took himself very seriously. His prefaces to the later volumes treat the whole enterprise with a ponderous solemnity, as a series of studies that required doing and that only Wells could do; he came in the end to regard *Anticipations, Mankind in the Making* and *A Modern Utopia* as together composing a complete philosophical statement on social and political questions. The tone that Wells assumed is exemplified well enough in this remark from *A Modern Utopia*:

> since this may be the last book of the kind I shall ever publish, I have written into it as well as I can the heretical metaphysical scepticism upon which all my thinking rests, and I have inserted certain sections reflecting upon the established methods of sociological and economic science. . . .[15]

One of the interesting questions is how Wells, a writer of popular romances, was led to think of himself as a thinker whose metaphysical scepticism was worth recording. Another, equally interesting, is why intelligent and sophisticated contemporaries agreed with him.

There is no doubt that they did. The sales of Wells' "sociological" books might be explained away as representing a semi-educated taste, but this does not explain the fact that in November 1903—the year of *Mankind in the Making*— Wells was invited to read a paper to the Oxford Philo-

[15] "A Note to the Reader," *A Modern Utopia* (London: Chapman & Hall, 1905), p. vi.

sophical Society, or that the paper was subsequently published in *Mind*, or that another paper, *The Discovery of the Future*, was read to the Royal Institution and published in the Smithsonian Report for 1902. Wells' vogue as a philosopher seems to have been as sudden and extreme as his earlier success as a romancer, and is far less easy to explain.

The Oxford paper, "The Scepticism of the Instrument," suggests some reasons for Wells' success. He came before the society as a stranger from an unknown class—the undereducated lower-middle—and as a philosopher and metaphysician whose intellectual training had been entirely scientific. He must have seemed to be in touch with two "modern" sources of knowledge not open to most Oxford philosophers, and the strategy of the essay encouraged that assumption, being at once plain-speaking and scientific-sounding, the writing of an honest, no-nonsense man of science. The argument is essentially anti-logical, a rejection of the philosophical validity of general terms. Wells argued, by analogies drawn from science, that all terms are unique, and all generalizations, like the genera of science, merely approximations; he concluded from this argument that ethical, political, social, and religious ideas must be treated as personal expressions, without general validity.

At the time, Wells' point must have seemed most shocking in its application to morals, but the political implications were more ominous for his future as a Fabian. One wonders how the Fabians, reading this paper (and they must have read it, since Wells thought so well of it that he appended it to *A Modern Utopia*), could possibly have considered its author a Fabian Socialist, for it proposes nothing more than a pseudo-philosophical basis for anarchy. And in the end Wells' penchant for political and moral anarchy combined to his undoing in Fabian circles.

The swift growth of Wells' public stature as a popular philosopher is perhaps reflected in the rapidity with which he became a disturbance in the councils of the Fabians. In March 1904—scarcely two years after he had joined the Society—he resigned, partly, he explained, because he was leaving London, but not entirely:

... this alone [he wrote to the Secretary] would not justify my abandoning the privilege and honour of calling myself a Fabian. But I find also that I am by no means in sympathy with the attitude adopted by the society towards various contemporary political issues. Neither the matter nor the manner of the second tract upon "Free Trade" [the work of Shaw], for example, is to my taste. Were I able to attend the meetings with any regularity I would do my poor best to establish my views of methods against the prevailing influences, in spite of my distinguished ineptitude in debate. As things are however I do not see what service I can do the society by remaining in it.[16]

Three weeks later he withdrew his resignation, and over the five years that followed he did indeed do his poor best to establish his views.

He did so at first with the approval and apparently the friendship of the Webbs. During 1904 the Webbs visited the Wellses at Sandgate and gave a "carefully selected" dinner party for them in London (the other guests included the Shaws, the Prime Minister, and the Bishop of Stepney); though Mrs. Webb continued to write calculating analyses of Wells in her diary, her remarks were not hostile. In 1905 Wells published the third of his principal sociological books, *A Modern Utopia*, and *Kipps*, his second novel. He entertained the Webbs at Sandgate again in May and had a long talk with Mrs. Webb, which she recorded in her diary thus:

A long talk with H. G. Wells at Sandgate: two articles of our social faith are really repulsive to him—the collective

[16] Letter dated March 17, 1904. In files of Fabian Society.

provision of anything bordering on religious or emotional training, and the collective regulation of the behaviour of the adult.[17]

In the discussion Wells was obdurate and dogmatic, and everyone got hot and exaggerated in the argument; they parted without reaching any agreement. The clash seems a fundamental one, yet Mrs. Webb, though perceptive as usual in analyzing Wells' point of view, seemed to regard the whole thing as simply an interesting intellectual discussion, not the head-on clash of personalities that later events showed it to have been.

Two other events of 1905 should have warned the Webbs of the trouble that lay ahead. One was a lecture, "This Misery of Boots," which Wells delivered to the Fabians in December and later published as a pamphlet. The talk was an attack on private enterprise, but in no other respect was it a Fabian performance. It contained no statistics, and indeed no facts. It was simply an emotional appeal for a redistribution of wealth, novelistic in its methods (the cast of characters includes imaginary rich men and pitiful little girls in ill-fitting shoes), and emotional in its essential appeal. The pamphlet clearly demonstrates Wells' attractiveness for the Fabian leaders—he could make socialism both simple and touching—but it also shows the remoteness of his imagination from theirs. Further, the pamphlet makes clear Wells' deep hostility to the fundamental Fabian principles of gradualism and permeation. One passage was so bluntly antagonistic that the Fabian executive asked Wells to cut it from the published version; being Wells, he irritably refused; being Fabians, they allowed the offending passage to stand.

The other portentous event of the year was the publication of *A Modern Utopia*. In this book Wells tried to avoid what he considered the weaknesses of his earlier sociological studies by combining fictional and discursive methods. For a

[17] *Our Partnership*, p. 307.

framework he chose a miraculous journey, in the manner of other utopias, and in this story he imbedded some of his pet ideas as they might appear in ideal action. Wells' utopia embodied two general principles that might have alarmed the Webbs: the subordination of regulation to freedom (of which Wells said characteristically that the fundamental freedom is the freedom to love) and the elevation of artists and aesthetic concerns above administrative issues. The book gives scarcely any attention to forms of government—in fact Wells took it as a condition of utopia that there should be no government—and though there is a chapter entitled "Utopian Economics," it contains little that would have made sense at a Fabian meeting. Indeed the whole idea of a utopia is contrary to the way in which Fabians dealt with society; the Webbs worked for precise and particular reforms within the existing social fabric, whereas *A Modern Utopia* abandons the present for a spacious, self-indulgent daydream.

The most emphatic element of daydream in Wells' book is in his conception of ideal rulers, his "Samurai." The Samurai are a "voluntary nobility," bound by ascetic vows, who control the state and its wealth. They live strenuous intellectual lives and obey rules of health, industry, discipline, costume, and religion that would please Baden-Powell. They are the only voters and are not themselves elected. They have no defined class origins. It is striking that Wells' idea of utopia included an all-powerful, anti-democratic elite. It is equally striking that the society he imagined governed by this Samurai caste was a precisely class-structured society, though class is defined in ways that make men like Wells the aristocracy. Below the Samurai, a class based on energy, there are four other classes: The Poetic, based on creative imagination; the Kinetic, based on unimaginative intelligence; the Dull, based on lack of intelligence; and the Base, a class containing all those who lack moral sense. Wells' profoundly anti-democratic turn of mind reveals itself here not only in the *fact* of this class division, but also in the very language he used—the Dull and the Base classes. It is not, one would think, a Fabian world: it is a world made *by* Wells especially *for* Wellses. Yet Mrs. Webb considered the Samurai to be the literary expression of her influence on Wells' thought, which suggests that she too fancied a class structure rule by a voluntary nobility.

But however un-Fabian Wells' views became, the Webbs managed to maintain the ties of friendship; Wells was apparently still more valuable than irritating. The first sign that trouble was coming appears in Mrs. Webb's diary in March 1906:

H. G. Wells has broken out in a quite unexpectedly unpleasant manner. The occasion has been a movement to reform the Fabian Society. The details are unimportant for I doubt whether he has the skill and the persistence and the real desire to carry a new departure. But what is interesting is that he has shown in his dealings with the executive and—with his close personal friends on it— Shaw, Bland, and Webb—an odd mixture of underhand manoeuvres and insolent bluster, when his manoeuvres were not successful. The explanation is, I think, that this is absolutely the first time he has tried to co-operate with his fellow men—and he has neither tradition nor training to fit him to do it. It is a case of "Kipps" in matters more important than table manners. It is strange for so frank a man that his dealings have been far from straight—a series of naive little lies which were bound to be found out— when at last he forced the executive to oppose him he became a bully and remained so until he found they were big enough to knock him down. I tell Sidney not to be too hard on him and to remember there was a time when "the Webbs" were thought not too straight and not too courteous in their dealings (and that after a dozen years of mixing with men and affairs). But we have shown our displeasure by slight coolness; G. B. S. has expressed himself with his usual scathing frankness, and it is more than likely that H. G. W. with his intelligent sensitiveness will feel he has taken false steps into semi-public affairs and retire into his own world of the artist. It is more for "Copy" than for reform that he has stepped out of his study; when he has got his "copy" he will step back again.[18]

As usual, Mrs. Webb was partly right, and shrewd in her analysis of what she saw. But she left a good deal unseen and unsaid, and she was quite wrong in her analysis of Wells' motives. He was clearly not moved by a desire for copy; his imagination provided more copy than he could use. He was simply drunk on his own messianic possibilities, a prophet with a vision of a Great Society, who wanted not mere administrative reforms but a radical change of heart. It was his messianic certainty that blurred his sense of propriety and led him to offend Mrs. Webb, not his humble breeding.

But Wells would have had no success with his scheme if there had not been a mood in the Fabian and in English socialism in general to which his ideas appealed. In the General Election of January 1906, the Liberals had won 377 seats, a majority of 84 over all other parties combined, and this victory had convinced many Socialists that the time was at hand to bring socialism directly into British political life. For more than twenty years the Fabians had carried this motto:

For the right moment you must wait, as Fabius did most patiently, when warring against Hannibal, though many censured his delays; but when the time comes you must strike hard, as Fabius did, or your waiting will be in vain and fruitless.[19]

[18] Passfield Papers.
[19] This motto, for which no source has been found, was supplied by Frank Podmore, one of the founders of the Fabian Society, and was printed at the head of Fabian Tract No. 1.

For many Fabians, the time had come in the spring of 1906; they wanted to strike hard. When on February 9 Wells delivered a severely critical address on "The Faults of the Fabian," he spoke to an audience that contained many sympathetic members. (The pamphlet is reproduced in Appendix C.) "My list of the society's faults grows long," he told them.

> Our society is small; and in relation to its great mission small minded; it is poor; it is collectively, as a society, inactive; it is suspicious of help, and exclusive; it is afflicted with a giggle, and a deliberate and intended "sense of humour." And all these faults I have, I think, traced back to the conditions of its early origin. It met socially—to this day it meets socially. It has never yet gone out to attack the unknown public in a systematic and assimilatory manner. At a certain stage in its development its effort seemed to cease, it ceased to grow, ceased to dream, ceased to believe in any possible sort of triumph for socialism as socialism. It experienced just that arrest of growth one sees in a pot-bound plant.[20]

This is not only an attack on Fabian methods; it is also an attack on the old guard, those originators who had given the society its peculiar definition and who continued to control it, and on the *class* bias of the society. To say at that time that the Fabian was exclusive and social was to say that it was self-perpetuatingly middle-class. Wells urged an end of snobbishness, delay, and socialism-by-permeation, and a new era of vigorous propagandizing and expansion. The society he proposed—large, moneyed, and militant—was a Fabian Society without the Fabianism, a Socialist action group with Wells as chief Propagandist.

The files of the present Fabian Society show that Wells' attack was well received by many rank-and-file Fabians, who,

[20] Wells, *Faults of the Fabian* (London: privately printed for the Fabian Society, 1906), p. 9.

it seems, resented the way the old guard monopolized meetings instead of encouraging and instructing the neophytes. One letter to Wells from a working-class member of a provincial Socialist league ended "People in the provinces think H. G. Wells is a great man, and I can assure you they pay great attention to anything you say. Your audience is assured already, let the prophet appear."

The prophet was quite willing to appear and to reorganize and direct the Fabian Society. In this endeavor he had the support of enough members to organize a Reform Group and to force the establishment of a special committee to consider the reformers' proposals. The committee, formed in February, included both Wells and his wife, as well as Mrs. Shaw and a number of other old guard members. A report was submitted in October; it was in general support of Wells' suggestions (which is not surprising, since Wells had been allowed to select the members) and was sent to all Society members in December 1906, along with a witty, arrogant reply by Shaw. A series of meetings was arranged to discuss the two documents. At the first meeting, Wells attempted to force the issue by moving an amendment that would, in effect, have driven the old guard out and turned the Society over to him. At the next meeting Shaw replied in a speech that was the most impressive he ever made in the Society, according to the Secretary, Edward Pease. Overpowered by Shaw's parliamentary skill, Wells withdrew his amendment. Mrs. Webb noted in her diary for December 15,

> H. G. Wells made a bad failure of his effort to capture the Fabian Society by turning out "with dishonour" the old executive. The odd thing is that if he had pushed his own fervid policy or rather enthusiasm for vague and big ideas without making a personal attack on the old gang, he would have succeeded.[21]

But Wells was not leaving the field; he was simply with-

21 Passfield Papers.

drawing to a new position, already prepared for further battle. In October 1906, before his defeat at Shaw's hands, Wells read to a Fabian meeting a paper on "Socialism and the Middle Classes" in which he argued that "Socialism repudiates the private ownership of the head of the family as completely as it repudiates any other sort of private ownership," and urged in place of parental ownership "the State family." What this meant in effect was the endowment of motherhood, making women financially independent of their husbands and vice versa. The Socialist, Wells continued, "no more regards the institution of marriage as a permanent thing than he regards a state of competitive industrialism as a permanent thing."[22] In taking this line, Wells was grievously violating the Fabian principle, as formulated by Shaw, of avoiding unnecessary controversies and sticking to "practical Democracy and Socialism." But he was doing more—he was attacking the foundations of the bourgeois, benevolent, bureaucratic middle-class society from which the Fabians drew their membership. The Society's reaction was extremely hostile. "I am afraid Wells' lecture did no sort of good to the propaganda," wrote old-guard member Hubert Bland to the Secretary. "Judging by what I heard afterwards a lot of people were quite upset. I am inclined to think one might do worse than force this 'sex and child' question to an issue as among Fabians. We had to do that with the Anarchists and we may have to do it with the Free Lovers."[23] It is interesting that Bland, the most notorious philanderer in the Fabian, should have taken this moral stand—though if one looks again at his remarks it is clear that he is at least partly concerned with public relations. But the labelling of Wells as a defender of free love and a sexual anarchist expresses what seems to have been a general attitude.

This attitude was a general one partly, at least, because

[22] Wells, *Socialism and the Family* (London: A. C. Fifield, 1906) , pp. 29 and 30.

[23] Hubert Bland to Edward Pease, Oct. 14, 1906, in the files of Fabian Society.

Wells had invited it. In the fall of 1906 he had published another scientific romance, *In the Days of the Comet*. In some ways it was simply more of the old Wells—a mixture of lower-middle-class grubbiness and a vision of a Socialist utopia. The story is a before-and-after account of a comet which strikes the earth and releases a curious green gas. Before the comet, the world is the world of Mr. Polly and Kipps; after the gas, it is a utopian world in which men are natural Socialists and brotherly love is the human condition. Wells used his book to attack the idea of private property and all the evils that he thought sprang from it: class hatred, poverty, imperialism, war; but he could not resist adding in an epilogue a few remarks on his idée fixe, the idea of monogamous love as a form of private property. Conservative readers pounced on the epilogue with delight and used it to club both Wells and his Socialist associates. The *Times Literary Supplement*, for example, ended its review with these remarks:

> He foresees the objection that, even if men could be persuaded not to quarrel about property, they would still be liable to quarrel about women, and he is prepared with his solution of that problem also. Socialistic men's wives, we gather, are, no less than their goods, to be held in common. Free love, according to Mr. Wells, is to be of the essence of the new social contract. One wonders how far he will insist in the tracts which he is understood to desire to write for the Fabian Society, and what the other Fabians will say.[24]

The other Fabians had a good deal to say, most of it hostile. Sidney Webb was furious, and Shaw accused Wells of "playing against his own side." Beatrice Webb's reaction to Wells' new line of attack was curious, but entirely characteristic. On October 18 she wrote,

[24] *Times Literary Supplement*, Sept. 14, 1906, p. 314.

H. G. Wells gave an address to the Fabian Society on Socialism for the middle-classes, ending up with an attack on the family. Some of the new members welcomed his denunciation, but the meeting, which was crowded, was against him, for the simple reason that he had nothing constructive to suggest. Since then I have read *The Days of a Comet*, which ends with a glowing anticipation of promiscuity in sexual relations. The argument is one that is familiar to most intellectuals—it has often cropped up in my own mind and has seemed to have some validity. Friendship between particular men and women has an enormous educational value to both (especially to the woman) . Such a friendship is practically impossible (or, at any rate, impossible between persons who are attractive to each other—and, therefore, most remunerative as friends) without physical intimacy; you do not, as a matter of fact, get to know any man thoroughly except as his beloved and his lover—if you could have been the beloved of the dozen ablest men you have known it would have greatly extended your knowledge of human nature and human affairs. This, I believe, is true of our present rather gross state of body and mind. But there remains the question whether, with all the perturbation caused by such intimacies, you would have any brain left to think with? I know that I should not—and I fancy that other women would be even worse off in that particular. Moreover, it would mean a great increase in sexual emotion for its own sake and not for the sake of bearing children. And that way madness lies.[25]

As so often, Mrs. Webb saw some of the implications of Wells' book with great clarity, but missed the fundamental point on which her way of thinking was most remote from his. The utopia of Wells' book depends on a miracle, a uni-

[25] *Our Partnership*, pp. 359-360.

versal and unmotivated change of heart; what he describes is the dream of the prophet, not the plan of the reformer.

Nevertheless, though Sidney Webb was cross with Wells, Mrs. Webb thought it important not to dislike him; "he is going through an ugly time," she noted in her diary, "and we must stand by him for his own sake and for the good of the cause of collectivism."[26] But the standing-by was becoming difficult, for Wells, as he grew more confident of his capacity for settling social and economic questions, grew more contemptuous of Fabian drudgeries. Mrs. Webb found it increasingly difficult to preserve amicable relations, and she prophesied in private that five years would see Wells out of the Fabian. She was, as so often, overcautious in her prediction; he was out in a little more than two.

The socialism-and-sex issue was not the only source of conflict between Wells and the old guard, but it was the most inflammatory. Shortly after he had delivered his address to the Society on "Socialism and the Middle Classes," Wells published it in a pamphlet called *Socialism and the Family*. The little book was immediately seized upon by Tories who were then campaigning against Socialist-Labour candidates. William Joynson-Hicks, the Conservative candidate campaigning against a Socialist in Lancashire, told working-class audiences that the Socialists would separate husband and wife and subject every woman to communal prostitution. Wells complained, with justice, that he had been misquoted. But the point is that he had taken a public position that exposed him (and socialism) to misrepresentation; to the degree that the Fabian Society had become a political organization it had to regard him as an expensive liability.

Wells recognized this and set about to modify his opinions. In 1907 he published a series of essays, later collected as *New Worlds for Old* (1908), in which he recanted his extreme views and observed simply that socialism had not

26 *Our Partnership*, p. 360.

worked out a theory of marriage and at present simply maintained an attitude of neutrality. But the Tories were understandably reluctant to abandon such a rich emotional issue and continued to condemn socialism in general for Wells' heresies. For example, in October 1907 the *Spectator*, a journal that viewed Wells with particular and repeated abhorrence, published an editorial entitled "Socialism and Sex Relations," in which the following points were made:

> . . . we may feel certain that the triumph of Socialism must mean the overthrow of the Christian moral code in regard to marriage and the relations of the sexes, and must end in free love and promiscuity. . . .
>
> The clearer-eyed Socialists realise that Socialism, if triumphant, will not leave the relations of the sexes as they are. For example, we find Mr. Wells in his novel, "In the Days of the Comet," making free love the dominant principle for the regulation of sexual ties in his regenerated State.
>
> Instinctively most Socialist theorizers have realised that the family is inimical to Socialism, owing to the desire which it creates for the possession of private property, private life, and an existence based on individualism. Therefore the family must be destroyed.
>
> . . . Socialism has always resulted in the advocacy of some form of promiscuity, open or covert. . . .[27]

This association of socialism with other, less acceptable forms of advanced thought was just what the Fabians had striven to avoid. The natural instinct of the Webbs had always been to ally themselves with the established sources of political and social power—all those bishops and cabinet ministers who came to eat the Webbs' bleak dinners—and to work from that position of strength to effect particular changes in society. "Socialists," Mrs. Webb was fond of saying,

[27] *Spectator*, 4,138 (Oct. 19, 1907), 558.

"should be respectable." But Wells was not being respectable, and his improprieties were giving ammunition to the enemies of progress.

By the end of 1907 Wells' views (or perhaps more precisely his publishing of his views) had cost him the trust and support of the Fabian leadership, though he still had a large following among the rank-and-file (in the 1907 elections to the Fabian Executive, Wells had the support of seventy-eight percent of the members). He continued to write about the Family, and to campaign for the Endowment of Motherhood, but without much enthusiastic support; in the end he did succeed in forcing the Society to publish a tract on the subject, but it was a pallid, actuarial treatment that did not mention Wells, even in the bibliography.

Wells was re-elected to the Executive in the following year, along with his wife, but by this time his Fabian adventure was nearly over. He served for only a few months and then resigned. In his letter of resignation, which was printed in full in the *Fabian News* (October 1908), he wrote,

Essentially the position is this: I find myself disagreeing with the Basis which forms the Confession of Faith of the Society and discontented with the general form of our activities. So long as I could consider the Basis a document that might presently be altered and the policy of the Society as a policy that would develop and change, I have remained a member. I have had it in my mind that I might presently take part in a vigorous campaign for a revised Basis and a revived Propaganda. But when I calculate the forces against such a campaign, the inevitable opposition and irritation that must ensue and the probable net results of what would certainly be an irksome and distressful conflict, I am forced to conclude that the effort is, for me at least, not worth making. Moreover I want very much to concentrate myself now upon the writing of novels for some years, and so I have taken the alternative course and sent in my resignation.

My chief objection to the Basis is its disregard of that claim of every child upon the State which is primary and fundamental to my conception of Socialism. A scheme which proposes to leave mother and child economically dependent upon the father is to me not Socialism at all, but a miserable perversion of Socialism. It forbids the practical freedom of women and leaves the essential evils of the Industrialist system untouched. I see the hopelessness of any attempt to force this recognition upon the Fabian Society at the present time, and I do not care to remain permanently identified with formulae that mis-state my views by this tremendous omission. . . .[28]

Prophetic to the end, Wells concluded his letter with the gloomy observation that the opportunity to reach the British middle classes by Fabian propaganda had passed while Fabians stood divided in theory and undecided in action. They had not rallied to his crusade; their cautious Fabian hearts had not been changed. Expounding his lost cause and prophesying doom, Wells stepped from the Fabian stage.

Wells' letter does not mention a motive for resigning that was at least as strong as his distress with Fabian views on Motherhood. He had become involved in a love affair that shocked both Mrs. Webb's sense of decency and her sense of Fabian solidarity.[29] The girl was a young Cambridge graduate, a Fabian, and the daughter of one of the Fabian old guard. She was a vital and intelligent person— she had taken a double first in the Moral Science tripos— but she was also vain and careless, and the affair was conducted with a maximum of indiscretion. Mrs. Webb was especially shocked that the union had been consummated

[28] *Fabian News*, vol. 19 (October 1908), 77-78. The *News* mis-transcribes "Industrialist" as "Individualist." The original letter is in the files of the Fabian Society.

[29] Her private account of the scandal is in the Passfield Papers.

within the very walls of Newnham College: it seemed to her the sort of thing that the author of *In the Days of the Comet* would do.

The uproar that surrounded this liaison continued for nearly a year and involved both the Webbs and Shaw in attempts to settle it quietly. The moral issue involved was one on which Wells and the Webbs had quarrelled years earlier: "The collective regulation of the behaviour of the adult," as Mrs. Webb put it, was repulsive to Wells, while to her it seemed a necessary condition of a decent society. While this difference was an abstract point of social theory she was content to argue and go away disagreeing, but when it became a particular case she put morality above Fabian utility and eventually broke off her relationship with him. (She was not the only one of Wells' acquaintances to react strongly; his club, the Savile, dropped him from its membership—perhaps because the girl's father had taken to spending his afternoons sitting in the club's front window with a pistol in his lap, waiting for his daughter's seducer to appear.)[30]

At least one old-guard Fabian—Wells' antagonist Hubert Bland—expected a wave of resignations to follow Wells' and was pleased at the prospect. "I fancy we shall have a goodish few resignations following Wells'," he wrote to Pease in September 1908. "During the last year a whole lot of people have joined us for every sort of reason but that of belief in Socialism. It will be an excellent thing to shed these."[31] But in fact the membership continued to grow. The principal and indeed the only visible effect of Wells' break with Fabianism was on Wells' own writing. Mrs. Webb had said years earlier that Wells had come out of his study into the world of public affairs more for copy than for reform, and though this was not true at the time, it is true that he habitually turned the immediate events of his life more or less

[30] The story is told in Compton Mackenzie's *My Life and Times. Octave Four* (London: Chatto & Windus, 1965), p. 114.
[31] Dated Sept. 23, 1908. In files of Fabian Society.

directly into books. One may explain this half-autobiographical habit in various ways. In part, no doubt, it was a consequence of Wells' enormous productivity; he simply did not have time to let imagination transmute experience. It also seems in part to have been a matter of conviction, for Wells clearly thought of the novel as a running commentary on current affairs and an act of propaganda. But on some occasions the motive was simply spleen; Wells used his fiction to revenge himself upon his enemies. Having broken with the Fabians, he promptly turned them into fiction.

Both *Tono-Bungay* and *Ann Veronica*, Wells' two novels of 1909, contain attacks on the Fabian Society. The latter book also reflects Wells' recent history in that it centers on a love affair between an emancipated young girl and an older man who is a trained scientist. Mrs. Webb thought Ann Veronica was a near-anagram of the real girl's name and shrewdly described the book as a portrait of Wells from the girl's point of view. Like the *Utopia*, *Ann Veronica* is a daydream book, a philanderer's idealizing of his behavior. The book was violently attacked in the *Spectator*, in what Mrs. Webb believed was a veiled personal attack on Wells for his immoral behavior.

Still, even with these copious materials for conflict, the Wells-Webb relation was a year in finally breaking up. In the meantime, Mrs. Webb further strained the connection by preferring *The War in the Air*, Wells' latest scientific romance, to *Tono-Bungay* and telling Wells so in a letter (the letter apparently accompanied a gift of the two-volume *Minority Report of the Poor Law Commission*, which was published in 1909). In her diary she wrote of the novel,

Tono-Bungay, on the other hand, sets out to be a straightforward description of society as it exists today—a sober estimate of the business world. But it turned out to be a veritable caricature—and a bitter one. Moreover, it bores me, because its detail is made up, not of real knowledge of the world he describes, but of stray bits he has heard from this or that person. There are quite a lot of things he has picked up from me—anecdotes about business men that I have told him are woven into his text, just all wrong—conveying an absurd impression of meaningless chaos.[32]

Apparently she managed to convey the burden of this negative judgment to Wells in her letter, though no doubt she omitted the sentences that followed:

But he is a useful missionary to whole crowds of persons whom we could never get at. It will be sad if he turns completely sour: if after all, it turns out to be a misfortune to the cause we both believe in that we should have known one another.

The points that Mrs. Webb makes in these comments are essentially those that defined her relation with Wells throughout the decade: that he was a useful contact with the lower classes, but that he was ignorant of the ways society really worked—ignorant, that is, of the kind of facts that the Webbs prided themselves on knowing, and ignorant because of his own background. As so often, Mrs. Webb was accurately heartless in her judgment.

Wells, who was neither accurate nor heartless, retaliated with a wild attack on the Minority Report. "What a mass of stuff it all is!" he exclaimed. "I had hoped for a fuller and more illuminating introduction. . . ."

You don't by any means make the quality of your differences from the Majority Report plain, nor your case in the slightest degree convincing. Perhaps I had been led to expect too much but at any rate I am left wondering just what it is that you think you are up to. All literature and science is digestion and I've been wondering at times lately whether your later views as to dietary couldn't with advantage be applied to intellectual things.[33]

[32] Feb. 27, 1909. Passfield Papers.
[33] Letter dated Feb. 22, 1909. Passfield Papers.

A few days later he followed this with another letter, shifting from the professional to the personal level:

Dear Mrs. Webb,

Perhaps my letter was ungenerous but the provocation to treat your good piece of work as you treated mine and to be just willfully unsympathetic was too great. You and Sidney have the knack of estranging people and I think you have to count me among the estranged. I've tried to do something toward educating the big popular socialist movement and I've never had a generous moment from Webb. He's been the ready ally of Bland or any one to minimise my influence. And now here you are in the ridiculous position of forcing your Minority Report upon the Fabian Society, after a session spent in reiterating that stale Basis, paragraph by paragraph, and with the society just publishing a tract, to show that it has learnt nothing and forgotten nothing since the beginning, a tract which expressly repudiates the essential principle of your Report. I gave up trying to cooperate with the two of you. I don't see what you are up to in relation to me.

But really your Report is as you know a very great piece of work, and quite after my own heart.

Very sincerely yours,
H. G. Wells[34]

Mrs. Webb's response to this rage and abuse was coldly serene: "Bless the man!" she wrote in her diary. "We never think of him, now he has resigned from the Fabian Society." But indeed she did think of him, and a few months later, when his scandalous affair continued, she noted simply: "The end of our friendship with H. G. Wells."

Wells' resignation from the Fabian Society was the end of his organized political activities, but not quite the end of his connection with the Webbs. During 1910 he began to publish in *The English Review* a new novel called *The New*

34 Passfield Papers. Undated (note added: "Feb/Mar 1909").

Machiavelli. The novel appeared as a book in 1911 under the imprint of John Lane, who advertised it as containing "a striking picture of the unequal contest between love and duty, and a stern moral of the inevitable consequence. It is a remarkable exposition of the political condition of the present day, and a masterly indictment of the fundamental hypocrisy of the modern point of view."[35]

The novel is in fact a fictionalized account of Wells' Edwardian political life, improved and elevated, as one improves an unsatisfactory conversation after the fact; it is, as so many of Wells' topical novels are, a kind of daydream version of actuality. It has for its hero one of Wells' alter egos, a poor boy called Richard Remington, out of a Kentish town, who enters Parliament as a Liberal, revolutionizes British politics with a campaign for the Endowment of Motherhood (the slogan that sweeps the nation is "Love and Fine Thinking!"), switches parties, and finally throws his career away to go off with the woman he loves.

Wells' account of Remington's political career reveals a good deal about Wells' own political commitments. In the fourth chapter, where he describes how Remington evolved from a sentimental Socialist sympathizing with the miseries of the poor, to a technocrat who hated inefficiency above all, one gets what seems a fair account of Wells' own development to his final highest value—the Ideal Efficiency of the Great State. Remington's concern for the poor is treated as immature (the chapter is entitled "Adolescence"), and the technocracy as an obvious advance. Little attention is given to the thought that Democracy might also have value. It is not surprising that Remington shifts his allegiance from one party to another, for there is no necessary connection between Efficiency and any political philosophy (any more than there are political or social implications in Remington's fatuous slogan, "Love and Fine Thinking!"). The connection between the slogan and the efficient ideal is not

[35] Quoted in Compton Mackenzie, *Octave Four*, p. 113.

explained, nor is Wells clear on just why such a banality should catch on. Social change comes about as it does in *In the Days of the Comet*, through miracle—an inexplicable change of heart.

The New Machiavelli is a bad novel, ill-conceived as fiction and preposterous as political theory, but it is full of interest if one is interested in Wells. The daydream element prevents it from being anything like a straightforward, trustworthy account of Wells' life, but it is nevertheless a kind of history of the political life in which he was involved. It is a biography, one might say, of a generation and a class—of Edwardian reformers and would-be reformers. And it is a suggestive record of the political disorder of that time, the confusion of principles and intentions, the vagueness of party definition, the uncertainty of political directions. Formally it is incomplete—the political theme is not properly resolved—but that very incompleteness takes on meaning if one considers the title; Wells, sitting down in exile to write an Edwardian version of *Il Principe*, can only lead his hero from one party to the other and eventually away from politics and England altogether.

Defeat had sharpened Wells' political eye. It had also sharpened his tongue as far as the Webbs were concerned. They figure prominently in the novel as Altiora and Oscar Bailey, "two active self-centered people, excessively devoted to the public service," who are in fact the real Machiavellians of the novel. Wells expended a considerable store of venomous imagination in creating these two figures, with their odd appearances, their cheerless house, the "shameless austerity" of their table, their taste for "things harsh and ugly," their intellectual miserliness. But there is more than mere venom in the portrait. There is also an intelligent account of the differences of mind between Wells and the Webbs which made their quarrel inevitable. As Wells observed, he was by nature a nominalist (the epigraphs to *The New Machiavelli* are a nineteenth-century reference to

Abelard and a quotation from William James' *Pragmatism*), while the Webbs "were, in the scholastic sense . . . 'Realists.' They believed classes were *real* and independent of their individuals."[36] "This is the common habit," Wells continues, "of all so-called educated people who have no metaphysical aptitude and no metaphysical training. It leads them to a progressive misunderstanding of the world." What Wells was unable to grasp was that he had no metaphysical aptitude either; the difference was that the Webbs understood that metaphysics had no place in social reform, whatever one's aptitude, and that Wells did not. He was all his life a man with a metaphysical itch, a prophet without a religion, and his errant career in Fabianism is best understood as a furious attempt to turn a political philosophy into a religion, with himself as John the Baptist. That such an effort failed is not surprising, and is certainly not to be regretted. But the waste of a decade in the creative life of an imaginative and original mind is. Wells devoted most of his energies between his thirty-fifth and forty-fifth years to his Fabian schemes. His campaign divided the Society at a time when circumstances seemed most propitious for it, deflected Fabian energies from public issues to internal conflicts, provided the opponents of socialism with powerful weapons, and in the end accomplished nothing but his own alienation from the group. He wrote constantly in the cause of socialism, and reached larger audiences than any other Socialist writer did, but in the end the great Socialist document of the period was not his, but that "mass of stuff," *The Minority Report of the Poor Law Commission*, of which Mrs. Webb was the chief author.

Wells ended his political career an example of that saddest and least necessary of men, the unsuccessful Messiah. One cannot doubt that his account of the emotions of Richard Remington, as he leaves London for the last time, were

[36] Wells, *The New Machiavelli* (London: John Lane, 1911), p. 216.

close to Wells' own as he bid farewell to his dreams of Fabian greatness.

We were leaving London; my hand, which had gripped so hungrily upon its complex life, had been forced from it, my fingers left their hold. That was over. I should never have a voice in public affairs again. The inexorable unwritten law which forbids overt scandal sentenced me. . . . And suddenly all the schemes I was leaving appeared fine and adventurous and hopeful as they had never done before. How great was this purpose I had relinquished, this bold and subtle remaking of the English will![37]

But that bold remaking—the Parliamentary Labour party and the Welfare State—were left for the victors, who knew, as Fabius knew, how to wait.

One could make too much of Wells' failure—it is not, after all, the function of novelists to blueprint the future— but it is a perplexing question why the movement that appealed so strongly to imaginative minds during the Edwardian period found no major literary expression either in Wells' work or anywhere else. Surely at that time, if ever, great Socialist literature should have been written. But it wasn't; one wonders why.

One answer is that the two principal leaders of Fabian thought—Beatrice and Sidney Webb—were persons without aesthetic sensibility, who not only were not themselves imaginative, but seemed to pride themselves on their limitations ("two second-rate minds but curiously complementary" was Mrs. Webb's judgment of herself and her husband) . Insofar as they understood literature at all, they saw it as an instrument of propaganda, a way of reaching large popular audiences who were beneath the appeal of Fabian Tracts. Mrs. Webb remarked, without apparent regret, that she was "poetry-blind" as other people are color-blind; she was also fiction-blind and drama-blind, and so, apparently, was Sid-

[37] *New Machiavelli*, p. 525.

ney. They numbered among their associates and friends some of the best writers of the time—men like Shaw and Wells and Granville Barker—and they managed to work with these men in the common cause. But they showed no sign of understanding what the literary imagination was, and their judgments of their friends' works were bleakly moralistic and utilitarian. In the end Wells, who wanted a revolution of the imagination, was left as "one of the estranged," and Barker, the intellectual actor who wanted to be a man of affairs, gradually resigned from life, leaving first the Fabians, then the theater, and finally England. Only Shaw, indestructible in his ironic genius, survived—perhaps because he put his socialism into his speeches and pamphlets and wrote his plays, as he told Mrs. Webb, "about psychology and conduct."

The relation of Fabianism to the literary imagination can be sketched briefly in terms of Mrs. Webb's connections with her writing friends. Her great work during the later Edwardian years had been the Minority Report, and it is characteristic of the way her mind worked that when she had finished it she turned at once to the playwrights she knew to help her in making the report popular. The work was finished in January 1909; in May she was working on Granville Barker—both by direct letter and through Sidney—to write a Minority Report play. Barker's reply was amiable, but evasive:

> The difficulty about a big play such as you want [he wrote] is that it generally takes a year's thinking about and then a year's work. I'm far slower than either G.B.S. or J. G. [John Galsworthy]. *And* the ideas for these things come as God decides *and* though they begin one way— suppose this one ended with a eulogy of Lord George [the head of the Royal Commission on the Poor Law, and presumably author of the Majority Report which Mrs. Webb opposed]!

But I'll tell you—when you come across any curious pro-
voking twisted point in the problem—tell me—it is such
that I manage to hang things on.

Sidney spoke to me about this on Friday and on Sunday
morning (see how obedient I am) I made a note for a one
act play on the subject—but a mere nothing compared to
what you want.

I'll certainly back you up with Galsworthy—he's your
likeliest quarry too. And indeed it is a great notion—if
only the *ideas* would come. You see the practical side of
my trade I can do as slick as you like—but the ideas![38]

Barker continued to think about the play, and a year later
Frank Swinnerton could write, "Mr. Granville Barker wants
plays to embody great social ideas; he says he wants a play
setting forth the principles of the Minority Report."[39] But
though Barker may have wanted such plays, he could not
write them.

Evaded by Barker, Mrs. Webb turned at once to Galsworthy, apparently asking for general support of her cause
this time, rather than a play. To her appeal Galsworthy
replied,

You honour me with your request, for I do think your
Minority report a wonderful document.

I don't feel however that my name must be added. First,
because I haven't given the subject sufficient scientific
study. Second, because it's my business *not* to belong to
leagues and so forth. I don't know if you'll understand me,
but I regard it as my business to visualise things and set
them down in terms of art (when I'm lucky enough to win
the smile of that goddess). In visualising what one finds
round one, if one has any sense of proportion and love of
justice, one naturally reverses a good many prejudices;

[38] Passfield Papers. Undated (note added: "May 1909").
[39] "Modern Realism," *New Age*, vol. 7 (March 31, 1910), 518.

but the influence of one, who tries to work in my department, as a reverser of prejudice, (if he has any influence, which I often doubt) depends on his liberty, and his impartiality.

So, I'm sorry.[40]

Galsworthy's letter shows that if he was the least Socialistic of her literary friends, he was also the least an artist. In the process of declining to join her he confessed having designs on his readers' prejudices—and thus defined himself as being, like Mrs. Webb, a propagandist concerned above all to change human behavior.

It is not surprising that when Mrs. Webb saw plays by Barker, Shaw, and Galsworthy during the next few months, Galsworthy's was highly praised and Shaw's and Barker's deplored.

I went to Granville-Barker's *Madras House* this afternoon [she wrote in her diary in March, 1910]. After listening to this and to G. B. S.'s *Misalliance,* one wonders whether these two supremely clever persons are not obsessed with the rabbit-warren aspect of human society? G. B. S. is brilliant but disgusting; Granville-Barker is intellectual but dull. They both harp on the mere physical attractions of men to women, and women to men, coupled with the insignificance of the female for any other purpose but sex attraction, with tiresome iteration. That world is not the world I live in. . . .[41]

Two days later she saw *Justice,* and found the world she did live in. She thought it a great play,

great in its realistic form, great in its reserve and restraint, great in its quality of pity. Its motive, that all dealings with criminals should be treatment *plus* restraint in the

[40] May 21, 1909. Passfield Papers.
[41] *Our Partnership,* p. 447.

interests of the community, are all worked in with the philosophy of the Minority Report.[42]

Her world, and Galsworthy's, was a simple one, in which moral indignation and a desire for reform gave all the form that was needed, and themes could be cross-referenced to sociology. It was not a world for the imaginative and the brilliant. But the Webbs mistrusted brilliance and were glad they didn't have it, and after the Wells affair they must have been more than ever convinced that the most useful instrument of reform is one that is not too sharp.

Justice was a perfect example of Fabian art, as Mrs. Webb saw it. It was based on careful research—Galsworthy visited prisons and interviewed more than a hundred prisoners at Lewes, and it had measurable social consequences—the periods of solitary confinement in British prisons were reduced. The play fulfilled itself as art (in Fabian terms) on the day in July when the Home Secretary, Winston Churchill, rose in Parliament to announce his program of prison reform. But it had already reached audiences of the most varied political complexions, and Galsworthy's mail was full of admiring testimonials to his powers as a propagandist. Only one correspondent suggested that in this respect the play was inadequate. Wells wrote,

> But it isn't a system that is wrong. Another system will give kindred cruelties. If people abolish solitary confinement, for example, some new horror will creep into the substituted treatment. We've got to go further back into the sources of law and control.[43]

But it was Wells' desire to "go further back" that had made him a bad Fabian and had separated him from the Society. For those who remained, *Justice* was what a Fabian play should be, even though—and Mrs. Webb did not seem to

[42] *Our Partnership*, p. 449.
[43] H. V. Marrot, *Life and Letters of John Galsworthy* (London: Heinemann, 1935) , p. 260.

see the irony of this—it was written not by a Fabian but by a man whose political ideas were limited to upper-class benevolence and indiscriminate compassion, and who came so close to being the average Edwardian man-of-good-will that he could set out to propagandize for reform and emerge with a commercial success. In Galsworthy's *Justice*, Mrs. Webb had what she wanted—her Minority Report play. She must have felt that at last the arts had done their duty by her.

....

SCIENCE, SEERS, AND SEX

....

In February 1909, George Bernard Shaw read a paper on "Socialism and Medicine" before the Medico-Legal Society. It began,

> I was born in the year 1856. That does not seem—if I may judge from the expression of your faces—to convey very much to you; but if you will remember that Darwin's Origin of Species was published in 1859 you will understand that I belong to a generation which, I think, began life by hoping more from Science than perhaps any generation ever hoped before, and, possibly, will ever hope again. I give the date in order to get out of the minds of any of you who may entertain such an idea that I am in any way hostile to science. Science will always be extraordinarily interesting and hopeful to me. At the present moment we are passing through a phase of disillusion. Science has not lived up to the hopes we formed of it in the 1860s; but those hopes left a mark on my temperament that I shall never get rid of till I die.[1]

In his hope and in his disillusion Shaw was characteristic of his generation as it passed from the Victorian period to the Edwardian. Victoria's reign had been a triumphant Age of Science; advances in geology, biology, and physics had not only affected the way men thought about their physical environment but had altered men's ideas of their relation to that environment—had brought, that is, a new cosmology

[1] Dan H. Laurence, ed., *Platform and Pulpit* (London: Rupert Hart-Davis, 1962), p. 50.

and a new conception of the nature of change. It had been a scientific revolution, and, as is often true of revolutions, the revolutionaries in their moment of victory saw only their successes and not the new problems that success had created. To Victorian scientists like Lord Kelvin it seemed reasonable to predict in the 1870's that in a few years science would have discovered all the properties of matter and "all the marvels of the Sun," and this prospect filled him with optimistic enthusiasm: the contemplation of new discoveries made him feel, he said, "as if led out from narrow waters of scholastic dogma to a refreshing excursion on the broad and deep ocean of truth."[2]

Recalling this jubilant Victorian mood, the psychologist Frederick W. H. Myers wrote,

> It must be remembered that this was the very flood-tide of materialism, agnosticism—the mechanical theory of the Universe, the reduction of spiritual facts to physiological phenomena. It was a time when not the intellect only, but the moral ideals of men seemed to have passed into the camp of negation. We were all in the first flush of triumphant Darwinism, when terrene evolution explained so much that men hardly cared to look beyond.[3]

In the years that followed, triumphant Darwinism affected thoughtful men in various ways. For some (H. G. Wells, for instance) it remained a promise of human progress; but for others the effect was a gloomy feeling of restriction and loss. Masterman, in *The Condition of England*, described the fading of the scientific dream in this way:

> The large hopes and dreams of the Early Victorian time have vanished: never, at least in the immediate future, to

[2] Sir William Thomson (Lord Kelvin), *Popular Lectures and Addresses*, 3 vols. (London: Macmillan, 1894), vol. 2, p. 177. The quotation is from Lord Kelvin's Presidential Address to the British Association in 1871.

[3] Frederic W. H. Myers, *Fragments of Inner Life* (London: The Society for Psychical Research, 1961), p. 15.

return. The science which was to allay all diseases, the commerce which was to abolish war, and weave all nations into one human family, the research which was to establish ethics and religion on a secure and positive foundation, the invention which was to enable all humanity, with a few hours of not disagreeable work every day, to live for the remainder of their time in ease and sunshine—all these have become recognised as remote and fairy visions. . . . Civilisation, in the early twentieth century in England, suffers no illusions as to the control of natural forces, or the exploration of natural secrets furnishing a cure either for the diseases from which it suffers in the body, or the more deep-seated maladies of the soul.[4]

The soul had no scientific existence, but Masterman was speaking for a good many of his contemporaries when he worried about it; Victorian science may have made metaphysics obsolete, but it had not destroyed men's metaphysical itch, and much of what one might generally call Edwardian science is concerned with the problem of restoring metaphysics to the human world.

One strong intellectual line through the late Victorian and Edwardian years is made up of reactions to Victorian materialism—both in the sense of the physical explanation of phenomena and in the more general sense of an exclusive concern for material things, and it is important to see the extent to which reactions to these two meanings of "materialistic" were related and how often apparently unconnected movements shared a common concern for the liberation of men from the restrictions of materialistic thought and materialistic values. Here, as an example, is a contemporary account of the last decades of the century, by the Edwardian sage, Edward Carpenter:

The years from 1881 onward were certainly a new era for

4 Masterman, *The Condition of England*, pp. 214-215.

me. They not only brought me *Towards Democracy* [his epic poem, begun in 1881 and finished in 1902], but they marked the oncoming of a great new tide of human life over the Western World. . . . It was a fascinating and enthusiastic period—preparatory, as we now see, to even greater developments in the twentieth century. The Socialist and Anarchist propaganda, the Feminist and Suffragist upheaval, the huge Trade-union growth, the Theosophic movement, the new currents in the Theatrical, Musical and Artistic world, the torrent even of change in the Religious world—all constituted so many streams and headwaters converging, as it were, to a great river.[5]

Carpenter was inclined to find Unity everywhere—it suited his doctrine of the Universal or Omnipresent Self—but historians of less mystical intentions will have to acknowledge that in fact an unusual amount of activity of a radical-eccentric nature did take place around 1880. Within a few years of 1880 the following organizations were established in England: the Democratic Federation, the Hermetic Order of the Golden Dawn, the National Anti-Vaccination League, the National Anti-Vivisection Society, the Society for Psychical Research, and the Theosophical Society. These movements, ranging from socialism to spiritualism, had one thing and only one thing in common—they were all opposed to conventional Victorian ideals. One can read in the list a large social and intellectual restlessness that in turn made members of established society nervous and led to various official and unofficial efforts to tighten control over the more wayward elements of society.[6] The restlessness continued through the Edwardian period, and the variety of its manifestations is characteristic of Edwardian radicalism—a point

[5] Edward Carpenter, *My Days and Dreams* (London: George Allen & Unwin, 1916), p. 245.

[6] For example the Criminal Law Amendment Act of 1885 and the Indecent Advertisements Act of 1889. For a more detailed account see below, Ch. VIII.

that can be demonstrated by noting how many important figures of the period were involved in several movements of the kind that Carpenter mentions: Yeats is a good example, and so are Shaw, Havelock Ellis, Ramsay Macdonald, Annie Besant, and Carpenter himself. Each movement had its appeal as a possible way out of the mechanistic world that triumphant Darwinism had made.

One way out of that world seemed to lie, paradoxically, through science. In the 'nineties the discovery of the X ray, of radioactivity, and of the electron had made the Victorian version of matter as obsolete as Genesis; and it seemed that further investigations might reveal new forces and new freedoms, by which the universe might be made teleological again. Carpenter, writing in 1912, described before-and-after versions of the world of science: about the middle of the nineteenth century, he said, the old cosmogonies finally perished and gave way, for the most part, to a simple negative attitude:

It was allowed that intelligences and personalities (human and animal) moved on *this* side of the veil, and were plainly distinguishable in the actual world; but they, it was held, were more or less isolated and probably accidental products of a mechanical universe. That mechanical arrangement of atoms, and so forth, which we could now largely map out and measure, and which doubtless in the future we should be able completely to define— that was the universe, and somehow or other included everything. One of its properties was that it could run down like a clock, and would eventuate in time in a cold sun and a dead earth—and there was an end of it! Any intelligent existence behind or on the other side of this veil of mechanism was too problematical to be worth discussing; in all probability on that side was mere nothingness and vacancy.

Such, very roughly stated, was the attitude of the fairly

intelligent and educated man about fifty years ago, but since that time the outgrowths of science and human enquiry have been so astounding as to leave that position far behind. The obvious signs of intelligence in the minutest cells, almost invisible to the naked eye, the very mysterious arcana of growth in such cells . . . the myriad action of similarly intelligent microbes, the strange psychology of plants, and the equally strange psychic sensitiveness (apparently) of *metals*, the sudden transformations and variations both of plants and animals, the existence of the X and N rays of light, and of countless other vibrations of which our ordinary senses render no account, the phenomena of radium and radiant matter, the marvels of wireless telegraphy, the mysterious facts connected with hypnotism and the subliminal consciousness, and the certainty now that telepathic communication can take place between human beings thousands of miles apart— all these things have convinced us that the subtlest forces and energies, totally unmeasurable by our instruments, and saturated or at least suffused with intelligence, are at work all around us. They have convinced us that gloomy phrases about cold suns and dead earths are mere sentiment and nonsense.[7]

Carpenter's account of the new conception of existence contains an odd mixture of elements; along with the findings of biology and physics he mentions matters like hypnotism and telepathy, as though they belonged to the same order of scientific acceptability. And it is one of the striking features of end-of-the-century thought that for many serious investigators this was indeed true; the new discoveries had, for the time, made the world of science open and receptive to new hypotheses: "I believe," William James wrote at the time, "there is no source of deception in the investigation of na-

[7] *The Drama of Love and Death* (London: George Allen & Co., 1912), pp. 112-113.

ture which can be compared with a fixed belief that certain kinds of phenomenon are impossible."[8]

One field of scientific investigation in particular seemed to offer an escape from Darwinism—the field of mental events. Victorian psychology had, inevitably, developed as a biological science, concerned with the physiology of the nervous system and subject to the laws of evolution; the limitations of this approach had retarded the progress of psychology in England, and the further resistance of the universities to what seemed an irreligious treatment of mind had left psychology out of the late-Victorian scientific picture. At the end of the century the best English-speaking psychologist was an American, William James, and the best work was being done everywhere but in England: when the *British Journal of Psychology* was established in 1904, there were only six lectureships in psychology in all England and almost no experimental facilities.[9]

One effect of this condition of English psychology in the late-Victorian years was that the field was left open for less disciplined, less professional workers. The very term "psychological" was appropriated by the most disparate groups: on the one hand spiritualists used the term to describe their experiments (both the *Psychological Review* and the *Psychological Magazine* were journals devoted entirely to the esoteric and the occult), while on the other hand researchers into "psychic phenomena" regarded themselves as empirical scientists engaged in extending the frontiers of psychological knowledge. What these heterogeneous groups had in common was simply this: they were all pushing back against the cramping limits of a purely mechanistic materialism. Psychology, taken in a large (and somewhat imprecise) sense to include all these movements, became in late-Victorian and Edwardian times the liberating movement in science, as the

[8] Henry James, ed. *The Letters of William James*, 2 vols. (Boston: Atlantic Monthly Press, 1920), vol. 1, p. 248.
[9] See L. S. Earnshaw, *A Short History of British Psychology* (London: Methuen, 1964).

suffrage movement was in social relations, and socialism was in politics; and as such it attracted many of the same people.

This side of English psychology found its first organized expression in England in 1882, when a group of Cambridge friends led by Frederick Myers, Edmund Gurney, and Henry Sidgwick organized the Society for Psychical Research, "for the purpose of inquiring into a mass of obscure phenomena which lie at present on the outskirts of our organised knowledge."[10] The members shared a conviction that realities existed which could not be described or accounted for by existing scientific methods, and they intended to seek proof of these realities by means which would be scientifically acceptable. The Society therefore was scrupulous in its testing of evidence and ruthless in exposing frauds: a member was sent all the way to India to expose Madame Blavatsky, and did so to the Society's satisfaction (though faithful followers like Yeats were unconvinced by the exposure). The Society's publications—the *Proceedings* and the *Journal*— were from the beginning meticulously scientific in tone and presentation, even when presenting the report of, say, the Haunted Houses Committee.

Still, for all the scientific gestures, psychic research appealed to a need that was essentially religious. Myers' own motive, as he confessed in his autobiography, was simply to recover the sense of meaning in the universe that he had lost when triumphant Darwinism deprived him of his Christian faith: "re-entering by the scullery," as he put it, "the heavenly mansion out of which I had been kicked through the front door."[11] Myers was an intelligent, educated man— a classical scholar and minor poet, as well as one of the first men in England to recognize the importance of Freud. He was also, it would seem, an intellectually honest one: he did

[10] Letter from Myers to editor of *The Psychological Review*, vol. 5 (Nov. 1882) , 459.
[11] Myers, *Fragments of Inner Life*, p. 15.

not want to be soothed with lies, though at the same time he wanted with all his heart to believe that his phenomena were true. Masterman, who knew and worked with him at Cambridge, wrote of Myers' faith,

> It was not an opinion, but a conviction. . . . I shall never forget the eagerness with which he essayed the work of investigation, the welcome to all obscure and remote testimony, the sense almost of awe with which he would announce some fresh fragment of evidence, however grotesque or ridiculous. No devotee of the older religion hunted for souls more eagerly than Myers hunted for news of ghost stories and telepathy and roaming personalities and inexplicable tricks of hypnotism and magic.[12]

This mixture of scientific method and religious enthusiasm characterized much of the Society's early work and no doubt had something to do with its extraordinary success.

For the Society was successful, even fashionable, from the first. Among its members and associates in its first year were Arthur Balfour, Leslie Stephen, John Ruskin, John Addington Symonds, the biologist A. R. Wallace, the Rev. C. L. Dodgson (Lewis Carroll), and the wife of the Archbishop of Canterbury. By 1885 Gladstone, Tennyson, and G. F. Watts had accepted honorary memberships, William James and Nicholas Murray Butler were corresponding members, and S. L. Clemens, of Hartford, Connecticut was an associate; the vice-president that year was the Bishop of Ripon. In 1894 Balfour, then Leader of the Opposition in the House of Commons, became president of the Society; he was succeeded by William James, who was followed by another distinguished scientist, Sir Oliver Lodge, a physicist who was also Principal of the University of Birmingham. None of the discreditable aura of table-tipping in darkened rooms seems to have attached itself to the Society, and its membership lists during the Edwardian period might well be lists of

12 Masterman, *In Peril of Change*, p. 66.

the members of some rather intellectual West End club, or the pew-holders of a fashionable church.

Two explanations of this success suggest themselves: first, that at a time when English society was still stratified and, within those strata, homogeneous, the founders of the Society were so impeccably acceptable, so very Cambridge and wellborn, that they carried their social position with them, even into the seance. At the social center of the Society was Balfour; Sidgwick had been his tutor and later married his sister Nora; Myers was a Cambridge acquaintance who had been one of Balfour's examiners for the Tripos. Other early members were Balfour's younger brother, Gerald, and his brother-in-law, the mathematician and physicist Lord Rayleigh.

But another explanation is worth considering. If, as I have suggested before, English intellectual life was in a state of open uncertainty at the turn of the century, then it might well follow that a kind of investigation which now seems quackery would be regarded as at least unproven, and that serious investigation, under careful control, would seem no less reasonable than Lodge's experiments with the ether. Balfour, in his presidential address in 1894, put the case for such investigations, as well as acknowledging the difficulties for the investigator who wished also to be a scientist. "We are not endowed," he said,

with the appropriate physical senses, we are ill supplied with appropriate subjects for experiment, we are hampered and embarrassed at every turn by credulity, fraud, and prejudice. Nevertheless, if I rightly interpret the conclusions which many years of labour have forced upon our members, and upon others not among our number who are moved by a like spirit of inquiry, it does seem that outside the world of nature, as we, from the point of science, have been in the habit of conceiving it, there does lie a region in whose twilight some experimental knowledge

may laboriously be gleaned; and even if we cannot entertain any confident hope of discovering what laws its dim
and shadowy phenomena obey, at all events it will be some
gain to have shown, not as a matter of speculation or con-
jecture, but as a matter of ascertained fact, that there are
things in heaven and earth not hitherto dreamed of in
naturalistic philosophy.[13]

Balfour, soon to be Prime Minister of England, was not
alone among serious men in taking an interest in such matters: William James, Jung, and Freud were all corresponding members of the Society, and all contributed to the *Proceedings*. During the Edwardian years the membership lists
of the Society were an odd mixture of the kind of seriousness
that these names imply and what seems simply High Fashion. The list for 1901 contained more than 900 names, including on the one hand such distinguished scientists as Von
Hartmann, Lombroso, and Janet, and on the other hand a
dozen peeresses and the Ranee of Sarawak. The range of the
Society's appeal is suggested by the last three pre-war presi-
dents: in 1911 Andrew Lang; in 1912 W. Boyd Carpenter,
Bishop of Ripon; in 1913 Henri Bergson. It is suggestive of
the intellectual climate of those years that in their presidential addresses Bishop Carpenter and Bergson made much
the same point—that psychic research offered an extension
of, and a liberation from, the mechanistic limits of Victorian
scientific materialism.[14] At the same time that he was President of the Society for Psychical Research, Bishop Carpenter was also President of the National Council of Public
Morals, an organization dedicated to the preservation of Victorian limits in moral matters.

The investigations undertaken by the Society during these
years covered a wide range of subjects, some of them within

[13] Balfour, "Psychical Research," in *Essays Speculative and Political*
(London: Hodder and Stoughton, 1920), pp. 190-191.
[14] *Proceedings of the Society for Psychical Research*, vol. 26 (Sept.
1912), 2-23, and vol. 27 (Jan. 1914), 157-175.

the range of psychological studies—multiple personality, for instance, extra-sensory perception, and hysteria—and others rather closer to spiritualism—dowsing rods, poltergeists, automatic writing. It is easy to ridicule some of these experiments, but one must recognize that for two decades the Society, by its very willingness to appear gullible, provided the only English audience for the most advanced thought in psychological matters. Myers' account of the Breuer-Freud work was delivered at a meeting of the Society and published in its *Proceedings* in June 1893. Myers included a summary of Freud's *Studien über Hysterie* in his major work, *Human Personality* (1901). This book, the last enormous product of decades of psychic research, was meant to make the case for psychic phenomena conclusively, but it was also an important contribution to psychological theory. William James reviewed it after Myers' death and wrote of it in a letter, "The general problem of the subliminal, as Myers propounds it, promises to be one of the great problems, possibly even the greatest problem, of psychology."[15] At a time when English academic psychology was concerned with consciousness and the nervous system, Myers, in search of the immortal soul, had found the subconscious.

One of the strengths of psychic research as a movement was the variety of its appeals. To Myers it was a new religion, to William James it was a set of hypotheses, to be entertained without metaphysical implications, by which new empirical knowledge might be acquired. For Oliver Lodge, the principal Edwardian figure in the Society, it was at first simply a scientific challenge: he was presented with phenomena in a spiritualist's performance that he felt obliged to explain in terms of physical laws. One can infer something about Lodge, and also about Edwardian intellectual life, from the fact that he was, in successive years at the turn of the century, President of the Physical Society and Presi-

15 *Proceedings of the Society for Psychical Research*, vol. 18 (1903), 22-33, and *Letters*, vol. 2, p. 141.

dent of the Society for Psychical Research; he was aware that some of his scientific fellows found this conjunction peculiar, but he thought it intellectually defensible. Throughout the pre-war years Lodge continued to be simultaneously a physicist, a psychic researcher, and a university administrator, and in fact only agreed to accept the post of Principal of Birmingham on the condition that he would continue publicly to pursue his psychic studies.

Lodge's initial defense of psychic research was, like Balfour's cautiously scientific. In 1906, in an introduction to a book called *The Physical Phenomena Popularly Classed Under the Head of Spiritualism*, Lodge wrote,

> With most of the evidence here adduced I have of course been familiar for years, in its original sources, and am well aware of the extreme difficulty or impossibility of understanding some of the alleged facts in any physical or physiological sense; nevertheless if I am asked whether such impressions can be actually received and honestly recorded by sane people, and whether I recommend experiment by careful and competent and unsuperstitious observers as if a *prima facie* case had been made out—that is to say, as if some of these unusual and hitherto quite unexplained occurrences might possibly turn out to be true—having laws of their own and constituting an unopened chapter of science, or rather a new science, uniting characteristics from physical, chemical, physiological, and psychological sciences, and throwing new light on the connection between mind and matter—then, though doubtless the answer will be received with scorn, I answer unhesitatingly yes.[16]

The style of this halting, backtracking, qualifying sentence suggests that Lodge's yes was anything but unhesitating; the passage is in fact one long hesitation. Nevertheless, Lodge

[16] Introduction to Edward T. Bennett, *The Physical Phenomena Popularly Classed Under the Head of Spiritualism* (London: T. C. & E. C. Jack, 1906), pp. 9-10.

did utter it, and became one of the psychic researchers' arguments against scientific scepticism (another was A. R. Wallace, the Victorian biologist who had shared in Darwin's discovery of the principle of natural selection; Wallace was seventy-eight when Edward became king, but his spectrum of interests—biology, psychic research, and socialism—make him an Edwardian radical in spirit).

As the Edwardian decade passed, Lodge's interests in psychic research became less and less scientific and more and more religious; his goal became the reconciliation of science and religion through the use of psychic evidence. In *Life and Matter* (1906) and *Man and the Universe* (1908), he attempted to refute scientific materialism and to find scientific support for spiritual reality; in *Reason and Belief* (1910) he interpreted Christian myths and doctrine in the light of current scientific knowledge. (The latter book is dedicated "To the right honourable Arthur James Balfour, Past President of the British Association and also of the Society for Psychical Research.") In these works Lodge expressed what must have been the principal motive of most members of the Society—the desire to restore the consolations of religion that Victorian science had denied. They were the heirs of the Victorian crisis of belief, and in psychic research they found a solution to that crisis—scientific proof that men survived death and that the universe was morally coherent. Lodge in his last years demonstrated this point in unhappy circumstances; when his youngest son was killed in the war, Lodge wrote *Raymond* (1916) to express both his grief and his consolation. The book is sad reading for many reasons. Raymond, as presented in his letters from the front, is an attractive young man, representative of the best of his class who were destroyed in the war; the specimens of spiritualist communications that Oliver Lodge quotes seem simply evidences of the credulity of grief and of nothing else; and the exposition of Lodge's own theories of life and death are depressing, coming from a man who had once made valuable contributions to scientific knowledge. The book was attacked by scientists as a scandal to the profession, but it had a wide circulation among persons bereaved, as Lodge had been, by the war.

One influence that Lodge's psychic work exercised, and an influence that he would undoubtedly have deplored, was on contemporary literature. When Arthur Machen wrote his ghost story, "The Black Seal" (1895), he took his idea from the researches of Lodge, who had suggested that seance phenomena might be caused by "a kind of extension of the medium's body."[17] The influence of psychic researchers on minor Celtic writers is of no importance; but there is nevertheless a point to be made here—the literature of the late-Victorian and Edwardian periods includes a strain of supernaturalism and fantasy that seems to relate to the main stream of English literature in something like the way that psychic research relates to science. From *The Yellow Book* to the Pan-ridden stories of E. M. Forster one finds the same fascination with pagan deities, under the hill or behind a hedge, with witches and wood nymphs, with supernatural visitors from above or below. Barrie's *Peter Pan* was the most successful play of 1904, and not, as is now happily the case, for audiences of children only (Rupert Brooke came down from Cambridge to see it and thought it was the best play he had ever seen). Pan is a particularly omnipresent figure of the period—even Kipling came across him in Vermont—though not always in forms that would have been recognizable to the Greeks; Barrie, as someone remarked, had robbed Pan to pay Peter, and other Edwardian Pans are similarly domesticated.

A considerable list of this sort of late-Victorian and Edwardian literature could be drawn up: H. G. Wells wrote a romance about a visiting angel, *The Wonderful Visit* (1895), and Ford Madox Hueffer imitated it in *Mr. Apollo*

17 Arthur Machen, *Things Far and Near* (London: Martin Secker, 1923), pp. 109-110.

(1908); M. R. James wrote popular ghost stories, and so did Henry James; Maurice Hewlett and Chesterton and Hueffer all blended Wardour-Street medievalism with vague supernaturalism. All of these examples may be taken, in their various ways, as expressions of religious instincts detached from the forms and dogma of established religion. After the social realism of the Victorians, from Dickens to George Moore, Edwardian novelists (some of them, at any rate) turned toward the mysterious and the unseen, just as the psychic researchers turned from the natural sciences to spiritualism: what William James called "the will to believe" was very much in the air. But if you remove doctrine and dogma from the religious instinct, what you have left is a debased or sentimentalized supernaturalism, things that go bump in the night, and that is, on the whole, what this strain of writing amounts to: of all the examples that one could cite, only "The Turn of the Screw" is a substantial work of art.

It might also be argued, in passing, that even the scientific romances that were so popular during the period were essentially anti-scientific. In Wells' *In the Days of the Comet* (1906), for example, the political and social problems of the modern world are miraculously solved by the arrival in the earth's atmosphere of a comet of green gas which transforms the entire human race into benevolent rationalists and makes earth a happy place. The point of this miraculous intervention seems to be a rejection of Wells' earlier scientific optimism, green gas playing the role formerly played by science. And E. M. Forster's "The Machine Stops" is a more direct attack on Victorian scientific aspirations; it was written, Forster said, as "a reaction to one of the earlier heavens of H. G. Wells."[18] Both Wells and Forster are anti-scientific in these works in two ways: first, both have liberated the imagination by repealing scientific laws (the cloud

[18] E. M. Forster, "Introduction," *Collected Short Stories* (London: Sidgwick & Jackson [1948]), p. vii.

of green gas has no foundations in the scientific knowledge of 1906) , and second by demonstrating in action the inadequacy of current science to accomplish human happiness.

WHEN the first English journal on psychological matters, *The British Journal of Psychology*, appeared in 1904, the editors were anxious to establish at once that their subject was a legitimate science.

> Psychology [said an editorial in the first issue] which till recently was known among us chiefly as Mental Philosophy and was mainly concerned with problems of a more or less speculative and transcendental character, has now at length attained the position of a positive science,

and one of the editors went on, in an article "On the Definition of Psychology," to divorce his subject further from unscientific matters:

> In whatever way our practical interest in such problems as that of immortality may be met, they have, at any rate, since Kant's day, ceased to be regarded as psychological problems, and psychology has now become entirely an empirical science, divested alike of theological and of metaphysical assumptions.[19]

It was no doubt because of psychology's uncertain status as a science that the *Journal* editors were so anxious to dissociate their subject from its doubtful fringes. In so doing they separated themselves from the investigation of the subconscious that runs from the psychic researchers to psychoanalysis; they also withdrew from one area of speculation—speculation about the nature of sex—in which Edwardian England's principal contribution to modern psychology was to be made. The *Journal* psychologists, in the infancy of their subject, already seem to have constituted an exclusive

[19] "Editorial," *British Journal of Psychology*, vol. 1, pt. 1 (Jan. 1904) , 1-2; James Ward, "On the Definition of Psychology," 14.

professional group, and it is not surprising that in this matter as in so many others, what was interesting was done outside the professional ranks, by men who were, strictly speaking, amateurs. Two men, both with scientific training but neither a practicing scientist, both with literary leanings, both with something of the prophet in them, created between them a new understanding of sex and a new climate in which the subject could be discussed. These two—Edward Carpenter and Havelock Ellis—were as close to being Edwardian Sages as anyone, and it is a significant point that the subject to which they applied their sagacity most effectively and dramatically was sex.

Edward Carpenter was born in 1844, the same year as Gerard Manley Hopkins. Like Hopkins he came from an educated middle-class family and went to the university intending to become an Anglican clergyman. But whereas Hopkins went to Oxford, met Newman, and became a Jesuit, Carpenter went to Cambridge and became a Socialist. But only gradually; until he was nearly thirty his career developed along entirely conventional lines: he read mathematics and took a good degree, was made a Fellow of his College, took holy orders, and became a curate under F. D. Maurice, the Christian Socialist. By 1873 Carpenter felt that he could no longer continue in the Church; he resigned his order and his fellowship and left Cambridge.

From this point on, Carpenter's life was a more and more complete rejection of Victorian conventions in politics, religion, and sex, and even in diet and costume. He became first a lecturer in science with the Cambridge University Extension Movement, but when he discovered that his provincial students were not working men but members of the "commercial classes," he quit and took up market gardening. He was one of the organizers of the Sheffield Socialist Society; he was a vegetarian; he made his own sandals; he was a professed homosexual and a defender of "Uranians," as he called them. He was also a writer, author of a long,

Whitmanesque poem, *Towards Democracy*, and of many books and pamphlets, principally on questions of socialism and on sex; he was a traveller who visited America to talk with Whitman and Ceylon to talk with a Guru (he wrote admiring accounts of both visits). Carpenter's life and works are a catalogue of late-Victorian liberating movements, and it is not surprising that by the beginning of the century socialists, anarchists, suffragettes, simple-lifers, free-lovers, spiritualists, anti-vivisectionists, theosophists, vegetarians, and homosexuals all claimed him as a patriarch. The inclusive eclecticism of much turn-of-the-century thought is nowhere better exemplified.

Carpenter's background provided him with three ways of interpreting experience: he had been trained as a scientist; he had been ordained a priest; and he had become a socialist-anarchist. All of these contributed to his later attitudes and to his methods: he was, as Mrs. Havelock Ellis said, a "democratic mystic" whose ideals for man's future combined political and spiritual liberation and were supported by evidence drawn from his own versions of the new science. His books draw on current work in biology and physics and on the researches of European psychologists like Krafft-Ebing, but they are not scientific books. Carpenter did no research of his own, nor did he make systematic use of other men's results; he was a seer, and his methods were the methods of sermon and prophecy.

It is important to note that, though Carpenter was the first modern writer on sex in England, he did not derive, as one might expect, from the great Victorian biologists. Carpenter acknowledged two chief influences on his thought, and they are as remote from Darwin as anything could be—they were Walt Whitman and the *Bhagavad Gita*. The theory of sex, in Carpenter's mind, was not an extension of Victorian science but a part of the reaction against it, an aspect of the general liberating movement; what he wrote was closer to philosophy than to physiology and was not separable from other movements which sought to free men (and women) from degradation and bondage. When he published his pamphlets on sex during the 'nineties, Carpenter gave them related titles: *Sex-love and its place in a free society*; *Marriage in a free society*; *Woman and her place in a free society*; *Homogenic Love and its place in a free society*. That common phrase points to the center of his interests: he sought human freedom, and when he wrote about sex it was about the sexual implications of the whole liberation of men. In *Love's Coming of Age* (1896; enlarged 1906) he referred approvingly to "the spirit of revolt which is spreading on all sides," and in all his books he stressed the interconnections between sexual reform and other aspects of freedom: "It is evident that no very great change for the better in marriage relations can take place except as the accompaniment of deep-lying changes in Society at large"; "the freedom of Woman must ultimately rest on the Communism of society"; "assuredly it is no wonder that the more go-ahead Women (who have come round to the light by their own way, and through much darkness and suffering) should rise in revolt; or that the Workmen (finding their lives in the hands of those who do not know what life is), should do the same."[20] He blamed the failure of love and the failure of society on the same two imprisoning institutions—Christianity and commercialism—and he believed that man, freed from these two, might fulfill his potentialities. The Democracy of his most ambitious work, *Towards Democracy*, is not simply a political term: it is rather a synonym for Love, and his use of the two terms suggests that they were for him simply two routes to the same millennium, in which all mankind, released from their bonds, could love one another. "I conceive a millennium on earth," he wrote,

—a millennium not of riches, nor of mechanical facilities, nor of intellectual facilities, nor absolutely of immunity

[20] *Love's Coming of Age* (Manchester: Labour Press, 1896) , pp. 111, 54n, 31.

from disease, nor absolutely of immunity from pain; but a time when men and women all over the earth shall ascend and enter into relation with their bodies—shall attain freedom and joy. . . .[21]

If this is socialism, it is a socialism that owes more to Whitman than to Marx, a socialism that is mixed in a very improbable way with anarchism.

In his writings on sex, Carpenter tried to put aside conventional institutional and legal considerations and to deal with men and women simply as creatures having certain physical and spiritual needs, which could be either fulfilled or suppressed by their sexual relationships. In some ways he seems to have arrived at conclusions resembling Freud's on the power of the sex drive, the ego and the id, and the role of violence in sex, but in other ways he was curiously unenlightened and old-fashioned. He believed, for instance, that sexuality comes late in children and should be encouraged to come later; he regarded physical love as the lowest level of desire, which reasonable beings would repress in order "to throw the centre of their love-attraction upwards"; and he accepted the Victorian view that for a substantial proportion of women sex could be no more than "a real, even though a willing, sacrifice."[22]

Because Carpenter's conclusions were opinions only, based on intuition and occasional selected secondary sources, they could not be tested and could have no permanent scientific authority. Insofar as he was writing about individual human psychology, he was bound to be superseded by more precise, scientific work (as he was, for example, by Ellis' *Sexual Inversion*). But Carpenter's most important contributions to a modern understanding of sex were not in individual but in social psychology—in his speculations on the relation of social organization to sexual behavior. In his

[21] *Towards Democracy* (London: George Allen & Unwin, 1905) , p. 5.
[22] *Love's Coming of Age*, p. 78n.

treatment of marriage, for example, he argued for a reasonable, human view of marriage that would recognize that love might end, and would allow for easier, honorable dissolutions of the marriage contract. His defense of homosexuality, in *Homogenic Love* (1896) and *The Intermediate Sex* (1908), was the first in English to argue that the condition might be both natural and socially useful. Some of his arguments have since become commonplaces (one finds them, for instance, in the pages of the Wolfenden Report) : that homosexuality may be an instinctive and congenital condition rather than a vice; that the condition is in many cases ineradicable and should therefore be accepted; that homosexuals often play important roles in the public work of society and in the arts. On the latter point he followed the usual line of citing famous artists who might be considered to have been homosexual, though he made one daring addition to the familiar list by claiming Tennyson, on the evidence of *In Memoriam* (Tennyson was still alive and Poet Laureate at the time).

Some of Carpenter's other arguments are odder: for example, he blamed heterosexuality for the growth of European materialism, because heterosexual love makes reproduction a desired end of sex; and he proposed that the class conflict might be solved by encouraging homosexuality, which often draws members of different classes into amiable relationships. The important point, though, is not the quality of Carpenter's arguments but the fact that he made them publicly when he did. His books on sex were gestures of liberation, and if they had no more permanence than gestures usually have, this is not a denial of their value to their time. The sage of one age may well become the bore of another; nevertheless, every age needs its sages.

For a fair and final judgment of Carpenter's importance, one can turn to his friend, E. M. Forster. "If my impression is correct," Forster wrote, he is not likely to have much earthly immortality. He will always be known to students of the late nineteenth and early twentieth centuries for his pioneer work; for his courage and candour about sex, particularly about homosexuality; for his hatred of snobbery while snobbery was still fashionable; for his support of Labour before Labour wore dress-clothes; and for his cult of simplicity. But I do not think he will be remembered long either as a man of letters or scientist. He will not figure in history.[23]

There is only one objection that might be made to Forster's judgment here; it seems possible that Carpenter may figure indirectly in literary history for his role in creating, by his courage and candor, the particular intellectual and emotional climate in which Forster so briefly flourished. Forster has acknowledged that he was "much influenced" by Carpenter,[24] and one can see that they shared ideas and attitudes. Forster's professed belief in tolerance and personal relations is very like Carpenter's, and his version of the Englishman with his "undeveloped heart" is anticipated in Carpenter's *Intermediate Sex*. Even the terms are the same: "Love the beloved republic," and "Two Cheers for Democracy." And through Forster (and perhaps in other ways) Carpenter stands among the ancestors of Bloomsbury, the formulators of that religion of art, intelligence, and human relationships that was born in Edwardian London and died in the Second World War.

Havelock Ellis first knew Carpenter not as a student of sex but as a Socialist—they met at a meeting of the Fellowship of the New Life during the 'eighties. When he came to read Carpenter, Ellis hit first upon *Towards Democracy* (and thought it was "Whitman and water") before he read the sex pamphlets. These first terms of contact say something about both men: both were Socialists, poets, men of letters,

[23] "Some Memories," in Gilbert Beith, ed., *Edward Carpenter in Appreciation* (London: Allen & Unwin, 1931), p. 80.
[24] Letter to the author, Jan. 18, 1965.

and philosophers, and for both the study of sex was a natural part of the intellectual curiosity that included their other interests. "By inborn temperament," Ellis once wrote, "I was, and have remained, an English amateur; I have never been able to pursue any aim that no passionate instinct has drawn me towards";[25] the sentence would apply just as well to Carpenter. There were other resemblances too; Ellis had been trained as a doctor, but he did not consider himself a scientist, and he shared that hostility toward nineteenth-century scientific thought that Carpenter and other advanced thinkers of the time felt. Also like Carpenter, Ellis had lost his Christian faith but had retained a vague religious sense that sometimes gave to his writing a mystical or prophetic tone (though he never became as Biblical, or as Whitman-esque, as Carpenter often was). One can treat the two together, as English amateurs in the study of sex, with a common conception of the nature of their work—that it was to be a service done for the liberation of men from the conventions and repressions of the past.

Ellis' own attitude toward the Victorian past is wittily expressed in his Socratic dialogue, *The Nineteenth Century* (1900), in which a wise philosopher, living at some unspecified time in the future, explains the past to his pupil. The philosopher, who speaks for Ellis, is particularly critical of the nineteenth-century "cult of science": "it was common at that period," he says, "to treat metaphysics with contempt; it seemed to them that the making of machinery and all that that involved might well cover the whole of life. But as we know, there is always scope for the philosophic impulse. It is natural to man, in so far as man is a thinking being, and the development of specialisation in thinking merely gives it a larger field to work in. The philosopher is the amateur of all the sciences."[26] This is clearly Ellis' own conception of himself—the "English amateur" of all the sci-

25 Havelock Ellis, *My Life* (London: Heinemann, 1940), p. 89.
26 *The Nineteenth Century* (London: Grant Richards, 1900), pp. 44-45.

ences, concerned not simply to practice, but to judge the practice of scientific disciplines.

Ellis' relation to science is in some ways like Carpenter's and Wells'; all were trained scientists, but all were also reformers who regarded Victorian scientism as socially undesirable. "Science," Ellis' philosopher explains to his pupil,

> was merely mechanical aptitude, the aptitude to make and to measure. It was a condition of human civilisation, and one of its most essential conditions. But it was not more than that, and in itself could never furnish any guide to life. It was a mere instrument, as good to slay as to save. . . . Science never taught the art of thinking, for the most skilful mathematical thinkers could make the grossest elementary blunders in thought. Science never taught the art of living, for a man who was a perfect instrument for scientific thought could yet remain on a lower moral level than the lowest of the savages. And how little science could do for the other arts, the whole nineteenth century remains an everlasting monument.[27]

What the philosopher is attacking here is not science as a body of knowledge but the Victorian belief in the progressive role of science in human affairs. Ellis was concerned to reduce the place of science in society to an instrumental role and to remove from it all suggestions of inherent human value. His motive in this was simple enough: a faith like Lord Kelvin's in the imminent discovery of perfect scientific knowledge could be used as a reactionary argument in support of a laissez-faire attitude toward social reform. Ellis was a Socialist who wished to use science as an instrument for the improvement of men's circumstances; but if socialism and science were to go hand in hand, socialism must do the leading and provide the values.

It is in this idea of science as an instrument of reform that men like Ellis differ most fundamentally from the Victorian

[27] *The Nineteenth Century*, pp. 48-49.

scientific giants. Darwin, in developing the theories of evolution and natural selection, had provided established society with a scientific reason for neglecting social reform; evolution could be trusted to arrange for changes in a natural way (though only if one took society to be a biological form). Thus in a pamphlet on *Problems of Sex* written for the reactionary National Council of Public Morals, the authors (both academic scientists) could conclude, "Admitting the idea of evolution, we are not only entitled to the hope, but logically compelled to the assurance, that these rare fruits of an apparently more than earthly paradise of love [they had been talking, with unscientific lyricism, about poets and the women they write about], which only the forerunners of the race have been privileged to gather, or it may be to see from distant heights, are yet the realities of a daily life toward which we and others may journey."[28] Ellis, writing in the same year, took an exactly opposite view:

> . . . as Whitman put it, "There will never be any more perfection than there is now." We cannot expect an increased power of growth and realisation in existence, as a whole, leading to any general perfection; we can only expect to see the triumph of individuals, carrying out their own conceptions along special lines, every perfection so attained involving, on its reverse side, the acquirement of an imperfection. It is in this sense, and in this sense only, that progress is possible.[29]

During the late-Victorian and Edwardian years, Ellis was a sort of all-purpose prophet, defending Zola and Ibsen, supporting socialism and the women's movement, speaking always for what he called The New Spirit. But during these years he was also at work on the books which he regarded as his major life work—the *Studies in the Psychology of Sex*.

28 J. Arthur Thomson and Patrick Geddes, *Problems of Sex* (London: Cassell, 1912), p. 58.
29 Ellis, *The Task of Social Hygiene* (London: Constable, 1912), p. vii.

The first volume was published in England in 1897 and immediately suppressed; the sixth appeared in 1910; the whole is not only Ellis' greatest work, it is also Edwardian England's principal contribution to psychological knowledge. The *Studies* is primarily a work of synthesis, derived from a vast range of scientific and literary sources rather than from primary research; but the value of the work is not reduced by this fact. For what Ellis did in his synthesis was to document a new attitude toward sex, which is essentially the twentieth century's attitude. He took sex as a category of human behavior, available to study from many points of view—biological, psychological, historical, anthropological—and expressed in many ways. His approach is not pathological—that is, he is not concerned simply with the abnormal in sexual behavior but with all sexual behavior, and indeed the concept of normality has little meaning in the work. Ellis was the first English scientist to write about homosexuality as a natural human condition; he was also the first to study auto-eroticism (a term which he coined) and the evolution of modesty. But most of all he was the first English writer to be at once objective and readable on the subject of sex. Before Ellis, writers on sex had either elaborately avoided details, or they had followed Krafft-Ebing's practice: "In order that unqualified persons should not become readers," Krafft-Ebing had written in the preface to *Psychopathia Sexualis*, "the author saw himself compelled to choose a title understood only by the learned, and also, where possible, to express himself in *terminis technicis*. It seemed necessary also to give certain particularly revolting portions in Latin."[30] Ellis, on the contrary, assumed that sex was a subject in which all adults were qualified to take an interest, and he wrote for the general reader. It is one of the ironies of the Edwardian situation that Ellis' *Studies*, one of the intellectual monuments of the period, could only be

[30] Dr. R. von Krafft-Ebing, *Psychopathia Sexualis* (Philadelphia and London, F. A. Davis Co. and F. J. Rebman, 1893), p. v.

published in America; it was not published in England until 1935.

The contribution that Carpenter and Ellis made to the modern world is best understood if they are seen not as scientists, or as psychologists, but as philosophers of sex. Between them they made a beginning in the long task of persuading Englishmen that sexual behavior was instinctual as well as moral. And they gave circulation to two important but unpopular ideas: that sexual deviants were not all vicious and that judgments of sexual behavior should be based on natural and humane considerations rather than on social conventions. Ellis' own judgment of his achievement in the *Studies* is a just one:

> I had done mankind a service which mankind needed, and which, it seemed, I alone was fitted to do. I had helped to make the world, and to make the world in the only way that it can be made, the interior way, by liberating the human spirit.[31]

That is a fine thing to be able to say, but it is not a scientist's judgment; Ellis and Carpenter did help to liberate the human spirit, but to say this is to place their work among the battles in the Edwardian war against social conservatism rather than in the history of the evolution of a scientific discipline. Neither man worked as a scientist works; neither performed experiments or applied his knowledge to clinical cases. The principal effect of their efforts was not on the science of psychology; it was on the attitudes of the informed lay public.

William James once defined the difference between the professional and the amateur by saying that the latter interests himself especially in the result obtained, the former in the way in which we obtain it. In these terms, both Ellis and Carpenter were amateurs in the study of sex, and their successors were even more so. The British Society for the

[31] *My Life*, p. 363.

Study of Sex Psychology was organized in 1914, largely through the efforts of Carpenter and Laurence Housman, to provide a forum for "the consideration of problems and questions connected with sexual psychology from their medical, juridical, and sociological aspects." At the first meeting Housman, who became the Society's first president, defined its principles and aims; it is characteristic both of the Society and of the time that the aims of a psychological organization should be defined not by a psychologist but by a novelist-poet-dramatist who was active in the suffrage movement. Among the sex problems that Housman proposed for discussion were

> the admitted evil of prostitution, male and female; the attendant and wide-spread existence of blackmail which takes criminal advantage of the law as it now stands; the lack of proper safeguards for consent in sex-relations, free from all compulsion social, economical, or physical; the unsatisfactory conditions of marriage and divorce; the failure to deal equitably and soundly with the spread of venereal disease; the almost total absence of sex-training from education. . . .[32]

Each of these is primarily a social problem rather than a psychological one, and it is clear from this list that the Society was organized to continue the work that Carpenter and Ellis had started, to create an informed public that would accept and support reforms in the laws governing sexual behavior and in time modify the general social attitudes toward sex.

Over the next ten years the Society published another dozen papers—including two by Ellis and one by Carpenter —but less than half were by medical men, and none was of any special importance to psychology. The Society's expressed aims were not, however, primarily scientific; they

[32] *Policy and Principles. General Aims.* British Society for the Study of Sex Psychology, Publication No. 1. (London: Beaumont & Co., n.d. [1914]) , pp. 3-4.

were rather educational, and in this direction the Society's achievements are more difficult to measure. Years later, when Housman wrote an appreciation of Carpenter's work, he seemed to have the Society in mind when he said,

> In the last ten years that enfranchisement of the public conscience in sex matters, for which Carpenter worked all his life, has come largely into being. The law—as is usual in all reforms tending toward human freedom—still lags behind. But between the general attitude of people claiming to be intelligent thirty years ago and that of the same class to-day, there has come a change of enormous significance—a great and hopeful revolution. Carpenter, one of the quietest revolutionists ever known, lived to see the beginning of it; a beginning which without his help, might not have been discernible.[33]

The last ten years that Housman referred to are the decade of the 1920's, and one can surely argue that the activities of the Society did play a part in the post-war enfranchisement; but a more direct and brutal cause of that liberation was the war itself. There is a sadly ironic sentence in Housman's speech to the Society at its first meeting, when he declared that the Society "intends activity so soon as the sinews of war are given to us."[34] He made that speech on July 12, 1914. Like so many other Edwardian movements for reform, this one came too late to come peacefully.

The actions of men like Carpenter and Ellis to liberate sex from ignorance and repression produced equal and opposite reactions from spokesmen for the established order. The points at issue, in their view, were these: Was man's sexual behavior to be treated as instinctual or as volitional and therefore moral—in short, was man an animal? Were the young to be taught about sex, and if so what and

[33] "A Peaceful Penetrator," in Beith, ed., *Edward Carpenter In Appreciation*, p. 111.
[34] *Policy and Principles*, p. 7.

when? Were the results of scientific investigations in sexual matters to be made public? If so, what would be the social effects? There was obviously a good deal more at stake in these questions than simply the right attitude toward sex; the answers, one way or the other, implied ideas about the relation between the public and their rulers, about the place of women in society, about the morality of monogamous marriage, about the role of education in society. A revolution in the public attitude toward sex seemed to conservative minds to threaten larger and even more sinister revolutions, and they consequently set about a counter-revolution.

Conservative defenses were of two kinds: first, efforts to suppress new ideas, either by active censorship or by professional indifference; second, the circulation of counter-publications on sex and sex education. Of the first sort, both Carpenter and Ellis had experience of censorship (see below, Chapter VIII). Ellis' first volume in the *Studies, Sexual Inversion*, was seized and destroyed by the police, and the books of other writers on sex were also suppressed by police action—those of the German, Iwan Bloch, for example, in 1909. The common justification of such suppressions was that the book might fall into the hands of the young and ignorant, the assumption being that even scientific knowledge of sex would be inflaming and corrupting to young minds. Occasionally this defense turned up in rather odd places. The *Lancet*, for instance, did not review *Sexual Inversion*, and after the book had figured in an obscenity trial, the *Lancet*'s editor defended his decision:

> When Mr. Havelock Ellis' book was sent to us for review we did not review it, and our reason for this neglect of the work of the Editor of the "Contemporary Science Series" was not connected with its theme or wholly with the manner of its presentment. Mr. Havelock Ellis' book is written in a purely dispassionate and scientific style and the only exception we take to the treatment is that we consider

some of his quotations unnecessary because a scientific public is already familiar with the originals, and some of them useless, being drawn from tainted sources. We may say also that we do not agree with his view of the question, for we consider that such matters are far better treated from the psycho-pathological standpoint of Krafft-Ebing than from that of Ulrichs, with whose theory as to the naturalness of homo-sexuality Mr. Havelock Ellis seems in agreement; but a difference of opinion would not have prevented us from giving publicity to the author's labours. What decided us not to notice the book was its method of publication. Why was it not published through a house able to take proper measures for introducing it as a scientific book to a scientific audience? And for other reasons, which it would serve no purpose to particularise, we considered the circumstances attendant upon its issue suspicious. We believed that the book would fall into the hands of readers totally unable to derive benefit from it as a work of science and very ready to draw evil lessons from its necessarily disgusting passages. It must be pointed out, too, that a more than ordinary danger is attached to Mr. Havelock Ellis' work as a book for laymen in that the author's views happen to be that sexual inversion is far more prevalent than we believe it to be and that the legislature does injustice to many by regarding as crimes the practices with which it is bound up. He has failed to convince us on these points; and his historical references and the "human documents" with which he has been furnished will, we think, fail equally to convince medical men that homo-sexuality is anything else than an acquired and depraved manifestation of the sexual passion; but, be that as it may, it is especially important that such matter should not be discussed by the man in the street, not to mention the boy and girl in the street.[35]

[35] "The Question of Indecent Literature," *Lancet* (Nov. 19, 1898), p. 1344.

Since the *Lancet* would scarcely reach the man (or the boy and girl) in the street, it is difficult to see the editor's action as anything but a personal punishment meted out to a writer who had offended the editor's conservative moral sensibilities. One finds the same attitude in many other Edwardian reviews of controversial books by Carpenter, Ellis, and Freud.

Freudian psychology offers another example of the way in which the established order—in this case the medical establishment—resisted new ideas. Psychoanalytic ideas had spread more slowly in England than anywhere else in Europe or America. When Freud was made an honorary member of the Society for Psychical Research in 1911, he wrote to Jung that it was "the first sign of interest from dear old England";[36] the London Psycho-Analytical Society was not founded until two years later, in 1913, and then with only nine members, of whom only four ever practiced. Freud's methods became acceptable to the British medical world only after they had been proved in war-time treatment of shell-shock cases; before the war the official attitude was bleakly and uniformly hostile. In 1911, when Dr. David Eder presented the first paper on clinical psychoanalysis to be read at a British Medical Association meeting, the chairman waited until he had finished and then stalked out of the room without a word, followed by the entire audience. Even Freud's books were treated as indecent literature: the 1913 English edition of *The Interpretation of Dreams* contains a slip reading: "Publisher's Note. The sale of this book is limited to Members of the Medical, Scholastic, Legal, and Clerical professions."

While Carpenter, Ellis, and Freud were meeting such resistance, other writers, men of impeccable qualifications (at least from the established order's point of view) were at work to provide more acceptable ideas of sex for the general

36 Ernest Jones, *Sigmund Freud. Life and Work*, 3 vols. (London: Hogarth Press, 1955) , vol. 2, p. 99, n. 2.

public. The first in time, as well as in the perfection of his social station, was The Reverend The Honourable Edward Lyttelton, author of *The Causes and Prevention of Immorality in Schools* (1887) and *Training of the Young in the Laws of Sex* (1900). The word "Establishment" is one that I have tried to avoid, but if it could ever be applied precisely to anyone, that person is the Rev. Mr. Lyttelton. He was the son of an earl, had been educated at Eton and Cambridge, was a priest and a canon of the Church of England; from 1905 to 1916 he was Headmaster of Eton; his brother, General the Right Honourable Sir Neville Lyttelton, was Chief of the General Staff from 1904 to 1908. (See Appendix B.) He was the author of a number of other books, including *Cricket* (1890) and *Are we to go on with Latin verses?* (1897). At the time of Lyttelton's appointment as Headmaster of Eton, his former colleague, A. C. Benson, wrote this note in his diary:

> May 8, 1905. Found Edward, brown as a berry, full of tranquillity, good spirits and confidence. . . . I felt an odd mixture of confidence in his strength, and entire mistrust in his judgment.[37]

Lyttelton's first book on sex was published by the Social Purity Alliance and was intended for private circulation; for this reason Lyttelton must have felt free to speak frankly. He acknowledged that schoolboy homosexuality existed and proposed some ways of dealing with the problem. He returned to the subject in 1900 in a very different spirit. In the intervening years Carpenter had published *Homogenic Love* and Ellis had written *Sexual Inversion*; but far more important than either book in affecting public opinion, Oscar Wilde had been tried and imprisoned for the "love that dare not speak its name" and had been released to die in France. Lyttelton devoted his second book to denying the charge

[37] Percy Lubbock, ed., *The Diary of Arthur Christopher Benson* (New York: Longmans, Green, 1926), p. 114.

that public schools bred perversion—a charge that both Carpenter and Ellis had made; the real origin of depravity, he wrote, "is to be found in the common predisposition to vicious conceptions which is the result of [parental] neglect."[38] He went on to offer suggestions as to how to explain conception and birth with a maximum of delicacy (and a minimum of information).

Lyttelton's attitude toward sex is essentially the Victorian attitude, as expressed in the standard Victorian work on the subject, Acton's *Practical Treatise on the Diseases of the Urinary and Generative Organs*:[39] sexuality is treated as a matter of voluntary moral or immoral acts, which can be controlled and postponed by an act of will or by wise guidance and can only properly be expressed within the conventions of monogamous marriage. There are no direct references to biological facts and almost none to the role of the father; Lyttelton's advice was to concentrate on the boy's feelings for his mother, "with emphasis laid on the suffering involved to his mother, and the wonderful fact given as a reason why the mother so dearly loves her son."[40]

But the most interesting point made in Lyttelton's little book is not on sex education, but on the social history of sex.

> Unless a great many careful observers are wrong [Lyttelton wrote], there is a certain urgency of need at the present day which has perhaps not existed before. There are some reasons for supposing that the most startling symptoms of unnatural social corruption which manifest them-

[38] Rev. the Hon. E. Lyttelton, *Training of the Young in Laws of Sex* (London: Longmans, Green, 1900), p. 8.

[39] William Acton's *Practical Treatise* was first published in 1841, and reached its sixth and last edition in 1875, though it remained a standard reference for years after—Lyttelton's *Cause and Prevention of Immorality in Schools* (1887) leans heavily on it. For a shrewd and entertaining analysis of Acton, see Steven Marcus, *The Other Victorians* (New York: Basic Books, 1966), Ch. I.

[40] *Training of the Young*, p. 80.

selves to careful observers of to-day were not to be discerned a century ago; and anyhow, in this question to lull ourselves into security by a contemplation of England's past history is an idle kind of optimism.[41]

That is to say, the motive for sex education is not past ignorance (which was presumably all right in that secure and natural past) but present social anxieties. This is characteristic of conservatives in their attitudes toward such problems, that they only begin to concede the need for change when that need can be argued in terms of general social danger. Lyttelton, combining nostalgia (in this case a kind of sexual pastoralism) with vague fears of the present, was very much an Edwardian of his class.

He was also typical of his class in that, once the immediate threat seemed to be past, he lapsed into a more comfortable position opposing change, freedom, and intellectual liberation. When the question of censoring indecent literature was being argued in the press in 1913, Lyttelton wrote, in his role as Headmaster of Eton, to the *Times*:

Those who are working and hoping, however feebly, to encompass the lives of our boys and girls with wholesome atmosphere must know that in regard to sexuality two facts stand out. First, that in proportion as the adolescent mind grows absorbed in sex questions wreckage of life ensues. Secondly, that sanity and upright manliness are destroyed, not only by the reading of obscene stuff, but by a premature interest in sex matters, however it be excited.[42]

These propositions would seem to contradict the practice implied in Lyttelton's earlier pamphlet; but in fact his practice was probably much the same—a policy of protection, ignorance, and English reserve.

[41] *Training of the Young*, pp. 114-115.
[42] *Times*, Nov. 22, 1913, p. 11.

Lyttelton, though as representative of his class as any man could be, nevertheless spoke officially only for himself. Two conservative writers who followed him brought organization to the fight against sexual knowledge. Lt. Gen. Sir Robert Baden-Powell regarded sex in much the same way that he regarded smoking and spectator sports—as an unhealthy practice that good Scouts would avoid in order to make themselves stronger and healthier servants of the crown. (He practiced what he preached, at least to the extent of not marrying until he was fifty-one.) The first edition of *Scouting for Boys* (1908) and *The Handbook for Girl Guides* (1912), written by Agnes Baden-Powell with her brother's collaboration, contain much the same advice on adolescent sexual practices, though oddly the girls' book is rather more emphatic:

> All secret bad habits are evil and dangerous, lead to hysteria and lunatic asylums, and serious illness is the result. . . . Evil practises dare not face an honest person; they lead you on to blindness, paralysis, and loss of memory.[43]

Cold baths and exercise are recommended.

Another organizer of conservative morality was the Rev. James Marchant, a professional moral crusader who directed the National Council of Public Morals and was later knighted for his work on the birth-rate problem (an unusual honor for a clergyman, as it was an odd clerical job). In the cause of sexual purity Marchant wrote *Aids to Purity* (1909), a series of letters to young men. In the book Marchant argued that the "psychological moment" had come for a purity crusade because of "the recent Parliamentary Report on Indecent Advertisements, the great International Moral Education Congress just closed, the outcry resulting therefrom against poisonous literature and debasing postcards raised

---

[43] Agnes Baden-Powell, in collaboration with Lt. Gen. Sir Robert Baden-Powell, *The Handbook for Girl Guides* (London: Thos. Nelson, n.d. [1912]), p. 340.

and echoed again and again by the responsible journals of the country." But the particular crusade that these letters addressed themselves to was rather narrower—the old clean living and cold baths program of headmasters like Lyttelton. Marchant made some attempt at a hearty, men-together tone, but when he got down to the theme of impurity he took a view of the effects of sex that is essentially Victorian:

> Impure and pure alike agree in this—if you, it is a personal matter, give way to impurity, you are lost. You will fail in your examinations, you will lose your chances in business, you will weaken and sicken, body and soul, you will go under. Let me repeat the terrible truth, you will lose your character, you will be ruined. . . .
>
> And impurity is not, as is sometimes thought, a secret, solitary vice. It is seen and known from the beginning. The face, the eyes, the hands, the walk, the attitude, the temperament, all betray the sinner.[44]

There are two striking things about this passage: first, it does not give the slightest suggestion of what kind of impurity is being discussed (nor does the rest of the book); therefore, one must conclude that the author takes it that his readers know (in which case it must be too late, and their faces, eyes, hands, and walks are already marked with vice). Second, the expense is, in the protestant-evangelical tradition, the loss of status and worldly success.

Marchant's later activities were principally the organization and administration of the National Council of Public Morals. One of the projects of the NCPM was a series of pamphlets, "New Tracts for the Times," dealing with aspects of "race regeneration"—the conservative conviction that British society was in a state of progressive decadence, but that the process could be reversed by firm moral action. For this series two professors of biology, Thomson of Edinburgh

[44] James Marchant, F.R.S.L., *Aids to Purity* (London: "Health and Strength" Ltd., n.d. [1909]), pp. 9-10.

and Geddes of St. Andrews, wrote *Problems of Sex* (1912), a pamphlet which may be taken as the informed conservative view of the matter. The authors set out to deal with their subject "fundamentally from the biological and evolutionary point of view, and its associated psychological and social ones," but moved almost at once to a moral position: "We wish to say at once," they wrote,

> that we do not share the mood of extreme toleration which is sometimes cultivated today. It would pardon all evil without perhaps understanding any; and it must be despised even by the condoners themselves. To have a good stock of wholesome prejudices against dirt and deviltry, against lust and unnatural vice, is a sounder social position than that milk-and-water timidity of decision which condones all that "evolution" evolves, which would indeed soon make a very drab affair of our social fabric. Such excessive leniency, which is afraid to stamp down, or it may be to stamp out, what is evidently bringing man nearer to, not farther from, the beast, betokens a slackening of intellectual and moral fibre.[45]

Aside from occasional references to evolution (most of them doubtful extensions of the concept) there is nothing in *Problems of Sex* to identify the authors as scientists; the work is as much an exercise in propaganda as Carpenter's pamphlets were on the other side of the argument.

These representatives of the established Edwardian order share certain significant attitudes. For all of them, sex was only a problem when it was unhealthily indulged in. For all of them the problem was related to recent social change rather than to man's physical nature—and indeed none acknowledged animal nature as a constant to be dealt with. They shared the notion that there had been a time in the past when modern problems (including the problem of sexuality) did not exist, when Englishmen were somehow

[45] *Problems of Sex*, p. 28.

healthier and decenter than Edwardian Englishmen were. All of them treated sexual activity in the young as depravity (though one must add that liberated men like Ellis, Carpenter, and H. G. Wells also shared the idea that human sexuality normally began in late adolescence; Freud's theory of infant sexuality was resisted in England even by those who were sympathetic to his other ideas; it was the last of his theories to gain general acceptance).

In the conservative view, sex was essentially a social problem involving behavior that was subject to rational choice and control and therefore could properly be made subject to the prescriptions of law. This view was antithetical to what Ellis called the "New Spirit," which would liberate individual sexual feelings from social definitions ("There is no rule," Carpenter wrote, "except that of Love"). The conflict between these two opposing ideas of sex—the repressive and the liberating—continued through the Edwardian period, increasing in intensity in the later years as the Edwardian sexual revolution advanced. One finds it evidenced in the activities of legislators, reformers, and the police, in the public statements of artists and clergymen, in sermons and editorials and letters to editors, and in some of the most important plays and novels of the time. No aspect of human life changed more in the transition from Victorian England to modern England than the way Englishmen thought about sex.

....

THE TROUBLE WITH WOMEN

....

Because of men like Carpenter and Ellis, Englishmen thought about sex in a different way, but that change was only a part of a larger, slower, and more complicated one—the vast change that took place in the relations between the sexes, and in the place of women in English society in the years before the war. This social revolution had many implications besides the sexual: it also involved legal, political, and economic issues, and touched on property ownership, the franchise, higher education, the birth rate, laws of marriage and divorce, the protocol of the court, and the future of the Empire—in short, on nearly every aspect of Edwardian society. In all these aspects, the question asked was, what should be the role of woman here? (Or by Tories, what is the trouble with women *now?*) Before the Edwardian years were past, the trouble with women had been blamed on everything from contraceptives to bicycles and had been the subject of novels, poems, and plays, of debates in the Lords and the Commons, and of rallies in Trafalgar Square.

When the war brought a sudden end to controversy, women still had their problems: marriage and divorce were legally what they had been twenty years earlier, women still did not have the vote, and the double standard was still double. In fact, men and women seemed more thoroughly alienated from each other than ever, and one might argue that the relations between the sexes, like the relations between rich and poor, employers and employees, English and Irish,

Conservatives and Liberals, had deteriorated during the Edwardian years.

But though this seems true, it is only part of the truth. The campaign for women's rights, in its more dramatic and militant forms, did effect an alienation of men from women and harden the Conservative opposition to reforms, even those reforms which had nothing to do with suffrage. And it is true that the militant suffrage campaign achieved no positive goals before the First World War. But the women's revolution of the late-Victorian and Edwardian years was fought on a wider field than suffrage, and if there were political defeats there were also social victories—less flamboyant, but important ones. If laws did not change, attitudes did. By the end of Edward's reign many thoughtful people had come to believe that the institutional forms of man-woman relations in England were outmoded and unjust at best and were often immoral and degrading. Attitudes were changing toward marriage and divorce, toward the double standard (which the existing divorce laws made official), and toward irregular sexual behavior. The pages that follow will deal with this aspect of the women's revolution as it is recorded in Edwardian writing, in the theater, and in public discussion.

It is generally true of revolutionary situations that the beginnings of change increase the desire for change, and that revolutions therefore flare up, not in the worst circumstances, but in improving circumstances. Certainly this is true of the revolution of women. During the last third of the nineteenth century women had entered the professions and the universities, had gained the franchise in some local elections, had won the right to serve on school boards and as guardians of the poor. Their economic circumstances had been improved by the Married Women's Property Act and by the increase in office employment for women. But as women's circumstances improved, so did their appetites for improvement. Once reasonable alternatives to marriage as a career existed, the institution of marriage itself became the object of examination and criticism. The idea of a divinely sanctioned lifetime of subjection and inferiority began to be questioned and discussed, by men as well as by women.

Of all the aspects of the women's movements, the Marriage Question was the most central, for it brought into question the entire social structure, government of men, the bases of sexual morality, and the authority of the Church. It was also the most inflammatory. Just as discussions of racial integration tend to be reduced in opening arguments to the question of one's daughter marrying a Negro, so discussions of women's rights over the Edwardian years tended to dissolve into emotional questions of sexual purity and motherhood. The woman's revolution is a dramatic demonstration of the truth that all relations between the sexes will sooner or later be treated as sexual.

Shaw acknowledged this problem in his Fabian pamphlet on policy (1896), in which he wrote that the Fabian Society "has no distinctive opinions on the Marriage Question." The fact that he felt the need to make such a disclaimer suggests that he recognized the controversial nature of the question and wished to save the Fabian Society from the sex war. The fact that the Fabians did manage to avoid the issue of women's rights for another ten years is testimony to their diplomatic skills, for even when Shaw was writing his pamphlet the Marriage Question was a lively public issue, and Shaw had done his bit toward making it so. One might say that the Marriage Question became public on the night of June 7, 1889—the occasion of the first English performance of *A Doll's House*. The vogue of Ibsen that followed—with Shaw as a principal publicist—made the "problem play" a popular dramatic form, but it also made the marriage problem a popular subject for serious playwrights.

During the next few years most of the important English plays produced dealt in some sense with the Marriage Question: *Lady Windermere's Fan* in 1892, *A Woman of No Importance* and *The Second Mrs. Tanqueray* in 1893, *The Case* of *Rebellious Susan* and *The Masqueraders* in 1894, *The Notorious Mrs. Ebbsmith* and *The Benefit of a Doubt* in 1895 are examples. These plays touched various aspects of the problem—male infidelity vs. female infidelity, the present effects of a woman's past, the conflict of love and marriage, but all have this in common—that they took marriage seriously. Because Ibsen was being publicized at the time, and because these plays dealt with sexual matters, they were sometimes called "Ibsenish" and criticized as improper. They were also well attended, no doubt because they were thought wicked; all were successful, and two or three had extremely long runs. One might infer from this that advanced thought had seized the Victorian theater; but such an inference would be quite wrong, for these plays are only superficially "problem plays" in the sense that Ibsen's were; the playwrights were simply using the Marriage Question as another way of writing melodramas on "that dullest of stock dramatic subjects, adultery."[1] In the course of the play some advanced ideas might be expressed, and some sympathy shown for the Woman Who Pays, but in every case the final attitudes were conservative: sin was punished, marriage was preserved, and the double standard was treated as a natural law. No play in this group would have disturbed the average Victorian playgoer or have shaken his confidence in the fundamental morality of English society.

The playwrights themselves sometimes protested at the complacent and provincial conservatism of the audiences they served, but to some extent they also shared it. Henry Arthur Jones, for example, directed a heavily ironic attack at English Mrs. Grundy in a prefatory letter in his *Case of Rebellious Susan*:

I am aware [he assured Mrs. Grundy] that I have no warrant in the actual facts of the world around me for placing

[1] Preface to *Mrs. Warren's Profession* (dated Jan., 1902), in Shaw, *Prefaces* (London: Constable, 1934), p. 223.

on the English stage an instance of English conjugal infidelity. There is, I believe, madam, a great deal of this kind of immorality in France, but I am quite sure you will rejoice to hear that a very careful and searching inquiry has not resulted in establishing any well-authenticated case in English life.[2]

But while he denied any connection with English Grundyism, he was equally anxious to dissociate himself from Ibsen. In 1891 (the year of the English production of *Ghosts*) he publicly protested against "a school of modern realism which founded dramas on disease, ugliness, and vice," and, though he had once collaborated on an adaptation of *A Doll's House* he became very indignant at the suggestion that he had been influenced by Ibsen.

Rebellious Susan is a good example of the forms that the Marriage Question took in the late Victorian theater. It is a play about a wife's revenge, or attempt at revenge, on her husband for his infidelity. The principal theme is set out in this exchange in the first act:

LADY SUSAN: I want somebody to show me some way of paying him back without—without—

SIR RICHARD [her uncle]: Without losing your place in society and your self-respect. Ah! that's the difficulty. There's an immense reputation to be made as a moralist by any man who will show you ladies the way to break the seventh commandment without leaving any ill effects upon society.

LADY SUSAN: Well, he'd better make haste, or we shall find out the way ourselves.

SIR RICHARD: [Shakes his head.] My dear Sue, believe me, what is sauce for the goose will never be sauce for the gander. In fact, there is no gander sauce. . . ."[3]

[2] "To Mrs. Grundy," in *The Case of Rebellious Susan* (London: Macmillan, 1897), pp. vii-viii.
[3] *Rebellious Susan*, pp. 7-8.

Lady Susan nevertheless leaves her husband and travels to Cairo, where she has a brief romance. She then returns and is reconciled with her husband, though she refuses to confess all to him unless he will confess as much to her. The point about the double standard is made—that it is unjust of the husband to demand greater fidelity of his wife than he offers her—but the play ends with a reconciliation and the preservation of marriage, and no one questions Sir Richard's proposition that there is no gander sauce.

In his published preface Jones tried to make the play more daring than it in fact is. The moral, he suggested, was this: "That as women cannot retaliate openly, they may retaliate secretly—and *lie!*" But this is not the point of the play; Lady Susan's romance is a case of true love, not of retaliation, and it is love that she renounces in the interests of convention and her place in society. Perhaps this is what Jones meant when he called the play "a tragedy, dressed up as a comedy"—that he had distorted the proper ending of the play to fit the public taste for happy and moral endings. (Thomas Hardy shared Jones' box on opening night; one wonders what he thought of this gingerly account of the Marriage Question, being engaged as he was on his own version, *Jude the Obscure*.)

Yet even as written the play caused some qualms. The producer, Sir Charles Wyndham, and the star, Mary Moore, were anxious that Jones should revise his text so as to leave the question of Lady Susan's sin ambiguous; Wyndham in fact preferred that she should be made clearly innocent of any actual infidelity.

I stand as bewildered to-day as ever [he wrote to Jones] at finding an author, a clean living, clear-minded man, hoping to extract laughter from an audience on the score of a woman's impurity. I can realise the picture of a bad woman and her natural and desirable end being portrayed, but that amusement pure and simple should be expected from the sacrifice of that one indispensable quality in respect for womanhood astounds me.[4]

Wyndham's concern was practical as well as moral. He was the operator of the theater in which the play was to be performed, and he was worried about box office receipts.

I am equally astounded at a practical long-experienced dramatic author believing that he will induce married men to bring their wives to a theatre to learn the lesson that their wives can descend to such nastiness, as giving themselves up for one evening of adulterous pleasure and then return safely to their husband's arms, provided they are clever enough, low enough, and dishonest enough to avoid being found out.[5]

In Wyndham's view, propriety was good business, and good business was good theater: "the tendency of the drama should always, if possible, be elevating," he told Jones. "If we depart from this ever, as in the case of *Mrs. Tanqueray*, and such like, the subject has to be grappled with seriously."[6] The trouble with *Lady Susan* was that it was insufficiently serious —that is to say, Jones saw the comic aspects of the Marriage Question.

Wyndham saw that if serious questions really had to be dealt with in the Victorian theater, Pinero offered the model of how to do it, for he had superlatively the gift for grappling seriously with shocking subjects without saying anything shocking about them. Shaw regarded him as an acquisitive tradesman of the drama who wrote serious plays because they sold, a man "with the Jew's passion for fame and effect and the Jew's indifference to the reality of the means by which they are produced,"[7] and though this is an unpleasant

[4] Doris Arthur Jones, *Life and Letters of Henry Arthur Jones* (London: Gollancz, 1930), pp. 164-165.

[5] *Life and Letters*, p. 165.

[6] *Life and Letters*, pp. 166-167.

[7] Dan H. Laurence, ed., *Bernard Shaw. Collected Letters 1874-1897* (New York: Dodd, Mead, 1965), p. 501.

judgment, Pinero's career supports it. A measure of his success at his trade is his knighthood, conferred in 1909.

In *The Notorious Mrs. Ebbsmith* Pinero offered his version of The New Woman and the Marriage Question, and his attitude toward the matter is clear enough in his treatment of the title character. He made her a revolutionary agitator opposed to marriage, religion, femininity, and sex; he dressed her in dowdy clothes; and he provided her with a personal history of suffering and privation to explain how she had become the character known to her audiences as "Mad Agnes." This last point is an important one, for Pinero's easy assumption that the desire for rights and freedom in a woman is a neurotic symptom is one that continued through the two decades that followed, and not only among writers of Pinero's conservative slant. Mrs. Ebbsmith is useful, not because she is a well-drawn character—she isn't—but because she defines a persistent male attitude toward women.

In Pinero's play this extraordinary creature is in love with an ailing young English politician, with whom she plans a sexless and unmarried life devoted to pamphleteering against marriage. Against her Pinero brings two antagonists —her lover's uncle, the Duke of St. Olpherts, and a Yorkshire clergyman. The Duke speaks for Society and a career; the clergyman speaks for mercy (and offers a pocket Bible). Together these two figures of the established orders persuade her to renounce her advanced views and to restore her lover to his wife and to politics.

The subject of *Mrs. Ebbsmith*—free love vs. social convention—one might describe as both serious and modern, but the play is neither. It has in fact all the elements of traditional Victorian melodrama. The scene, for example, is Venice; as so often in Victorian literature (and no doubt also in Victorian life) sinning is something that one does while abroad. The cast of characters includes a duke, a baronet, and a knight, for Pinero shared the conviction of his contemporary playwrights that really dramatic materials were only to be found among the upper ranks of society. And the resolution of the play is melodramatic in the extreme: Mrs. Ebbsmith exclaims "My sex has found me out!" and accepts her womanliness and the subordination and self-sacrifice that go with it; she also finds religion and is prepared by it for a life of renunciation. In short, she becomes a conventional Victorian heroine. It is said that when Mrs. Patrick Campbell, who played Mrs. Ebbsmith, read the last act she groaned audibly; she pleaded with Pinero to revise it and make his heroine a real woman, but Pinero refused. He knew what the market wanted.

To writers of more genuinely advanced views, *Mrs. Ebbsmith* was offensive in many ways. Shaw said of the play that it "not only shews awkwardness, constraint, and impotence on its intellectual side, but apparent exhaustion and sterility on its inventive side,"[8] and Max Beerbohm complained of "its pretentious air of being somehow philosophic and Ibsenish."[9] The attribution of "Ibsenism" to this dreary play and others like it must have been particularly hard to take, for between the liberation of Norah's exit from her doll's house and the submissions of Lady Susan and Mrs. Ebbsmith no philosophical connection is conceivable. Ibsen's success may have drawn late-Victorian playwrights toward new problems, but he had not taught them to see new solutions; on the English stage the Marriage Question was still a question without an answer.

Ironically, the most Ibsenish play of the 'nineties was too advanced to be produced. Shaw called *The Philanderer* (1893) a "topical comedy": the topic was Ibsen, converted to the needs of Shavian farce. It was, as Shaw said, extremely advanced. When actor Richard Mansfield read the script, he complained that "it turns Ibsen inside out, and the spectacle, as a result, is not a pleasant or agreeable one."[10] Mans-

[8] *Letters*, p. 500.
[9] Max Beerbohm, *Around Theatres* (London: Rupert Hart-Davis, 1953), p. 133.
[10] *Letters*, p. 487.

field refused the play, and it was not professionally performed until 1907, when the Edwardian era had advanced
sufficiently to meet it, and even then it was not well received
—the Webbs disliked it, and so did Granville Barker.

In *The Philanderer* Shaw ridiculed conventional ideas
of marriage, while mocking those who try to avoid it, the
Ibsenish New Woman and the Philanderer. The play is full
of Ibsen; a bust of him dominates the second and third acts,
and the advanced characters identify their views with his,
but the tone is hardly reverent. The heroine talks like a slap-
stick Mrs. Ebbsmith, and the hero, involved in a triangular
situation that Shaw took from his own amatory experience,
talks like Shaw. The play is really *beyond* Ibsen—it is a
parody of his ideas. It is not surprising that a theater that
was not ready for the real thing was not ready for a parody
of it.

Shaw recognized—indeed insisted on—the radical differences between his own kind of theater and that of his late-
Victorian contemporaries: "My school," he said, "is in violent reaction against that of Mr. Pinero."[11] If Jones, Pinero,
and Wilde wrote plays that were advanced in subject matter, they were conservative in their attitudes toward marriage and toward women. They took as given that happiness
is not possible for women outside marriage, that extra-
marital sex required suffering and punishment, that the
power of society to compel behavior is right, and that there
is no sauce for the gander. None of their plays really questions the basic assumptions of marriage, and when a questioner does appear in a play, like Mrs. Ebbsmith, she is
plotted out of her position rather than refuted.

At the same time that Shaw was writing *The Philanderer*,
another advanced thinker was writing a novel on the Marriage Question. Grant Allen's *The Woman Who Did* was
in its day as notorious as *Tess of the D'Urbervilles*, and it

[11] Bernard Shaw, *Dramatic Opinions and Essays* (New York: Brentano's, 1907), vol. 1, p. 47.

remained for many years the type of the "daring" novel that one would not allow one's daughters and servants to read. The "woman" of the title is a New Woman; though she is the daughter of a Dean, she has advanced views and has been to Girton. What she does is enter into a "Free Union" with her lover, on principle:

> If I would [she tells the world] I might go the beaten way you prescribe, and marry him legally. But of my own free will I disdain that degradation; I choose rather to be free. No fear of your scorn, no dread of your bigotry, no shrinking at your cruelty, shall prevent me from following the thorny path I know to be the right one. I seek no temporal end. I will not prove false to the future of my kind in order to protect myself from your hateful indignities. I know on what vile foundations your temple of wedlock is based and built, what pitiable victims languish and die in its sickening vaults; and I will not consent to enter it.[12]

When she becomes pregnant, she goes with her lover to Perugia (once more, sin flourishes better on the other side of the Channel), where he suddenly dies. She bears his child and returns to London. Homeless, penniless, friendless, and *déclassée*, there she is forced to earn her living as a journalist and to associate with Bohemians and Fabians. The daughter grows up, reverts to the philistinism of her ancestors, and marries a country gentleman. She also learns her mother's story and renounces her for her depravity. The mother, heartbroken, commits suicide.

Allen said that he wrote the book "wholly and solely to satisfy my own taste and my own conscience," and it clearly is an attempt to treat love and marriage frankly and honestly. Plot and characterization are subordinated to didactic intent, and whole chapters are devoted to elaborating the heroine's opinions. Unlike Mrs. Ebbsmith, she is made to

[12] Grant Allen, *The Woman Who Did* (Boston: Roberts Bros., 1895), p. 47.

appear wholesome, intelligent, and psychologically normal; her views are the consequences of thought not of suffering. Still, she is defeated by philistinism, and like Mrs. Tanqueray she commits suicide. And though her views on marriage are revolutionary enough, the book assumes other ideas about women that are conservatively Victorian: that every good woman is by nature a mother, that women suffer less from celibacy than men, that suicide is an appropriate, and perhaps inevitable, end for a woman who chooses to defy the power of society. In tone and style the book is not at all shocking; it is in fact as anaphrodisiac as any Victorian mother could wish. There is perhaps a bit of fin-de-siècle decoration to the prose, as there is to John Lane's design (one can see that it comes from the publisher of the *Yellow Book*), but there is nothing scandalous except the heroine's opinions. The moral of the story is beyond reproach; the heroine pays with her life for defying convention, and Society, as always, wins.

The Woman Who Did was attacked by reviewers as indecent, but to one critic, at least, it was bad on other grounds. H. G. Wells, then a young contributor to the *Saturday Review*, sympathized with Allen's ideas on the emancipation of women but was infuriated by the novel; it was hasty and headlong and incompetent, he thought, a treason to a great cause. Allen's failure, Wells thought, was in part simply bad writing, but it was also, and more seriously, a failure to understand what emancipation really meant:

He does not propose to emancipate them from the narrowness, the sexual savagery, the want of charity, that are the sole causes of the miseries of the illegitimate and the unfortunate. Instead he wishes to emancipate them from monogamy, which we have hitherto regarded as being more of a fetter upon virile instincts. His proposal is to abolish cohabitation, to abolish the family—that school of all human gentleness—and to provide support for women who may have children at the expense of the State. We are all to be foundlings together, and it will be an inquisitive child who knows its own father. Now Mr. Grant Allen must know perfectly well that amorous desires and the desire to bear children are anything but overpowering impulses in many of the very noblest women. The women, who would inevitably have numerous children under the conditions he hopes for, would be the hysterically erotic, the sexually incontinent. *Why* he should make proposals to cultivate humanity in this direction is not apparent. We find fine handsome sayings about Truth and Freedom, but any establishment for his proposition a reviewer much in sympathy with him on many of his opinions fails altogether to discover in his book. A fellowship of two based on cohabitation and protected by jealousy, with or without the marriage ceremony, seems as much the natural destiny of the average man as of the eagle or the tiger.[13]

Here is Wells, in 1895, asserting his claim to the forefront of advanced thought on sexual matters by defending monogamy, the family, and "a fellowship of two based on cohabitation and protected by jealousy." In the ten years that followed, his ideas on all these matters changed radically, and the change in Wells is symptomatic of, if not identical with, the general change that took place in Edwardian advanced ideas about women and marriage. But in 1895 he was of his time, a late-Victorian.

Two points are to be made, then, about the early 1890's. First, it was a time when serious thought about marriage and women was finding public utterance, both in the theater and in fiction. And second, it was still a very Victorian time, and the serious thoughts took their form from Victorian attitudes. By comparison with the previous decade, it was a time of free thought; by comparison with the Edwardian years it was a time still ruled by the Widow of Windsor.

The last five years of the century were much less open to

[13] Quoted in Wells, *Experiment in Autobiography*, p. 465.

discussions of love, sex, and marriage. Explanations of such changes of mood are speculative at best, but one can venture the observation that 1895, the turning point, is the year of the Wilde trials. *Mrs. Ebbsmith* opened on March 13, and *The Woman Who Did* was published before February 14 (the date in the British Museum copy). The first Wilde trial, his suit against the Marquis of Queensberry, opened on April 3, and Wilde was finally sentenced on May 26. Performances of his own plays immediately stopped; but so, in a general way, did those of "advanced" plays. It was as though the Victorian age, in its last years, had determined to be relentlessly Victorian while it could.

Victoria died on January 22, 1901; six weeks later *The Notorious Mrs. Ebbsmith* was back in London. But alas she was not what she used to be. Max Beerbohm, reviewing the revival, used the metaphor of an old suit of clothes to describe the play's decline:

> The garment seems to show its age pretty clearly. It is of the fashion set six years ago. It is not threadbare, certainly. There is plenty of "wear" in it. It need not be given away yet. But it would need a good many alterations before one could look smart in it. In other words, the play is still an exciting, almost an absorbing, story; but on no one save the average critic could it possibly impose as being what it pretends to be: a solemn and wide-eyed consideration of life.[14]

Somehow, during that last Victorian interval, the avant-garde had ceased to be advanced. The Marriage Question, if it was to be discussed, would have to find new, Edwardian terms.

That the terms would be new, the character of the new monarch alone guaranteed. Edward VII was a man who had had his share of experience of the Marriage Question: he had appeared as a witness in the divorce court (in the

[14] *Around Theatres*, p. 131.

Mordaunt Case in 1870) and had narrowly avoided a public scandal for his involvement in the Aylesford affair in 1876. His affairs with Lily Langtry and Mrs. Keppel were common knowledge and were accepted by society hostesses and by his wife. He himself was tolerant of the irregular behavior of others so long as it was discreet. He exemplified the practical morality of his class: "It doesn't matter what you do, so long as you don't frighten the horses."

But if the King's standards of private morality were indulgent, his standards of public behavior were as severe as his mother's. He denounced Lord Blandford (the third party in the Aylesford case) for inviting scandal, and when the Duke and Duchess of Marlborough were in the process of separating he gave instructions that they "should not come to any dinner, or evening party, or private entertainment at which either of Their Majesties are expected to be present." Though divorce and the threat of divorce were common in his circle, and must have been continually discussed, he rebuked the Home Secretary for putting women on the Royal Commission on Divorce in 1908 on the ground that divorce is a subject "which cannot be discussed openly and in all its aspects with any delicacy or even decency before ladies."[15]

These being the social conditions in the upper classes at the turn of the century, one must admire the courage of Earl Russell (the older brother of Bertrand Russell, the present Earl) in bringing before the House of Lords, not once but twice, a bill to amend and liberalize the laws governing marriage and divorce. In doing so Lord Russell was not merely questioning the customs of his class in the citadel of that class; he was also attacking the ecclesiastical bases of marriage in the presence of the Lords Spiritual, the English Bishops. For any suggestion that the marriage contract might be regarded as a terminable one struck at the conception of man-woman relations defined in Scripture and endorsed by

[15] Philip Magnus, *King Edward the Seventh* (London: John Murray, 1964), pp. 406 and 442.

the Church—that marriage was a holy sacrament, not a contract, and that the relationship it sanctified was binding for life. The Bible sanctioned one kind of divorce only—a husband's divorce of a wife taken in adultery, and the Church opposed any extension of this limit. In debate on the Divorce Bill of 1857, the Bishop of Oxford expressed the Church's absolute opposition to change in the law:

> The Bill proposed [he observed] not only that a husband should be permitted to put away his wife for adultery, but also that a wife should be allowed, under certain conditions, to put away her husband. Now, would any of their Lordships tell him that there was the shadow of a foundation in the Gospel for such an extension of the right of divorce? It was distinctly stated that a husband might put away his wife, but no general principle was asserted in the Gospel which would equally entitle a wife to put away her husband. It seemed to recognise an equality in the sexes; but the truth was, that though the sin might be equal in each—yet the social crime was different in magnitude as committed by the one or the other; and our blessed Master, while allowing a husband to put away his wife for adultery, because all the highest purposes for which marriage was instituted by God would be defeated by the infidelity of the wife, never extended the same right to the other side.[16]

The bill passed in 1857 had slightly modified this ecclesiastical view by providing means of divorce for both parties, but one would hardly call it liberal. It provided that:

> a husband may obtain a dissolution of his marriage on the ground that his wife has, since the celebration thereof, been guilty of adultery, and a wife may obtain a dissolution of her marriage on the ground that, since the celebration thereof, her husband has been guilty of incestuous

[16] *Hansard*, 3rd series, vol. 143 (July 3, 1856), cols. 233-234.

adultery, or of bigamy with adultery, or of rape, or of sodomy or bestiality, or of adultery coupled with such cruelty as without adultery would have entitled her to a divorce *a mensa et thoro* [that is, a judicial separation], or of adultery, coupled with desertion, without reasonable excuse, for two years or upwards.[17]

Thus the God-given right of a man to put away his wife was preserved, and the woman's inferior situation confirmed. No grounds for divorce other than adultery were recognized, though cruelty and desertion were considered grounds for a judicial separation—an arrangement by which the parties were freed from their conjugal ties but were not free to re-marry. The law was extremely wary of collusion: divorce was not granted if both parties were guilty of adultery, nor was a judicial separation possible if husband and wife parted by mutual consent. In every case it was necessary that an offense be committed and that one party be innocent and the other guilty; in effect, the law required that divorce be criminal.

It was to humanize this severe Mosaic system that Lord Russell rose in the House of Lords in the spring of 1902 and presented his bill. Lord Russell's bill proposed three kinds of modification of the existing law: to extend the grounds for divorce to include cruelty, penal servitude for three years, lunacy, three years' separation, or one year's separation if both parties concurred; to make the legal positions of men and women equal; and to move divorce actions into County courts, thus reducing the cost of a suit and making divorce feasible for the poor. In his speech in defense of the bill Lord Russell pointed out that English divorce law was a distorted remnant of ecclesiastical law and was neither logical nor just; that it encouraged immorality rather than morality by deny-ing unhappy persons release; that a more generous law in

[17] Summarized in *Report of Royal Commission on Divorce and Matrimonial Causes* (London: H. M. Stationers' Office, 1912), vol. 1, p. 159.

Scotland had not caused greater moral laxity; and that the changes he proposed would not affect the bond of marriage where that bond genuinely existed. The speech was a model of temperate, rational discourse, and one could imagine the Peers rising at its end to applaud the speaker.

Instead, the Lord Chancellor, the Earl of Halsbury, rose in a rage to attack Lord Russell and to denounce his bill as an attempt to abolish the institution of marriage. So outraged was he by what he took to be an insult to the House of Lords, that he took an unusual course in disposing of the bill. It was the custom of the house to defeat a bill by moving its postponement; Lord Halsbury moved instead that Russell's bill be *rejected*, a method that had not been practiced in Parliament in modern history. The rejection passed, and Lord Russell was both defeated and snubbed.

Nevertheless, he returned in the next session to resubmit his divorce bill. He had modified his proposed grounds for divorce, removing the one-year-by-concurrence clause, which had so offended the Lord Chancellor, but the balance was the same. His arguments once more were humane and modest, and his peroration was a persuasive summary of the case for a liberalizing of the laws governing divorce:

I submit this Bill to the House [he concluded] as an honest attempt to remedy an intolerable state of things. I ask whether among all the Members of this House there are none who recognise that the present marriage laws do inflict upon a vast number of men and women in this country great hardship; that the present marriage laws lead in many cases to the contracting of immoral alliances between separated men and women, and that the granting of a judicial separation is really to throw upon the world two potential adulterers. It is easy to legislate for human nature, but it is less easy to control it after your legislation. The present law offers a divorce as a reward for immoral conduct. It can be obtained where immorality has taken place, but where both parties are unwilling to be guilty of immorality, the present law denies divorce; and where, as so often happens, women have been deserted by their husbands for an indefinite number of years, they are precluded from ever contracting a fresh alliance, and are compelled to remain for the rest of their lives neither married nor unmarried, with no possibility of establishing a home and all that is dear to the heart of a woman. Is there no one in this House who feels that this state of things needs a remedy? Are your Lordships satisfied, because in your individual cases the law may not bear hardly upon you, to leave such a blot upon the social legislation of this country? The proposals which I have put before you, and I say this unhesitatingly, make for the increase of social purity and for the absence of adultery. They make for a legitimate dissolution of unions that have long since become impossible, and their adoption would tend to purify the marriage relation, to make marriage a more real thing than it is at present, and to make adultery looked upon, as it is not often looked upon now, as a disgraceful, a discreditable, and an unnecessary crime. I beg to move the Second Reading of this bill.[18]

Lord Halsbury once more spoke in rebuttal and once more defeated the bill. He concluded his remarks by saying,

I hope that we may not have the same proposal repeated over and over again, for the noble Lord and everybody else must know that it is only in the nature of a protest by himself against the marriage law as it exists. . . .[19]

Though this reference to Lord Russell's personal affairs was in dubious taste, it was accurate in its implication; for Lord Russell had indeed had experiences in marriage and divorce

18 *Hansard*, vol. 124 (June 23, 1903), cols. 211-12.
19 *Hansard*, vol. 124 (June 23, 1903), col. 213.

that would lead the most phlegmatic man to protest. The story of his marital difficulties provides a fair example of just why he felt it necessary that the laws of marriage and divorce should be revised.[20]

Lord Russell married, for the first time, in 1890. A year later his wife brought an action for divorce, charging cruelty and "heinous crimes"; the action was dismissed. In 1894 she brought an action for restitution of conjugal rights. The following year her husband obtained a decree of judicial separation, but the decree was successfully appealed. In 1900 Lord Russell went through a form of marriage with an American divorcée named Mrs. Somerville, which caused him to be cast in damages of £1500 for adultery and tried by his peers for bigamy. In passing sentence, the Lord Chancellor said:

> My Lords, for my own part, speaking with considerable knowledge of this unfortunate litigation which, as Earl Russell has explained, has led to this terrible catastrophe, while I think he was undoubtedly suffering under almost intolerable provocation, the circumstances of his domestic life being such as might lead him to do almost anything to get rid of the person who had poisoned the whole atmosphere in which he lived; on the other hand, of course, it is impossible for your Lordships to pass over that defiance of law which I cannot forbear from saying I think he exhibited. . . .[21]

Defiance of the law could not be tolerated in a man of Lord Russell's position; he was sentenced to three months in jail. He did, however, achieve his end; his marriage to his first wife was dissolved, and his second marriage was made legal.

The point of this rather sordid recital is that it describes a marriage that was obviously a disaster from the beginning.

[20] For Lord Russell's account of his marital troubles see his *My Life and Adventures* (London: Cassell, 1923).
[21] *My Life and Adventures*, p. 284.

Yet though the parties were persons of position and wealth, it was dissolved only after ten years of complicated legal maneuvering, and then at the cost of large sums of money and a term in jail. Lord Russell could apparently afford both the cost and the scandal, but persons with less money and more anxiety about social position would have had the greatest difficulty in achieving what Lord Russell achieved. In moving his bill, Lord Russell was simply asking that some of the sordidness, and some of the expense, be removed from the circumstances of divorce.

Lord Russell failed in his immediate goal, and no changes were made in the divorce laws; but in a sense one might say that he succeeded, for he put the issue of divorce before the public, and it remained there, a lively public issue, for the rest of the Edwardian period. The Society for Promoting Reforms in the Marriage and Divorce Laws of England was founded in 1903, and the Divorce Law Reform Association shortly after. In 1906 the two groups merged as the Divorce Law Reform Union, and Sir Arthur Conan Doyle was made president, a post which he held for ten years; funds were sought, public meetings held, and pressure was applied to the government to appoint a Royal Commission "to investigate the existing English laws of divorce and separation with a view to their reform." In the Commons, members began to ask questions about divorce reform, while Lord Russell continued his campaign in the Lords. Finally, in 1909, a Royal Commission was appointed to consider reforms in the laws of marriage and divorce. A remarkable change in English attitudes had occurred in a rather short time—no more than seven years—and for that change Lord Russell deserves a good deal of credit.

The same change of mood is apparent in the literature of the period, as compared with that of the previous decade. For example in *Whom God Hath Joined* (1906), Arnold Bennett wrote a novel that is entirely about divorce (the first devoted entirely to the subject, as far as I know). The book concerns two divorce suits: a solicitor's clerk against his wife, and the solicitor's wife against her husband. They are the sort of people that Lord Russell's bill was designed to relieve, ordinary middle-class persons who cannot afford scandal or great expense, and who are more unhappy than wicked. In following the two suits, Bennett dwelt on the suffering and humiliation that the process of English divorce law imposed upon the principals, innocent and guilty alike, and he contrived the two cases so that both made just claims and both failed. Everyone is degraded, and no one gains happiness or freedom from the law.

Although Bennett was knowledgeable about the inequities and complexities of the law, his book was not primarily an attack on the injustice of divorce but upon its inhumanity and sordidness. The solicitor's clerk, Lawrence Ridware, sits in court, watching the suit that precedes his own:

And gradually the secret imperious attraction of the Divorce Court grew clearer to the disgusted and frightened Lawrence than it had ever been before. Here there was no pretence that the sole genuine interest in life for the average person is not that which it is. Here it was frankly admitted that a man is always "after" some woman, and that the woman is always running away while looking behind her, until she stumbles and is caught. Here the moves of the great, universal, splendid, odious game had to be described without reservation. Nothing could be left out. There was no Mrs. Grundy. All the hidden shames were exposed to view, a feast for avid eyes. The animal in every individual could lick its chops and thrill with pleasure. All the animals could exchange candid glances and concede that they were animals. And the supreme satisfaction for the males was that the females were present, the females who had tempted and who had yielded and who had rolled voluptuously in the very mud. And they were obliged to listen, in their prim tight frocks, to the things which they had done dishevelled, and they were obliged to answer and to confess and to blush, and to utter dreadful things with a simper. The alluring quality of this wholesale debauch of exciting suggestiveness could never fail until desire failed. As an entertainment it was unique, appealing to the most vital instinct of the widest possible public. It had no troublesome beauty to tease the mind or disturb the sleeping soul. In short, it was faultless. And only the superhuman and commanding mien of the judge, who was capable of discussing the foulest embroidery of fornication as though it were the integral calculus, saved the scene from developing into something indescribable.[22]

Unlike Russell, Bennett had no reforms to suggest in the letter of the law. What appalled him was the existence of an institution devoted to making public the most private and degrading actions of its appellants. His novel is an appeal for human decency in the conduct of divorce rather than for reform of the legal conditions. Nevertheless, it was a liberating book in two ways: it called attention to the ugliness of divorce procedures, and it made moral judgments of its protagonists that were generous and relative; the clerk's wife, though guilty of adultery, is not condemned, while the solicitor, also guilty, is. The basis of judgment is not the act of sin, but the motive.

One can find similar views in other novels of the period like Galsworthy's *Man of Property* (1906) and Ford's *A Call* (1910), and the same loosening of the old moral attitudes is also evident in certain advanced plays of the mid-Edwardian period. St. John Hankin's *Last of the de Mullins* (1907), for example, takes the melodramatic situation of *The Woman Who Did* and turns it into light-hearted comedy in which the ruined maid and her bastard son reach a happy ending. Granville Barker's *Madras House* (1910) is comical about

[22] Arnold Bennett, *Whom God Hath Joined* (London: David Nutt, 1906), pp. 222-223.

polygamy, bastardy, and infidelity. Shaw's *Getting Married* (1908) calls into question all the conventional views of marriage and divorce, and it is surely the first English play to treat the circumstances of English divorce farcically. It is clear that a radical change has taken place since the marriage plays of the 'nineties. The Edwardian plays start with the biological facts of sexual attraction and the urge to reproduce, and work toward solving human relations in those terms; the tone is tolerant and amused, sex is more a physiological and social problem than a moral one, and resolutions are pragmatic and tentative. (Shaw's preface to *Getting Married* develops the argument for marriage reform at greater length, but in the same tone.)

These plays seem mild enough now, but it is worth remembering that they did not seem so to all Edwardians. Beatrice Webb, for example, was not at all amused by Shaw and Barker. In her diary for December 27, 1909, she wrote,

> G.B.S. read his new play [it was *Misalliance*] to us the other night—a good three hours. It is amazingly brilliant —but the whole "motive" is erotic—everyone wishing to have sexual intercourse with everyone else. . . . S[idney] and I were sorry to see G.B.S. reverting to his studies in anarchic love making.[23]

And the following March, when she had seen Granville Barker's *Madras House*, she recorded her opinion that both Shaw and Barker were "obsessed with the rabbit-warren aspect of human society," and that they harped on the single theme of sexual attraction. "That world," she concluded, "is not the world I live in."[24] Mrs. Webb was a poor describer of plots, but she was quite right in thinking that the world that Barker and Shaw wrote about was not hers. They were not concerned in these plays with the lives of intellectual feminists or of Tory socialists: the characters of *The*

[23] Passfield Papers.
[24] The passage is quoted on p. 129 above.

Madras House are the staff of a women's clothing store and their families, and *Misalliance* is set in the country house of an underwear manufacturer. Mrs. Webb held the conservative view that only people at the top and bottom of the social structure indulged themselves sexually, but Shaw and Barker were arguing that even the middle classes had urges.

Yet though Mrs. Webb deplored the rabbit-warren activities of Shaw and Barker, she herself was playing, if inadvertently, a role in the current changing ideas of marriage. For her own marriage, lived as it was in public, was a public demonstration that the marriage relationship need not imply home, children, and a hot stove. Mrs. Webb worked with her husband as a colleague and an equal; she bore him no children, and indeed one does not feel any sexual dimension to the union in her writings about it, though there was obviously deep, reciprocal love. The Shaws were another variant case—a marriage apparently unconsummated, yet close and long-lived. The Havelock Ellises provided a third —a wife who was a professed lesbian, and who lived apart from her husband, yet who seemed to have close, affectionate ties with him. Together these three marriages demonstrate a new and freer conception of the marriage relationship, of the woman's right to define her commitment, and of her freedom from chatteldom. If they did not significantly alter the nature of the average English marriage, they at least brought the unexamined assumptions of the marriage laws into question.

Clearly a lot of Englishmen were re-examining the laws of marriage and divorce—the appointment of the Royal Commission proves that point, for Royal Commissions follow public opinion. Liberal ideas about marriage were spreading; but, as with other liberating ideas during the Edwardian period, they met aggressive opposition. The most vocal antagonist of liberation was, as one might expect, the Established Church, the views of which had not substantially changed in the fifty years since the laws were written.

The Church spoke directly in the House of Lords through the Bishops, and indirectly in both Houses through secular opponents of reform, who leaned for support upon the "higher sanction" of their views that religion offered.

In the debates preceding the appointment of the Royal Commission (1909), the Church once more led the fight against reform. The Archbishop of Canterbury spoke feelingly against the un-Christian nature of the proposal, but in his concluding remarks he revealed a rather different motive. "I look with profound anxiety and alarm," he said, "on any proposal in favour of extending, almost lavishly, those facilities to other classes than those who take advantage of them now."[25] One principal motive of the reformers was to allow the poor access to the same relief in marital matters that the rich had. The Church, like other conservative establishments, regarded this as socially dangerous, as one of many unstabilizing agitations in an increasingly unstable lower class.

Divorce was sometimes associated with another source of Edwardian anxiety—the falling birth rate. Between the mid-seventies and 1910 the birth rate in the United Kingdom dropped by nearly thirty percent. Most Englishmen regarded this decline as a clear and present threat to the country: a high birth rate meant men for the armed forces, men for the Empire, and men to swell the industrial labor force at home. Men as unlike as H. G. Wells and the Rev. Mr. Marchant agreed on this point and published their solutions to the problem in articles and pamphlets. Only a few thoughtful persons (Havelock Ellis was one) recognized that, since there was also a decline in infant mortality and an increase in longevity, the decline was not in fact alarming, and the population of England was not decreasing.

The birth-rate panic was felt by Edwardians of every political view and was used to buttress both sides of the Marriage Question. The Divorce Law Reform Union's pamph-

[25] Quoted in *Times*, July 19, 1909, p. 4.

let, *Divorce and Morality* (1912), argued that the falling birth rate might rise if marital mistakes were made less irrevocable, and H. G. Wells defended the morality of *Ann Veronica* by asserting that the existing matrimonial system was "not giving the modern State enough children, or fine enough children, for its needs." The Tory editor of the *Spectator*, St. Loe Strachey, snapped back:

> the notion that the kind of promiscuity which he [Wells] advocates will people the earth with sound children is, as all experience shows, utterly untenable. One man and one woman is the law of fecundity.[26]

Though probably not many biologists would have accepted Strachey's Law, his conservative clerical readers certainly did. Nobody, apparently, doubted that fecundity, whatever its laws, was a good thing.

Strachey and his kind took as given that the law of fecundity should not be tampered with, and they were therefore alarmed and offended by another feature of Ann Veronica's career—the fact that she lives with a man she is not married to and is not punished for her sin by bearing illegitimate children, because she chooses not to be. She is liberated from society's moral code by her knowledge of birth control. To members of the established orders, birth control encouraged immorality by removing the social penalty, and they invoked both the law and extreme social pressure to prevent the spread of knowledge and the use of contraceptives. As is often the case, the efforts to suppress knowledge actually publicized it and spread the news about birth control to the people.

Contraception for the masses was one of the many achievements of Victorian practical science; it was the discovery of the vulcanizing process in 1843-44 that made inexpensive rubber condoms possible.[27] However, the general popula-

26 *Spectator*, 4,247 (Dec. 4, 1909), p. 945.
27 The account that follows is based on Norman E. Himes, *Medical History of Contraception* (New York: Gamut Press, 1963).

tion remained for some time ignorant of this and other methods of contraception: the best-known Victorian work on the subject, Knowlton's *Fruits of Philosophy*, sold only a thousand copies a year between 1834, when it was first published in England, and 1876. In that year, after forty years in print, the book was suppressed, and the publisher prosecuted for obscenity. In protest against this action two free-thinking radicals, Charles Bradlaugh and Annie Besant, printed their own edition and announced their intention of distributing it. They were arrested, tried, and convicted, but won on appeal. The publicity that attended their trial increased sales of the *Fruits of Philosophy* to about 50,000 copies a year.

A decade later another attempt at suppression of a book on birth control was made, this time by the medical establishment. In 1887 Dr. H. A. Allbutt, a Leeds physician and a Fellow of the Royal College of Physicians in Edinburgh, published *The Wife's Handbook*, a book of advice on hygiene, prenatal care, care of infants, and methods of birth control. The secretary of the Leeds Vigilance Association protested to the medical societies, and the case was brought before the General Medical Council in London. The Council found Allbutt guilty of "infamous conduct in a professional respect," and ordered that his name be dropped from the Medical Register; his offense, the verdict read, had been to publish his book "at so low a price as to bring the work within the reach of the youth of both sexes, to the detriment of public morals." Allbutt continued to sell the book, however, and by the middle of the Edwardian period it was in its forty-first edition.

The extraordinary sales of *The Fruits of Philosophy* and *The Wife's Handbook* are evidence that in the closing years of the nineteenth century the practice of contraception was becoming widespread in England. If this fact were set beside the fact of the falling birth rate, it was possible to conclude that the Marriage Question and the problem of Imperial Defence were related, and to blame the impending decline and fall of England on women. But beyond even this imperial anxiety, the practice of birth control implied another and perhaps a greater threat to established social order. A woman who could choose not to bear children was liberated from one of the strongest bonds that held her subordinate to men; she became at once both independent and mobile. If at the same time the laws governing divorce were also relaxed, then the family—both as husband-wife and as parents-children—might cease to be the stable social unit that conservatives thought it had to be.

Fears, then—fears of a declining and degenerate population, of a dissolute and unstable poor, and of a liberated womanhood—were together one cause of opposition to marriage and divorce reform. The reference to Wells above suggests another—the fear of socialism, which Wells' campaign for endowed motherhood had identified in the public mind with promiscuity and sexual license. Wells' argument that the family was a form of capitalistic ownership had the dubious merit of shaking two pillars of conservative security at once, and the prospect of a future society without either families or private ownership was upsetting to many who might otherwise have been willing to allow the wives of drunkards and criminals legal relief.

Still another factor contributing to the growing sense of moral crisis in man-woman relations was the militant suffrage movement. During the summer of 1909, while debate on the Royal Commission was going on in Parliament, members of the Women's Social and Political Union were rioting in Parliament Square outside, and hunger-striking in Holloway Prison. Now insofar as the WSPU was an organization devoted to winning the franchise for women it had no views on the Marriage Question; but its goals, even as most narrowly defined, did imply a radical change in the relations between men and women, and the public pronouncements of its leaders left no question but that they were engaged in a sex war. "The struggle has begun," Mrs. Pethick-Lawrence, the militant leader, announced in 1906. "It is a life and death struggle. . . . What we are going to get is a great revolt of the women against their subjection of body and mind to men."[28] The gestures of this great revolt, begun as demonstrations of solidarity in pursuit of the vote, increasingly became mindless acts of aggression and protest against Maleness and even against sex itself. For the women, sex was the means by which men exploited them; whether a woman became a housewife and mother, or worked in a factory, or turned to prostitution, she was imprisoned in her sex, and man was the jailer. And it was an easy grammatical step from saying, "The trouble with women is the exploitation of their sex," to saying, "The trouble with women is sex"—to shift the blame from sexual discrimination to sex itself. The movement never made sexual freedom a goal, and indeed the tone of its pronouncements was more likely to be puritanical and censorious on sexual matters than permissive: "Votes for Women and Chastity for Men" was one of Mrs. Pankhurst's slogans. Beneath the sense of political injustice was a deeper feeling, the women's sense of the fundamental injustice of sexual relations.

This feeling is vividly created in a good but forgotten play by an interesting but forgotten woman: *Votes for Women!* by Elizabeth Robins. Miss Robins was an American actress who made her reputation in England in the early productions of Ibsen; she had played Mrs. Linden in *A Doll's House*, and had been a brilliant Hedda Gabler. She wrote romantic novels that were popular, and even gained some critical approval (Edward Garnett admired her *Dark Lantern*, for example), and she was friendly with men like Shaw and Henry James. Beautiful, successful, and admired, Elizabeth Robins seemed to have everything. But she had another side, which expressed itself in the

[28] Quoted in Roger Fulford, *Votes for Women* (London: Faber and Faber, 1957), p. 143.

WSPU. She was a member of the Union's governing committee and an active speaker and agitator in the women's cause, and it was for that cause that she wrote *Votes for Women!* The play was produced in April 1907, at Granville Barker's Court Theatre, with a cast that included Aubrey Smith, Lewis Casson, and Edmund Gwenn; it was a brilliant success.

Votes for Women! is a variation on the woman-with-a-past play, of the kind so popular in the 'nineties. The woman, Vida Levering, turns up at a country house weekend where the Hon. Geoffrey Stonor, a Tory politician, is a guest with his fiancée, an heiress called Jean Dumbarton. Miss Levering's "past" includes the customary betrayal and an abortion, and Stonor is the betrayer. Act II is a suffragette meeting in Trafalgar Square. Jean Dumbarton is there with her fiancé and is converted, though in the process she learns of the Vida-Stonor relationship. In the third act she confronts Stonor and asks him to make amends. He offers Vida marriage and is refused; Vida then threatens to take Jean into the movement unless Stonor gives it his political support. He agrees, and Vida leaves him, to return alone to her cause.

The play is obviously melodramatic, but it has something else as well, and that something else is its peculiar tone. Miss Robins called the play a tract, and her didactic intentions are obvious, but when she put her characters to debating, she struck hardest on one note—the sexual exploitation of women. As a consequence, the tone is not that of a debate but of a bitter, deep-felt, intimate quarrel, like a husband and wife on the brink of divorce. When the standard cases of suffering women are brought up—the ruined maids, the Piccadilly whores, the tramp women, the starving working mothers—they are invoked in order that their sufferings may be laid to one cause, the sexual viciousness of men. The sex war has begun, and the play is a dispatch from the front, fiercely partisan and militant. This is clear, for example, in this dialogue between Vida Levering and the lady of the country house in Act I:

LADY JOHN: We oughtn't to do anything or *say* anything to encourage this ferment of feminism, and I'll tell you why: it's likely to bring a very terrible thing in its train.
MISS LEVERING: What terrible thing?
LADY JOHN: Sex antagonism.
MISS LEVERING (rising) : It's here.
LADY JOHN (very gravely): Don't say that.
MISS LEVERING: You're so conscious it's here, you're afraid to have it mentioned.
LADY JOHN: If it's here, it is the fault of those women agitators.
MISS LEVERING (gently): No woman *begins* that way. Every woman's in a state of natural subjection—no, I'd rather say allegiance to her idea of romance and her hope of motherhood. They're embodied for her in man. They're the strongest things in life—till man kills them. . . . Let's be fair. Each woman knows why that allegiance died.[29]

Votes for Women! is perhaps a dramatic failure in the sense that T. S. Eliot thought *Hamlet* was a failure—that is, it is dominated by emotions which are in excess of the facts as the play gives them. Vida Levering is a woman with personal emotions far more bitter than is appropriate to the suffrage movement alone, and Stonor is right when he accuses her of using the movement for revenge against men. But that is just what makes the play significant—it does express this quality of the movement, its passionate and irrational revengefulness.

If we compare Vida Levering with that earlier agitator, Agnes Ebbsmith, we can measure the distance that the lib-

[29] Elizabeth Robins, *Votes for Women!* (London: Mills & Boon, n.d. [1907]), p. 44. Miss Robins' novel, *The Convert* (London: Methuen, 1907) is a narrative version of the same story with the same characters.

erating movement had come in twelve years, and perhaps also something of the cost. Vida Levering is deaf to the sort of appeals that moved Mrs. Ebbsmith and Rebellious Susan; as she says, her allegiance to man has died, and she has filled the emptiness with a cold passion for the women's cause. She is a woman who cannot be moved, and to whom no amends can be made, and because she is implacable, she wins her battle. But the price, for her, is total separation from men and their world: at the end of *Votes for Women!* the alienation of the sexes is complete.

Elizabeth Robins was a dedicated woman, but she seems to have been a normal one. It is not surprising that the women's movement attracted other supporters who were less so, women who regarded their own exploited sex as the only worthy one, who regretted God's male folly in dividing his creatures into two sexes and then compounding the error by giving dominance to the wrong one. The works of Miss Frances Swiney, who seems to have been both a suffragette and a theosophist, are rich in examples. In her *Cosmic Procession* (1906) she argued that

> woman at present is incomplete woman, having within her potentially the perfect woman, and has attained to the second phase of consciousness to a greater extent than man; her actions are dirigated by love more than by desire. Man, on a lower plane, is undeveloped woman.[30]

And the following year, in a book called *The Bar of Isis, or the Law of the Mother*, she blamed racial degeneracy on man's failure to honor the natural law of continence during the periods of gestation and lactation—his failure to reproduce only at intervals three to five times the length of the gestation period. Her system, if followed, would virtually eliminate sexual intercourse from the marriage relation,

[30] Frances Swiney, *The Cosmic Procession, or the Feminine Principle in Evolution* (London: Ernest Bell, 1906), p. 221.

and that, for Miss Swiney, would be a good thing, since she believed that sperm was a virulent poison.

Miss Swiney is something of an oddity, but many less eccentric suffragettes shared her views of the inferiority of men. Letters from women to the *Times* during the years of agitation argued the eventual superfluity of man (as the race evolves) and the superiority of women, a view summed up in one brief slogan: "Life is feminine." One suffragette argued that in the original text of the book of Genesis, where we now read "male and female created He them," the pronoun should in fact be feminine.[31]

It was women like Miss Swiney, no doubt, who made H. G. Wells antagonistic to the women's movement. His *Ann Veronica* (1909) is about a rebellious New Woman who joins the suffrage movement and takes part in a raid on the Houses of Parliament (the raid Wells describes did occur, on February 11, 1908). She is arrested and sentenced to prison, and while there she comes to some conclusions about men and women:

One of these was a classification of women into women who are and women who are not hostile to men. "The real reason why I am out of place here," she said, "is because I like men. I can talk with them. I've never found them hostile. I've got no feminine class feeling. I don't want any laws or freedom to protect me from a man like Mr. Capes [her lover]. I know that in my heart I would take whatever he gave. . . .

A woman wants a proper alliance with a man, a man who is better stuff than herself. She wants that and needs it more than anything else in the world. It may not be just, it may not be fair, but things are so. It isn't law, nor custom, nor masculine violence settled that. It is just how things happen to be. She wants to be free—she wants to

31 *Times,* Aug. 7, 1912, p. 2.

be legally and economically free, so as not to be subject to the wrong man; but only God, who made the world, can alter things to prevent her being slave to the right one.[32]

It seems at first strange that a writer of such radical leanings should show such hostility to the women's movement, but on reflection it seems understandable enough. Wells' own liberating movement was toward the liberation of sexual love from economic and legal restrictions (as Ann Veronica says). He saw heterosexual union as a great human fulfillment, and obviously a sex war was not the way to go about it. But further, Wells had a strong streak of bourgeois sentimentality in him; he wrote about the emancipation of women, but his idea of felicity was romantic, domestic, and monogamous. The family group remained for him, as for so many advanced thinkers of his time, a powerful image of security in a troubled world—more powerful, perhaps, for not being acknowledged, except indirectly through the happy endings of novels like *Ann Veronica*.

Wells clearly identified the suffrage movement with women's failure *as women*; Ann Veronica does not belong in it because she is successful—she likes men, and they like her. This attitude toward suffragettes turns up frequently in the writing of the period—and not unjustly, if Miss Swiney is a fair example. D. H. Lawrence, for example, links marital failure and the women's rights movement in Clara Dawes (in *Sons and Lovers*), and the lesbian schoolmistress who seduces Ursula Brangwyn in *The Rainbow* is also a suffragette.

It is less surprising that conservative opponents of suffrage took up the idea that suffragettes were psychologically abnormal (an idea that, as I said, had been around since Mrs. Ebbsmith), but the ferocity with which the case was argued is a bit startling. The most extreme statement appeared in a

[32] H. G. Wells, *Ann Veronica* (London: T. Fisher Unwin, 1909), p. 248.

famous letter to the *Times*, written by Sir Almroth Wright, an eminent bacteriologist who had provided Shaw with the model for Sir Colenso Ridgeon in *The Doctor's Dilemma*. Sir Almroth argued that the suffrage movement was made up of the sexually embittered, the incomplete (sexually atrophied), and the intellectually embittered, and he traced the whole movement to the fact that there were a half million "excess women" in Britain:

> . . . no doctor can ever lose sight of the fact [he wrote] that the mind of woman is always threatened with danger from the reverberations of her physiological emergencies. It is with such thoughts that the doctor lets his eyes rest upon the militant suffragist. He cannot shut them to the fact that there is mixed up with the woman's movement much mental disorder; and he cannot conceal from himself the physiological emergencies which lie behind.[33]

Sir Almroth's letter appeared on the morning that the government's second Conciliation Bill (offering *some* women the vote) came up for its second reading in the Commons. The bill was defeated by fourteen votes, and it seems possible that the letter influenced the result. Responses to Sir Almroth's statement came quickly and fiercely. Two fellow doctors wrote to the *Times* that the letter was an insult to women and to the medical profession; another doctor described it as "essentially pornographic." May Sinclair wrote a brisk denial of Sir Almroth's interpretation, insisting that the women's movement was a sociological not a psychological phenomenon. Even Mrs. Humphrey Ward, a leader of the anti-suffrage movement, publicly repudiated Sir Almroth (though the National League for Opposing Woman Suffrage, of which she was an official, circulated complimentary copies of the letter).

The "bitter and unseemly violence" that Mrs. Ward complained of was certainly in the letter, as it was in much

[33] *Times*, Mar. 28, 1912, p. 7.

male opposition to women's rights. Nevertheless, Sir Almroth's charges cannot simply be dismissed: there was an element of aggressive, hysterical hostility in the militant movement that cannot be explained in terms of political aims and political frustrations. The movement offered man-haters an outlet and a form of expression, and in so doing it played an important role in that deterioration of relations between the sexes that marked the course of the period. By taking women out of the home and putting them on the barricades the movement also added to the growing mood of anxiety about home, family, and domestic stability that gave to the end of Edward's reign an atmosphere of moral crisis. It was in that troubled atmosphere that in 1910 the Royal Commission on Divorce and Matrimonial Causes began its hearings.

The Royal Commission was the first full inquiry into marriage and divorce ever held in England, and probably the first anywhere. Its chairman and motive force was Lord Gorell, the president of the Probate Divorce and Admiralty Division of the Supreme Court, a man dedicated to liberalizing the laws of divorce, particularly in the direction of making divorce possible for the poor. Other members included the Archbishop of York, the Solicitor-General, Sir Rufus Isaacs, and two women: Lady Frances Balfour, sister of Arthur Balfour, and May Edith Tennant, sister-in-law of Mrs. Asquith. The Commission was appointed on November 10, 1909, and submitted its report three years later, almost to the day. In those three years the Commission held seventy-one hearings, and heard 246 witnesses, most of them official representatives of legal, medical, social, and religious groups.

The questions that the Commission considered were of five kinds: jurisdiction; extension of grounds for separation; the placing of the sexes on equal legal footing; the extension of grounds for divorce; and control of publication of reports of matrimonial cases. Their recommendations in all these matters were modestly liberalizing: that jurisdiction be given to County courts (thus making divorce cheaper for the poor); that the grounds for separation and divorce be extended; that men and women be equal under the law; and that judges have power to close the court and to restrict publication of reports. It all seems obvious and unobjectionable, a simple matter of doing the overdue right thing. But in fact the issue was a highly emotional one that was bitterly fought on both sides; for some combatants, at least, it was England's last holy war.

One of the most attractive warriors to take the field was Maurice Hewlett, a writer of highly successful historical romances, whose behavior was sometimes rather like something out of one of his books. Hewlett profoundly believed that there should be no marriage where there was no love, and he considered it his duty to testify to his beliefs before the Commission, even though he was persuaded that public testimony to such heretical views would be the end of him. "No moral cause can be successful until a leader has been crucified," he told his friend Newbolt; "someone must go, and it will be me."[34] And so he went, spiritually at least in shining armor, and explained that marriage was a contract "contingent upon the presence of the bodily desire and spiritual intention which are essential to the marriage." His most interesting contribution was the proposal that conjugal rights should be treated separately from other aspects of marriage, thus making possible a contract without sexual rights where desire was absent but the existence of children made divorce impossible.

The Commission treated Hewlett with the careful courtesy that such bodies extend to the impractical and idealistic. When he had finished the chairman dismissed him with these words:

[34] Laurence Binyon, ed., *Letters of Maurice Hewlett* (London: Methuen, 1926), p. 112.

Thank you very much for your evidence. You have presented a certain view of this matter which will have to be considered of course.[35]

There is no reason to think that it ever was considered, and there is certainly no sign of Hewlett's views in the Commission's report. Nor is there any indication of martyrdom in Hewlett's subsequent career. He had been heroic where heroism was impossible.

The forces marshalled on the other side of the argument, though perhaps less romantic than Hewlett, were a good deal more powerful. They included three representatives of the conservative Church party: the Archbishop of York, Sir William Anson, a baronet and Conservative member of Parliament, and Sir Lewis Dibdin, whose title was Dean of the Arches.[36] These three wrote a minority report on the Commission, which appeared in a large edition and was circulated by the Central Office of the Church to every diocese. The *Times* also printed the minority report in its entirety. An address on the Commission's report by the Archbishop of Canterbury was also published.

The Church's view of the matter was simple. It opposed all extensions of grounds for divorce, on the unexamined assumption that any increase in numbers of divorces would per se be evil. The minority report agreed on the equalizing of the sexes, but it made no other concession. The situation, therefore, was an impasse: on the one hand the majority of the Commission, with the support of legal, medical, and social experts; on the other hand the Established Church, militant and intransigent.

Faced with this problem, the Liberal government did what it did in every such crisis—it delayed. Three months after the submission of the majority report the Prime Min-

[35] *Report of the Commission*, vol. 3, p. 525.
[36] Dean of the Arches: in English ecclesiastical law the principal judge of the Court of Arches, the court of appeal of the archbishopric of Canterbury, to which matrimonial causes were referred.

THE ILLUSTRATED
LONDON NEWS.

REGISTERED AT THE GENERAL POST OFFICE AS A NEWSPAPER.

No. 3610.—VOL. CXXXII.   SATURDAY, JUNE 27, 1908.   With Special Photogravure Supplement: "Fishing for Jack." ONE SHILLING.

The Copyright of all the Editorial Matter, both Engravings and Letterpress, is strictly Reserved in Great Britain, the Colonies, Europe, and the United States of America.

THE KING'S GARDEN - PARTY AT WINDSOR: HIS MAJESTY PASSING THROUGH THE RANKS OF THE GUESTS.

DRAWN BY MAX COWPER, OUR SPECIAL ARTIST AT WINDSOR.

The King and Queen gave a most successful garden - party at Windsor on Saturday, and entertained more than 8000 guests. Our Illustration shows the royal party passing through the ranks of their visitors, who seemed to be drawn from all classes, and to represent every shade of political opinion.

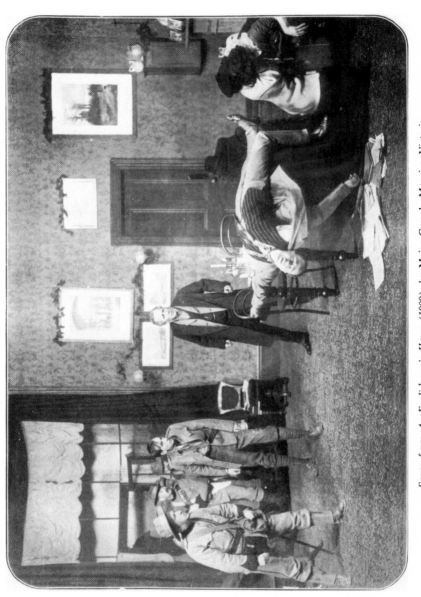

Scene from *An Englishman's Home* (1909), by Major Guy du Maurier. Victoria and Albert Museum. Crown Copyright.

Cover of P. G. Wodehouse's parody, *The Swoop* (1909).

"Mr. John Galsworthy envisaging Life and giving it—for he is nothing if not judicial—credit for the very best intentions." By Max Beerbohm.

"C. F. Masterman preserving his ideals." By Max Beerbohm.

The Fabian Window at Beatrice Webb House, Leith Hill, Surrey. The large figures are, left to right, Edward Pease, Secretary of the Fabian Society, Sidney Webb, and G. B. Shaw. The kneeling figures, all Fabians, include H. G. Wells, thumbing his nose, at the left, and Caroline Townshend, who made the window, at the extreme right. The books composing the altar include works by Shaw and the Webbs and *Fabian Tracts*. Shaw commissioned the window in 1910.

G. B. Shaw and H. G. Wells, by Alvin Langdon Coburn.

Edward Carpenter, by Alvin Langdon Coburn.

THE
NEW AGE

A WEEKLY REVIEW OF POLITICS, LITERATURE AND ART.

New Series. Vol. VI. No. 14.   THURSDAY, FEB. 3, 1910.   [Registered at G.P.O. as a Newspaper]   **THREEPENCE.**

THE CENSORSHIP.

"The Censorship." Cover cartoon, *The New Age*, February 3, 1910.

"Earl Russell tried by his peers for Bigamy, July 1901. The Lord High Steward (Lord Halsbury) reading the sentence." *The Illustrated London News.*

Scene from Votes for Women! (1907), by Elizabeth Robins. Victoria and Albert Museum. Crown Copyright.

Four playwrights: Granville Barker, Shaw, Galsworthy, and Barrie, by Alvin Langdon Coburn.

"Mr. Asquith in Office." By Max Beerbohm. He is surrounded by his problems:
the House of Lords, the Germans, the miners, the Suffragettes, and Ulster (in
the person of Sir Edward Carson).

Scene from the Russian Ballet's *Le Sacre du Printemps*, London, 1913.

"The Unknown God," by Henry Tonks (Roger Fry lecturing, with Clive Bell as acolyte). In the front row are Sickert, MacColl, George Moore, Steer, Maclagan, Sargent, and Hutchinson.

The funeral of Edward VII: The royal procession passing the statue of Queen Victoria on Castle Hill, Windsor. In the first row, left to right, are the German Emperor William II, King George V, and the Duke of Connaught. The boys following are the Duke of Cornwall (later Edward VIII) and Prince Albert (later George VI). Behind them are the kings of Norway, Greece, Spain, Bulgaria, Denmark, and Portugal.

ister was asked in the Commons what he intended to do. He replied that the matter was under consideration; "the whole ground," he explained, "is very contentious." A private bill was introduced in April 1913 but did not get a second reading. In June, Asquith was again asked if he intended to introduce a bill for reform of the divorce law; he replied that he did not. Similar questions were asked in March, April, and May of 1914, and the same answer given: "I fear it is not possible," said the Prime Minister, "to undertake legislation on this subject this Session." It was the last chance, for there was no time for humane legislation in the session that followed; and so the issue moves out of our period, still hopelessly unresolved, still unjust.

The trouble with women during the Edwardian period was simply that their troubles could not be kept separate and distinct, but kept getting mixed up with each other and with other social issues: contraception threatened the family and the birth rate, divorce threatened the Church and the stability of society, suffrage threatened political balances, and so even the most moderate move toward liberation seemed a rush toward chaos. The women themselves contributed to this state of affairs in the closing years of the period—that is to say the suffragettes did—by the extreme and increasing violence of their demonstrations. Edwardian Englishmen, seeing women rioting, burning, destroying property, and even dying, drew back in alarm from a cause that threatened to loose that rage for chaos upon the world of men. And since men governed England, it is not surprising that, after more than two decades of considering the problems of women, they went to war in 1914 with apparent relief, as a husband might leave a nagging wife, and left the problems unsolved, the liberating actions not even begun.

Chapter VII

....

THE THEATER
AND THE LORD CHAMBERLAIN

....

An ordered society is necessarily a censoring society, because any society that is stable enough to have established values will naturally act to protect them against disturbance. An act of censorship is therefore in a sense a political act, in defense of the existing order. Whether the censor is officially appointed or self-delegated, whether he claims to defend religion or purity or the Good Old Ways, he is in fact acting politically when he tries to protect an established order from the wrenches and abrasions of change. New ideas, on the other hand, tend to be anarchic, and therefore against censorship, and clash with the social status quo. The clash will be more or less violent, according to the width of the gap between the established values of a society and the values of the creative element in it; there have been times—the middle of the nineteenth century in England was one—when the gap was slight, and censorship seemed to have had little repressive effect. But by the end of the century the gap was widening, and during Edward's reign censorship in England—and particularly censorship of the stage—came to be felt by authors and intellectuals to be intolerably repressive.

For this change there are two explanations: first, the English theater, under the influence of new ideas from the continent, and particularly the influence of Ibsen's problem drama, had become a medium for serious thought for the first time in a century; and second, the system of stage censorship in England was a tangle of anomalies that made it a peculiarly "establishment" office, free of all controls and influences except the influence of the past.

Like many peculiar institutions, the English system of stage censorship began as a simple administrative office which over the centuries accumulated new and often conflicting functions and standards, without ever quite discarding old ones, until, by the twentieth century, it was a system which not only was inefficient, but was radically incapable of performing its function.

The history of the censor begins with Henry VIII, who placed control of court amusements under the Master of the Revels. In time this official came under the authority (and quite reasonably) of the principal administrator of the court, the Lord Chamberlain. As the theater developed into a public and commercial enterprise, this authority became anomalous, but naturally it was never removed from the Lord Chamberlain, who remains today the official censor of plays (as well as directing the activities of the Keeper of the Swans, the Bargemaster, and the Poet Laureate). In 1737 the Lord Chamberlain's censoring powers became statutory, when Sir Robert Walpole passed his Theatres Act to suppress the personal and political satires of playwrights like Henry Fielding.[1] This act gave the Lord Chamberlain licensing power over all theaters in the City of London and liberties of Westminster and in places of royal residence; it also required that plays be submitted to him for approval before performance, thus giving him the power of prior censorship which he still retains. It was quite sim-

---

[1] 2 George II. c. 28 (1737). "An Act to explain and amend so much of an Act made in the Twelfth Year of the Reign of Queen Anne, intituled, *An Act reducing the Laws relating to Rogues, Vagabonds, sturdy Beggars, and Vagrants, into one act of parliament; and for the more effectual punishing such rogues, vagabonds, sturdy beggars, and vagrants, and sending them whither they ought to be sent,* as relates to common players of interludes."

ply a political instrument and not at all a moral one in intention; it prohibited attacks on political personages, but it did not provide for the prohibition of indecent plays unless they were also libellous or seditious.

During the 1830's a Select Committee of Parliament reviewed Walpole's Act, and in 1843 a new Victorian version was passed. "Victorian" is used here in its connotative sense, for this Act, which remains the law under which the stage is controlled in England, has a distinctly Victorian moral bias that is quite in contrast to the eighteenth-century act. In the new version the Lord Chamberlain retained his power of prior censorship and control of theater licensing, but the grounds on which he might forbid performances were markedly changed. "And be it enacted," the Act reads, "That it shall be lawful for the Lord Chamberlain for the Time being, whenever he shall be of opinion that it is fitting for the Preservation of good Manners, Decorum, or of the public Peace so to do, to forbid the acting or presenting any Stage Play, or any Act, Scene, or Part thereof, or any Prologue or Epilogue, or any Part thereof, anywhere in Great Britain, or in such Theatres as he shall specify, and either absolutely or for such Time as he shall think fit."[2] "Good Manners" and "Decorum" were not defined, nor have they ever been since. The Act was subjected to reconsideration by various Parliamentary committees during the latter half of the nineteenth century, but there was never substantial opposition to it (in the hearings of 1892 only William Archer, the translator of Ibsen, testified in favor of abolishing censorship), and at the turn of the century the system was still Victorian, and still under the absolute authority of the Lord Chamberlain.

For many reasons, the Lord Chamberlain was a peculiarly inappropriate official to exercise this authority. As a member of the Royal Household, and one chosen principally

[2] 6 & 7 Vict., c. 68. "An Act for Regulating Theatres."

for his sense of propriety in terms of quite other functions (the present Lord Chamberlain recently announced, for example, that miniature medals may be worn with dinner jackets, thus signing the death warrant of the tail coat), he was a person whose standards of judgment were likely to be both conservative and punctilious. As a member of the Household he was appointed by the Crown, and paid from the Civil List; he was therefore not accountable to Parliament, and questions concerning his conduct in office could not be asked in the Commons, nor could the Commons exercise any control over his actions by controlling the purse strings. He was not required to state the principles on which he censored or to explain the grounds of any particular prohibition, and from his decisions there was no appeal. He dealt with theater managers only—in fact he did not legally recognize that dramatists existed—and most frequently by informal consultation and private correspondence.

The Lord Chamberlain's power over the public stage was therefore absolute. But in practice he did not do the censoring himself; the task of reading and judging plays was performed by an assistant called the Examiner of Plays. This official (who in fact has no existence in law but has simply been appointed as a convenient advisor to the Lord Chamberlain) was expected to read every play that was accepted for performance by a London manager; this amounted to 297 plays in 1890, 466 in 1900, and 604 in 1910 (or two a day during fifty six-day weeks). Most years the Examiner refused licenses to only two or three plays, but his influence on the English theater is not adequately measured by this small number, for he was likely to ask informally that many other plays be altered before production, and furthermore the very fact that his power existed affected the attitudes of both playwright and theater manager. His power was great and intimidating because it was applicable before the fact, and because its principles were mysterious: "The essence of my office," said an Examiner of the early 'nineties, "and its advantage to the art and the professors of the stage is that it is preventive and above all secret."[3] That was its essence, all right, but to the playwright its advantage was undiscoverable.

The Examiner of Plays from 1895 through Edward's reign was one G. A. Redford, a former bank manager whose principal qualification for the post was that in the past he had filled it illegally and without pay while his friend and predecessor, E.F.S. Pigott, was away on holidays. Redford was a man of strong convictions and limited intelligence, blandly confident of his own (that is, his society's) standards, and apparently incapable of entertaining an idea. He never suggested, by word or deed, that he had the slightest feeling for literature or for the drama as an art form; certainly he made no distinctions between serious drama and popular prurience, except perhaps to favor the latter. When asked what the principles were on which he proceeded in licensing plays, he replied: "I read them from an official point of view, but it is really impossible to say on what principles I proceed. There are no principles that can be defined." And later he added, more succinctly: "I have no critical views of plays. I simply have to maintain a standard."[4]

It is clear that to Redford the intuitive Victorianism that he exercised was "official" (the expression, that is, of established attitudes), and therefore a "standard" that reasonable people would agree should be maintained. With this official standard in mind he forbade the discussion on public stages of those subjects which, in the High Victorian tradition, One Did Not Discuss: sex, religion, and politics. In short, he proceeded by simply transferring the code of a gentleman's club, or an officers' mess, to the stage. In doing so, he was acting quite outside the defined areas of prohibition,

[3] "Report from the Select Committee on Theatres and Places of Entertainment," *Reports from Committees*, 1892, vol. 8, para. 5189.

[4] "Report from the Joint Select Committee of the House of Lords and the House of Commons on the Stage Plays (Censorship)"; *Reports from Committees*, 1909, vol. 3, para. 194.

as set down (however vaguely) in the Act of 1837. He forbade, for example, plays on Scriptural subjects, and even refused to read them on the grounds that the "rule" against them was an absolute one, though in fact such a rule did not exist. He also disapproved of plays dealing with political subjects: "the stage is not a political arena," he announced, "and it is not considered desirable that important political questions, involving, perhaps, diplomatic relations with foreign Powers, should be dealt with there."[5] And he was so sensitive to the impropriety of sexual matters that he could not even mention in public the scene from Edward Garnett's *The Breaking Point* to which he objected. Only by the broadest possible interpretation of the statute can *all* references to politics, religion, and sex be considered to be breaches of "good Manners, Decorum, or the public Peace."

Redford's "principles" suggest two points about the attitude of England's governing class toward the Edwardian stage. First, they seem to have felt no legalistic qualms about imposing their judgments of what was desirable for the public upon helpless artists and audiences; Redford's actions consistently imply the assumption that knowledge of the public good resides in official minds, and is not to be foolishly questioned. Second, their acts of censorship can be read pretty consistently as acts in defense of an established order, and therefore as fundamentally political and social in nature. Censorship of religious subjects, for example, meant in effect a defense of the Established Church: Redford's invented category of "Scriptural" subjects protected only Christianity from stage representation; he did, to be sure, once refuse to license a play about Mohammed, but his motive in that case was clearly political, not religious. And the particular political prohibitions reflect the Edwardian concern for social order in a time of strikes, suffragette demonstrations, and anarchist threats. Even sex

[5] "Report from the Joint Select Committee," para. 259.

seems to have offended most when it involved correlative disturbances of the social order, as in cases of adultery in high places and abortion; French farces continued to be allowed throughout the period.

When he came to apply his principles, Redford demonstrated with startling clarity that he meant it when he said he had no critical view of plays. Acting on his anti-Scriptural principle, he forbade the performance of the Oberammergau Passion Play; to protect England from sexual improprieties he refused a license to *Oedipus Tyrannus* (though he rather surprisingly allowed *Lysistrata*—funny classical sex was apparently acceptable, but tragical incest among monarchs might set a bad example); and to avoid offending a foreign potentate he cancelled a revival of *The Mikado.* All of these examples are absurd, but it would be a mistake to laugh Redford away as simply a quaint fool, for he had a hangman's power over the London stage at a time when English drama was beginning to show signs of life. Nor was his stupidity in any way extraordinary: indeed his usefulness is precisely in the degree to which he was ordinary, a typical managerial mind applying itself to managing morals.

In the end it must have been the waywardness of Redford's "official standards" that was hardest to bear. He was like the philistine art lover who doesn't know what's good, but knows what he likes: he was unclear about the bases of his judgments, but he never doubted that they were right judgments, which decent people would not question. His sense of his own infallibility was so papal that he was impatient of small inconsistencies, and he never condescended to learn exactly what the law under which he ruled actually said. His censoring career began in flat illegality, and it continued to be, if not exactly illegal, at least ethically dubious, as when he licensed a play that he had written himself (when questioned about this, he could not be made to see that he had behaved improperly—after all, wasn't he the censor?).

Like his predecessor, Redford drew upon the services of an unpaid, unofficial assistant. In his case the assistant was his wife, who, as he explained, could read German and so took care of all German plays; Redford could read French himself, and in the case of plays in Italian seems to have settled for an English précis.

Like previous censors, Redford regarded his dealings with managers as privileged; he relied primarily on personal pressure to compel revisions—often after a play had been licensed and performed. He often accepted the authority of newspapers reviews or even private opinions when he had not seen a play himself, and would require changes in the text of any play described as indecent, regardless of the length of its run. He threatened to close *A Gaiety Girl* after fifty uncensored performances when it was brought to his attention that a parson in the play resembled the Dean of Windsor (the play was allowed to continue after the parson had been turned into a doctor); and a successful provincial run of something called *Secrets of the Harem* was stopped after an official of the Turkish Embassy protested (it later reopened as *Secrets – – –*). In most of these dealings the Examiner assumed a "let's talk this over as men-of-the-world and gentlemen" attitude, and he considered that anyone who revealed his "Private and Confidential" communications was behaving in a most ungentlemanly fashion.

Since Redford's letters often revealed his lack of either intelligence or clear critical principles, it is not surprising that he wanted them kept secret, but it is scarcely a reasonable demand, coming from a public official on official business. As an example, here is a letter from Redford to Laurence Housman concerning Housman's nativity play, *Bethlehem* (1902):

Dear Sir,—I have no power as Examiner of Plays to make any exception to the rule that Scriptural plays, or plays founded on or adapted from the Scriptures, are ineligible for license in Great Britain. It would appear from your letter that your play would come under this rule, and I may say for myself that I am glad to be relieved of the difficult and delicate duty of deciding on the fitness of treatment in each particular case.[6]

The rule, as I have said, did not in fact exist. Nor was it true that no exceptions were made: a play called *Eager Heart* staged a nativity scene without interference from the authorities, and *Everyman* and the Chester Mystery Plays were done regularly at Christmas. It is also characteristic of Redford that he blandly admitted rejecting Housman's play without reading it—a form of judgment which he seems to have used frequently.

In spite of Redford's total lack of qualifications for his job, serious resistance to his office did not develop until he had been at it for some ten years; it was not until the developing Edwardian dramatists began to feel the Examiner's Victorian decorum as a serious restriction—that is to say, when their dramatic ideas began to clash with his social ideas—that the issue became a public one. In 1906, Edward Garnett wrote a play called *The Breaking Point* and submitted it to a number of theater managers, including Granville Barker, who turned it down for the Stage Society, and Frederick Harrison, who accepted it in December 1906 for the Haymarket. Garnett was not a gifted playwright, and he had not written a good play; but he was serious about literature, and his play was a serious effort to write about real human issues. In accepting it, Harrison was quite aware that he was not getting a money-maker; "the general public," as he wrote to the author, "sets its face stubbornly against sad plays. And yours is more than sad—it is tragic." But he was anxious to produce plays that would "take us out of the dull, dreary round of conventionality,"[7] and he rightly saw

[6] "Report from the Joint Select Committee," para. 2519.
[7] Quoted in preface to Edward Garnett, *The Breaking Point* (London: Duckworth, 1907), p. ix.

that *The Breaking Point* was such a play. The Examiner, like the general public, set his face against it, and what followed was typical of the methods he used. First Redford suggested privately to Harrison that the play should be withdrawn before it opened. Garnett refused to accept this surreptitious execution of his work and wrote to Redford asking the reasons for refusing the play a license; Redford replied as follows:

> Dear Sir,—I trust you will absolve me from any discourtesy if I point out that my official relations are only concerned with the Managers of Theatres. It is always painful to me to decline to recommend a licence, and in this case I hoped to avoid any possible appearance of censure on any one by suggesting privately to Mr. Harrison the desirability of withdrawing this piece. I cannot suppose that he has any doubts as to the reason.—I am, Dear Sir, Yours faithfully.[8]

This letter, so politely insulting and so precisely vague, expressing the odd aspiration of a censor to avoid any possible appearance of censure, was marked, as always, "Private and Confidential." Garnett nevertheless published it in full in the prefatory material to the printed text of his play, along with a wrathful "Letter to the Censor."

The offensive contents of *The Breaking Point* are clear enough in Garnett's own succinct summary of the plot: "A girl, Grace Elwood, has intimate relations with her lover, Sherrington, a man whose wife has previously left him. Her father, Dr. Elwood, and her lover quarrel for control of her. The girl, fearing she is *enceinte*, cannot stand the strain, and succumbs." ("Succumbs" is a delicate way of saying that she throws herself into the river and drowns.)[9] Two things should be plain from this summary: first, that the play is scrupulously moral, if the punishment of transgressions is

[8] *Breaking Point*, pp. xxii-xxiii.
[9] *Breaking Point*, p. x.

what "moral" means; and second, that Garnett has treated the sexual aspects of his play with extreme reticence (*enceinte* is characteristic—how long has it been since ladies got pregnant in French?). *The Breaking Point* has no literary merit to speak of: it is stilted, talky, and creakingly melodramatic, the kind of play a Man of Letters might be expected to write if he were serious without being gifted. It is important, not because it is good and not because it says anything revolutionary about sex or writes about it with real frankness, but because Garnett refused to play the Examiner's game by gentlemen's rules. When he published the play, the war against the system began.

At the same time that Garnett was preparing his censored play for publication, Granville Barker was submitting his own play, *Waste*, for licensing. Like *The Breaking Point*, *Waste* concerns the tragic consequences of adultery. Henry Trebell, a prominent M.P., has a casual affair at a house party with a married woman; when she learns that she is pregnant, she submits to an abortion and dies of the operation; Trebell is protected from scandal by his party leader but is rejected by his party and kills himself. Barker had treated sin with greater severity than Garnett; nevertheless, the Examiner refused to grant the play a license. When Barker asked for specific objections, Redford replied that it was not necessary to indicate particular allusions, but that Barker "must be prepared to moderate and modify the extremely outspoken references to sexual relations."[10] In the course of further correspondence he added that Barker must eliminate all references to "an illegal operation"; since the plot turns on the abortion, Redford's demand is rather like asking the producer of *Hamlet* kindly to remove all mention of regicide.

One of the immediate consequences of Redford's action against *The Breaking Point* and *Waste* was a petition

[10] "Report from the Joint Select Committee," para. 1232.

from a group of dramatic authors to the Prime Minister, requesting a meeting to discuss stage censorship in general. (Neither play is mentioned, but the petition, coming as it did immediately after the publication of one play and the suppression of the other, must surely be regarded as an expression of outrage at the Examiner's actions in these cases). In the interval between the petition and the conference, the following letter was also sent to the Editor of the *Times*:

Sir,—The Prime Minister has consented to receive during next month a deputation from the following dramatic authors on the subject of the censorship of plays. In the meantime may these authors, through your columns, enter a formal protest against this office, which was instituted for political, and not for the so-called moral ends to which it is perverted—an office autocratic in procedure, opposed to the spirit of the Constitution, contrary to common justice and to common sense?

They protest against the power lodged in the hands of a single official—who judges without a public hearing, and against whose dictum there is no appeal—to cast a slur on the good name and destroy the means of livelihood of any member of an honourable calling.

They assert that the censorship has not been exercised in the interests of morality, but has tended to lower the dramatic tone by appearing to relieve the public of the duty of moral judgement.

They ask to be freed from the menace hanging over every dramatist of having his work and the proceeds of his work destroyed at a pen's stroke by the arbitrary action of a single official neither responsible to Parliament nor amenable to law.

They ask that their art be placed on the same footing as every other art.

They ask that they themselves be placed in the position enjoyed under the law by every other citizen.

To these ends they claim that the licensing of plays shall be abolished. The public is already sufficiently assured against managerial misconduct by the present yearly licensing of theatres, which remains untouched by the measure of justice here demanded.[11]

The list of seventy-one names that follows is an impressive one: a few of the signatories were Barker, Barrie, Conrad, Galsworthy, Garnett, Gilbert, Hardy, Hudson, Hueffer (Ford Madox Ford), James, Masefield, Maugham, Meredith, Pinero, Shaw, Swinburne, Synge, Wells, and Yeats. The deputation, introduced by Barrie and supported by a large following of playwrights, did not in fact see the Prime Minister; instead, on February 22, 1908, they were received by the Home Secretary, the Right Honourable Herbert Gladstone.

Barker thought Gladstone an ass and expected nothing of the meeting, as he told Murray in a letter;[12] and indeed press reports of the conference were not encouraging. Pinero made an emotional speech urging the rights of dramatic authors, and was cheered by his fellows; Gilbert spoke more cautiously, offering a very modest modification of the existing system of censorship in the form of a court of appeals. Gladstone replied in one of those marching-in-place speeches so dear to the politician's heart. Censorship was not really in his department, he began, and in fact "it was one of those curious questions, not infrequently found in the British Constitution, which seemed not to belong to any distinct Department of State."[13] Since this was one of the dramatists' objections to the system, it could hardly have comforted them to be reminded of it. Gladstone went on to warn that of course, if reform required a change of law, "difficulties must arise," and he would not presume to offer a personal opinion of the issue; he would, however, represent their

[11] *Times,* Oct. 29, 1907, p. 15.
[12] Quoted in C. B. Purdom, *Harley Granville Barker* (London: Rockliff, 1955), p. 78.
[13] *Times,* Feb. 26, 1908, p. 18.

view to the Prime Minister. And so the delegation filed out again. Much had been spoken, but little had been said.

Writing of the interview in the *Academy*, the playwright St. John Hankin related its failure to the failure of the Liberal party.

> The Liberal Party [he wrote] may be unwilling or afraid to abolish the Censorship of Plays. It is a thorny problem, into which all kinds of questions, including that of party tactics, may conceivably enter. Still, a touch of enthusiasm, a spark of generous heat in the cause of free speech in all departments of life, would not, I think, have been amiss.

The basic source of failure, he concluded, was in Liberalism, which "as a vital force is at such a low ebb in this country at the moment and almost threatens to be crushed out altogether between the upper and nether millstones of Conservatism and Socialism."[14]

Nevertheless, the authors' protest did have results, though they came slowly. According to Herbert Samuel, who had been present at the dramatists' interview with Gladstone, the Prime Minister's decision to appoint a committee to examine the question of stage censorship was a direct result of this protest.

Another event of 1907 which may have had some influence on the Prime Minister's decision was the farcical *Mikado* affair, which entertained the Commons and the readers of the daily papers during the spring. It was appropriately enough on April first that Mrs. D'Oyly Carte announced that, "owing to representations which have been made . . . as to the inadvisability of reviving *The Mikado*, she has come to the decision not to produce that opera." A question was promptly asked in the Commons as to the reason for these "representations"; the answer given was that the

[14] St. J. H[ankin], "The Censorship of Plays," *Academy*, vol. 74 (Feb. 29, 1908), 514-515.

opera had been prohibited "owing to buffoonery in certain parts," the implication being that the buffoonery would cause distress to the head of a foreign state—a principle that had been invoked in defense of political censorship on other occasions. It may seem at first odd that *The Mikado* had been allowed more than twenty years of freedom from censorship before this principle was applied to it; but the Lord Chamberlain's decision (and this time it *was* his decision, and not, as was usually the case, his rubber-stamping of Redford's judgment), was based on two factors that had not existed before. The Japanese had become British Allies in 1902, and presumably offenses to foreign potentates were especially censorable when those potentates joined the British side; and further, His Imperial Highness General Prince Fushimi was on his way to England on a state visit. He arrived on May 6, and while he was in Britain not only was *The Mikado* not performed but all naval and marine bands were instructed to remove the music of the opera from their programs. Only one military band violated this ban; the band of the Japanese warship *Tsukuba*, lying at anchor at Chatham, cheerfully played selections from *The Mikado* to welcome a visiting British naval party aboard. The prohibition was removed in June, by which time Prince Fushimi was in Ottawa and presumably out of range of the offense; a revival in 1908 ran without official interference and without any indication of distress from Tokyo.

The significant point in this absurd affair is that the control of stage productions was considered a legitimate power of the state where matters of diplomacy were concerned, and that offenses to Crowned Heads were regarded as particularly undesirable. One might perhaps argue that the Heads were already lying uneasily, and that in this instance, as in many others, insecurity and defensiveness about established institutions led to restrictive measures that now seem grotesquely excessive. (This was not a practice peculiar to the British; Verdi's *Un Ballo in Maschera* had similar troubles with the authorities for representing an historical Swedish regicide. Verdi solved the problem by changing his locale to Massachusetts, but when a similar device was proposed to solve the *Mikado* problem, the Lord Chamberlain refused. A pity, for otherwise we might have had a production in which Titi-pu was in Boston, and the Mikado the Mayor.)

The authors' letter of protest brought the censorship issue into the open, but it also served to unify the supporters of the existing system. These were principally the managers of theaters in London and the provinces, and within a month the Theatrical Managers' Association had passed a resolution opposing abolition of censorship and urging that the Lord Chamberlain's powers should be extended "to prevent the performance of stage plays anywhere until such plays have been duly licensed." (This extension would have added provincial and private theaters to those already under his control.) Thus from the beginning of the controversy the lines were clearly drawn: opposing censorship were the authors, who sought a theater in which ideas could be freely discussed; supporting censorship were the managers (and later some actors' groups), for whom the theater was a commercial enterprise, and who sought maximum financial security. Security is exactly what the Theatre Act provided: a license from the Lord Chamberlain was in effect an official assurance that a play was morally correct, and even when provincial authorities disagreed (as the burghers of Hull did when *The Merry Widow* played there) they did not close a play if it had been licensed. A theater without this protection would be exposed to arbitrary interference by local officials, and in the managers' eyes it was not worth freeing authors if you also freed country constables.

The fact that the managers did not seriously consider the rights of dramatic authors points to an important distinction between the two opposed groups. Most of the managers were actor-managers—men who both produced and starred in their own productions and in some cases owned their own theaters. They were managers in the tradition of Sir Henry Irving—floridly romantic actors who chose romances and romantic comedies for their vehicles. The attractions that their shows offered were first the stars and second the elaborate sets; the play was adequate if it provided sufficient opportunities for the display of these attractions without offending young ladies in the audience. Many of the most successful actor-manager plays were adaptations of popular novels (like Tree's greatest success, *Trilby*); others were adaptations of French melodramas and farces; the serious theater was represented almost entirely by over-staged productions of Shakespeare. (Of the 46 major productions that Tree mounted at his Haymarket Theatre during the eighteen years of his occupancy, 12 were by Shakespeare, and all of these were spectaculars: the wood in *Midsummer Night's Dream* had real rabbits in it, and the sheepshearing scene in *The Winter's Tale* included a real brook that really babbled.)

It does not seem fanciful to see this actor-managers' theater as an analogue of the Edwardian established order in general. It appealed by splendor and spectacle (both a little vulgar), and by repetitions of the familiar; it never offended, either by rude language or by ideas. It had a kind of aristocracy in its actor-managers, and valued them above any other property of the stage (a valuation which the court confirmed by knighting Tree, Bancroft, and Alexander.) And it regarded its authors as far down the social scale, somewhere between prop men and jugglers, perhaps.

This "establishment" theater was an expensive, though often financially rewarding, enterprise; it made a great deal of money when it made any, but such success depended on long runs, with provincial tours at the end. The actor-managers, who were financially involved in two ways—as stars and as entrepreneurs—were therefore understandably anxious to minimize the risk of being closed by arming themselves with the Lord Chamberlain's license. It was not sufficent that the plays they produced were innocuous: they must also be certified to be innocuous. This demand for official sanction surely points up the moral uncertainty of the time; but it also suggests something specious about the morality, that audiences and authorities should accept with evident relief and satisfaction an official judgment that relieved them of the necessity of making their own moral choices. If the authorities at Hull really thought the *Merry Widow* was "immoral," why didn't they close it? Because the authority of the Lord Chamberlain was a superior authority? Or because it was easier to accept his opinion than to defend their own?

In the censorship controversy, the managers were therefore in natural league with the Lord Chamberlain's office. In defending the censorship, they may have been thinking of their commercial commodities, the licensed plays, but when they spoke they uttered the censor's opinion that a play was capable of great harm if it dealt with controversial ideas or spoke frankly about the relations between the sexes. What the dangers of theatrical freedom were, W. S. Gilbert made clear in his statement to the investigating committee in 1909: "I think," he said, "that the stage of a theatre is not a proper pulpit from which to disseminate doctrines possibly of Anarchism, Socialism, and Agnosticism. It is not the proper platform upon which to discuss questions of adultery and free love before a mixed audience composed of persons of all ages, of both sexes, of all ways of thinking, of all conditions of life, and of various degrees of education."[15] The dangers that Gilbert feared are, predictably enough, all radical ideas; but note that what Gilbert opposed was not the advocacy of radical ideas, but the discussion of them— he was simply expressing the typical conservative hope that new ideas, if not acknowledged, will go away. In spite of the "alls" in his last sentence, it is clear that Gilbert, like most supporters of censorship, was not thinking of himself and

[15] "Report from the Joint Select Committee," para. 3421.

other educated males as endangered by these radical threats, but only those less wise and more susceptible souls, the young, the female, the poor, and the foreign. This paternalistic assumption that it was a proper function of the English gentleman to shelter the minds of weaker vessels is just what the significant social movements of the Edwardian period violently opposed, and the gentlemen's blindness to their own relation to suffragettes, Socialists, and lesser breeds is an important contributing cause of the decade's vast disorders.

But what did the other side of the conflict want? What did the writers expect from the elimination of censorship? They wanted, first of all, a theater in which serious contemporary ideas and problems could be discussed seriously. The new movement in the English theater had been profoundly influenced by Ibsen, and from Ibsen it had taken the idea of the stage as a forum for the discussion of human problems.

> Not merely to depict life as it is [wrote Max Beerbohm], but to point therefrom some moral, is the aim of all the dramatic authors who count for anything at all to-day. Very often their moral fervour, their wish to do good, gets in the way of their artistic achievement. Their anxiety to be helpful to mankind does very often make their work clumsy. Propagandism in drama is a passing fashion, I daresay, and the playwrights of the near future will be as little anxious to do good as they will be to do harm. Meanwhile, being even more definitely moralists than artists, our playwrights have especial reason for resenting an official whose effect is so often to prevent them not merely from depicting life, but from exerting a moral influence.[16]

It was one of the playwrights' bitterest complaints that the Examiner forbade their serious treatment of sexual matters

16 "The Censorship Report," *Saturday Review of Literature*, vol. 108 (Nov. 20, 1909), 625.

while he continued to license trivial and vulgar farces dealing with adultery and prostitution as the materials for broad humor.

To perform their moral exercises, the playwrights wanted modern theaters in which plays could be mounted in a style appropriate to modern ideas. It is true that one finds less reference to methods of staging in the writings of these playwrights than in the next generation and that the conception of play production implied by the plays of Shaw, Galsworthy, and Barker is a conventional one; still producers and designers like William Poel, Gordon Craig, and Granville Barker were thinking of staging in symbolic, non-representational terms, and one can see in the Barker-McCarthy productions of Shakespeare in 1912-13 a determination to escape from the bloated realism of Beerbohm Tree to a new, bare, modern style. One critic called these productions "post-Impressionist," thus recognizing the connection between the new theater and the new art then on exhibition in London, though on the other hand two literary men who were also art critics disagreed: George Moore said the setting of *The Winter's Tale* made the stage look like a public lavatory, and Arnold Bennett thought the sets "unimportant."[17]

Finally, the opponents of censorship wanted a rational theater, in which the restraints of authority, if they were applied, would at least be applied intelligibly. The Edwardian Examiner of Plays was an anachronism, operating on principles that were, like the laws themselves, Victorian, and that could not be applied consistently to twentieth-century plays. His ideas of decency, propriety, and blasphemy were simply not relevant to the plays (and the world) of Shaw. Consequently, playwrights who wrote for the present found their works sacrificed capriciously to what Sir Thomas Beecham called "the unknown English gods," the lingering vague decorums of the past.

17 Both in Arnold Bennett, *Journals*, vol. 2 (London: Cassell, 1932), pp. 52 and 50.

The enemies of the new drama, one might say, were Mrs. Grundy, Beerbohm Tree, and the Unknown Gods. All these were profoundly, almost institutionally English, and the English theater at the turn of the century was built upon what they represented—prudery, empty spectacle, and Anglo-Saxon insularity. Consequently, to oppose these was to behave in un-English ways: to introduce foreign works and foreign methods and—most un-English of all—intellectual vigor to English stages. The playwrights' attack on censorship must be seen as something more than simply an attack on an official institution: it was an attack on an idea of Englishness, an idea that had become outmoded and restrictive and irrational but was more vigorously defended by the established order as it became less defensible.

Although the issue of censorship was clear and public by the end of 1907, it was not officially recognized in Parliament until 1909. In April of that year Mr. Robert Harcourt, the member from the Montrose Burghs, and a minor playwright, introduced a Theatres and Music Halls Bill designed to abolish censorship in Britain, and he continued to ask questions about censorship in the Commons until in June the Prime Minister agreed to appoint a Joint Committee of the two Houses to consider the question.

Harcourt emerges as something of a hero in this action, but he was not the only one. Shaw also did his bit, in his own characteristic way, to goad the government into action. Between the time of Harcourt's first question in the Commons and the Prime Minister's announcement, Shaw submitted for licensing two one-act plays—*The Shewing Up of Blanco Posnet* and *Press Cuttings*. Both were refused licenses, and one can hardly avoid concluding that Shaw had written both plays as intentional exercises in Examiner-baiting, in order that he might ridicule the system in the press while preliminary plans for committee hearings were going on. *Blanco Posnet* is a play about a horse thief's reluctant conversion to religion; it is a religious work in that

it celebrates God's power, but the language Shaw used is
hardly orthodox (James Joyce described Blanco's climactic
speeches as "theological insofar as their subject is God, but
not very churchly in diction").[18] In fact, Shaw refers to
God in terms that make Him sound like a superior faro
dealer, and it is not surprising that Redford banned the
play. Shaw immediately made a public statement in which
he protested that his play was a pious one, and defended
himself in a manner worthy of Graham Greene: "What is
called the struggle of a man with God is the most dramatic
of all conflicts; in fact, the only one that makes really good
drama."[19] In Shaw's hands, what that conflict made was
really good farce; and he managed to contrive another good
farce out of the Examiner's prohibition.

A month later Shaw was back again with *Press Cuttings*,
"A topical sketch compiled from the editorial and correspondence columns of the daily papers during the women's
war of 1909." The play is short and trivial—Shaw later collected it among his "Trifles and Tomfooleries"—and obviously designed mainly to annoy a number of public figures.
In it a General Michener and a Prime Minister called Bals-
quith are harassed by suffragettes, and converted to votes
for women and civil rights for the Army. The Lord Chamberlain objected to the names, and Shaw rushed to the letters columns of the *Times*, arguing that *Punch* used "Bals-
quith" all the time, and that in any case neither Balfour nor
Asquith nor Kitchener was referred to.

Shaw was altogether successful in making the system of
censorship ridiculous with his two little plays. Neither
could conceivably be regarded as dangerous to morals or to
the public peace; yet, given the Examiner's principles, both
had to be refused licenses. *Blanco Posnet* violates both the

---

[18] "Bernard Shaw's Battle with the Censor," *Critical Writings of
James Joyce*, ed. Mason and Ellmann (London: Faber & Faber, 1959),
p. 208.

[19] *Times*, May 24, 1909, p. 12.

religious prohibition and the prohibition against straight talk in sexual matters (in his testimony to the Joint Committee Beerbohm Tree confessed that he found Shaw's treatment of sex in the play "rather too strong"); *Press Cuttings* makes undignified references to easily identifiable public figures and current political issues. If wit were enough to sway governments, the Lord Chamberlain's power over the English stage would surely have been destroyed by Shaw's attack. But in fact cleverness seemed to frighten and offend the English ruling class, and Shaw may have done his cause some harm by being funny about it. Not only in his plays, but also in his testimony before the committee, he indulged in a certain amount of paradox-making and foolery, and the tone of the recorded interrogation reflects a good deal of irritation with his behavior.

The tone of Shaw's remarks, on the other hand, reflects his feelings about them; he described the committee members from the Lords as dunderheads, and he took no particular care to conceal this opinion. The committee was in fact better than Shaw said it was. Among the Commons members were two playwrights: Harcourt, who had had a play produced by Granville Barker at the Court, and A.E.W. Mason, a popular dramatist-novelist best known for his novel, *Four Feathers*. The chairman, Herbert Samuel, was probably given the job simply because he was the only cabinet member who had time (all the others were busy in the battle over the Parliament Bill) ; but he was an able, literate man, something of a scholar, and probably the best available person. The peers were Lord Gorell, the distinguished justice who chaired the Divorce Commission a few months later; the Earl of Plymouth; Lord Ribblesdale, brother-in-law of the Prime Minister and a sensitive and intelligent man; Lord Willoughby de Broke, who was at the time deeply involved in the "backwoods" resistance to the Parliament Bill, and may well have been put on the committee to distract him; and Lord Newton, an independent-minded diplomatist. Not, perhaps, a particularly distinguished group, but not dunderheads, either; as the testimony shows, the peers were on the whole reasonable and open-minded men—in fact two who began as supporters of censorship were eventually converted by the evidence of the opposition.

The committee began its hearings on July 29, 1909, and had its fourteenth and final meeting on November 2. Nearly fifty witnesses were called, representing the government, playwrights, managers, actors, critics, and the Roman and Anglican churches. They divided about three to two in favor of continuing the censorship—a ratio which is roughly proportional to the ratio of managers to playwrights examined. Among the witnesses were Shaw, Barker, Barrie, Galsworthy, Gilbert, Gilbert Murray, Pinero, Tree, Bancroft, and Alexander; "with such a galaxy," Lord Samuel recalled, "it is not surprising that our doings received much publicity; the evidence filled columns in the Press, and our sittings even competed with the most sensational murder trials in the posters of the evening papers."[20] The published report of the hearings is a full and fascinating record of Edwardian opinions on the conduct of the theater: "few books of the year 1909 can have been cheaper and more entertaining," as Shaw observed. It has moments of high comedy, as when Shaw appeared with a book-length printed statement, which he proposed to read into the record, and was, as he put it, kicked out of the room;[21] there were moments verging on farce, as when the committee felt compelled to empty the hearing room before they could read aloud the improprieties of a play that had already been granted a license; and there were moments when admirable clarity and intelligence prevailed, as when the Anglican

[20] Rt. Hon. Viscount Samuel, *Memoirs* (London: Cresset Press, 1945), p. 59.
[21] Shaw's account of the hearing and his rejected statement are included in his preface to *The Shewing Up of Blanco Posnet*.

Bishop of Southwark made a moving defense of freedom of conscience. The committee issued its report on November 11, 1909. Its principal recommendations were these:

The Lord Chamberlain should remain the Licenser of Plays.

It should be optional to submit a play for license, and legal to perform an unlicensed play, whether it had been submitted or not.

The Director of Public Prosecutions should have power to prefer an indictment against both the author and the theater-manager involved, if he considered an unlicensed play open to objection on the ground of indecency.

The office of Examiner of Plays should be continued.

The existing practice of having only managers submit plays to the Examiner should be continued.

These recommendations were far from ideal: censorship was left in the hands of unqualified officials, and the existence of playwrights remained unacknowledged (except when they were indecent); but the principle of optional licensing was an important improvement, which made censorship *after* the offense at least a possibility. The only official voice of the playwrights, the Dramatic Committee of the Society of Authors, greeted the report as "a notable advance on anything of the kind that has appeared before," and in general response to the report was favorable.

Some of the committee members—notably the playwriting members—must have been disappointed, but the two who left memoirs of the occasion were evidently satisfied with their work. The chairman, in his *Memoirs*, wrote that "the methods of the dramatic censorship were much modified as the result of the inquiry, so that the question soon ceased to be a burning one, and has rarely attracted public attention since";[22] and Lord Newton recalled that "the Report recommended a compromise which, on the whole,

[22] Samuel, *Memoirs*, p. 62.

seems to have given satisfaction, for during recent years we have heard little about it."[23] Unfortunately, neither noble lord is correct; both seem to have indulged a politician's instinct for regarding all completed past actions as successful ones. But in fact only those recommendations that preserved the established system were enforced, and the "compromise" existed only on paper. Max Beerbohm judged the committee's work precisely when he wrote, "Ten gentlemen in frock-coats, five lords and five commons, at a long green table—not by them ever are dawns of new eras ushered in."[24] The committee had sat, the report existed, and from time to time some opponent of censorship raised a question in the Commons about it, but nothing was done, and at the Lord Chamberlain's office the business of preventing the presentation of sex, religion, and politics on the stage continued much as usual.

The question of religion turned up in a farcical incident that occurred in the following year, when Sir Thomas Beecham applied for a license for the English premiere of Strauss' *Salomé*. The Lord Chamberlain refused the license, on the familiar grounds that the opera treated a forbidden Biblical subject; Beecham appealed through friends and was summoned to a conference at which the Lord Chamberlain explained that he had received a large number of letters protesting against the presentation of a sacred figure on the stage. Beecham pointed out that *Samson et Delilah* had been given in London for many years, to which the Lord Chamberlain quickly replied: "There is a difference— a very great difference; in one case it is the Old Testament and in the other the New." (Beecham might have countered this parry with Massenet's *Herodiade*, which had recently been licensed, though only after the names had been changed.)

Compromises were at length agreed upon: Saint John

23 Lord Newton, *Retrospection* (London: John Murray, 1941), p. 172.
24 "The Censorship Report," p. 626.

was to be referred to only as "The Prophet," Salomé's desire was to be not for sexual gratification but for spiritual guidance, and The Prophet's head was not to appear on stage (the producer was allowed a platter completely covered by a cloth so long as there was nothing under the cloth that might suggest a head; Granville Barker described the result as a "bedaubbed tea-tray"). "It is only fair to say," Beecham remarked of this absurd conference, "that my collaborators in this joyous piece of nonsense were, in spite of their outward gravity, as exhilarated as myself; for we all of us alike felt that we were making a solemn sacrifice on the altar of an unknown but truly national god."[25] On the opening night the cast strove to sing the bowdlerized text of the opera, but soon lapsed into the original version. Nobody noticed, however, and the production continued with official approbation.[26]

Except for this one comic crisis, the years 1910 and 1911 were relatively quiet ones for the censors—perhaps because their opponents were naively waiting for official action on the committee's report. But at the end of 1911 censorship once more became a matter of public controversy. One apparent cause was the resignation of Redford as Examiner of Plays. He was succeeded by Charles H. E. Brookfield, a man who was unlike his predecessor in at least one respect— he had some apparent qualifications for the job. Brookfield had been an actor (he had worked with Beerbohm Tree) and a prolific playwright; he had written a large number of farces—plays with titles like *What Pamela Wanted* and *Dear Old Charlie*, often adapted from French sources, and sometimes very successful. He had been around theaters professionally for more than thirty years.

[25] Sir Thomas Beecham, *A Mingled Chime* (London: Hutchinson, 1944), p. 103.

[26] Three years later Sir Thomas once again offended the Lord Chamberlain by producing *Der Rosenkavalier* with a bed onstage, to which reference was made in the sung text. He was told that either the bed or the reference to it must go. The bed went.

Nevertheless, the appointment of Brookfield as Examiner was received by the theatrical world with derision and distress and was severely criticized in the Commons. One objection was that Brookfield's plays were the sort of worthless, indecent farces that managed to get licenses while serious plays were banned: indeed *Dear Old Charlie* was cited by more than one witness at the committee hearings as an example of offensive but uncensored filth. The text of *Dear Old Charlie* has not, alas, survived, but contemporary reviews describe it in considerable detail; it was an elaborately plotted comedy of multiple sexual infidelity, with a happy ending for Charlie, the seducer of his friends' wives. This sort of play was common and popular at the time, but *Dear Old Charlie* seems to have been a particularly vulgar example of the type, though a cleverly made one. When Brookfield revived it in 1912 (shrewdly taking advantage of the publicity that his appointment as Examiner had given the play), the *Times'* critic observed that "there really cannot be two opinions about the cynical, shameless immorality that underlies the play—none the less cynical and shameless because it is conveyed by innuendo, by double meanings, by nods and winks." Still, the play would probably not have been so conspicuously condemned were it not for the fact that while *Dear Old Charlie* prospered, plays like *The Breaking Point* and *Waste* were refused licenses. (Brookfield had gratuitously called attention to this injustice by inserting into his play a satiric reference to a play called "Sewage," by "Mr. Bleater.")

But Brookfield had not contented himself with being an offensive playwright; he had also, on the eve of his appointment as Examiner, published an article, "On Plays and Playwriting," which seems designed to alienate everyone associated with the English theater with the exception of the Lord Chamberlain. In the article, Brookfield described the years from 1865 to 1885 as the Golden Age of English drama, and complained of the contrasting dullness of more recent years (the years, that is, of Shaw, Wilde, Galsworthy, Barker, Barrie, and Yeats). His explanation of the decline was simple and sweeping: "The British nation is not an artistic nation; the British public does not know good art from bad and the British newspaper-reporter critics cannot guide them because they are handicapped by a similar dead weight of ignorance."[27] He condemned playgoers, playwrights, and actors, and heaped particular abuse on "the earnest young writer who, far from underestimating the importance of the drama, pays it the highest compliment he can imagine by regarding it as the heaven-sent trumpet through which he is to bray his views on social problems of his own projection" (a direct attack on the didactic moralism that Beerbohm had said was "the aim of all the dramatic authors who count for anything at all to-day"). Brookfield's own view of morality in the theater was this:

> Personally I think the influence of the theatre either for good or evil is much overrated. But if a young person *could* be harmed by seeing a play, I think it would more probably be by a sombre dissertation on the right of a wife to desert a degenerate husband—or one of the many kindred topics so dear to the New Dramatist—than by the frivolous burlesque of ill-assorted marriages, such as one finds in the old French vaudevilles.[28]

Quite apart from this scarcely veiled approval of his own sort of play at the expense of Ibsen's sort, the article is a shocking display of philistinism and stupidity—the opinions of a Garrick Club Colonel Blimp. Yet one can hardly avoid inferring that it was Brookfield's public application for the Examiner's job, and a successful one. And small wonder, for though the article contains not the slightest suggestion that Brookfield recognized the drama as an art form, or as a pos-

[27] Charles H. E. Brookfield, "On Plays and Play-Writing," *National Review*, no. 345 (Nov., 1911), 429.
[28] "On Plays and Play-Writing," p. 421.

sible medium for the expression of ideas, it does repeat the "established" notions of a theater of jolly, harmless entertainment written by "harmless, necessary authors," for audiences of wholesome, thick-headed British philistines.

Brookfield's tenure of office did not begin quietly. On the day after his appointment, at the first private performance of Laurence Housman's banned play, *Pains and Penalties*, Granville Barker turned an intermission into an anti-Brookfield protest meeting, and a resolution condemning the appointment was passed. A few days later Robert Harcourt asked in the Commons that Brookfield's appointment be cancelled "in view of the character of the evidence given before the Joint Committee as to Mr. Brookfield's own plays," and another M.P. asked what considerations could have led the Lord Chamberlain to make such an appointment. The Home Secretary replied that the Lord Chamberlain had made the appointment without consulting the government (as it was his right to do) and that the considerations which moved him in making the appointment were "the special qualifications which in his judgement Mr. Brookfield possesses, by training and experience, to execute the duties of the post."[29] The Lord Chamberlain did not think that the evidence regarding *Dear Old Charlie* disqualified Brookfield, and since the Lord Chamberlain was not in any case responsible to the House of Commons, the matter was closed. The protest and the questions might, under the circumstances, be taken as a vote of no confidence in the Examiner, but it is characteristic of the operations of the Lord Chamberlain that no notice was taken, and Brookfield continued to serve as Examiner until his death in 1913.

In the early months of 1912 Brookfield imposed a number of prohibitions that brought him a good deal of publicity, all of it bad. There is no point in reviewing all of his mistakes: three examples, embodying one offense against each of the "gentlemanly" categories of politics, religion,

[29] *Hansard*, Commons, vol. 32 (Nov. 30, 1911) col. 580.

and sex will suffice to show that Brookfield, for all his experience of the theater, operated on moral principles as simple and rigid as Redford's.

In January 1912, London papers announced that the Examiner had refused a license to *The Coronation*, a play by Christopher St. John and Charles Thursby. *The Coronation* is a militantly propagandist play—militantly suffragette, militantly Socialist, militantly pacifist. It is set in the country of Omnisterre and concerns the coronation of King Henricus XVI. Henricus, appearing at the cathedral to be crowned, is stopped by a poor woman who appeals for food and for protection for the people; Henricus is touched by her plea, and uses the fact that he must be crowned before the government can function to blackmail his officials into granting relief for the poor and universal suffrage. The play is extremely topical (as when a character remarks of the peers of Omnisterre that "they have realised very sensibly that, although they may no longer make or mar their country's laws, they are irreplaceable when it comes to bearing a big sword, or a hat on a cushion"—this less than six months after passage of the Parliament Act).

The *Times*, in announcing the prohibition, reported that "the play is said to be Socialist and anti-military in its tendencies," but a week later, in a review of the first private performance, concluded that it had not been banned for its socialism or anti-militarism, but because it was anti-monarchist and thus offensive to members of the Royal Household. It was presumably also offensive to members of the House of Lords, which included, of course, the Lord Chamberlain. It is worth noting that this play, like most other banned plays, had no trouble in evading the Lord Chamberlain's ban. Since his powers did not extend to private performances, the ticket purchasers had simply to become a club—in this case they called themselves "The Coronation Club"—and the show could go on. It did go on, and after the first performance the "club" passed a resolution condemning the Lord Chamberlain. But even if the ban could have been enforced, the "danger" of the play's ideas would not have been significantly reduced, since it had already been in print for several months as a pamphlet publication of the International Suffrage Shop.

Israel Zangwill's *The Next Religion* was refused a license a few months later on religious grounds: not, as in previous cases, because it dealt with Scriptural subjects—it is set in modern England—but because it treated Christianity in a critical, unorthodox way. In the play a country vicar rejects supernatural religion and leaves the Church to found a new "religion of law." His new church is financed by an arms-maker and is successful until, at the dedication of his new temple, a religious maniac bursts in and kills the clergyman's son. The play ends ambiguously, with the clergyman and his wife asserting opposite views of life after death.

The Next Religion is a crudely didactic play, a long and clumsy debate on faith and science, that was not, in 1912, even contemporary—Huxley and the Higher Critics had played out the drama of doubt fifty years earlier. Reviewers found it dull and old-fashioned, and it is hard to imagine Edwardian audiences paying to see it in a public theater; nevertheless the Examiner refused the play a license. Ideas that were hackneyed to a critical audience were still controversial to the Examiner, especially if they were ideas about Christianity; in this case, as in many others, the stage was treated as the last bastion of an antiquated propriety that had long since been eliminated from books and from public discussions.[30]

[30] Public discussions of religious issues were not entirely free in Edwardian England. In 1908 one Harry Boulter was convicted of blasphemous libel for saying in a public speech, "I don't believe Jesus Christ ever lived," and "If I knew a man who believed in Christianity I would kill him." In 1911 there was a conviction for blasphemy in Leeds. See Hypatia Bradlaugh Bonner, *Penalties Upon Opinion: or Some Records of the Laws of Heresy and Blasphemy* (London: Watts and Co., 1912). See also E.S.P. Haynes, *The Decline of Liberty in Eng-*

The Examiner demonstrated the same sort of extravagant decorum when Eden Phillpotts presented for licensing a dramatic adaptation of his novel *The Secret Woman*. The novel had been in print since 1905 and had gone through three editions; it had been widely and favorably reviewed, and without any suggestion that it was improper. The circulating libraries, which at that time were organized and alert to suppress the slightest indecency, had raised no objection to handling the book. Brookfield nevertheless refused to issue a license. Once more a group of distinguished authors protested in a letter to the *Times*. The letter, signed by Barrie, Conrad, Conan Doyle, Galsworthy, James, Masefield, George Moore, Shaw, and Wells, among many others, testified that the authors had read the play and considered it "worthy work." They observed that Phillpotts, in all his years of novel writing, had never been criticized for impropriety, "but the moment he has the ambition to write a play in the same spirit that inspired his novels he is at the mercy of an official who knows no better than to use him thus."[31]

Five days later the Home Secretary was asked in the Commons why the play had been refused a license. McKenna replied that it could be licensed, subject to the elimination of five short passages, but he declined to specify what had caused offense: "I should be most unwilling," he said, "to read out in public passages of so objectionable a character." Forty years after, Phillpotts remembered that "the Censor demanded expulsion of two sentences that mattered nothing to the play and involved no sacrifice of art; but compliance with his direction did involve sacrifice of principle and I declined to erase the sentences."[32] But whether

---

land (London: Grant Richards, 1916). Haynes, a lawyer, argues that the discussion of heresies was allowed among the well-to-do but suppressed among the poor.

[31] *Times*, Feb. 14, 1912, p. 10.

[32] Eden Phillpotts, *From the Angle of 88* (London: Hutchinson, 1951), p. 78.

five passages or two sentences, the identity of the objectionable matter must remain a mystery to a modern reader; it
is not even possible to determine from the text whether the
Examiner objected to language or to situation. The raciest
passages are probably one in which a man's mistress is
described as a harlot and another in which a comic rustic
discusses sex and drunkenness in obvious imitation of the
Porter Scene in *Macbeth*. Neither, surely, was as improper
as *Dear Old Charlie*. The plot, to be sure, might be considered shocking, involving as it does adultery, murder, suicide, and an abnormally close relation between a mother
and her son: but so does *Hamlet*, and Phillpott's treatment
of his material is a good deal more cautious than
Shakespeare's.

Since there was no appeal from the Lord Chamberlain's
verdict, the play had to be performed privately, and once
more Barker, who was the producer, turned the private performance into a public protest. He and his wife, Lillah Mc-
Carthy, advertised that, because of the Examiner's refusal,
the play would be performed at six free matinees; they then
saw to it that lists of the distinguished peers and men of letters who attended were published in the daily papers. The
play was a notable success, and even had the distinction of
converting a member of the Joint Committee, who had previously supported censorship, to the side of the authors.
Lord Ribblesdale, having seen the play, returned to his club
and wrote the following letter to the *Times*:

> Sir,—On balance and after hearing most of the evidence,
> as a member of the Stage Censorship Parliamentary Com-
> mittee, I came, with some misgiving, to the half-hearted
> conclusion that no sufficiently strong case had been made
> out for the abolition of this authority.
>
> But I have just returned to this club from seeing *The
> Secret Woman* at the Kingsway Theatre—in the original
> text, as I am assured—and I feel most uneasy about the
> notions I then entertained.

We all know that the old Censorship moved in a mysterious way—it is the nature and essence of that kind of engine to do so—but what is going to happen now that it has been reconstructed?

I confess that I do not like the look of things, by the light of its most recent performance: the refusal of a licence to Mr. Eden Phillpotts' play. We must look out.

I remain, Sir,

Ribblesdale[33]

There is a certain arrogant candor in Ribblesdale's public recantation that is worthy of the proud peer of Sargent's great portrait—it is the sort of gesture that noblemen would make, if they were really noble. It had, unfortunately, no effect whatever on the Lord Chamberlain, who had, one must conclude, a superior arrogance.

The Secret Woman must have been refused because of the way that sex was treated in the play—either because the language was considered offensive or because it concerned adultery and the sexual rivalry of a father and his son. If the play seems altogether inoffensive now (and it does), this simply points up the fact that an extravagantly genteel standard of decorum obtained among Edwardian audiences generally, of which the Examiner was the agent but not the only representative. Even the best of the newspaper critics shared this sense of propriety to some degree. A. B. Walkley, the *Times*' dramatic critic, is a fair example; he was an intelligent and literate man, conservative and a bit cynical in his views, but also witty and urbane. He wrote of *The Secret Woman*:

There are, however, two things which, we must admit, could have been cut out, or toned down, without injury to the play. We have lately seen the *Oedipus Tyrannus* [Gilbert Murray's translation had at last, after many years, been allowed a license]; but the marriage of Oedipus and

33 *Times*, Feb. 28, 1912, p. 6.

Iocasta is ancient legend and of the very stuff of the story. *The Secret Woman* would not have suffered if Jesse Redvers had not been shown pining with love for a woman who was (though he does not know it) his father's mistress. And though Salome Westaway, in the great scene where she forces the truth on her lover's widow, would very likely have expressed it in real life much as she expresses it in the play, we could have supplied for ourselves without loss of effect something of what she insists upon in detail.[34]

This is the testimony of an intelligent Edwardian man of good will. He admires the play, finds the climactic scene "great" and the language realistic; yet he wishes that it had been "toned down" in the direction of conventional propriety. He makes no charge of indecency, but he finds too much reality shocking. It is important to recognize that the new movement in the Edwardian theater was opposed by such men as Walkley, for in the end it was through men like him that the restraints and prohibitions of Victorian England continued to work most effectively to slow, with the best intentions, the public acceptance of new theatrical ideas.

On the other hand, there were also still some Victorian sensibilities around, working less effectively, perhaps, but no less vigorously to resist change. There was, for example, Lord Newton, a peer who had fought against the Parliament Bill, and the only member of the Joint Committee on Stage Censorship to oppose any change at all in the censorship procedure. On March 10, 1912, Lord Newton rose in the Lords to speak in defense of the Lord Chamberlain, observing crustily as he did so that he was "exercising one of the few remaining privileges of this House."[35] The defense was no doubt occasioned by the authors' protest of the pre-

[34] *Times*, Feb. 23, 1912, p. 11.
[35] *Hansard*, Lords, vol. 11 (Mar. 19, 1912), cols. 506ff.

vious month; but what Lord Newton was in fact defending was not the Lord Chamberlain but his own attitudes toward ideas, art, and artists. His speech is a fascinating exposure of a mind altogether untouched by the new ideas in the world around it: distrustful of cleverness, fearful of agitation, contemptuous of art and artists, and capable of valuing achievement only in men who were members of his own world.

Lord Newton made three main points. First, there was not really a censorship problem at all: it had simply been stirred up by egotistical, clever artist-fellows. Second, the office of censorship was in the best possible hands: a peer "who had been considered good enough to govern a good many millions of our fellow-subjects, and who had also been considered good enough to form part of a Liberal Ministry, was, upon the whole, good enough to decide whether a play was or was not fit for presentation"; and his second-in-command was a knight who was not only an admirable linguist, but had filled "an important military post at two of the most fashionable cities in Europe." And third, there were two publics, one an enlightened public interested in "advanced ideas," the other the general public, and the censor existed to protect the latter from the ideas of the former.

In making this last point, Lord Newton was not being contemptuous of the general public. On the contrary, like the current Examiner, Mr. Brookfield, he rejoiced in his representative British insensitivity, as in this sentence from his speech, describing the Joint Committee hearings:

There were managers, actors, solicitors, agents, critics and dramatic authors, and the members of the two latter classes enjoyed themselves enormously, as was not improbable in view of the fact that everything had been arranged for their especial benefit, and they came with books and bags crammed with jests and epigrams and impromptus and paradoxes, which no doubt to some extent bewildered the intellect of dull and conscientious persons like myself and other noble Lords who were there to adjudicate and report upon the question.[36]

The capering jester, one need hardly add, is Shaw, with his printed volume of evidence. Lord Newton was expressing a typical established distrust of cleverness as something suspect and foreign; only dullness was altogether British and therefore trustworthy.

Lord Newton was at the extreme right wing of his party, and many members of the House of Lords must have found his views alarming (as some indicated in their replies to his speech); but there were nevertheless many influential people in England who shared them. As Lord Newton had remarked, the Parliament Bill had shorn his sort of much of their political power; and it may be just because of this loss that they defended the Lord Chamberlain so vigorously. For the Lord Chamberlain's right to judge and forbid plays must have seemed to them symbolic of the established order's right to decide what was best for that "second public," the common people, and his immunity from Parliamentary interference symbolic of their privilege. There were not, after all, many areas left in 1912 where noblesse oblige had more than ritualistic significance.

If the Lord Chamberlain is regarded as a last stronghold of direct established authority, the astonishing inflexibility of the office becomes more intelligible. Certainly it is true that the exercise of stage censorship during Edward's reign showed a Bourbon-like inability to respond to change. The attack on the office that began in 1907 forced the government to examine its practices, but after five years it had not compelled any significant reforms, and indeed in 1912 the situation was worse than ever. It is true that an advisory committee had been formed to assist the Lord Chamberlain in difficult decisions, but a glance at the composition of that

[36] *Hansard*, Lords, vol. 11 (Mar. 19, 1912), col. 507.

committee will show much that was wrong with the system, and indeed with the governing of England. For his advisors the Lord Chamberlain had appointed two members of Parliament, Sir Edward Carson and Mr. Buckmaster; one member of the theatrical profession, Sir Squire Bancroft; one professor of English literature, Sir Walter Raleigh; and the Comptroller of the Lord Chamberlain's office, Sir Douglas Dawson (he of the linguistic gifts and the experience in foreign capitals). Of these five, four were knights, and all were as established in position and outlook as one could expect. Furthermore, to expect Sir Edward Carson to judge the morality of plays in 1912, engaged as he was in the complex moralities of the Home Rule issue, was patently absurd. The committee could hardly have been regarded by the dramatic authors as anything but a further offense.

And so in June of 1912 those patiently unsuccessful appellants, the Edwardian men of letters, once more composed a letter, this time in the form of a petition to the new king, and signed this time not only by more than sixty dramatists, but also by representatives of repertory theaters and dramatic societies, by critics, musicians, artists, professors, members of Parliament, editors, and authors. The petition, after describing the development in recent years of a new and powerful British drama, submitted that the Lord Chamberlain's department had by its arbitrary and unwarranted prohibitions been grossly unjust to managers, authors, and the public, and that the present situation was "more burdensome and grievous" than before the Joint Committee met.

The petition was sent in June, but in April, hearing of the authors' plans, the Society of West-End Theatre Managers hastily forwarded their own petition to the King. As one might expect, they begged that the existing system should be preserved; the public was entitled to protection from "blasphemous or immoral plays," and the managers were entitled to protection from their old bugaboo, police interference. If the King read either petition, he must have attended to that of the managers; at any rate, nothing was done, and the censorship continued.

In fact, it not only continued, but expanded. In February 1912, operators of the new "cinematograph exhibitions" had called on the Home Secretary to request a censor of their own. Their motive was clearly the same as that of the theater managers—to protect themselves against the moral whims of local authorities. In the discussions of the Committee on Lotteries and Indecent Advertisements of 1908, cinemas had been treated as a problem comparable to indecent sporting papers and advertisements for contraceptives; control over films had therefore been left in the hands of local police. Any form of uniform control would be preferable to such uncertain freedom, and when the Home Secretary declined to provide an official censor, the operators organized and appointed their own. The man they chose for the job was G. A. Redford, the retired Examiner of Plays; he announced at once that he hoped to be able "to keep the tremendous number of cinema theaters throughout the country clean and free from any stigma even of vulgarity," and in this hope he ruled as film censor until his death in 1916.

In the years just before the war, the Examiner continued to exercise his powers with steady inconsistency. In 1913 he allowed Beerbohm Tree to produce *Joseph and His Brethren*, apparently finding nothing offensive in this Scriptural subject or in Tree's appearance as the patriarch Jacob, surrounded by a *corps de ballet* of voluptuously gyrating maidens (Granville Barker suggested somewhat unkindly, in a letter to the *Times*, that perhaps there was a connection between Sir Herbert's support of the Lord Chamberlain and the Lord Chamberlain's support of Sir Herbert). But lest this lapse might be taken as a sign of weakening censorial vigor, the Examiner forbade the Irish Players to perform a play called *The Supplanters* until they had deleted from the script the expression "a bloody brat." (Shaw may have thought that he had made the world safe for "bloody" when he put it into Eliza Doolittle's mouth, but the Examiner clearly saw every battle as a new war.) The phrase was deleted, under protest from Lady Gregory.

Then, in the summer of 1914, there was a sudden relaxing of the censor's restraining hand; in one week in July, Ibsen's *Ghosts* and Maeterlinck's *Monna Vanna*, two long-banned plays, were given their first licensed performances in London. It was as though, in that last month of peace, Edwardian England had tried to enter the modern world (England was the last country in Europe to allow *Ghosts* to be performed). But the effort came too late—decades too late, perhaps. There would be no more serious theater in London until the veterans of the war not yet begun would return home, to denounce and condemn their Edwardian elders for causing the war, and in the violence of their rejection turn away from that once-promising new movement, the Edwardian theater.

And the Lord Chamberlain? He would go on, though less oppressively, examining plays for their threats to "good Manners, Decorum, or the public Peace." Authors might write letters to editors and kings, and old committee members might congratulate themselves on their success in ending controversies by wise compromise, but in fact nothing important had changed. And indeed nothing has changed yet. Over the years the Lord Chamberlain has become a bit more lenient, perhaps, but he continues to invoke the same basic rules that governed the judgments of Redford and Brookfield. In 1965 he banned John Osborne's *A Patriot for Me* (homosexual); in 1966 he refused to license a student production of Chaucer's *Miller's Tale* for the Edinburgh Festival (racy language); in 1967 he forbade public performance of Barbara Garson's *MacBird* ("it represents a head of state of a friendly power in an unfavourable light"). The report of a Parliamentary committee on theater censorship issued in June 1967 suggests that the office of the censor may be abolished; the report recommends the repeal of the 1843 Act for Regulating Theatres, arguing—as opponents of censorship have argued all along—that sufficient laws exist elsewhere to protect the public against libellous, blasphemous, and obscene performances. If the committee's recommendation becomes law, England will have an uncensored theater for the first time in more than 400 years.

Chapter VIII

....

THE ORGANIZATION OF
MORALITY

....

The peculiar institution of the Lord Chamberlain's office made Edwardian stage censorship a strong, focussed expression of established social and moral values. The same motives were at work to control books and the other arts, though in the absence of an official censor these motives found expression in more varied and often unofficial ways. There were, indeed, evident reasons for considering books a more serious threat to English social stability than plays were: late-Victorian education acts had increased the literacy rate (or perhaps more precisely the semi-literacy rate), free libraries were increasing in number and circulating more volumes, and publishers were experimenting with cheap editions of books that had previously been restricted in circulation by price. And more books were being written that questioned conventional ideas of religion, politics, and sex. Conservative elements of society read this increased circulation of ideas as a threatening tide of immorality, which had to be fought and defeated if society was to survive.

Weapons for the battle were drawn from a well-stocked Victorian armory. There were, first of all, the laws and legal precedents which gave magistrates and local police considerable independent power to suppress indecency; and second, there were the unofficial, extra-legal forms of intimidation, which worked even more efficiently and, being unofficial, required no tiresome justifications.

The construction of the legal bases for Edwardian censorship of books and art began in the spring of 1857, when the Lord Chief Justice, Lord Campbell, rose in the House of Lords to comment on a bill to control the sale of poisons. There was, he said, a far worse poison abroad in the land uncontrolled; he referred to poisonous publications, and he urged that Parliament enact legislation to control this poison (the poison metaphor was to become so common in discussions of indecent literature that in time it almost ceased to be metaphorical and was used in ways that suggested that Balzac's *Droll Stories* might literally cause convulsions). A month later "An Act for more effectually preventing the Sale of Obscene Books, Pictures, Prints, and other Articles" was given its first reading in the House of Lords, and before the end of the session it was law—a law that was to last for a hundred years. What the law provided, chiefly, was greater power for magistrates and justices of the peace to issue search warrants and to order seized materials destroyed if they judged them to be obscene. It provided the magistrates with no definition of the offense that they were so empowered to suppress.[1]

The Obscene Publications Act was fiercely supported by the Lord Chief Justice—so much so that it came to be known as Lord Campbell's Act—but it was opposed by many thoughtful men in both Houses. Lord Lyndhurst objected that there was nothing in the bill to protect works of art, and mentioned Ovid, Correggio, Rochester, and Wycherley as possible victims of over-zealous magistrates; in the Commons Mr. Roebuck remarked that "a more preposterous bill had never been sent down from the House of Lords—and that was saying a great deal."[2] But against all reasonable concerns for individual liberties and the rights of art to exist, Lord Campbell countered with horrible examples—at one point he brandished a translation of *La Dame aux Camélias*—and the support of the Archbishop of

[1] 20 & 21 Vict. c. 83.
[2] *Hansard*, 3rd series, vol. 147 (Aug. 12, 1857), col. 1475.

Canterbury. Against the combined forces of moral indignation and ecclesiastical authority, opponents of the bill
wilted, and it passed easily. (It is an interesting coincidence
that the Divorce Bill, another Victorian legacy that plagued
progressive Edwardians, was passed at the same session.)

Ten years later, Lord Justice Cockburn, trying a case of
obscene libel, offered a definition of obscenity that became
the accepted one in law. "I think the test of obscenity," he
said, "is this: whether the tendency of the matter charged as
obscenity is to deprave and corrupt those whose minds are
open to such immoral influences, and into whose hands a
publication of this sort may fall."[3] This definition has some
virtues: it requires a degree of offense beyond mere taste-
lessness or vulgarity, and it recognizes the relevance of circumstances of publication (thus protecting—at least in
theory—serious professional works). But Cockburn's definition also has one weakness that is characteristic of his
time: it assumes that in circumstances which allow an audience of the young and innocent, such an audience must be
made the standard of purity. Cockburn may well have been
right in assuming that most of the people who read novels
in his day were vicarage-garden virgins, but he did serious
literature a disservice by writing that assumption into his
judicial opinion. We are still, a hundred years later, restoring to general circulation books that Cockburn's definition prohibited.

One other Victorian statute is relevant here. The Indecent Advertisements Act (1889) made "any advertisement
relating to syphilis, gonorrhea, nervous debility, or other
complaint or infirmity arising from or relating to sexual intercourse" an indecent publication.[4] The effects of this Act
on the intellectual life of England were not great, but its
implications are significant; it said, in effect, that *all* mention of sex in public is indecent, and this indiscriminate

[3] R. v. Hicklin (1868). L. R. 3o.B. 367 & 371.
[4] 52 & 53 Vict. c. 18.

prohibition of any reference to sexual realities explains why, in the same year, Zola's English publisher went to prison for publishing *La Terre*, and why, twenty years later, an Edwardian committee on Indecent Advertisements thought it proper to treat abortion-inducing drugs and ordinary contraceptives as indecent in the same sense.

Campbell and Cockburn provided the laws, but Victorian magistrates seem to have made little immediate use of them, and one must conclude either that the mid-Victorians were more tolerant than we are accustomed to assume or that Victorian propriety was so universal as to extend even to pornographers. In the 'eighties, however, the mood of England changed, and indecency in literature became an issue as it had never been before. One evidence of the change was the establishment in 1885 of the National Vigilance Association, an organization of unofficial censors that was to act as England's moral watchdog for the next several decades. Another and more dramatic manifestation appeared three years later in the form of a resolution in the House of Commons. The author of the resolution was a zealously evangelical M.P. named Samuel Smith. Smith's resolution read,

> That this House deplores the rapid spread of demoralising Literature in this Country, and is of opinion that the Law against obscene publications and indecent pictures and prints should be vigorously enforced and, if necessary, strengthened.[5]

The debate on Smith's resolution reveals a number of characteristic Victorian attitudes, all of which survived into the twentieth century. First, Smith reflected the dominant attitudes of the Victorian ruling class toward Europe: he blasted France for its degeneracy, and he praised Germany, where novels of "the Zola type" were forbidden. Secondly, he said specifically what Cockburn had only implied, that

[5] *Hansard*, 3rd series, vol. 325 (May 8, 1888), col. 17.

children should provide the basis for literary standards, and suggested that the Elementary Education Act had failed because it had taught children to read and then turned them out on the street where they might be exposed to a Zola novel. (Smith's point was intended to encourage censorship, but one cannot avoid noting that the same end could be achieved by reducing literacy among children.)

Another common attitude was expressed in the debate by a Mr. De Lisle, who observed complacently,

> Unfortunately, the evil affected the class of persons who were least able to resist it. Those who were rich and had comfortable homes [a class which obviously included those listening to the speaker] might keep the evil from their doors; but the poor, who had little scope for the higher enjoyments of life, naturally picked up the literature which was nearest at hand.

This is a typical example of the censoring mind at work: it is generally both paternalistic and patronizing, assuming, as De Lisle assumed, that a class exists (always including the censor) that is especially well equipped to protect other classes (in Victorian and Edwardian times the young and the poor) from evils which they could not defend themselves against. If indecent art is a poison, it is usually a poison with a class consciousness.[6] Such a conception of

6 Hansard, vol. 325, cols. 1717-1718. This attitude did not die with the Edwardians. A magistrate in 1935, trying an obscenity case against *The Sexual Impulse*, by Edward Charles, asked a witness: "Do you consider them [passages from the book charged] fit and decent for people of the working class to read?", and during the trial concerning *Lady Chatterley's Lover* the prosecuting attorney asked the jury of mid-century, middle-class Englishmen whether they would want such a book around where their servants could read it (and lost the case). See Alex Craig, *The Banned Books of England* (London, 1937), p. 69, and *The Trial of Lady Chatterley* (London: Penguin Books, 1961), p. 17.

The reference to the Dulwich Venus is from R. v. Hicklin:
For the appellant: "What can be more obscene than many pictures

censorship must necessarily have been offensive to intelligent members of the working class and (more importantly) to their spokesmen among artists and writers. As the producers of art became less oriented toward the established order, and more inclined toward liberation (as they did during the Edwardian years), they naturally objected to seeing their work screened from a working-class audience, or censored to suit an upper-class idea of what the working class should have, and so became the principal opponents of existing systems of censorship. In their opposition, the class motive was of course not the only one, but it was an important factor.

One of Mr. Smith's examples—and in fact the one circumstance that seems to have led him to offer his resolution—was the success of Henry Vizetelly in selling the novels of Zola. At the time of the resolution, Vizetelly had eighteen volumes of Zola in print and had sold—or so he said—a hundred thousand copies of *Nana* alone. None of these books had had any trouble with the authorities until in the spring of 1888 Vizetelly made the mistake of boasting in print of the extent of his sales;[7] Smith heard of the boast, and the thought that a million copies of "the worst class of French novels" had been sold in England filled him with a sense of moral crisis. It is not surprising that Vizetelly found himself in Criminal Court a few months later, charged with publishing an obscene libel titled *The Soil: A Realistic Novel*. (Vizetelly had made another mis-

---

publicly exhibited, as the Venus in the Dulwich gallery."
Mr. Justice Lush: "It does not follow that because such a picture is exhibited in a public gallery, that photographs of it might be sold in the streets with impunity."

[7] Edward [a publisher's error for Henry] Vizetelly, "My Life and Publications," *Pall Mall Gazette*, Mar. 24, 1888, pp. 2-3. Vizetelly claimed that his firm published each year "far more translations from the French and Russians than all the other London publishers put together." In addition to Zola, Vizetelly & Co. published Flaubert, the Goncourts, Maupassant, Tolstoy, Dostoevsky, Gogol, and Lermontov.

take when he attached that subtitle to the book; in 1888 "realistic" was almost an obscenity in itself, and certainly in many minds it was a promise of obscenity to follow.)

The prosecuting attorney in the case was young Herbert Asquith, who was to come up against the problem again twenty years later when as Prime Minister he had to deal (or rather avoid dealing) with stage censorship and the control of indecent publications. On this occasion he began his case by reading aloud to the jury the offensive passages from the novel in charge. Before he had finished, the jury, deeply offended, asked if it was necessary to read any more; Vizetelly took their hint and changed his plea to guilty. He was fined £100 and required on his own recognizances of £200 "to keep the peace and to be of good behaviour for twelve months."

Six months later, in May 1889, Vizetelly was back in the dock. He had turned his translations of Zola over to his son to be expurgated and had then re-issued them. The Solicitor-General argued that the expurgation had been insufficiently rigorous and added, as further evidence of Vizetelly's depravity, that he specialized in "the publication of works of this class . . . not only with respect to French novels, but also unexpurgated books." Faced with this charge, Vizetelly once more pleaded guilty, forfeited his £200, and went to prison for three months. He died shortly after, and the Vizetelly list slowly dwindled, though the firm did publish *L'Assommoir* without trouble in 1897.

One must recognize that a concentration of censorial actions took place at the end of the 'eighties—the National Vigilance Association, the Smith Resolution, the two Vizetelly trials, the Indecent Advertisements Act—though it is difficult to say just why such a concentration should occur. No doubt one explanation is simply that one act of suppression encourages another: Smith's speech in the Commons called attention to Vizetelly and made a prosecution possible; the Vizetelly trials created an atmosphere in which the Indecent Advertisements Act seemed necessary. But one still must go back to the basic question: why did Smith feel the need of starting the whole disturbance? The answer is that he felt that indecencies from abroad—and specifically from France—were threatening the stability of the Victorian social order. Smith's anxieties, as expressed in his resolution and accompanying speech, were for the nation's strength, judged not in terms of moral absolutes but by comparison with continental competitors. To Smith, England's relative power seemed at stake, and his resolution was offered to protect that power; as we shall see, a similar period of social anxiety masked as moral indignation occurred toward the end of Edward's reign.

In the mid-nineties another case reached the courts which, though it was not directly concerned with censorship, nevertheless had repercussions in the suppression of books—the trials in which Oscar Wilde was involved in 1895. In the two trials in which he was a defendant, Wilde was charged with committing acts of gross indecency with men, contrary to the Criminal Law Amendment Act of 1885. To a society that did not wish to be reminded even that "complaints or infirmities" might arise from heterosexual intercourse, the public airing of the problem of homosexuality must have seemed offensive to a degree. In Wilde's own case, society expressed its outrage by first imprisoning and then exiling him, and by suppressing his plays during his lifetime (revivals began to appear as soon as he had purified his art by dying). But these were not the only anti-homosexual effects of the case. The publishing experience of Edward Carpenter offers another and for our purposes a more significant result.

Edward Carpenter lived in Manchester, where he was active in Socialist causes, and it was there, at a Socialist-operated press that he had printed his long, Whitmanesque poem, *Towards Democracy*. In 1892 Carpenter arranged for the London firm of Fisher Unwin to take over the printing and distribution of the poem, though it was still done at the author's expense. Carpenter continued to write and publish books and pamphlets, including a series on sex and love, and this series was accepted by Unwin for publication as a book in 1895. The title was to be *Love's Coming of Age*. In January 1895, Carpenter published a new pamphlet, *Homogenic Love*, which was a defense of homosexuality; it was not to be included in *Love's Coming of Age*, but when, after the Wilde trial, Unwin heard of the pamphlet, he promptly cancelled his contract for the new book and even refused to continue to handle *Towards Democracy* (neither of which contained anything offensive). Carpenter had to go back to his Manchester press, taking the unsold copies of his poem with him. He did not find a London publisher again until 1901, and even then his position was not secure. At the beginning of the First World War, a representative of Scotland Yard called on Carpenter's publisher to advise him that complaints had been received concerning *Love's Coming of Age* and to ask him whether he would withdraw it from circulation. The book had by this time become, as Carpenter put it, "quite a little old-fashioned and demure"; his publisher refused to suppress it, and the book remained uncensored and in print.[8]

Carpenter's pamphlet had been offensive in the way that advertisements for syphilis cures were offensive—he had mentioned one of the "unpleasant" aspects of man's sexual nature in public. But one must also consider the fact that he was a Socialist and had first published his books from a Socialist press. In cases of censorship through the late Victorian and Edwardian years, it is usually the case that an offense against morality is aggravated by offensive attitudes toward property or the state. (I mean in cases of serious

[8] See Edward Carpenter, *My Days and Dreams* (London, 1916), p. 197; and Stanley Unwin, *The Truth About Publishing* (London, 1926), pp. 324-325.

works—the sort that a modern reader would wish to defend.) This is understandable if one thinks of the established order as a network of imperatives and prohibitions holding a traditional society together. From the established, inside point of view, any attempt to cut one strand of this net must loosen others, and so if the exponent of sexual knowledge is also a Socialist he is not simply a man with two separate advanced ideas but a doubled threat to the social order. From the outside, on the other hand, the very intricacy of the network makes it almost impossible to act for one kind of freedom without attacking other kinds of restraint. Very few cases of late Victorian and Edwardian censorship involve only one kind of offense against society.

A case in point is the curious legal history of Havelock Ellis' *Sexual Inversion*. This book, the first written of his *Studies in the Psychology of Sex*, was published in England and Germany in 1897. The German edition included "A Problem in Greek Ethics" and other contributions by John Addington Symonds, and carried Symonds' name on the title page, but at the last minute Symonds' executor—perhaps influenced by the notoriety of Wilde, who had just been released from prison—withdrew permission to include this material in the English edition, and it appeared with only Ellis' work. (One might say that the book had been censored before it even appeared.)[9] Ellis, never a shrewd businessman, placed the English edition of his book with a dubious publisher who called himself—at the time—De Villiers, and who operated a press variously called the University Press and Wilson and Macmillan (it had no connection either with any university or with the Macmillan Com-

[9] Although the Ellis-Symonds volume was suppressed, there is a copy in the British Museum "cupboard" of restricted books: Havelock Ellis and John Addington Symonds, *Sexual Inversion* (London: Wilson and Macmillan, 1897). The circulated version is titled *Studies in the Psychology of Sex, vol. I, Sexual Inversion* (London: The University Press, 1897).

pany, but both names sounded respectable). The book was published and received some favorable notices. Then the network principle began to work.

De Villiers had placed some copies of Ellis' book in the quarters of one George Bedborough, secretary of the English branch of the Legitimation League, an organization devoted to winning the rights of legitimate birth for bastards. (Why De Villiers thought that a book on sexual inversion would sell to League members is another, unanswerable question.) Scotland Yard became convinced that the Legitimation League harbored anarchists and sent a detective named Sweeney to investigate. Sweeney confirmed their worst suspicions, and, as he later put it, "we applied for a warrant . . . convinced that we should at one blow kill a growing evil in the shape of a vigorous campaign of free love and Anarchism, and at the same time, discover the means by which the country was being flooded with books of the 'Psychology' type."[10] Bedborough's rooms were raided, two tons of literature was seized, and Bedborough was arrested.

It is interesting to note that although the Yard saw the prosecution of Bedborough as primarily a blow against sexual and political anarchism, neither of these concerns was mentioned in the charge. Bedborough was simply accused of publishing and selling obscene libels—of which Ellis' book was the principal evidence. Many of Ellis' acquaintances thought the case could and should be contested, and a Free Press Defence Committee, including among its members Grant Allen, Shaw, and Carpenter, was formed. Sweeney's version of this committee's efforts is characteristic: "Bedborough's personal popularity made his many friends anxious to secure his release, and this fact was taken advantage of by a nice little gang of Secularists, Socialists, Anarchists, Freelovers and others anxious to ob-

[10] John Sweeney, *At Scotland Yard* (London, 1905), p. 186.

tain a little cheap notoriety by defending Ellis' book on principle."[11] There, in capitals, are the enemies of Society arraigned; note that the three recurrent categories, sex, religion, and politics, were all apparently endangered by Bedborough's friends.

In the end Bedborough defeated the committee's efforts by pleading guilty, and was let off on recognizances of £100, with a severe lecture by the presiding judge. "I am willing," this official said, "to believe that in acting as you did, you might at the first outset perhaps have been gulled into the belief that somebody might say that this was a scientific work. But it is impossible for anybody with a head on his shoulders to open the book without seeing that it is a pretence and a sham, and that it is merely entered into for the purpose of selling this obscene publication."[12] This opinion, which implied criminal motives on the part of both the publisher and author, drew a gentle rebuke from the editor of the *Lancet*: "Mr. Havelock Ellis," he wrote, "seems to us to have been badly treated in the matter," but he added that he had also been unfortunate in his publisher and concluded: "The moral of the story for scientific writers, who must often publish what would be obscene if appearing in doubtful channels or confided to dirty hands, is obvious. It is—be careful about the publisher."[13] It was because of the method of publication of Ellis' book that the editor of the *Lancet* decided not to review it: "We believed," he explained, "that the book would fall into the hands of readers totally unable to derive benefit from it as a work of science and very ready to draw evil lessons from its necessarily disgusting passages." It is not clear why this should prevent the publication of a review in a journal which circulated entirely among medical men; what the editor was in fact doing was im-

[11] Sweeney, pp. 187-188.
[12] The record of the trial is printed in Houston Peterson, *Havelock Ellis, Philosopher of Love* (Boston & New York: 1928), pp. 255-256.
[13] *Lancet*, Nov. 19, 1898, p. 1345.

posing a penalty on the book on moral grounds, refusing to assist its circulation because he disapproved of the conditions of publication. His editorial makes it clear that he did not question Ellis' motives or think that the book was inherently indecent; but he did think that "it is especially important that such matters should not be discussed by the man in the street, not to mention the boy and girl in the street," and because he doubted the motives of the publisher in this respect, he denied his readers information about an important contribution to the psychology of sex; and not only did so, but explained his action with obvious self-approval. Thus in this case Justice Cockburn's principle that circumstances of publication are a factor backfired. Ellis took his book, and the other volumes of *The Psychology of Sex* that followed, to an American publisher.

In terms of censorship actions, the twentieth century began more promisingly than the nineteenth had ended. In June of 1900 a bookseller named Isabel Thomson was arrested and charged with selling an obscene book—*The Heptameron of Margaret Queen of Navarre*. During the trial, one point of some historic importance was raised. The defense, in arguing that the *Heptameron* should be regarded as a classic and thus in that class of books "against which proceedings ought not to have been instituted" (quoting Cockburn), had referred to discussions in the *Encyclopaedia Britannica* and the *Edinburgh Review*. The Common Serjeant, summing up to the jury, countered,

> The questions for you are—(1) did the defendant publish the book in question, *i.e.* did she put it out to other people under such circumstances as to be responsible for its contents? (2) is it a book of a lewd and lascivious character manifestly calculated to corrupt public morals? We do not require the help of critics, or of antiquarian research, to help us to decide the above questions.[14]

14 R. v. Thomson (1900) 64 J. P. 456.

In his maneuver, the defense counsel was nearly sixty years ahead of his day: expert testimony on literary quality was first admitted as evidence in England in the case of *Lady Chatterley's Lover* in 1960. The Common Serjeant, on the other hand, seems very much of his time. I take it that the "we" in his last sentence above refers not simply to prosecutor plus jury, but more expansively to the class of society of which he assumes they are all a part—the men who run the country and make the moral judgments. (The same attitude is evident in the prosecution's remarks to the jury in the *Lady Chatterley* case, and it may well have inclined the jury toward the defense.)

In any case, the jury in the Thomson case ignored the Common Serjeant's plea and found for the defendant—one of the rare instances of a serious book successfully defended in a British court against an obscenity charge.[15] It would be nice if one could point to the case as a turning point in the history of British prosecution of books; but in fact it was nothing of the sort. Cases continued to be brought against serious books in the decade that followed: Balzac's *Droll Stories* was seized, and copies destroyed, on at least three occasions.

Nevertheless, although the police seemed to have no trouble at all in suppressing books almost at will, the opponents of impropriety were not satisfied and applied increasing pressures to the government to make the statutes even more efficient. Finally, in March 1908, a Joint Committee was appointed to consider two matters: Lotteries (which were increasing in England through the popular press, but need not concern us here) and Indecent Advertisements. The committee met through April, May, June,

[15] Nine years later Mrs. Thomson returned to the dock under less sympathetic circumstances. Once more the charge was the selling of obscene libels, but the texts in this case were *Maison de Flagellation* and *Le Tour du Monde d'un Flagellant*. In spite of the defendant's plea that she couldn't read French, she was convicted.

and July—ten meetings in all—and submitted a report on July 29.

The report of the hearings[16] is interesting, both for what it contains and for what it leaves out. The committee heard testimony from twenty-seven witnesses, including seven police officials, five newspaper publishers, four government officials, two clergymen, two representatives of the stock exchange, the secretary of the National Vigilance Association, and one man who can only be described as an enthusiastic amateur censor. Witnesses testified on subjects that went far beyond questions of lotteries and advertising —on indecent paintings and books, on the definition of an obscene photograph, and on methods of intimidating newsagents. The Bedborough case was once more reported from the Scotland Yard point of view ("a number of grossly obscene books, purporting to be works of a classical or medical character. . . .") , and a representative of the Home Office explained how a show of French pictures had been forced to close by threats of prosecution. No one testified on behalf of writers and painters, perhaps because no painter, writer, editor, gallery owner, bookseller, or critic was invited.

The testimony on the whole gives an impression of a collective English moral force composed of officials (Post Office, Home Office, Metropolitan Police) and persons sympathetic to officialdom (the National Vigilance Association, the clergy) , banded together to enforce standards of morality that they all took to be established and incontrovertible. Many of their assumptions now seem wrong-headed or stupid or immoral: that all contraceptives are obscene, for instance, or that the French are more given to indecency than the English, or that a magistrate who flouts the law in

16 "Report from the Joint Select Committee on Lotteries and Indecent Advertisements; with the Proceedings of the Committee, Minutes of Evidence, Appendices, and Index," *Reports from Committees*, 1908, vol. 4, pp. 375-498. (H.C. 275) .

the interests of censorship is not to be condemned. But no one questioned these assumptions during the hearings. Perhaps it is not a function of a government committee to examine its own assumptions.

The committee's recommendations were principally concerned with making the enforcement of morality more efficient. They recommended that police be given greater freedom of search, and magistrates wider summary authority, and urged the extension of the powers of the magistrates to include cases "where it would be desirable to take proceedings, but in which the matter complained of, although objectionable and indecent, cannot with any accuracy be described as obscene." They also, to their credit, recommended that books of literary merit and works of art should be exempted from prosecution. In terms of the committee's mandate, the recommendations were reasonable ones and should have pleased those persons who concerned themselves with the condition of public morals. Yet not one of the recommendations became law under the government that appointed the committee. In this case, as in the case of the committee on stage censorship of the following year, the Liberals seem to have felt that the mere appointment of a committee could be taken as a favorable gesture by the morally concerned, but that changes in the status quo would surely offend someone. And so in both cases they published the report and then spent the rest of their Parliamentary time countering demands of action and pleading the press of more urgent legislation (and with considerable justification, since the Parliament Bill, Home Rule, naval estimates, and labor problems were all at issue). The laws, in the meantime, remained what Victorian legislators had made them.

THE LAWS concerning obscenity were not the only way of imposing censorship, however. The most interesting Edwardian cases did not reach the courts at all but were dealt with in ways that were unofficial, but were nonetheless effective.

The simplest method, and a fairly common one, was a direct appeal from one member of the established order to another. A typical example occurs in the biography of William Walsham How, Bishop of Wakefield in the 'nineties. Bishop How's son had been reading a realistic novel, "sent up from Smith's library to fill up the number of volumes required" (library customers seem to have ordered their books by weight and number rather than by title, a practice that contributed to the libraries' troubles in many cases besides this one).

> Finding it impossible to go on with it, he took it down to the library [the Bishop's, not Mr. Smith's], and told his father that though not over-particular, he was quite unable to wade through the unclean matter contained in the book in question. The Bishop's sole reply was to take an envelope out of his paper-stand and address it to W.F.B. Smith, Esq., M. P. The result was the quiet withdrawal of the book from the library, and an assurance that any other books by the same author would be carefully examined before they were allowed to be circulated.[17]

The Bishop's son (and biographer) offers this story as an example of his father's high standards of purity, and also no doubt of the force of his moral censure, but one cannot help noticing that the Bishop did not read the book and that he took a somewhat unfair advantage of the fact that the head of a circulating library was also in public office. But he clearly did not doubt for an instant that a bishop, a

[17] Frederick Douglas How, *Bishop Walsham How: A Memoir* (London, 1889), pp. 343-344. Bishop How is remembered for another act of censorship; he was so disgusted with the "insolence and indecency" of one of Hardy's novels that he threw it into his fire. Or so he said; Hardy expressed polite doubt that the Bishop would have had a fire in the summer, or, if he had, that he could have burnt a thick book in it (*Later Years of Thomas Hardy*, London, 1930, p. 48).

bishop's son, and a Member of Parliament would agree on what was indecent; nor did he consider that perhaps the author of the book might have a relevant opinion, or a right to be heard. The incident illustrates the moral arrogance that goes with class censorship.

Nor did the censor have to be a bishop to get results. In 1909, for instance, a country vicar named Herbert Bull wrote to the *Spectator* to report that he had persuaded the publisher John Long to withdraw a book from circulation merely by threatening a prosecution.[18] The book had been in print for several months, had gone through five editions, and was being circulated without restriction by all but one of the circulating libraries; nevertheless, when Bull uttered his edict, Long capitulated without a struggle.

The intimidating power of the clergy was a frequent instrument of censorship, but there were others, including one that derived from the curious feature of English libel law which makes not only the publisher and author but also the printer of a libel subject to legal action. This means in practice that, for his own protection, a printer has to exercise a private censorship of the things he sets; not to do so is to chance a fine or imprisonment. An author therefore might write a book that satisfied his publisher— he might for that matter satisfy the Archbishop of Canterbury—but until he has satisfied the printer he cannot see his book in print.

The most celebrated case in which the printer-as-censor figured is that involving James Joyce's *Dubliners*, which was suppressed for eight years by the contagious nervousness of a printer. The story begins in December 1905, when Joyce, in Trieste, sent his manuscript to Grant Richards in London. In March, Richards accepted the book, signed a

[18] *Spectator*, no. 4,248 (Nov. 27, 1909), 881-82. The book in question was a romance called *The Hazard of the Die*, "by a Peer." The publisher was John Long, who had been prosecuted the preceding December for *The Yoke*.

contract, and sent the manuscript to his printer. The printer sent it back: he refused to print Joyce's "Two Gallants," and also marked in the manuscript the word "bloody" (in "Grace"), and the following passages in "Counterparts":

> a man with two establishments to keep up, of course he couldn't. . . . Farrington said he wouldn't mind having the far one and began to smile at her. . . . She continued to cast bold glances at him and changed the position of her legs often; and when she was going out she brushed against his chair and said "Pardon," in a Cockney accent. . . .[19]

Joyce reluctantly made concessions to the printer's sense of delicacy, but for every concession that he made, Richards found a new objection. Clearly the printer's fear had infected the publisher; a month after he had signed the contract, Richards confessed that he feared prosecution for publishing an indecency and wrote to Joyce that "no publisher could issue such a book." And no publisher did issue it for eight years.

Throughout his negotiations with Richards, Joyce maintained an attitude of high artistic indignation that was understandable but not strictly justified in the light of the legal circumstances. He wrote in wrath to Richards, "I cannot permit a printer to write my book for me,"[20] but under British law he had to permit it; he could only publish the moral history of his country if it satisfied the man who set the type. Nor was he quite right in attributing his troubles to the "printer's conscience"; what was in danger was the printer's purse. Richards' man was afraid of indecency; the next publisher to refuse it was worried by references to the King; and when Richards finally agreed to publish the book in 1914, he did so still in fear of prosecution, but this time

[19] Herbert Gorman, *James Joyce* (London, 1941), p. 149.
[20] Gorman, p. 155.

because Joyce had used the actual names of Dublin firms in his stories.

Dubliners went unpublished for eight years because first a printer and then two publishers feared prosecution; they were afraid because the law was imprecise and the execution of the law capricious, and they were swayed by the special pleadings of private persons. Their fears, it is worth noting, were not based on a single clear offense; "bloody" was presumably objectionable because it is blasphemous, the passages from "Counterparts" were evidently considered obscene, and the reference to the King was political. Joyce had thus offended against all three forbidden subjects—sex, religion, and politics—in a single volume. The book finally appeared, in June of 1914, in its original form—all seven bloodies, ladies' legs, King Edward, and all. It is one more example of that curious last-minute plunge toward the twentieth century that marked so strikingly that last peacetime summer.

In the case of *Dubliners*, one can't say that intimidation was imposed, exactly—it was simply there, in the peculiar form of British libel law. But there were other cases in which intimidation verging on but yet avoiding official action was used with crushing effect; one such case was that involving John Lane and *The Song of Songs*.

John Lane had established himself as a publisher in the 'nineties, when his Bodley Head press published the *Yellow Book* and books by Ernest Dowson, Oscar Wilde, John Davidson, Francis Thompson, and John Addington Symonds. In the years that followed he added the English translation of the works of Anatole France and books by Chesterton, Saki, Bennett, Wells, and Beerbohm; by the middle of Edward's reign the Bodley Head list, though rather small (Lane was virtually a one-man firm), was an impressive one. Among Lane's foreign authors was the German novelist Hermann Sudermann: in 1898 the Bodley Head had published *Regina (Der Katzensteg)*, in 1906 *The Undying Past*

(*Es War*), and in 1908 *John the Baptist* (*Der Täufer*). But when Sudermann's new novel, *Das hohe Lied*, appeared in 1909, an American firm bought world rights to the English-language version, and Lane had to be content with buying sheets of the American translation and publishing it, under a joint Bodley Head–B. W. Huebsch imprint, as *The Song of Songs*.

The novel appeared in England in October 1910. In early December, two police inspectors called at the Bodley Head to inform Lane's manager (Lane was ill) that "serious objections were raised to it in certain quarters"; what the objections were and from what quarter they came were never explained, but Lane took the visit as a warning from the Public Prosecutor that a charge of obscene libel might be brought and that if it were he would not be able to plead ignorance of the objectionable character of the book. The officers who called were particularly anxious to make it clear that, though they had read the novel in question, they were not making a charge: the Chief of the Criminal Investigation Department of Scotland Yard did not associate himself with the complaint "at the present juncture." In short, someone had said that there was something objectionable in the book, and Lane couldn't say he hadn't been warned (though he also couldn't say that he'd been told what his offense was).[21]

Looking at the novel now, one can scarcely find anything either objectionable or daring in it. It is the story of a poor girl who marries a lecherous old nobleman for his money and position, is caught in an infidelity and thrown out, lives for a time as a kept woman, and eventually, faced with a choice between a loveless marriage and suicide, chooses marriage. The style is direct and frank, but not shocking, and the morality is as sound as anyone could wish—unless one

[21] Lane's account and the texts of letters concerning the case appear as "The Publisher's Note" to Hermann Suderman, *The Song of Songs*, a New Translation by Beatrice Marshall (London, 1913).

takes the Victorian view that death should always follow upon dishonor. The book is indecent only if reality is indecent, and it could only be attacked on the ground that the truth about man's sexual nature should be suppressed. It hardly seems the right book on which to fight the battle of moral censorship.

Furthermore, Sudermann was a writer of international stature, to whom unofficial (or indeed official) suppression on an unspecified charge would be an intolerable insult. Lane could not submit to intimidation without some attempt to defend his author; yet there was no specific charge that he could fight against. Faced with this dilemma, he acted with prudence and considerable dignity. He sent copies of the novel to fourteen well-known novelists, with letters requesting an opinion on the propriety of publishing it, and at the same time he appealed to the Society of Authors for help. He also notified booksellers of the problem and offered them the option of returning their copies. And he wrote to the Chief of the CID, explaining what he had done.

In calling on the novelists Lane was attempting a defense that had previously been tried in the Thomson case, and which had been recommended by the Joint Committee of 1908—he was calling expert witnesses. The assumption behind the defense, that the testimony of artists has a special relevance to the judgment of the morality of art, is an important one, not only for the freedom of writing but for the status of the writer as well, and the fact that the principle was never accepted by Edwardian authorities reveals something of the place of the arts in Edwardian society.

The experts that Lane selected seem at first an oddly mixed group: Arnold Bennett, E. F. Benson, Mrs. W. K. Clifford, Sir Arthur Conan Doyle, Thomas Hardy, Beatrice Harraden, A. E. W. Mason, Sir Gilbert Parker, Eden Phillpotts, G. B. Shaw, May Sinclair, H. G. Wells, M. P. Willcocks, and Israel Zangwill. Lane's reasons for selecting some of these writers is obvious: Bennett had been fighting the cause of the authors against library censorship in recent issues of the *New Age*; Wells' *Ann Veronica* had recently been suppressed by the libraries; Shaw and Zangwill had opposed stage censorship in the Joint Committee hearings of the previous year, and Mason had been a sympathetic member of the committee; Hardy had suffered from ignorant censoriousness with both *Tess* and *Jude*. Of the four women, three at least are explicable choices: Miss Harraden, Miss Sinclair, and Miss Willcocks were all, in their own ways, "modern" thinkers, involved in the suffrage movement and likely to respond sympathetically to the story of a woman victimized by men. They were also all productive professional novelists who might be expected to support a novelist's right to treat reality as he saw it. Four of the fourteen writers addressed—Bennett, Phillpotts, Wells, and Miss Willcocks—had been published by the Bodley Head, and two—Hardy and Shaw—had had Bodley Head books written about them.

The replies that he received from this carefully selected group can hardly have fulfilled Lane's expectations. Some, like Shaw and Wells, performed as expected: Shaw wrote a long letter protesting that the suppression of *The Song of Songs* would be a deliberate protection of vice, and concluded with a shrewd appeal to the fear of Germany that was then widespread, "If Germany may read Sudermann and we may not, then the free adult German man will presently upset the Englishman's perambulator and leave him to console himself as best he may with the spotlessness of his pinafore." Wells was less metaphorical but equally definite: "I cannot understand anyone who is not suffering from some sort of inverted sexual mania wanting to suppress it," he wrote.

Of the others, only one—Hardy—flatly advised the suppression of the novel. Hardy was by far the oldest of the group, and, as so often in his opinions, he revealed himself to be essentially a High Victorian. "A translation of good literary taste," he wrote to Lane, "might possibly have made such an unflinching study of a woman's character acceptable in this country, even though the character is one of a somewhat ignoble type, but unfortunately, rendered into the rawest American, the claims that the original (which I have not seen) no doubt had to be considered as literature, are largely reduced. . . ." One can see, in this sentence, Hardy silently comparing Sudermann's Lilly ("ignoble") with his own Tess ("a pure woman") and deciding that, if one must make an unflinching study of a woman's character, one had better choose a virtuous woman. The remark about the rawness of the American translation is not, to an American eye, supportable in the text; perhaps what Hardy meant is simply that the translator had not modified the original words into acceptably bland English euphemisms.

All of the other writers who answered Lane's letter had favorable things to say about the novel, but most of them mixed enough condemnation or caution with their approval to give Lane cold feet. Their judgments are revealing enough of Edwardian attitudes to be worth examining. Many accepted the convention that realistic treatment of sexual matters implies a special audience: Mrs. Clifford thought *The Song of Songs* "a book . . . for the student of literature and the mature, certainly not for the young person," and added, "the student, I take it, would be able to read it in the original," a remark which seems to advise Lane to leave the book in German; and Doyle, while denying that the book was obscene, found it "unnecessarily coarse" and therefore unsuitable for any woman under forty (the age, presumably, at which coarseness begins). Mason agreed on the coarseness, and other writers found it lacking in taste or in art—suggesting a relationship between literary excellence and propriety that was still generally taken for granted; I take it that Gilbert Parker was getting at some such point when he said that the book was "lacking in the essentials of that Art which makes all things possible if not expedient."

Faced with this cautiously conventional support from his handpicked panel of judges, Lane gave in and withdrew the edition—though it had still not even been officially charged. In an apologetic letter to Sudermann he explained that he did not want to take a chance on a British judge and jury without more support than he had gotten; "the verdict," he explained sadly, "might have been an insult to literature." Lane seized upon Hardy's remark about the "rawest American" as another, less embarrassing reason for withdrawing the book: "the present translation," he told Sudermann, "is fraught with Americanisms and has been made without due regard to the genius of the two languages and the prejudices inherent in the English character." He proposed that a new translation be made by the English lady who had done the earlier Sudermann novels. Sudermann agreed, and a new version was published three years later without incident.

A comparison of the suppressed edition of 1910 with the second English version of 1913 provides a clear explanation of what "the prejudices inherent in the English character" were: they were simply the manifestations of English prudery. Lane's lady translator, Miss Beatrice Marshall, had turned a direct, particular, physical style into abstraction and evasion. For example, this sentence in the 1910 translation:

> . . . his eyes lighted up as they scanned her tall, virginal body, her hips and bosom, already beginning to show delicate curves,

became in the 1913 version

> . . . his eyes rested with satisfaction on her tall, girlish

figure, already developing the soft rounded curves of womanhood.[22]

A better example, too long to quote, occurs in the fourteenth chapter, where Lilly dances and poses naked for her old husband. The 1910 version describes the scene in erotic detail; the later version reduces it to a single cold, abstract paragraph. This is typical of the treatment that Miss Marshall gave to the entire novel; the result is a book which is not so much a translation as a bowdlerization. The American version is a full and careful translation from the German—all the erotic details are there in Sudermann's text— but the English one is too concerned with "the prejudices inherent in the English character" to attend to the character of the book.

The Song of Songs was published, but it had been delayed for three years and was finally published in an inferior translation; a reputable publisher had been intimidated; a distinguished novelist had been insulted. Yet no charge had been made, no objectionable passage identified, no accuser presented. There is a Kafka-esque mystery about the whole case that shows the quiet power that "certain quarters" wielded in Edwardian England, and the unofficial uses to which they could put the official agencies of government.

THE TENDENCY to organize in the cause of morality is a characteristic of the whole of the nineteenth century in England, from the Society for the Suppression of Vice, through whose efforts publishers of obscenities were sentenced to the pillory in the early years of the century, to the National Vigilance Association at the end; but this sort of activity seems to have reached unusual heights during Edward's reign. Through the years before the war, organizations dedicated to the improvement of other people's morals

[22] *The Song of Songs* (trans. Thomas Seltzer), London and New York, 1910, p. 9; *The Song of Songs* (trans. Beatrice Marshall), London, 1913, p. 4.

so proliferated that by 1910 there were enough in London alone to be collectively organized as the Conference of Representatives of London Societies Interested in Public Morality.[23] These groups were voluntary and unofficial, but they were nevertheless extremely powerful. They had the support of the Church of England (or at least of its more evangelical wing) and later of non-conformists and Roman Catholics; they could draw upon the Metropolitan Police for help when they needed it, and, though their membership lists seldom included any important political figures, they could count on at least a telegram of sympathetic interest from a Home Secretary whenever they staged a conference (after all, what politician could resist expressing his approval of Public Morality?). The principal leaders and patrons were from the beginning clergymen, and this never changed; a few peers and M.P.s signed later manifestoes, but none of the moral improvement movements had important support outside the churches, and no support at all from the serious intelligentsia. The success of these groups is difficult to measure; certainly they got no legislation enacted and established no permanently effective organization. What they did do was to give public voice to certain conservative, repressive attitudes, and by doing so they affected the intellectual atmosphere of the time. They were at war with the twentieth century, and it was a war that could not be won; but in the process of losing they won many skirmishes and, like the Boers, succeeded in harassing for years the enemy that they could not defeat.

The most interesting and ultimately the most publicized

[23] The organizations present included the Church of England Men's Society, the Social Purity Alliance, the Friends' Purity Committee, the Young Men's Christian Association, the Alliance of Honour, the Society for the Rescue of Young Women and Children, the London Female Preventive and Reformatory Institution, the Church Army, the White Cross League, the Salvation Army, the London Council for the Promotion of Public Morality, the National Vigilance Association, and the Southwark Diocesan Association for the Care of Friendless Girls.

of these moral organizations began in 1901 as the National Social Purity Crusade. The Crusade was sponsored by the National Vigilance Association, which had of late turned its attentions primarily to the White Slave Traffic; the new organization was intended to offer militant guidance and encouragement on wider fronts and thus to raise the general moral tone of the nation. One of the Crusade's first acts was the publication of a volume of essays, largely by clergymen, called *Public Morals*, intended to fill the need for "a sound, readable text-book, explaining the duty of the State, the Church, the Parent, and the Individual in relation to Public Morals."[24] If the book had done all this, it would be an impressive document; but what it did in fact was to repeat the conventions and evasions of High Victorian morality, while insisting that a new kind of moral crisis was at hand. It seems to have had no effect at all, and the Crusade subsided into silence for nearly eight years.

Then, on April 4, 1908, the following announcement appeared in the *Times*:

> We believe that the time is ripe for more energetic action on the part of all religious and philanthropic communities to raise the standard of social and personal purity. Not only in London, but in all great cities and towns, there is an inevitable demoralisation that can only be arrested and replaced by a higher tone through combined action. For this object the forward movement of the National Social Purity Crusade has been inaugurated, and we desire to commend to all who realise the gravity of the issue, both the crusade and its director, the Rev. James Marchant, who has already rendered to this cause most efficient service both by voice and pen.

The announcement was signed by a number of clergymen, including three bishops. The Forward Movement (henceforth it would be capitalized) for Purity had begun.

[24] *Public Morals*, ed. Rev. James Marchant (London, 1902), p. 8.

Why did these clergymen think the time was ripe? First, they could scarcely have been unaware of the activities of recent months for and against censorship; the previous year had seen the suppression of *The Breaking Point* and *Waste*, the publication of Garnett's play with its aggressive preface, and the letter of protests by the authors in the *Times*. In February 1908, the deputation of authors had called on the Home Secretary. The Joint Committee on Lotteries and Indecent Advertisements had been appointed in March and was about to begin hearings. The combatants in the Edwardian struggle between new ideas and the old order were engaged, and the Church Militant cried Ha-Ha among the trumpets, and strode into the fray.

But one must also recognize a larger, vaguer source of the Crusaders' concern. Through the early years of the century Englishmen showed a growing anxiety about what one might call the threat of Europe. The Entente Cordiale, the growth of German sea power, the European reaction to the Boer War had made the British aware both of the hostility of some European powers and of the possibility of being involved in a European war. One result of this anxiety, on the part of the more conservative elements of society, was a "moral" reassessment of England's strength. Such assessments are usually based on two assumptions: first, that moral and martial strength are related (the Galahad Concept); and second, that the standard of measurement is the manhood of the past ("Get you the sons your fathers got, / And God will save the Queen," as A. E. Housman put it). The apparent terms of reference are moral, but the real issue is social and political—as it must always be when morals are considered as a public problem. Thus it is not an accident that as English awareness of the possibility of war with Germany increased, the Crusade for Social Purity also gained momentum.

The first meeting of the new Crusade was held on November 29 in London. By this time the Joint Committee had completed its hearings and submitted its report, and the Crusade's first act was to express support for the Committee's recommendations. A resolution was also passed repeating the gist of the April announcement that the time was ripe for energetic action. In spite of this militancy, however, no line of action was proposed, and the meeting closed without giving any indication of how Public Morals were to be promoted. For a Forward Movement, it was an oddly stationary start.

A clearer notion of the Crusade's particular aims can be extracted from the writings of the Rev. Mr. Marchant, whose voice and pen had been commended by the Crusade's first supporters and who had from the beginning held the office of secretary of the movement. During 1909 Marchant published two pamphlets in support of the cause: *Aids to Purity*, a series of letters to young men, and *Social Hygienics*, an outline of his views on the problems that Purity Crusaders should deal with. *Aids to Purity* repeats the assertion that the "psychological moment" had come, but it does not suggest that Marchant had much sense of his own time (this was, after all, the year of *Ann Veronica*). His advice to young men is essentially the prudential morality of that great Victorian, Martin Tupper: think clean thoughts, take exercise and cold baths, avoid modern novels, practice abstinence, and when you marry use your "sacred relations" only to nurture "the beautiful flower of parenthood." The book is extravagantly delicate and elliptical in its treatment of the dangers that it was presumably written to prevent; it achieves the curious feat for such a work of never even mentioning the word sex or specifying any kind of sexual activity beyond the collective term "impurity," which is to be avoided.

In one of the most revealing passages in the book, Marchant brings science to the aid of morality by citing the genetic consequences of the misdeeds of one Ada York, who died about 1800, "a victim of vice." Some 700 of Ada's descendants had been traced; of these Marchant reported the following enormities:

Born out of wedlock 106
Beggars 142
Inmates of Mendicity Institutions 64
Fallen 181
Gaol-birds 69
Murderers 7

This list scarcely requires comment. The author places illegitimacy, poverty, prostitution, imprisonment, and murder on the same moral scale and attributes all these "crimes" to poor Ada's vice (which is not, of course, specified, but seems to have been sexual incontinence). The sentence that follows this catalogue is also interesting: "In 75 years these victims have cost the State in relief, prison charges, and damages, a sum of close upon £250,000."[25] In remarks like this (and the literature of the movement is full of similar statements) the Purity Crusade revealed a social bias that allied it with established wealth and privilege, and against the neglected and victimized, and which gave economic foundations to moral anxieties. Purity is economical, and presumably if everyone were pure, the tax rate would drop. It is also patriotic. Marchant quoted and requoted Doctor Saleeby, the founder of the Eugenics Society, who had written: "modern biology is teaching historians to explain such phenomena as the fall of Rome in terms of the quality of the national life";[26] this sentence is characteristically eva-

[25] James Marchant, *Aids to Purity* (London, n.d., prob. 1909), pp. 15 and 20.

[26] This was in 1909. The following year Dr. Saleeby was converted by the Webbs from his conservative eugenist's position to a Socialist one. Mrs. Webb wrote in her diary on September 4, 1910: "Perhaps one of the important results of the [Fabian Summer] School is the alliance between ourselves and Dr. Saleeby. The 'Eugenists' have always been our bitter opponents on the ground that all attempts to alter environment are not only futile but positively mischievous as such improvements in environment diminish the struggle for existence and retard

sive in its language, but I take it that since it claims the authority of biologists, it must mean that a culture can preserve itself from decline by practicing sexual restraint.

A more militant expression of this nationalistic slant appeared in the *Times* on May 31, 1911, in the form of a manifesto addressed to "the people of Great and Greater Britain" from the National Council of Public Morals. (The Council was the Purity Crusade under a new name; apparently some historian had pointed out the moral aspects of earlier crusades, or perhaps the word crusade simply suggested a too aggressive stance.)

As an example of the crusading frame of mind, the manifesto is worth quoting in its entirety.

> We, the undersigned, desire to express our alarm at the low and degrading views of the racial instinct which are becoming widely circulated at the present time, not only because they offend against the highest ideals of morality and religion, but also because they therefore imperil our very life as a nation.
>
> Many causes, old and new, are conducing to the evasion of the great obligations of parenthood, and the degradation of the marriage-tie: evidence of this being found, to some extent, in the decline of the birth-rate.
>
> Our youth of both sexes is in danger of being corrupted by the circulating of pernicious literature for which no defence can be offered—a circulation which has to-day reached an extent and developed a subtle suggestiveness without parallel in the past. This is an evil that can be controlled, and, so long as we knowingly permit it to continue, the serious consequences lie at our door.

the elimination of the unfit. Eugenics have, in fact, been used as a weapon against socialism. Dr. Saleeby, who is one of the most prominent of the apostles, now joins not only the National Committee for the Minority Report but the Fabian Society. We spent two days talking to him. . . ." From the Passfield Papers.

The situation is further aggravated by the fact that our systems of education too frequently ignore the sacred and responsible functions which confront the young on reaching maturity. The tendencies of the age make it imperative that they should be taught to entertain high conceptions of marriage, as involving duties to the future of the nation and the race. The great truth must be enforced that the racial instinct, as this term declares, exists not primarily for individual satisfaction but for the wholesome perpetuation of the human family. Such physiological knowledge should also be imparted as shall protect our youth, at any rate to some extent, from those who would seduce their innocence or trade upon their ignorance.

Certain laws of heredity and development, no less natural or divine than other laws which are universally acknowledged, must also receive due recognition, and govern our national policy. A high proportion of immorality and inebriety is due to neglect of the incurably defective-minded, whose progeny, lamentably numerous under present conditions, too frequently resemble their parents, and largely reinforce the ranks of degradation and shame. These cases must receive permanent care apart from the community, that they and posterity may be protected.

We believe that only along these lines—by raising the ideals of marriage, by education for parenthood, and by intervening to prevent degeneracy—can we cope with the demoralisation which is sapping the foundations of national wellbeing. We earnestly recommend these suggestions, therefore, to all who love the good cause, and desire to maintain through the coming time our national traditions of marriage and the home.[27]

Among the sixty-six signatories to the manifesto were eight

[27] *Times*, May 31, 1911, p. 5.

peers, an archbishop, six bishops, three M.P.s, the heads
of two Cambridge colleges and a number of distinguished
professors, the editors of the *Lancet* and *Mind*, and the
heads of the Free Church of Scotland, the Primitive Meth-
odist Conference, the Congregational Union of England
and Wales, the Wesleyan Conference, the English Presbyterians and Baptists, and "General" William Booth of
the Salvation Army. (In the cause of purity, the evangel-
icals joined with the established orders.) Only two names
in the list are at all surprising: Ramsay Macdonald and
Mrs. Beatrice Webb.

The manifesto is a clear example of the way conservative
fears interconnected and supported each other: fear of national decline; fear of the fall in the birth rate; fear of the
spreading knowledge of birth control; fear of the corrupting power of "pernicious literature"; fear of the growth of
a degenerate lower class. The fact that these anxieties appear to center on sex is incidental; sex is treated not as an
individual human drive but as a national and racial matter: the sexual instinct becomes the *racial* instinct, a phrase
that Marchant had coined in his *Social Hygienics* (1909)
as being "in some ways a more acceptable phrase than sex
attraction, because of the selfish and merely animal element not necessarily in it but which does seem to accom-
pany it."[28] The essential fear is far greater, however, than
fear of animality; it is a fear that society will change so
radically under these liberating pressures as to remove it
from the authority of the established order and of the abstractions that that order depended on: property, the family,
Christianity, class, the dominance of men. To prevent this
revolution, the manifesto proposed two solutions that,
when stripped of the cautious language, are authoritarian
and extreme: control of the minds of the young and genetic
control of the subnormal.

The publication of the manifesto was the high point of

---

[28] *Social Hygienics* (London, 1909), p. 90.

the Crusade insofar as support is concerned; it never again captured such dignitaries. Yet even at this height, certain limitations are noticeable. First, the Crusade was conceived and directed from the center of the established order; it aimed at enlisting wider support, because it had to if it was to survive and succeed, but there is no evidence that it ever spread, either to the lower social ranks or to the intelligentsia (Rider Haggard is the only artist whose name ever appears on the statements of the Public Morals movements).[29] Second, though Crusaders spoke largely of Public Morals, the expressed goals of the Crusade were fairly narrow: all were related to sexual behavior, and it is important to note that the non-sexual aspects of public morality—probity in office, financial integrity, protection of the poor, the guarantees of justice—were never mentioned. Such issues scarcely could be mentioned by members of a movement so firmly based in the established order, for the class that provided the leadership in the Moral Crusade also provided leadership in government, law, and finance.

[29] It is surprising to find Havelock Ellis among the men who wrote for the NCPM. In 1911 he wrote the first of the Council's New Tracts for the Times, *The Problem of Race-Regeneration*, with a General Introduction by the Rev. Mr. Marchant. Why Marchant considered Ellis a suitable contributor it is impossible to guess; certainly everything Ellis had written or said showed him to be an open antagonist of the Council's purposes. Ellis' motives for accepting the commission are easier to work out: he was a professional writer who supported his psychological studies by literary journeywork; but he was also a popularizer of the "New Spirit," and he must have seen this as an opportunity to defend that spirit against the threat of regimentation and repression. His pamphlet is a direct rebuttal of the principal arguments of the Council; he says flatly that the race has not degenerated, or at least that there is no evidence to support that view, he argues for the use of birth control, and he warns against the very principles that the Council represented: "We have to be on our guard—and that is our final problem, perhaps the most difficult and complex of all— lest our efforts for the regeneration of the race lead us to a mechanical and materialistic conception of a life regulated by codes and statutes, and adjudicated in law courts." [*The Problem of Race Regeneration* (London: Cassell, 1911) p. 70.]

(This is not to say that a conspiracy existed, but simply that members of a governing class tend not to question the principles by which they govern.) The Crusade therefore took the curious form of urging purity in entirely sexual terms, while finding in sexual purity and impurity far-reaching social, racial, and economic consequences, which provided the principal arguments for continence. The whole movement has a parochial quality about it; it did not offer a moral judgment of Edwardian life in the light of clear moral principles; rather it sought to marshal the vague moral pieties of a past life against the social anxieties of a fearful present. The movement failed, insofar as one can measure success and failure in such an enterprise; but it is an indication of the power of established attitudes during the Edwardian years that the Crusade for Social Purity was loud and long in its failing.

The Crusaders' most important battles were fought against what they called "pernicious literature." They generally took a firmly anti-intellectual, anti-aesthetic line—as when the chairman of the first meeting of the Crusade remarked that "he would destroy even the best form of art if he believed it was inimical to true morality"[30]—and they tended to associate literary impurity with Godlessness (the Archdeacon of London thought that poisonous literature "was encouraged by clever reviewers and Agnostics"—note also here the conservative distrust of cleverness, an attitude embodied in Lord Newton in the preceding chapter). But their most vigorous attacks were reserved for the modern novel; Marchant advised his young men, "You should yourself resolve to read no doubtful novel. . . . If you miss almost all the modern novels you will not lose much," and this categorical dismissal is typical of his followers; in all the literature of the Crusade, there is no word in defense of the novel as a possibly worthy art form.

Within a month of the Crusade's first meeting, its parent

[30] *Times*, Nov. 30, 1908, p. 16.

organization, the National Vigilance Association, had summoned a publisher, John Long, into court on charge of publishing "a certain wicked and scandalous libel in the form of a book entitled 'The Yoke,' containing divers gross and obscene matters." *The Yoke*, a novel by a writer who signed his books "Hubert Wales," takes its title and its theme from a stanza of the *Rubaiyat*:

> What! out of senseless nothing to provoke
> A conscious something to resent the yoke
>   of unpermitted pleasure, under pain
> Of everlasting penalties, if broke!

The book is about "unpermitted pleasures" and the wisdom of permitting them. The heroine, Angelica Jenour, is a forty-year-old spinster who is appointed guardian of Maurice Heelas, the son of her dead suitor. Maurice, a young man of twenty, is tortured by sexual needs, which he suppresses out of a mixture of prudent and moral motives. His friend, Christopher, suffering the same strain, succumbs to prostitutes, contracts syphilis, and commits suicide. To save Maurice from the same fate, Angelica takes him as her lover. The effects on both are salubrious; of Angelica, Wales writes:

> Her sound constitution, in spite of so many years of unnatural conditions, responded vigorously, now that the check on normal development was withdrawn, and gave her not only glowing health but rejuvenation.[31]

Later, having "borne him safely through the perilous zones between manhood and marriage," she delivers Maurice over to a clean young wife and settles down to her own "Indian summer."

The novel makes two points that were new at the time and had certainly not been made in fiction: that sexuality is a natural appetite that must be gratified for a normal,

[31] Hubert Wales, *The Yoke* (London: John Long, 1907), p. 143.

healthy life; and that women may feel sexual desire as strongly as men. Such sentiments were probably more distressing to the National Vigilance Association than the action of the novel was, though the scene in which Angelica and Maurice agree to become lovers is frankly erotic, at least by Edwardian standards. Still, one may question whether it was really "harmful to the community, and especially damaging to young people of both sexes."[32] Nevertheless, when the NVA suggested that this would be only the first of many improper novels to be suppressed, Long, no doubt thinking of his long and vulnerable list of popular romances, withdrew *The Yoke* from circulation. One odd fact is that at the time of the summons *The Yoke* had been in print for nearly two years and was in its eighth edition. It had been widely if rather gingerly reviewed, and surely a searcher after improprieties as tireless as the NVA's Mr. Coote ought to have spotted it sooner. It seems reasonable to infer that the suppression of the book at that time was a contribution to the Purity Crusade, an attempt to give the Forward Movement a little initial impetus by publicizing the triumph of virtue over gross and obscene matters. One should add, though, another possible factor; *The Yoke* had appeared as a shilling paperback the preceding June, and it is consistent with the ways of censors to assume that the book under attack was not the six-shilling hard-bound edition but the cheap one. As in other cases, cost was considered a protection of the young and the impressionable poor, and low prices and low morals were taken as related.

The Crusaders had set a more ambitious goal, however, than the suppression of occasional naughty novels; they were determined to impose a voluntary pre-censorship on virtually all English fiction by forcing the circulating libraries to judge the moral level of all books by crusading standards before putting them into circulation, and to refuse to buy any books that might be offensive to the morally

[32] Both quotations from the *Daily Telegraph*, Dec. 15, 1908, p. 14.

sensitive. The libraries were in a vulnerable position on this point: their customers were on the whole not the advanced and literary readers, but rather the provincial ladies and their daughters who liked a good read and ordered their novels from Mudie's or Smith's by the bundle. George Moore's story that his *Modern Lover* was withdrawn from circulation because "two ladies in the country" complained may be slightly exaggerated,[33] but there is no doubt that these ladies existed and that they were alert for indelicacies in their fiction. The libraries were therefore in the difficult position of having to decide whether readers (and the parents of readers, like Bishop How) would object more if a book were circulated or if it weren't. The standard practice was largely a matter of wait-and-see, with some sorting out of clear cases before books went into circulation and hasty withdrawals if complaints were made. If someone objected —particularly if that someone was a clergyman—the book would be removed from general circulation and placed under the counter, where it would remain available to the persistent. This was, of course, an expensive system; if a book were withdrawn, the library lost its fees and had to dispose of copies at a loss. Further, other libraries that had not received complaints would continue to circulate the book and might win customers by so doing.

The libraries had much to gain, then, by a uniform system of pre-circulation censorship, and they must have welcomed the advances of the Crusaders. We have the testimony of an ex-librarian that by 1908 insiders in the book trade had expected a move for library censorship for some time;[34] they were aware of "the activity of a small, self-appointed committee, consisting of one or two clergymen and others, whose knowledge of the book world and of the read-

[33] George Moore, *Literature at Nurse, or Circulating Morals* (London, 1885).

[34] "The Library Censorship," by an Ex-Librarian, *Times*, Sept. 12, 1913, p. 4.

ing public was perhaps not quite equal to their moral fervour," and of other censorious groups like the Church of England's Mothers' Union which were also pressing for censorship. In the summer of 1908 the circulating libraries had even been denounced, in the inaugural address of the President of the Sanitary Inspectors' Association, as distributors of books that were "carriers" of spiritual infection. They could therefore offer plenty of evidence that their decision to impose a common censorship upon themselves was a public-spirited response to the moral will of society.

In the late fall of 1909 the cause of censorship received two fresh bursts of publicity, which further encouraged the libraries. The first was the Report of the Joint Committee on Stage Censorship, which, while it urged some changes in the existing system, approved of censorship in general and advised the continuation of the office of Examiner of Plays. The second and more dramatic issue concerned H. G. Wells' novel, *Ann Veronica*, which was published in October. Early reviews of the book were moderate: the *Saturday Review* thought the book dwelt too much on sex, but the *Times Literary Supplement* and the *Athenaeum* reviewed it favorably (the *Athenaeum* critic thought it "astonishingly brilliant").[35] Then, on November 20, St. Loe Strachey's *Spectator* spoke, in a long anonymous review entitled "A Poisonous Book." The review is significant because Strachey was the only London editor who actively supported the Purity Crusade and because his paper, with its strong Unionist and clerical ties, was the closest thing to an official voice of Toryism in Edwardian England. Consequently, the terms in which the *Spectator* attacked *Ann Veronica* are revealing of the actual nature of conservative moral concerns. The following two paragraphs are the core of the attack:

[35] *Saturday Review*, vol. 108 (Oct. 9, 1909), 445; *Times Literary Supplement*, no. 404 (Oct. 7, 1909), 364; *Athenaeum*, no. 4277 (Oct. 16, 1909), 456.

The loathing and indignation which the book inspires in us are due to the effect it is likely to have in undermining that sense of continence and self-control in the individual which is essential to a sound and healthy State. The book is based on the negation of woman's purity and of man's good faith in the relations of sex. It teaches, in effect, that there is no such thing as woman's honour, or if there is, it is only to be a bulwark against a weak temptation. When the temptation is strong enough, not only is the tempted person justified in yielding, but such yielding becomes not merely inevitable but something to be welcomed and glorified. If an animal yearning or lust is only sufficiently absorbing, it is to be obeyed. Self-sacrifice is a dream and self-restraint a delusion. Such things have no place in the muddy world of Mr. Wells' imaginings. His is a community of scuffling stoats and ferrets, unenlightened by a ray of duty or abnegation.

We do not wish to make an appeal solely to the principles of Christianity or to the sanctions of religion, though to our own mind that appeal is the strongest and greatest of all. What we want to do on the present occasion is to ask even those whose ears are deaf to such an appeal whether they think that it is possible to build up a self-sustained and a permanent State upon the basis which underlies not only Mr. Wells's latest novel, but so considerable a section of the thinking and writing which are described as modern. . . . Unless the citizens of a State put before themselves the principles of duty, self-sacrifice, self-control, and continence, not merely in the matter of national defence, national preservation, and national well-being, but also of the sex relationship, the life of the State must be short and precarious. Unless the institution of the family is firmly founded and assured, the State will not continue.[36]

[36] "A Poisonous Book," *Spectator*, no. 4,247 (Nov. 20, 1909), 846-847. Beatrice Webb took the review to be a veiled attack on Wells' personal life.

This is the style, and these are the opinions, of Strachey, and it seems likely not only that he wrote the review but that he held it back so that it would appear in time to support a move for censorship by the circulating libraries; it must be seen as a step in the Crusaders' campaign. Certainly the review is a frank presentation of the Crusaders' principles and anxieties. The essential point is that modern thinking and writing seemed to threaten the security of the state, by questioning the standards of behavior on which the state was based. These standards were taken as mutually supporting; thus Wells, by attacking conventional ideas of female purity and male good faith, was undermining not only the institutions of marriage and the family, but also religion, national defense, and England itself. The fundamental anxiety was not for the purity of women but for a threatened social system.[37]

Strachey expanded his range in his next issue with an editorial urging the establishment of an informal committee of "sensible men of the world," who, "without making any attempt to strangle literature because it might be couched in too free terms, would at the same time know how to deal with books which were likely to have a bad effect on the body politic." The kind of men who would fit the bill, said Strachey, were "the kind of men who get returned to Parliament by the best type of constituency," and not surprisingly, since Strachey's concern was with the body politic and the preservation of the state as it existed. This bare-faced appeal for extra-legal control by politically defined censors was received by Strachey's readers with enthusiasm: the issues of the *Spectator* immediately following contain approving letters from the headmaster of Westminster School, the officers of the Girls' Friendly Society, and the president of the YMCA. But before these letters appeared,

[37] Wells, in a reply published in the *Spectator* of Dec. 4, 1909, 945, agreed that his ideas about women's rights in sexual matters were anarchistic and anti-social, but insisted that they were nevertheless moral.

and only a few days after Strachey's editorial, a more important letter was published in the *Times*. On November 30, representatives of the major circulating libraries met and formed the Circulating Libraries Association. The first official act of the Association, and the reason for its existence, was the adoption of the following letter for circulation to publishers:

Dear Sir,—A meeting of the managers of the principal London circulating libraries has been held to discuss a matter which for some time past has been causing annoyance to their subscribers and inconvenience to themselves.

We refer to the circulation by the libraries of books which are regarded as transgressing the dictates of good taste in subject or treatment. Much undeserved adverse criticism has fallen upon the libraries, who in their endeavours to avoid giving offence, have repeatedly called in such books from circulation, and in consequence have suffered considerable loss. In order to protect our interests and also, as far as possible, to satisfy the wishes of our clients, we have determined in future that we will not place in circulation any book which, by reason of the personally scandalous, libellous, immoral, or otherwise disagreeable nature of its contents, is in our opinion likely to prove offensive to any considerable section of our subscribers. We have, therefore, decided to request that in future you will submit to us copies of all novels, and any books about the character of which there can possibly be any question, at least one clear week before the date of publication. Unless time is given to us to read the books before they are published it is impossible for us to avoid that annoyance to our subscribers for which we, and not the publishers, are generally held responsible.

We trust that you will not consider that the action we are taking in this matter is in any sense an attempt on our part to become censors, and we hope that you will co-operate with us by informing us that you consent to our request.

The members further agreed to classify all books as (a) satisfactory, (b) doubtful, and (c) objectionable, and to be bound by the following rules:

" (1) They will not circulate any novel until it has been submitted for reading at least one week.

" (2) They will at once advise the other members of any doubtful or objectionable book.

" (3) That they will not circulate or sell any book considered objectionable by any three members of the association.

" (4) That they will do their best to make the distribution of any book considered doubtful by three members of the association as small as possible."[38]

It was later revealed that the circular letter and the rules were meant to be confidential; and understandably so, if one considers the implications of the plan. The libraries were proposing a lowest-common-denominator censorship for commercial reasons; they were asking for powers of pre-censorship; and they were prepared to impose this control not only on their subscribers but on the book-buying public in general (the libraries controlled about two-thirds of the shops selling new books in London). The censorship that they imposed would be secret and without appeal.

The *Times*, in a leader of the same issue in which the libraries' plan was announced, expressed its complete approval of the libraries' action to suppress "the new immorality"; support came also from Strachey's *Spectator*, the Bishop of Hereford, and the Mothers' Union. Even the Council of the Publishers' Association was surprisingly docile; it expressed its "sympathetic approval of the aim of

38 *Times*, Dec. 2, 1909, p. 12.

the Circulating Libraries Association" and only suggested that perhaps the Society of Authors should be asked in to confer on methods. As in the case of dramatic censorship, only the authors rose in defense of freedom; the first, a rather surprising leader of the controversy, was Edmund Gosse, at that time Librarian of the House of Lords, a man widely regarded as "the official British man of letters."[39]

Gosse, in a letter to the *Times* of December 3, 1909, compared the proposed censorship to the Star Chamber and called it worse than the Lord Chamberlain's censorship of the stage. He wisely observed that it would operate to suppress any book "which promotes the advance of thought in a vigorous and startling manner," and added that if it had been in effect fifty years earlier it would have prevented the circulation of *On the Origin of Species*. He particularly objected to its polite and unofficial secrecy, "the veto," as he put it, "of a secret and irresponsible committee."[40] Like the Examiner of Plays, the committee would have had no legal existence, no stated principles, and no superior court of appeal. The assumption common to both authorities is that gentlemen of position and esteem will naturally act responsibly and for the good of society; but this is only true, of course, so long as responsibility means responsibility to that part of society which esteems them. If one adds the proposition that those who deal in books have a responsibility to allow a hearing to the "new immoralities" (in Shaw's sense), then the library officials become what Gosse said they were—irresponsible.

Gosse made another important point in a later letter. The libraries existed because a large reading public existed, and initially they simply provided that public with the books it wanted. But it is an inevitable danger of such a situation—perhaps it is built in to any society in which literacy becomes general—that the vendor of ideas should be-

39 H. G. Wells, *Boon* (London, 1914), p. 78.
40 *Times*, Dec. 7, 1909, p. 6.

come the censor of ideas. By the libraries' proposal, "the reading class in this country," Gosse wrote, "resigns its literary judgement and is bound hand and foot to the good pleasure of a group of commercial gentlemen." That last phrase sounds a bit reactionary—the old class bias in England against "persons in trade"—but here it operated in defense of a traditional and right notion of literary judgment, against a crude commercial one.

Gosse's view of the libraries as "a group of commercial gentlemen" was shared by many writers and explains in part the ineffectiveness of their opposition to the censorship scheme. The people who ran the libraries were in trade, and "trade" had two connotations, both of which interfered with successful resistance to the censorship. First, there was the traditional English view that tradesmen were inferiors, with whom one did not have relations as equals; this view was slowly breaking down, especially at the top of society (the King was friendly with Sir Thomas Lipton, for example), but it was still widespread. Thus Maurice Hewlett, a powerful figure in the councils of the Society of Authors, and a writer whose books rarely acknowledge the existence of the present, opposed a resolution urging conference with the libraries on the grounds that "he thought it not only undignified but almost indecent that representative writers should discuss these matters with tradesmen; that it was not for the tradesmen to dictate their terms to the Authors—a result that might follow such a discussion—but that the Authors should, if possible, dictate terms to the tradesmen."[41] It was *not* possible, but the resolution was nevertheless defeated.

The other meaning of "trade" is that in which one speaks of "free trade" and assumes the right of a trader to deal in whatever he chooses. This meaning also appears in Society of Authors' discussions: the Society's first response to the

[41] Minutes of a meeting of the Council of the Society of Authors, Oct. 16, 1913.

libraries' letter was a resolution which observed "that it is in the discretion of the libraries to select what books they will offer to their customers,"[42] and this view of booksellers as free traders in the same sense that fishmongers and greengrocers are, recurs in later discussions. Ironically, this is an argument that the authors shared with their opponents; it was asserted again and again in defense of the libraries that they were simply exercising their rights as traders. To take this line is, of course, to ignore the essential difference —that a fishmonger does not interfere with the intellectual life of either producer or consumer if he refuses to sell bloaters.

Burdened with these restrictive views of their art and the bookseller's trade, the authors were not conspicuously successful in their war with the libraries. Nevertheless, they went on fighting censorship, expressing their opposition to suppression and their sympathies for the oppressed, and though they did not win any important victories, one must conclude that their expressions of opposition had some effect on the libraries and won some modifications of the system of censorship. This is not a contemptible achievement when one considers the forces that were massed against them.

Circulating libraries' censorship remained a subject of controversy until the war made the question obsolete by imposing general censorship. On one side were the writers —Gosse, Bennett (in a brilliant series of essays in the *New Age*), William De Morgan, Anthony Hope, the Society of Authors—and a few liberal editors like A. R. Orage of the *New Age* and Clement Shorter of the *Sphere*; on the other were the Conference of Representatives of London Societies Interested in Public Morality, the Religious Tract Society, the Mothers' Union, the Bishops of Hereford and London, the Baptist Union of Great Britain and Ireland, and a number of other groups, mainly of the Organized

42 *Times*, Dec. 7, 1909, p. 6.

Morality kind. The first reaction of these groups to the circulating libraries' announcement was approval; the second was a movement to *extend* the censorship. The Bishop of Hereford urged the firms that supplied books and periodicals to railway bookstalls to censor them, and another correspondent to the *Times* asked, "What about free libraries?" Many supporters of censorship took up the poison metaphor once more, and some took the Purity Crusade line that the circulating libraries had saved England from Decline and Fall. All agreed that the issue was primarily the literary treatment of sex: whether, as one anonymous correspondent put it, the libraries "should continue to annoy the bulk of their subscribers by supplying them with 'literature' that disgusts a healthy-minded man and brings the blush of shame to the cheek of all but unsexed women."[43] When the Conference of Representatives of London Societies Interested in Public Morality met in January 1910, they officially expressed their thanks to the Circulating Libraries' Association "for combining to prevent the circulation of immoral, objectionable, and unhealthy books professedly treating of the sex problem."[44]

Clearly, the improvement of Public Morals, as it was applied to literature, was understood by the improvers as meaning the suppression of books dealing with sex (or, as they would have preferred to put it, with the "racial instinct").[45] What in fact they succeeded in suppressing was sometimes rather different. One library told a customer that Henry James' *Italian Hours* could not be supplied because, in the opinion of the manager, the circulation of the book

[43] *Times*, Dec. 10, 1909, p. 11; Dec. 13, p. 12.

[44] *Times*, Jan. 14, 1910, p. 11.

[45] The publisher, John Murray, was one exception to this generalization. In an address to a Public Morals Conference in 1910 he said that "he believed the books of Henry George, Karl Marx, and Nietzsche had done, and were doing a great deal of harm. He would class them as noxious literature." But apparently no one else did, for there is no evidence that books by any of these writers were suppressed.

"would be detrimental to the good name our library holds for the circulation of thoroughly wholesome literature";[46] and the Education Council of the London County Council withdrew from their list of books to be given as prizes *Dombey and Son*, *Hypatia*, and *Mary Barton*—the latter because the mother of a school girl had objected to "certain graphic but unpleasant details of maternity and imputations to the discredit of the medical profession"—and put in their places *What Katy Did*, *Little Women*, and *The Rose Coloured 'Bus*.[47] Balzac's *Droll Stories* were ordered destroyed in the same haul with books called *Sexual Abuses* and *Guilty Splendour*: "it was in the interests of public decency," said the prosecution, "that they should not be sold broadcast in this form and at the low price of one shilling"[48] (another example of the principle of censorship by price).

The forces of Morality continued to organize through 1910, 1911, and 1912. There was a Public Morals Conference in July 1910, a conference of the National Council of Public Morals in Edinburgh in February 1911, and the meeting of the London Societies etc. in November of the same year. In the same month the National Council of Public Morals called a conference on "Public Morals in relation to Race Degeneration." In July 1912 a public meeting was held in Dublin to promote the crusade of the Dublin Vigilance Committee against immoral literature and pictures, and in November 1913 a National Council of Public Morals conference met to discuss "the control of reports and literature of demoralising tendency" (whatever that may mean). The presiding officer was a bishop, and the con-

---

[46] Quoted in an unsigned letter to The *Times*, Dec. 15, 1909, p. 12. The Secretary of the Circulating Libraries' Association immediately wrote that some misapprehension must have occurred, but of course such an incident could neither be proved nor disproved.

[47] Letter to the *Times*, Jan. 27, 1912, p. 11, from Violet (Lady Edward) Cecil, and reply on behalf of the Education Council from Major Cecil B. Levita, *Times*, Feb. 1, 1912, p. 6.

[48] *Times*, Dec. 29, 1909, p. 2.

ferees were publishers, editors, booksellers, and representatives of circulating and public libraries. There were, as usual, no authors present.

The principal aim of these organizations was to force Parliament into taking action against "demoralising literature." During the winter of 1911-12 two conference-inspired deputations called on the Home Secretary. The first, on December 7, was led by the Bishop of London, who immediately made it clear that he was concerned with a particular kind of literary demoralization. He told McKenna that the deputation called first for the amendment of the Indecent Advertisements Act: "There was an unnatural and ominous decrease in the English birth rate . . . and the national conscience was concerned as to the cause."[49] (The cause, in the Bishop's mind, was clearly the circulation of advertisements for contraceptives.) He also expressed his disapproval of "classical dancing" (presumably the sort of thing that Gaby Deslys was doing) and of indecent postcards and "sex novels."

A month later another deputation, organized by the Council of Public Morals, was dispatched to the Home Secretary. This group was composed of publishers (mostly of religious works), booksellers, librarians, and journalists. St. Loe Strachey introduced the deputation and stated their purpose—to urge the introduction of a bill in accordance with the recommendations of the Joint Committee of 1908. The Secretary of the Circulating Libraries Association then appealed for the support of the law in the Association's censorship campaign—a curious appeal, since the Association had been operating without legal support for more than two years.[50]

McKenna's responses to these groups were in the tradition of his party's method of handling such requests. He expressed his gratitude for their visit and his sympathy for

[49] *Times*, Dec. 8, 1911, p. 4.
[50] *Times*, Jan. 24, 1912, p. 10.

their cause. The coming session was, however, a crowded one, and it would be impossible to pass controversial legislation. The answer is exactly the one given in response to earlier queries about the other Joint Committee report, the one on stage censorship. No legislation was passed in either case during Asquith's administration, though it was eight years in office after the first report was published. No doubt the Liberals felt that on the one hand they ought to take liberal views of intellectual freedom, but that on the other hand they could not afford to offend the powerful groups behind censorship. The politic move was no move, and that is the move they made.

By the end of 1913 the Forward Movement was once more almost motionless. The Crusaders' pressure on the circulating libraries had been countered by resistance of readers and authors, and what had been intended as a system of rigid control had become merely a "blocking" of sales and circulation of the more daring books. Even the blocking was not effective. In 1913 the libraries tried to suppress three books: *The Woman Thou Gavest Me*, by Hall Caine; *The Devil's Garden*, by W. B. Maxwell; and *Sinister Street*, by Compton Mackenzie. All three were nonetheless best sellers (Caine's book sold 180,000 copies within a few months of publication; the *Times Literary Supplement* included *The Woman Thou Gavest Me* and *The Devil's Garden* in its list of the twelve most popular novels of the year). Maxwell, not content with the stimulation of his sales that the censorship had provided, took the offensive in a series of letters to the *Times* in which he made the censors appear ridiculous simply by summarizing the extremely moral plot of his novel. And there were other letters to the press through the year expressing a growing discontent with the anonymity of the libraries' judges. In the end, the system simply ceased.

The true cause of the defeat of Organized Morality was not, however, primarily the resistance of individuals; at bottom the cause was economic. The power of the libraries was already on the wane when the Crusaders applied their pressure; and indeed it seems probable that the libraries would not have submitted so readily to such a scheme if they had not been worried about the loss of trade. The censorship scheme was an attempt to reach two desirable goals at one stroke: to reduce costs by not stocking expensive, short-lived books such as memoirs;[51] and to woo back an audience that was diminishing. But that audience was not withdrawing in moral indignation; it was simply fading historically away; those old ladies in the country could never be restored to their Victorian numbers, no matter what moral standards were waved. There was no way in which the libraries could have acted wisely under the circumstances; certainly they could not risk offending the imposing powers that confronted them, but on the other hand more and more of their readers must have been asking for *Ann Veronica* and *The Woman Thou Gavest Me* or going to the public library to get them. By the beginning of the war the public libraries in England had begun to render circulating libraries unnecessary, and though they held on— W. H. Smith and Boots survived into the 1960's—they became unimportant in the economics of publishing. The War of the Circulating Libraries was not a war that anybody won: the battlefield simply disappeared. And it was entirely characteristic of the conservative powers that forced

[51] On December 18, 1909, three weeks after the announcement by the Circulating Libraries Association's plan, Clement Shorter wrote in the *Sphere*: "It is quite an open question whether this action is really due to an ambition to preserve the daughters of England from infection or whether it is instigated by a trifling commercial circumstance. It is suggested in some quarters that the libraries were very much annoyed at the demand for Lady Cardigan's *Memoirs*; 17,000 copies of this book were sold at 10s. 6d., and a very large proportion of these must have been taken by the libraries.

"The libraries do not like buying large quantities of a high-priced book, and this was particularly the case with Lady Cardigan's *Memoirs*, which was not a book that many people would wish to preserve permanently in their libraries. The book, therefore, must have had a very poor sale in its second-hand stage." "A Literary Letter," *The Sphere*, vol. 39 (Dec. 18, 1909) , 268.

the battle that they should choose a field in which history and economics were aligned against them.

Neither official censors nor moral crusaders could stop the Edwardian revolution, any more than they could stop English women from reading the novels of Wells and pamphlets on birth control. All they could do was delay and perhaps distort the literary revolution that was the natural counterpart of the social revolution. By organizing or intimidating those members of their own order who controlled the production and distribution of art—the editors and publishers, the theater managers, the booksellers and library officials—they temporarily separated the artists with new ideas from their natural audiences. It was more than a coincidence that within a few months in 1912 a group of publishers asked the Home Secretary for sterner censorship of books and the theater managers petitioned the King to continue stage censorship. One need not infer complicity between these two appeals: it is enough to note that the same fear of freedom and the same desire for the security of official approval motivated both groups.

But though censorship did not stop the Edwardian social revolution, it did twist and stunt and delay the beginnings of modern literature. Joyce in his innocence wrote to his publisher that a change from Victorian attitudes was due, "and if a change is to take place I do not see why it should not begin now"; but though Joyce could not see why, we can: the change was delayed because the forces that ordered and controlled society were not ready for change. While on the Continent the intellectual and artistic movements that define the twentieth century were developing, conservative forces in England managed to a remarkable extent to hold new ideas at bay across the Channel. Such a state of affairs could not, of course, continue, and in the last years of the Edwardian period a sudden wave of European influences swept over England and ended at last its Victorian insularity and the power of its established order.

Chapter IX

··

HUMAN CHARACTER CHANGES

··

"For anything I see," said Dr. Johnson's friend, Old Meynell, "foreigners are fools." There has probably never been
a time when the majority of Englishmen would not have
agreed with this sentiment, adding, perhaps, that most foreigners are also frivolous and lubricious rascals. Certainly
at the end of the nineteenth century this insular mixture of
contempt and suspicion was general at nearly every level of
English society. No doubt a connection exists between England's imperial expansion at that time and the intensity of
national insularity that accompanied it; as the British Empire expanded, England withdrew from political and cultural contact with other European nations. When G. J.
Goschen, First Lord of the Admiralty, said in 1896: "We
have stood alone in that which is called isolation—our
splendid isolation. . . ," he was finding virtue in the fact that
England then had no allies whatsoever and had had none
since the end of the Crimean War; but his phrase might as
aptly have been used to describe the intellectual state of
England during the latter half of the century.

What England was splendidly isolated *from* was the great
intellectual ferment on the continent. In Europe those were
the years of the new realism in French fiction, of the great
Russian novels, of Ibsen, of French symbolism and Impressionism—the years when the foundations of twentieth century art and thought were laid. In England they were the
years of the laureateship of Tennyson, who wrote of "the poisonous honey spread from France" and "the troughs of Zola-

ism," the years of the Vizetelly and Wilde trials, of the ascendancy of the Royal Academy and academic painting, and of the National Vigilance Association. In the last decade of Victoria's reign one could not buy a translation of Zola's *La Terre*, or Dostoevsky's *The Idiot* or *The Possessed* or *The Brothers Karamazov* in London, or see a public performance of Ibsen's *Ghosts*, or look at any picture by a French Impressionist in any gallery, either public or private. The new thought of Europe had been kept out of England, as though by quarantine.

What the more-or-less official view of things European was during these late-Victorian years may be suggested by the following remarks by an M.P., a government official, and two journalist-critics. If none is particularly intelligent, that is a point to be noted about the late-Victorian view of Europe.

On French fiction:

Now, he asked, were they to stand still while the country was wholly corrupted by literature of this kind. Were they to wait until the moral fibre of the English race was eaten out, as that of the French was almost. Look what such literature had done for France. It overspread that country like a torrent, and its poison was destroying the whole national life. France to-day was rapidly approaching the condition of Rome in the time of the Caesars. The philosophy of France to-day was "Let us eat and drink, for to-morrow we die." (Samuel Smith, M.P., in debate in the House of Commons, May 8, 1888) [1]

On Ibsen:

I have studied Ibsen's plays pretty carefully, and all the characters in Ibsen's plays appear to me morally deranged. All the heroines are dissatisfied spinsters who look on marriage as a monopoly, or dissatisfied married women in a chronic state of rebellion against not only the conditions

[1] *Hansard,* 3rd series, vol. 325 (May 8, 1888), col. 1719.

which nature has imposed upon their sex, but against all the duties and obligations of mothers and wives; and as for the men they are all rascals or imbeciles. (E.F.S. Pigott, Examiner of Plays for the Lord Chamberlain, in testimony to the Select Committee on Theatres, 1892)[2]

On French Impressionism:
M. Degas has a right to exist, but the other members of the school are simply contemptible. (*Pall Mall Gazette*) Nothing so freely ridiculous has surely been seen in London of late as the Impressionist paintings, drawings, and pastels, now on view at 133 New Bond-street. (*Vanity Fair*)[3]

Europe's contribution to British culture during these years was substantially confined to two popular art forms, the yellow-covered French novel and the French bedroom farce, which together served to confirm the general view of France as a nation of seducers and coquettes, from which nothing serious or decent could be expected. During the 'nineties, fin-de-siècle figures like Wilde and Aubrey Beardsley provided further evidence of French depravity by their efforts to make their postures and perversions seem Gallic. Wilde wrote *Salomé* in French (it was the only play of Wilde's to be banned by the Lord Chamberlain) and carried a yellow-backed French novel, Pierre Louy's *Aphrodite*, on his trip to jail. Beardsley illustrated *Salomé* with characteristically decadent drawings, in which he placed, carefully titled, all the books that he considered important: *Les Fleurs du Mal, La Terre, Nana, Les Fêtes Galantes, Manon Lescaut*, and one book identified only as "Marquis de Sade."

This combination of bawdy farces, wicked novels, and decadent artists defined England's version of France. It made it possible for Englishmen to regard naughtiness as a

[2] "Report from the Select Committee on Theatres and Places of Entertainment," *Reports from Committees*, 1892, vol. 8, para. 5227.
[3] Quoted in an advertisement of Dowdeswell's Gallery, *Times*, June 21, 1883, p. 2.

titillating importation from the Continent, which could be indulged in without the feeling that essential English purity was threatened or the English imagination corrupted —an exotic taste, like champagne or rocquefort, not for everyday nutrition. France itself existed in the popular imagination as a wicked foreign place to which one went to indulge in immoralities that could not be tolerated (or perhaps even achieved) in England, or to hide, as in Wilde's case, when the immoralities had been discovered. "There was the dreadful little old tradition," Henry James wrote sadly in 1908,

> one of the platitudes of the human comedy, that people's moral scheme *does* break down in Paris; that nothing is more frequently observed; that hundreds of thousands of more or less hypocritical or more or less cynical persons annually visit the place for the sake of the probable catastrophe. . . .[4]

To James, the most devoted of Francophiles, this was a stupid idea; but to less intelligent and more insular men it was simply the geographical aspect of the truth about French novels and plays. Under such circumstances it was impossible that French culture should be taken seriously in England.

As for England's Russia, it scarcely existed in the popular mind before the turn of the century. Intellectuals knew about the great novelists: Gissing, for example, read Turgenev in a German translation in the 'eighties and made the heroine of his *Crown of Life* (1899) learn Russian in order to understand *War and Peace* better, and Robert Louis Stevenson read and admired *Crime and Punishment*. Vizetelly published five volumes of Dostoevsky in the 'eighties, translated by Frederick Whishaw, and Constance

[4] Preface to *The Ambassadors*, New York Edition, vol. 21 (New York: Scribner's, 1909), pp. xiii-xiv.

Garnett's translation of Turgenev's works was completed in 1899. But the Dostoevsky was very incomplete, and both editions soon went out of print. When Maurice Baring approached a publisher in 1903 with the proposal that he translate all the novels of Dostoevsky or Gogol, he was told that there was no market for such books in England, and at that time the publisher was right. It was not until great events—the Russo-Japanese War, the 1905 Revolution, and the Anglo-Russian agreement of 1907—had thrust Russia before the English people as a nation that Russian writing began to be recognized as great.

England's relation to Europe changed during the Edwardian years, and that change is probably the most important of all the transformations that took place in England before the war. It was a change that was vigorously resisted by the conservative forces of Edwardian society, for whom Europe was an infection and isolation was splendid. The liberating movement in this case was the sum of the efforts expended to persuade the English to become Europeans, or at least to take seriously what Europeans were doing.

In this liberating movement the King himself was a powerful influence. His fondness for France was well known— so well known, indeed, that his visits to Paris made his mother nervous. As Prince of Wales he had moved freely in fashionable Parisian society (Proust made him an acquaintance of Swann, to indicate the height of Swann's social connections). As king he visited Paris both officially and privately; his state visit of 1903 had important effects on the diplomatic relations between the countries, and four years later he took his queen on a private visit to the French capital, where she felt so liberated from English convention that she dined in a public restaurant for the first time in her life. Edward was so fond of Biarritz that when Asquith became Prime Minister the King insisted that he come to France to "kiss hands" rather than spoil the royal holiday; it was the only time in English history that this ritual conferring of office took place on foreign soil.

Edward had publicly urged closer Anglo-French relations even before he became king, and he continued his efforts toward that end after his succession. He took great pride in the part he had played in the Entente Cordiale, and he obviously worked very hard to win the affections of the French people. He also used his family connections with the royal families of Russia and Germany to influence diplomatic relations with those countries, and he was the first British monarch to visit the Pope. In all these personal negotiations the King played a role that was new in English diplomatic history. What his actual contribution to the political relations between England and the continental powers was is a question for political historians; the point for the present argument is that he thought closer relations with the Continent were desirable and that he used his position and his considerable personal attractiveness to achieve that goal. To the Englishman at home with his daily paper, the reports of the King's travels must have made Europe seem closer and more real than it had ever been in Victoria's time.

Edward might be described as a "good European," and he is surely the only modern British monarch to whom that phrase could justly be applied. The ideal that the phrase suggests—of a citizenship of the entire continent, a European culture and a European peace—became common after the Second World War, but at the turn of the century not many Englishmen subscribed to it, and probably not many would have understood it. There were in fact only two groups of Edwardian Englishmen that might have produced good Europeans: the nobility and the artists. Lord Ribblesdale, for example, born at Fontainebleau and a patron of the French turf, was one; Walter Sickert, who had learned about painting from Degas and had lived and painted in

Dieppe, was another. For these two aristocracies—one an aristocracy of class, the other of vocation—national boundaries were uncomfortably and unnecessarily narrow, and English insularity was provincial and boring; but even among peers and painters, there were not many who shared this view.

Even with the support of the King, the Europeanizing of England did not progress rapidly, and there is ample evidence that know-nothing, little-Englander insularity continued strongly into the twentieth century. Most Edwardian Englishmen would probably have shared the opinion of the character in Galsworthy's *Island Pharisees* that "what's right for the French and the Russians . . . is wrong for us,"[5] and would have found comfort as well as self-approval in the idea. Certainly Edwardian censors operated on this principle: the Lord Chamberlain refused to license plays by Ibsen, Brieux, and Maeterlinck, and Strauss' *Salomé*, and official action was taken to ban books by Zola, Balzac, and Sudermann, and *The Heptameron of Margaret of Navarre*.

This conservative view of Europe dominated the decade of Edward's reign. Important political alliances were made with France in 1904 and with Russia in 1907, and these brought changes in public attitudes, but it was only after Edward's death in 1910 that contemporary movements in European culture began to penetrate English insularity. Until 1910 there was little in English cultural life to suggest that contemporary Europe existed: the fine arts and literature were emphatically English, and they were most English when they were most serious, and though there were French and German theater seasons, the plays performed were generally popular trivialities. One can detect some stirring of protest among Edwardian intellectuals and artists against this aggressive Englishness, but none that had any immediate effects.

[5] *The Island Pharisees* (London: Heinemann, 1908), p. 55.

A case in point is the Chantrey Trust issue, which stirred English art circles in 1903 and 1904. Sir Francis Chantrey was an early-Victorian academic painter and sculptor who had been successful enough at his art to leave an estate of over 100,000 pounds "for the purpose of forming and establishing a Public National Collection of British Fine Art in Painting and Sculpture executed within the shores of Great Britain." His will directed that upon the death of Lady Chantrey the income from the estate should be used in the following manner:

> . . . the clear residue of the same monies shall be laid out by the President and other members composing such Council for the time being, of the Royal Academy, or of such other society or association as aforesaid, when and as they shall think it expedient in the purchase of works of Fine Art of the highest merit in painting and sculpture that can be obtained, either already executed or which may hereafter be executed by artists of any nation, provided such artists shall have actually resided in Great Britain during the executing and completing of such works, it being my express direction that no work of art, whether executed by a deceased or living artist shall be purchased unless the same shall have been entirely executed within the shores of Great Britain. . . . And my will further is that such President and Council, in making their decision, shall have regard solely to the intrinsic merit of the works in question, and not permit any feeling of sympathy for an artist or his family, by reason of his or their circumstances or otherwise, to influence them. And I do hereby further direct that such President and Council shall not be in any manner obliged to lay out and expend in every or any one year, either the whole or any part of the monies so paid over to them for the purpose aforesaid, or any accumulations that may arise therefrom, but that the same respectively may from time

to time be reserved and accumulated for a period not ex-
ceeding five successive years, if such President and Council shall see occasion. . . .[6]

Pictures bought were to be exhibited at the annual exhibition of the Royal Academy and were to become the property
of the National Gallery, though Sir Francis expressed hope
that when the collection became sufficiently impressive the
government would provide adequate separate space in
which to exhibit it properly.

In this benefaction Sir Francis seems to have had two
things in mind: he wanted to bring together a collection of
the best British painting, and he wanted to encourage foreign artists to work in England, and thus presumably to
enrich the artistic life there. The latter, "good European"
motive was unusually enlightened for his time—and indeed
for the time that followed, as the history of his bequest shows. For the Royal Academicians to whom he en-
trusted his admirable plan were the leaders of the English
artistic establishment in an extremely conservative and nationalistic period, and they interpreted the will as it might
have read if they had written it.

Lady Chantrey died in 1875, and two years later the
Council bought its first pictures for the Trust. Purchases
were made in nearly every year following, and by 1904,
when the administration of the Trust became a public
issue, the Council had spent £60,000 on 109 works of painting and sculpture, without buying one of the slightest distinction. In those twenty-six years the Council had bought
no picture by Madox Brown, Holman Hunt, Burne-Jones,
Rossetti, or Alfred Stevens, to name a few of the established
English artists painting then who might have been considered worthy in the terms of the will. Nor, among foreign
painters who had worked in England and were therefore
also eligible, were Corot, Degas, Delacroix, Fantin-Latour,

6 *Hansard*, 4th series, vol. 136 (June 21, 1904), col. 626.

Monet, Pissarro, Sisley, or Whistler represented. Instead, the Council had bought paintings by Clark, Cockram, Dicksee, Draper, Gotch, Hacker, Hunter, MacWhirter, Rooke, Stark, Tuke, and Yeames (this is a random but entirely representative list). In 1892 the Council had paid £800 for MacWhirter's "June in the Austrian Tyrol," while passing up Whistler's "Princesse du Pays de la Porcelaine," which sold that summer for less than £500; they had also overlooked Whistler's famous portrait of his mother, which went instead to the Luxembourg for £120. One might expect that sheer accident would have provided at least one good painting among all the Chantrey purchases; but even accident was helpless against the taste of the Royal Academy. And there was little chance of a happy accident occurring, since the Council consistently bought its pictures from its own Academy summer exhibition; only five of the 109 works bought were not first shown there.

The administration of the Chantrey Trust was obviously contrary to the donor's intentions, and from time to time this fact was remarked. In 1884 Sir Robert Peel brought the issue before the House of Commons; and in the early 'nineties critics in the *Saturday Review* and the *Speaker* attacked the administration of the Trust and the quality of the purchases (George Moore, the *Speaker*'s critic, described the Chantrey collection as "one of the seven horrors of civilisation"[7]). But protest had no effect; the Council claimed its authority to interpret the will as it chose and continued on its British way.

But in 1897 an important event in English art history occurred, which altered the circumstances of the Trust and made reform necessary. In July of that year the Prince of Wales opened the building that Chantrey had imagined would eventually exist for his "Public National Collection of British Fine Art"—the Tate Gallery. The gallery had

[7] George Moore, "The New Art Criticism," reprinted in his *Modern Painting* (London: Scott, n.d.), p. 281.

been endowed by Mr. Henry Tate to provide an "English Luxembourg" in which British art could be properly collected and displayed. As a nucleus for the collection Tate had given the gallery his own pictures (largely by Royal Academicians), and to these the National Gallery added the accumulated dreariness of the Chantrey collection, as well as other unwanted odds and ends from its own crowded rooms. The collection with which the Tate opened had some fairly good pictures in it, but considered as a national and representative collection of British art it was shamefully inadequate; the pomp and publicity of its opening simply emphasized its shortcomings.

The opening of the Tate did more than simply provide another public gallery in London; it called attention, by the very terms of its establishment, to *British* art, and to *modern* art. The Tate implied the existence of a taste in painting that was neither Old Masterly (as the National Gallery was) nor academic (as the Royal Academy's Burlington House was); it may even have helped to create this sort of taste, simply by existing to satisfy it. Taste for the modern did, of course, already exist in some British art circles. The New English Art Club, for instance, a group of French-influenced British Impressionists, including Walter Sickert and Wilson Steer, had been showing as a group for ten years before the Tate opened. And there were other painters and critics who were aware of modern art, and particularly modern French art; George Moore had made his pilgrimage to Montmartre and had returned to preach a gospel of Impressionism, Realism, and Symbolism in an assertive, if sometimes rather muddled way,[8] and most of the French Impressionists had visited and painted in England and had met English painters. By the end of the 'nineties a good many painters knew that in France things were happening in the art of painting that were not dreamt of in

[8] For a vigorously critical account of Moore's art criticism, see Douglas Cooper, "George Moore and Modern Art," *Horizon*, vol. 11 (Feb. 1945), 113-130.

Burlington House. These men were not, perhaps, strictly speaking an avant-garde; their impressionism was cautious, and they did not admire innovators like Cézanne. Nevertheless, they did much to liberate English painting from the domination of the Royal Academy and to bring it into the main stream of European art, and they brought their admirers with them. "There is fortunately a growing public that knows the difference between a good and a bad picture," a correspondent wrote to the *Saturday Review* in 1903, "though I am told that there are still a few benighted people who believe that all the pictures hung in the Royal Academy are works of art."[9]

Edwardian agitation against the handling of the Chantrey funds began in 1903, when D. S. MacColl, art critic of the *Saturday Review* and later keeper of the Tate, published an article entitled, bluntly enough, "The Maladministration of the Chantrey Trust," in which he accused the Council of ignoring the will and perverting its intentions and of grotesquely mishandling its funds. "The trust," he wrote,

> is being employed purely to reward exhibitors in current Academy exhibitions, and to penalise those who do not exhibit; not to get together the best obtainable works of art executed in this country. If no change be made in this policy, it will be the duty of Parliament to step in, as Chantrey provided, and arrange "some proper scheme."[10]

MacColl's attack caused a flurry in art circles, but had no immediate effects on the Council. Academicians made sedate statements to the press, and then went on, as before, spending Chantrey money on works from their own summer exhibition: that year they bought—as if to spite MacColl by the total obscurity of their selections—two sculptures,

9 *Saturday Review*, vol. 95 (June 13, 1903), 747.
10 *Saturday Review*, vol. 95 (April 25, 1903), 517.

"Springtide of Life" by Colton and "Remorse" by Armstead, and two landscapes, "Country of Constable" by Murray and "Autumn in the Mountains" by Stokes.

In the following year the attack was renewed, this time from a more powerful and somewhat surprising quarter. One thinks of the House of Lords as being to British politics roughly what the Royal Academy is to British painting. Yet it was in that House that the question of the Chantrey Trust was raised. In June 1904, the Earl of Lytton moved that a select committee be appointed to inquire into the administration of the Trust. "My justification for bringing the question before Parliament," he said,

> rests upon three grounds—(1) the accumulation of evidence over a series of years to the effect that the intentions of the testator in this matter have not been fully carried out and that the interests of the nation and of art generally have been sacrificed to those of the particular association of artists who belong to the Royal Academy; (2) the growing tide of hostile criticism which at the present moment is finding vent in almost every organ of public opinion in the country; and (3) the continued refusal of the Royal Academy to meet any of the charges against them or to give any explanation of their conduct, and their repeated assertions that they are responsible to no one, and that probably those who criticise them are actuated by motives either of wounded vanity or jealousy.[11]

In these remarks, Lord Lytton had put his finger on the source of the problem. The Academicians, with the arrogance that characterizes such established figures, acted on the assumption that they represented all English art worth mentioning and that their role in the art world was simply to perpetuate their own kind by using the Chantrey money as prizes for academic performances. Lord Lytton, on the other hand, spoke for the view that the Royal Academy was

[11] *Hansard*, vol. 136 (June 21, 1904), cols. 624-625.

merely one association of artists, as the New English Art Club was another, and Whistler's International Society of Sculptors, Painters, and Engravers another, and that it was not by any means the most excellent. What he was moving for was a recognition that contemporary art in England was not and could not be identified with English academic art, and that in fact its immediate roots were not English at all. Like Chantrey, Lord Lytton was reaching toward Europe.

The Lords committee on the Chantrey Trust was appointed on July 1, 1904, and presented its report on the eighth of August. That report is an extremely interesting social document; few Edwardian records show so clearly the abyss of mutual distrust and misunderstanding that separated the conservative established order from the spokesmen of liberation. This division is represented in the very form of the report: the first half contains testimony of the Academicians—twelve R.A.'s, three of them knights, all rigid with dignity, all hostile toward anything modern or foreign; the second half is the testimony of the art critics— all critical of the Chantrey collection and of the Academicians responsible, and all aware of the importance of contemporary European art. No painters who were not Academicians were invited to testify, although men like Sickert, McEvoy, Steer, and Whistler were available, and no critics sympathetic to the Royal Academy (a type more difficult to find, no doubt, but surely not entirely unknown). One gets the impression that the committee had arranged its hearings intentionally to dramatize the irreconcilable gap that existed between academic taste and the advanced taste of the day.

The testimony of the Academicians provides some interesting insights into the academic mind at work. The first witness was Sir Edward Poynter, Director of the National Gallery and President of the Royal Academy. When asked on what principles the Council selected pictures for the Chantrey collection, Sir Edward replied,

At the first Council, when the first purchases were made, I think there was an idea that the Council would do well to assist young artists by purchasing works which perhaps were not of the highest standard in Art, but good work of their kind and characteristic of the artist.[12]

To this principle another Academician, Sir William Richmond, added a second:

I think he [Chantrey] had in his mind that it was the unmarketable but admirable picture that ought to be purchased for the Chantrey Bequest. Therefore I should say he had in his mind rather what might be termed, and would be termed by a certain set of critics, academic pictures, dealing either with historical or imaginative subjects, and not domestic subjects.[13]

These assertions, neither of which has any support in the Chantrey will, describe what the Council had been doing with its hundred thousand pounds—it had been using the money to buy second-rate, unsellable academic pictures from painters who showed at Burlington House exhibitions. When Poynter was asked why the Council bought only from the Burlington House shows, he replied,

The best artists come into the Academy ultimately. I do not say that there have been no exceptions, but as a general rule all the best artists ultimately become Academicians. It is natural if we want the best pictures that we should go to the best artists. . . . We have been accused of buying an inordinate number of pictures from the Academy Exhibition; but all the best pictures come to the Academy Exhibition.[14]

[12] "Report from the Select Committee of the House of Lords on the Chantrey Trust," in *Reports from Committees* (H. M. Stationery Office, 1904).
[13] "Report," p. 39.
[14] "Report," p. 33.

Among the exceptions to Poynter's rule are all the Edwardian paintings that have any place in the history of British art.

When the R.A.'s had had their day, the committee turned to the art critics, among them MacColl and Roger Fry. Their testimony was unanimously disapproving of the Chantrey collection, and more than one pointed out that the present clumsy system of choosing pictures was not only contrary to the intention of the will but seemed designed to guarantee that all purchases should be of mediocre quality. If the goal of the Trust was a public collection of the finest work done in England, this was obviously not the way to go about acquiring it. A number of critics also emphasized Chantrey's clear intention of including the works of foreign painters and mentioned French Impressionists who were eligible. Academicians, on the other hand, resisted the notion of buying from foreigners, and leaned heavily on the *British* part of Chantrey's formulation.

In the end, the Committee's recommendations were mild and reasonable: that a smaller purchase committee be appointed and that the purchasing system be liberalized to allow for accumulation of larger sums and for purchase of foreign works done in England. These were only recommendations, and no move was made to give them the force of law. The Royal Academy was to be given reasonable time to meet the committee's suggestions, but no specific time limit was set. Questions were asked in the Commons in 1907 and 1909 as to what reforms were being introduced, but government replies were, as so often with the Liberals, evasive and equivocal. "I understand, then," the questioner, Mr. Middlemore, asked in 1909, "that the Government are able to do nothing?" Mr. Hobhouse, for the government, replied, "They are not inclined to do anything."[15] And so the matter rested.

15 *Hansard*, vol. 9 (August 12, 1909) col. 649.

The artistic establishment might be said to have won the Chantrey Trust battle. No important reforms in the buying of pictures were introduced, and the Academicians were allowed to continue their academic policies. But in a more general way the battle was a defeat for the cause that the Academicians represented. Academic art implies a number of things: a kind of subject ("historical or imaginative subjects," as Richmond put it, "and not domestic subjects"), an assumption of authority as represented by official notice ("all the best artists ultimately become Academicians") , and an assumed audience of picture-buyers from the upper-middle and upper classes—the sort of people who go to the summer exhibition at Burlington House. Men like MacColl held radically different views of these matters—that no subject was circumscribed, that excellence was recognized by informed modern taste and not by membership in any group, and that the audience for modern art was the liberated, intellectual class. MacColl and his colleagues lost their battle, but they called the attention of the public to new ideas about the nature and function of art and to excellent exemplars of those ideas. They helped to define the later character of the Tate and ultimately to separate it from the purchase policies of the National Gallery so that it was free at last to become what Sir Francis Chantrey had imagined more than a hundred years earlier—a great national collection.

Chantrey had visualized a gallery of British art; the Tate in fact came to include both British and modern foreign collections. The inclusion of foreign paintings among work by modern English painters makes an important point— that at the time the Tate was being established, and the Chantrey issue was being fought, British painting was in the process of losing its national identity; it was entering the mainstream of European modernism. The Chantrey controversy helped to make this possible, but it did not bring it about promptly and simply; the Academy had won, after all, and was still a powerful conservative force, resisting the Europeanizing of England. One might say, perhaps, that the Edwardian discovery of European art began with the Chantrey controversy, but the discovery was a slow process.

In the spring of 1905 the French dealer, Durand-Ruel, brought a large collection of Impressionist paintings to London, the first exhibition of Impressionists in England in more than twenty years. Coming as it did immediately after the Chantrey inquiry, the Durand-Ruel show suggests that MacColl had succeeded in creating an audience for modern French painting; the show attracted considerable curiosity and comment, which the gallery encouraged by quoting contradictory statements from reviews in its advertisements. Attendance was good—nearly 3,000 persons on a single Saturday—but sales were poor; fewer than ten pictures were sold, most of them to foreign collectors.[16]

In reviewing this show, the *Times* critic remarked, "It is natural that after the conquest of Paris and New York M. Durand-Ruel should wish to conquer London."[17] He did not seem to think the conquest tardy, although the Impressionists had been recognized in Paris for twenty years and were even known and accepted in America. (This must be the first time that New York moved ahead of London in the development of fashionable artistic taste.) To Englishmen of some sophistication (like the *Times'* critic), the Impressionists were still, in 1905, "the leaders of the modern movement," although Cézanne, Van Gogh, and Gauguin were already in high fashion in Paris; to more conservative judges, such as the officials of the National Gallery, even the Impressionists had not yet arrived: the Na-

---

[16] In the account that follows I am indebted to Mr. Douglas Cooper's history of modern British collecting in his introduction to *The Courtauld Collection* (London: Athlone Press, 1954).

[17] *Times*, Jan. 17, 1905, p. 6.

tional Gallery refused the gift of a Degas in 1904, and declined to exhibit Sir Hugh Lane's fine collection—which included a number of Impressionists—when it was offered in 1907.[18]

The ironic consequence of this insular resistance to modern French painting is that Impressionism was old-fashioned before it was fashionable in England. While the Chantrey committee was debating the acceptability of Monet, advanced taste in France had moved on to Post-Impressionism; in Paris, Matisse was in vogue, while in London the *Times* man was still worrying over the merit of Degas. In 1908, when an international show including work by Matisse, Gauguin, and Signac appeared in London, the *Burlington Magazine's* critic concluded his review by saying,

> Impressionism in France has run its course, and salvation for the next outburst of original talent must be expected from some entirely different quarter. Our national art appears to conspicuous advantage . . . chiefly because, whether consciously or not, it has recognised this vital fact, and thereby has avoided the senile puerilities to which we have referred. France may still dominate the world of sculpture, but the immediate future of painting seems to be with Great Britain. . . .[19]

The *Burlington* was often liberal and intelligent about modern art (largely because of Roger Fry's presence in its pages), but this review, with its insular regard for "our national art" belongs to the world of the Royal Academy and the Chantrey Collection.

And then, as Virginia Woolf put it, "on or about December 1910 human character changed."[20] Mrs. Woolf's choice

[18] For a description of the Lane collection, see Lady Gregory, *Hugh Lane's Life and Achievement* (London: John Murray, 1921), appendices I & II.

[19] *Burlington Magazine*, vol. 12 (Feb. 1908), 277.

[20] In a lecture, "Mr. Bennett and Mrs. Brown," delivered May 18,

of this date was not arbitrary: the first exhibition of Post-Impressionist paintings in London opened on November 8, 1910, and ran until January 15, 1911; and she chose that occasion as an appropriate symbol of the way European ideas forced themselves upon the insular English consciousness during the Edwardian years and so joined England to the Continent. With the arrival of Post-Impressionism, phrases like "our national art" ceased to have meaning distinct from the rest of twentieth-century western art. Perhaps the show did not exactly change human character, but it marked a point at which English attitudes toward Englishness, the Continent, and tradition changed radically.

The exhibition, called "Manet and the Post-Impressionists," was selected by Mrs. Woolf's friend Roger Fry.[21] It included eight canvases by Manet, among them the magnificent "Un bar aux Folies Bergère," to suggest a continuity between the generation of the great Impressionists and the painters who followed them, but the main substance of the show was work by the pioneer Post-Impressionists: 21 paintings by Cézanne, 22 by Van Gogh, 36 paintings and 10 drawings by Gauguin. The younger Post-Impressionists were also represented, but less copiously: Matisse showed 3 paintings, 12 drawings, and 8 pieces of sculpture, Picasso showed 2 paintings and 7 drawings, and there were paintings by Derain, Friesz, Redon, Rouault, Signac, Seurat, and Vlaminck. It was by any standards a distinguished show, and a striking testimony to the taste, judgment and courage of Roger Fry. (The contents of the exhibition are listed in Appendix D.)

Some small attempts had been made to prepare the British public for the newest French art: Fry had written about it in the *Burlington* and had translated an essay on Cézanne

---

1924, at Cambridge. It was published in *The Captain's Death Bed and other Essays* (New York: Harcourt, Brace, 1950).

[21] For an account of the events surrounding the show see Virginia Woolf, *Roger Fry* (London: Hogarth Press, 1940), Ch. VII.

by Maurice Denis. There had been one previous exhibition in England that included Post-Impressionist paintings; it was held in the summer of 1910 at the Brighton Municipal Galleries (like the Normans, the Post-Impressionists entered England through a Channel port). But London had not been attempted, and as Fry prepared for his opening at the Grafton Gallery he must have had serious qualms. In anticipation of hostility he gathered what defenses he could around him. He arranged for an Honorary Committee for the show, composed of titled patrons and directors of established and respectable galleries, and published the membership in his catalogue. It is an impressive-sounding list, including the Rt. Hon. the Earl of Plymouth; the Rt. Hon. Lord Ribblesdale; the Rt. Hon. Lewis Harcourt, M.P.; Sir Charles Holroyd, Director of the National Gallery; Sir Edgar Vincent; Claude Phillips, Keeper of the Wallace Collection; James Paton, Director of the Glasgow Art Gallery; Whitworth Wallis, of the Birmingham Art Gallery; Count Kessler; Princess Von Wrede; Madame Cohen Gosschalk Bonger; M. Paul Leprieur, Keeper of the Louvre Pictures; Le Comte Robert de Montesquiou-Fezensac and M. Octave Mirbeau. Some of these notables must have been reluctant to endorse Fry's advanced taste, for the catalogue contains, in two places, the following statement:

> The ladies and gentlemen on the Honorary Committee, though they are not responsible for the choice of the pictures, by lending their names have been kind enough to give this project their general support.

The catalogue also contains an unsigned introduction written by Fry's friend Desmond MacCarthy from notes supplied by Fry.[22] It is a low-pitched, conciliatory essay; MacCarthy made no claims for the greatness of the painters shown, but simply tried to explain what they were try-

[22] According to Virginia Woolf, MacCarthy was pulled from a sickbed and strengthened with champagne to write the essay. (*Roger Fry*, p. 153).

... 327 ...

ing to do and to persuade gallery visitors to be reasonably receptive. He conceded that the show was disconcerting, and he only asked that his readers be fair and consider the nature of the problems involved before they condemned the pictures as absurd. But modest as it was, MacCarthy's essay apparently claimed too much: "Here is the catalogue," the *Times* critic wrote, "with its cleverly-written Preface, trying to prove that the pictures are not only art, but almost the only logical art, the only possible art, at the present day."[23] (In this context, "clever" is, of course, a pejorative term.)

If the function of the committee was to reassure and of the preface to conciliate, then neither succeeded. The public came to mock, and stayed to mock. Fashionable ladies strolled through the galleries, tittering, and one gentleman laughed so hard at Cézanne's portrait of his wife that he had to be led outside into the open air. Those who did not laugh, raged; to nearly everyone who visited the show it was either a joke or a gross offense. Nor were these visitors merely Edwardian philistines; many sophisticated and intelligent persons were unable to see what Post-Impressionism was all about. E. M. Forster went to the Private View and confessed that "Gauguin and Van Gogh were too much for me";[24] and Wilfrid Blunt, the poet and diplomat, wrote in his diary,

> 15th Nov.—To the Grafton Gallery to look at what are called the Post-Impressionist pictures sent over from Paris. The exhibition is either an extremely bad joke or a swindle. I am inclined to think the latter, for there is no trace of humour in it. Still less is there a trace of sense or skill or taste, good or bad, or art or cleverness. Nothing but that gross puerility which scrawls indecencies on the walls of a privy. The drawing is on the level of that

[23] *Times*, Nov. 7, 1910, p. 12.
[24] Letter to Edward Marsh, quoted in Christopher Hassell, *A Biography of Edward Marsh* (New York: Harcourt, Brace, 1959), p. 168.

of an untaught child of seven or eight years old, the sense of colour that of a tea-tray painter, the method that of a schoolboy who wipes his fingers on a slate after spitting on them. There is nothing at all more humorous than that, at all more clever. In all the 300 or 400 pictures there was not one worthy of attention even by its singularity, or appealing to any feeling but of disgust. . . . Apart from the frames, the whole collection should not be worth £5, and then only for the pleasure of making a bonfire of them. Yet two or three of our art critics have pronounced in their favour. . . . These are not works of art at all, unless throwing a handful of mud against a wall may be called one. They are the works of idleness and impotent stupidity, a pornographic show.[25]

Blunt's concern that a few critics had approved the show was repeated by the *Times* critic, who feared that Fry's endorsement would persuade lesser critics to admire it and thus insinuate Post-Impressionism into general English taste. "It is lawful," he decided,

to anticipate these critics, and to declare our belief that this art is in itself a flagrant example of reaction. It professes to simplify, and to gain simplicity it throws away all that the long-developed skill of past artists had acquired and bequeathed. It begins all over again—and stops where a child would stop. . . . Really primitive art is attractive because it is unconscious; but this is deliberate—it is the abandonment of what Goethe called the "culture-conquests" of the past. Like anarchism in politics, it is the rejection of all that civilisation has done, the good with the bad.[26]

This is the common conservative argument, that civilized man lives on the accumulations of the past, and that lib-

[25] Wilfrid Scawen Blunt, *My Diaries*, Part Two (New York: Knopf, 1921), pp. 329-330.
[26] *Times*, Nov. 7, 1910, p. 12.

eration, whether in art or in politics, is a regression to primitive anarchy. The *Times'* formulation of the case was moderate, but it shared with more extreme reactions to the show the common fear that modern art would contribute to the decline and fall of English social order.

One of the most violent—and apparently one of the most widely read—conservative attacks on the show was Robert Ross' review in the *Morning Post*. Ross was scarcely a conventional figure; he had been on the fringes of the decadent movement in the 'nineties and had befriended Oscar Wilde, and he had lived a good deal in Europe. In 1910 he was a director of London's Carfax Gallery, where men like Orpen, John, and Beerbohm showed their work. Ross' view of the Post-Impressionists was very simple—they were all mad. He took from the catalogue preface the point that Post-Impressionists saw art as an expression of their emotions, and concluded that "the emotions of these painters (one of whom, Van Gogh, was a lunatic) are of no interest except to the student of pathology, and the specialist in abnormality."[27] He described Van Gogh as "a typical matoid and degenerate," and Matisse as a madman. The whole show seemed to him an imposition on the credulity of critics and an example of chicanery and charlatanism.

The surprising thing about Ross' review is that it was received with admiring approval by many respectable artists. Charles Ricketts wrote to the *Post* the following day, applauding Ross and congratulating his countrymen on the fact that "owing to the presence in England of work which is recognised abroad, post-impressionism has not touched us, and it is a novelty to our critics." Sir William Richmond wrote a week later,

> I hope that in the last years of a long life it will be the last time I shall feel ashamed of being a painter. . . . For a moment there came a fierce feeling of terror lest the

[27] *Morning Post*, Nov. 7, 1910, p. 3.

youth of England, young promising fellows, might be contaminated there. On reflection I was reassured that the youth of England, being healthy, mind and body, is far too virile to be moved save in resentment against the providers of this unmanly show.[28]

And the next day the *Post* carried a letter from Philip Burne-Jones, suggesting that the show was "a huge practical joke organised in Paris at the expense of our countrymen."[29]

These letters shared one common idea: all saw Post-Impressionism as a foreign threat to native English art and essential English morality. Richmond's letter added some familiar embroidery to this idea—the unmanliness of the French, the virility of the English, and the image of French influence as an infectious disease threatening English healthiness. The essential opposition was not to a new technique of painting, however primitive it might seem, but to the moral and social implications of the technique, and to its foreignness.

Although the initial response of established artists and casual gallery-goers was often aggressively hostile, a sympathetic reaction began almost at once. Sophisticated men of letters like R. B. Cunninghame Graham and E. F. Benson wrote to the *Post* protesting Ross' attack and regretting that the energies of artists should be expended in abusing other artists; and the more serious British journals carried thoughtful articles on the principles of Post-Impressionism.[30] In the *New Age*, Arnold Bennett, one of England's most articulate Francophiles, took the occasion to lecture Englishmen on their insularity.

The exhibition of the so-called "Neo-Impressionists" [he wrote] over which the culture of London is now

[28] *Morning Post*, Nov. 16, 1910, p. 5.
[29] *Morning Post*, Nov. 17, 1910, p. 3.
[30] See *Burlington Magazine*, Jan. 1911 and *English Review*, Dec. 1910.

laughing, has an interest which is perhaps not confined to the art of painting. For me, personally, it has a slight, vague repercussion upon literature. The attitude of the culture of London towards it is of course merely humiliating to any Englishman who has made an effort to cure himself of insularity. It is one proof that the negligent disdain of Continental artists for English artistic opinion is fairly well founded. The mild tragedy of the thing is that London is infinitely too self-complacent even to suspect that it is London and not the exhibition which is making itself ridiculous. . . . London may be unaware that the value of the best work of this new school is permanently and definitely settled—outside London. So much the worse for London. For the movement has not only got past the guffawing stage; it has got past the arguing stage. Its authenticity is admitted by all those who have kept themselves fully awake. And in twenty years London will be signing an apology for its guffaw.[31]

Bennett and the *New Age* had the ears of the radical young, and his article, coming as it did early in the show's run, must have affected the opinions of a part of the public. Among younger artists the judgments of Walter Sickert were also profoundly influential. In 1910 Sickert was widely recognized as the best living English painter; he was also the one most obviously influenced by French masters. He was England's chief Impressionist and a leader of the Impressionist-oriented New English Art Club, and he was the liveliest art critic writing in London. Roger Fry may have had freer access to conservative and academic circles than Sickert did, but among the young and liberated Sickert's voice carried more authority, as well as a good deal more wit.

Sickert's essay on Post-Impressionism[32] is an admirable

[31] Jacob Tonson [Arnold Bennett], "Books and Persons," *New Age*, vol. 8 (Dec. 8, 1910) , 135.

[32] "Post-Impressionists," *Fortnightly Review*, vol. 89 (Jan. 1911), 79-89.

example of how an intelligent and generous critic sets about assessing an alien school. Sickert confessed that he was repelled by Matisse, and that Van Gogh set his teeth on edge, yet he recognized the importance of the exhibition, both in itself and in its influence on England. He admired Cézanne, with reservations ("an incomplete giant," he called him); he thought some of Gauguin's pictures were of "National Gallery quality at its highest level"; and though he disliked Van Gogh's methods, he recognized his "fury and sincerity" and thought *Les Aliscamps* undeniably a great picture.

Sickert's appreciation carried weight, coming as it did from an established painter of a contrary school. But his essay made a further point that was equally important; Sickert observed that the show had shock value, and that it might force John Bull to acknowledge at last what Europe had known for a decade—that a non-English school of modern art existed. Taking the Royal Academy view that the issue at stake was Englishness vs. Foreignness, he turned it around and used it as a stick to beat his insular fellow-Englishmen. "We are citizens," he wrote,

> and nothing is gained by denying it, of a country where painting forms no living part of national life. Painting here is kept alive, a dim little flickering flame, by tiny groups of devoted fanatics mostly under the age of thirty. The national taste either breaks these fanatics, or compels them to toe the line. The young English painter, who loves his art, ends by major force, in producing the chocolate-box in demand.[33]

And while Englishmen were producing chocolate boxes, the French were creating the modern European tradition; "all modern painting," said Sickert, "is founded on the French school." The value of the show was therefore simply this, that it brought Englishmen into contact with the main stream of modern European art.

[33] "Post-Impressionists," p. 79.

One can estimate the impact of Fry's show by considering the contents of his second exhibition. The 1910 show was entirely French because it had to be: there were no non-French Post-Impressionists. Less than two years later Fry's second Post-Impressionist exhibition included several Russians and nine English painters: Vanessa Bell, Frederick Etchells, Fry, Eric Gill, Spencer Gore, Duncan Grant, Henry Lamb, Wyndham Lewis, and Stanley Spencer (see Appendix D).

> The scope of the present exhibition [Fry wrote in an introduction to the catalogue] differs somewhat from that of two years ago. Then the main idea was to show the work of the "Old Masters" of the new movement, to which the somewhat negative label of Post-Impressionism was attached for the sake of convenience. Now the idea has been to show it in its contemporary development not only in France, its native place, but in England where it has liberated and revived an old native tradition. It would of course have been possible to extend the geographical area immensely. Post-Impressionism schools are flourishing, one might almost say raging, in Switzerland, Austro-Hungary and most of all in Germany.[34]

The reviews of this show make it clear that by the end of 1912 Post-Impressionism was no longer regarded as a loathsome disease. Even unfavorable notices were moderate in tone, and if the friendly reviewers were not altogether admiring, this was because the show had fewer admirable paintings than the 1910 show and more second-rate imitations.

Still, it would be inaccurate to say that Post-Impressionism had spread widely in English art circles; its geographical limits, as Fry's show demonstrates, were essentially the limits of Bloomsbury. Clive Bell, Fry's friend and

[34] "Introduction," *The Second Post-Impressionist Exhibition* (London: Ballantyne, 1912), p. 19.

disciple, had selected the English paintings in the show and had included, in addition to Fry, Bell's wife, Vanessa (who was Virginia Woolf's sister), and his friends Duncan Grant (who had painted a portrait of Mrs. Woolf) and Henry Lamb. Wyndham Lewis was represented by a portrait of Lytton Strachey, another Bloomsburyite and a cousin of Duncan Grant. Among the collectors who had lent pictures were Lady Ottoline Morrell and J. M. Keynes, also members of the circle.

The show suggests that English Post-Impressionism was less a movement than a social group, and one might argue that it became acceptable partly for that reason—anarchy seemed unlikely in Gordon Square, among men who had been to public schools. Post-Impressionism entered England more readily because it was introduced politely through the intellectual middle class. But it was a somewhat pallid Post-Impressionism for the same reason. Fry and his friends had an historical right to be shown in the second Post-Impressionist exhibition—they were Post-Impressionists, all right—but the quality of their work scarcely deserved the company it kept. It must have been something of a shock to enter the Octagon Room of the Grafton Gallery and find there, among five Cézannes, two Matisses, and a Picasso, one painting by Duncan Grant (it hung between the Matisses). But the fact that it did hang there is important, for it represents in spatial terms what had happened to English painting: it had joined Europe.

The discovery of Europe is an important aspect of English cultural history in the last years of the Edwardian era, but one must add at once that Englishmen did not direct their attention toward all of Europe: the continent they discovered included their new allies, France and Russia, but it did not include Germany. This separation of Europe into good and bad, or friend and foe, is evident in many things: for example the second Post-Impressionist exhibition included work by English, French, and Russian painters, of whom the Russians were all unknown and unimportant artists, but it did not include paintings by Kandinsky or Kokoschka; and in the London theater the seasons of German drama, which had been annual events during the early years of the century, virtually stopped after 1906.

Russia in particular was discovered and extravagantly admired during those years. Russian literature, Russian modes of dress, Russian drama, Russian opera, and Russian ballet all had sudden vogues between 1910 and 1914. In one form or another, Russian influences reached most levels of English life; intellectuals discovered Dostoevsky, music-hall gallery goers fell in love with Pavlova, and society ladies wore dresses inspired by Bakst's ballet designs. Alexandra, the Queen Mother, so admired Nijinsky that she always moved from her box to an orchestra seat for performances of *Le Spectre de la Rose* so that she could see the great final leap better. Russia, it seemed, offered something for everybody.

The great Russian novelists were not, of course, unknown to English readers in 1910. The generation of writers that included James and Conrad—the men who had brought the idea of the novel as an art-form to England—had taken Turgenev in particular as their example; he was for them the superlative example of the artist in fiction—formal, sensitive, and controlled. Dostoevsky they considered the antithesis of Turgenev, with all Turgenev's artistry turned to disorder: James thought Dostoevsky's novels "fluid puddings," and Conrad regretted that Constance Garnett had wasted her time in translating them.[35]

But in the years before the war, Russian reputations shifted. Tolstoy and Turgenev declined in popularity, and Dostoevsky became the hero of a cult. The change be-

[35] Henry James, *Letters*, ed. Lubbock (New York: Scribner's, 1920), vol. 2, p. 237; Edward Garnett, ed., *Letters from Conrad 1895-1924* (London: Nonesuch Press, 1928), pp. 260-261.

gan in 1910, when Arnold Bennett wrote admiringly of *The Brothers* in the *New Age*. He had read it in a bad, incomplete French translation (it had never been translated into English); nevertheless he called it "one of the supreme marvels of the world."[36] Two years later Mrs. Garnett's translation appeared and immediately became a kind of holy book for the younger generation. Writers like Middleton Murry, Katherine Mansfield, and Frank Swinnerton made Dostoevsky their idol and declared *The Brothers* the greatest novel ever written.[37]

As in the case of Impressionists vs. Post-Impressionists, this change of taste was fundamentally a change of generations. The older writers derived their ideas of the novel from Turgenev and Flaubert and thought Dostoevsky formless and emotional; the younger writers found in Dostoevsky a link between literature and other liberating movements that engaged their interests—the new psychology, the revived interest in spiritual and mystical ideas, and the new experimental forms in the other arts. The very elements in the novels that repelled their elders attracted them.

At about the same time Englishmen began to be aware of Chekhov. There had been translations of his stories before this, but they had not attracted much attention, and he did not become known until 1911, when the Stage Society performed *The Cherry Orchard* for the first time in London. The play was not a success; half the audience walked out of the first performance, bored, indignant, or simply baffled, and the reviews were hostile and uncom-

[36] Jacob Tonson, "Books and Persons," *New Age*, vol. 7 (March 31, 1910), 519.

[37] Virginia Woolf considered the influence of Mrs. Garnett's translations an important factor in the change from the Victorian novel to the modern novel in England. "After reading *Crime and Punishment* and *The Idiot*, how could any young novelist believe in 'characters' as the Victorians had painted them?" "Mr. Bennett and Mrs. Brown," *Nation and Athenaeum*, vol. 34 (Dec. 1, 1923), 342. This is an earlier version of the more celebrated essay of the same title.

prehending. The *Times* took a familiar conservative position:

> Though Anton Chekhov's comedy may be a harmonious work of art, presented at home in its own atmosphere before people who know all about, if they do not actually live, the life it depicts, Mrs. Edward Garnett's *Cherry Orchard* cannot but strike an English audience as something queer, outlandish, even silly.[38]

It was left for Bennett—who sometimes seems to have been the only understanding critic in London—to explain the relevance of the play to English society, and to scold the audience for its collective stupidity.

> No such persons, I admit, exist in England; but then this play happens to be concerned with Russia, and even the men's costumes in it are appalling. Moreover, persons equally ridiculous and futile do exist in England, and by the hundred thousand. . . . Take the play in its entirety, and it is one of the most savage and convincing satires on a whole society that was ever seen in a theatre. It is a terrible play. It is a thoroughly unpleasant splendid play. And I am delighted that a fraction of London has had to swallow the pill.[39]

Other Chekhov plays were done in London—*The Sea Gull* in 1912 and *Uncle Vanya* in 1914—and two volumes of translated plays were published, but when the war came Chekhov was still relatively unknown except among intellectuals. At a time when Russian dance and Russian opera were drawing large and admiring crowds, his plays did not engage the popular imagination, but a few perceptive minds recognized the bitter relevance of his writing to the English scene. When Shaw wrote *Heartbreak House*, his denunciation of pre-war society, he called it "A Fantasia in

[38] *Times*, May 30, 1911, p. 13.
[39] *New Age*, vol. 9 (June 8, 1911), 132.

the Russian manner on English scenes," and made it clear in his preface that he had made Chekhov his model:

Chekhov's plays [he wrote], being less lucrative than swings and roundabouts, got no further in England, where theatres are only ordinary commercial affairs, than a couple of performances by the Stage Society. We stared and said, "How Russian!" They did not strike me in that way. Just as Ibsen's intensely Norwegian plays exactly fitted every middle and professional class suburb in Europe, these intensely Russian plays fitted all the country houses in Europe in which the pleasures of music, art, literature, and the theatre had supplanted hunting, shooting, fishing, flirting, eating, and drinking. The same nice people, the same utter futility.[40]

To men like Bennett and Shaw, Chekhov was more than a great writer; he was a great European prophet, who saw the fall of *Heartbreak House* before it came.

While French Post-Impressionism and Russian literature were absorbing English intellectuals, another European art form was entering England by a rather different route: Russian ballet, the most aristocratic of the arts, was introduced to English audiences in 1910 in that most democratic of institutions, the variety theater. It was the great age of the music halls, a time when stars like Marie Lloyd and Little Tich were as well known as royalty, and Gaiety Girls married dukes. The music halls were the one Edwardian institution that had no class identity; they had evolved as popular entertainment, but in their Edwardian heyday they appealed to all of England. Ford Madox Ford edited his *English Review* in a box at the Shepherd's Bush Empire, and the King himself preferred an evening of variety at the Empire or the Gaiety to G. B. Shaw at the Royal Court.

It was in these variety theaters that English ballet, such

[40] G. B. Shaw, preface to *Heartbreak House* (New York: Brentano's, 1919), p. x.

as it was, existed. Ballet was a form of popular entertainment, to be fitted into a program between the cycling act and the performing dogs. No full-length ballets were danced, and the dancers were more likely to be chorus girls than ballerinas. Then, in April 1910, Anna Pavlova came to London with a small company of dancers from the Russian Imperial Ballet, to dance at the Palace Theatre. The Imperial Ballet had had a brilliant success on tour in Europe the previous year, and Pavlova was billed, quite rightly, as one of Russia's greatest dancers. She appeared, in her first performance in England, on a variety program that also included a Bioscope film of the Punchetown Races; with the exception of one season in 1911, all her pre-war appearances in London were in variety, sharing star billing with other music hall performers like Harry Lauder.

In these somewhat unlikely circumstances, Pavlova was an instant and glorious hit; she became at once England's favorite dancer, the name and symbol of grace and beauty in ballet. Her success established serious ballet as a possible art in England; by giving English audiences a taste of great dancing in a traditional repertoire she prepared the way for the arrival in 1911 of Diaghilev's company and modern ballet.

The first London season of the Russian Ballet opened on June 21, 1911. The theater this time was not the Palace but the Royal Opera House, Covent Garden. It was the eve of George V's Coronation Day, and the gorgeous and extravagant mountings of the company's new dances suited the occasion, the last parade of pre-war royal elegance in England. On the twenty-sixth the company danced at the coronation Gala before the King and Queen—an unusual honor for foreign artists—in an opera house banked with thousands of roses and brilliant with the diamonds of tiaras and the gold and dazzle of dress uniforms. It was a far step from the Palace, and a step that ballet in England badly needed. The *Times* correspondent, reviewing the company's second performance, noted the significance of the change of scene:

> Our ballet-designing [he wrote] has always been a democratic art, so far as it can be reckoned among the arts at all. Our dancing has been to please the people without calling for any mental exertion on their part. It has been an essential principle of this, as in all democratic arts, not to divert any of the spectators' imaginative energy to the central inward idea, but to save it all for the enjoyment of the expression; to use only themes, such as coquetry, pursuit, evasion, the simplicity and familiarity of which would recommend them at once to the least cultivated spectator. In Russia, on the other hand, the ballet has been essentially an aristocratic institution, maintained by an autocratic Government for the use of the cultivated classes. It has not depended for its existence on giving immediate pleasure (the bane of all democratic art), but has been able to follow its own bent. It has not had to husband the imaginative energies of the spectators, but, on the contrary, has been able to pursue the proper aim of all arts—to trouble and exert their imaginations.[41]

The ballet that occasioned these remarks was *Le Spectre de la Rose*, with Karsavina and Nijinsky, and costumes and decor by Bakst. That it did trouble and exert English imaginations is evidenced in the notices that the opening received in the daily papers. All the critics agreed that they had had an extraordinary experience; some were stimulated by it, others clearly were upset. The reviewer for the *Daily Mail* seemed dazzled by the strangeness of it all; he called the troup "fantastic" and "amazing," and wrote of Nijinsky:

> no mood is too joyous and exuberant for this strange creature to express it with his gambols of incredibility

[41] *Times*, June 24, 1911, p. 13.

and grace. He seems half-boy, half-bird. No words can tell the airy gaiety of his leaping feet. He looks the realisation of some flight-gifted elf or faun.[42]

The more sedate *Morning Post* responded in a more English way, admiring but observing that it was, after all, very un-English:

Pinks, scarlets and blues are mingled together against a dull matt-green background, presenting a somewhat harsher colour-scheme than is general in British theatres. . . . The performances were the means of showing the remarkable attainments of the dancers, and though the colour combinations and the scenery are by no means designed with the feeling for harmony that distinguishes similar productions in England, the grace and perfect training of the dancers make up for a good deal.[43]

But though critical reactions varied in details, it was clear to all critics—and indeed to all spectators—that the dance in England had been profoundly changed.

The first season of the Russian Ballet ended in August 1911. A correspondent writing in the *Times* of August 5 summed up the experience:

This summer of 1911 has brought more than an aesthetic revolution with it; in bringing the Russian Ballet to Covent Garden it has brought a positively new art, it has extended the realm of beauty for us, discovered a new continent, revealed new faculties and means of salvation in ourselves. Alas! many pleasant illusions have been shattered thereby, many idols tumbled from their pedestals; we have grown up terribly fast and lost the power of enjoying things that pleased our callow fancies only a month or two ago.[44]

[42] *Daily Mail*, June 23, 1911, p. 12.
[43] *Morning Post*, June 23, 1911, p. 4.
[44] *Times*, Aug. 5, 1911, p. 9.

The images used here—a voyage of discovery, a religious conversion—suggest how profoundly the Russian dancers had affected their English audiences. This correspondent's reaction was not unusual; many others shared it—Hugh Walpole wrote in his diary, "The Russian Ballet has moved me more than anything I've ever seen in my life," and Leonard Woolf, recalling the season, remarked in his memoirs, "I have never seen anything more perfect, nor more exciting, on any stage."[45]

Diaghilev returned with his company in 1912, adding *L'Oiseau de Feu* and *L'Après Midi d'un Faune* to the repertoire, and twice in 1913, with *Petrouchka, Jeux,* and *Le Sacre du Printemps.* Edward Marsh saw a performance in June 1913, and wrote to Rupert Brooke about it:

> I went with Denis to the Ballet, *Scheherazade, Faune, Sylphides,* and the new Debussy *Jeux.* All the papers and most people hate it, but don't you believe them, it's *delicious,* I went thoroughly meaning to dislike it, so it isn't *snobisme* on my part. I was enraptured from the moment the curtain went up. It's a Post-Impressionist picture put in motion . . . it has almost brought me round to Matisse's pictures![46]

In calling the ballet Post-Impressionist, Marsh may have been noting visual similarities, or he may simply have been responding to a similarity of mood, a disturbing and dissonant modernness for which Post-Impressionist was a careless but not uncommon synonym (as for example when Granville Barker's production of *The Winter's Tale* was called Post-Impressionist because it dispensed with conventional scenery). With music by Stravinsky and Debussy, choreography by Fokine and Nijinsky, and costumes and decor by Bakst, the Russian Ballet was modern in many

[45] Quoted in Rupert Hart-Davis, *Hugh Walpole* (London: Macmillan, 1952), p. 85; Leonard Woolf, *Beginning Again* (London: Hogarth Press, 1964), p. 48.

[46] Quoted in Christopher Hassall, *Edward Marsh,* pp. 231-232.

disturbing ways at once; this was why it had such powerful effect on its audiences.

When Marsh wrote that "most people hate it" he was rather over-stating the case. Many may have gone to the theater, as he did, prepared to dislike what they saw, and some did hiss, laugh, or even walk out, but on the whole audiences were captured by the dances, and such hostility as was expressed was restrained. When *Le Sacre du Printemps* was first performed in Paris, members of the audience shouted and hissed, quarreled and even fought with each other, and made such a din that the dancers could not hear the music. In London, the ballet was received with some whistling and muffled laughter, but was performed completely and audibly, and without riots. The *Times*, reviewing the performance, observed,

> London takes both its pleasures and its pains more quietly than Paris. When *Le Sacre du Printemps*, the latest joint product of MM. Nijinsky and Stravinsky, was produced for the first time in England last night at Drury Lane, the applause was measured, but so were the cries of disapproval.[47]

This more civilized reception might be attributed to British phlegm, but one might also conclude that by the summer of 1913 English audiences had grown accustomed to the Russians; if they were still sometimes a little shocked, they were probably like the gentleman whom Arnold Bennett met on shipboard who was "strong on the indecency of the Russian ballet, which however he much admired."[48]

Certainly in the years before the war Englishmen had had ample opportunity to grow accustomed to Russians. In addition to Dostoevsky, Chekhov, and the Russian ballets, there were Russian singers and balalaika groups in the music halls, Russian Post-Impressionists at the galleries, Russian

[47] *Times*, July 12, 1913, p. 11.
[48] Arnold Bennett, *Journal* (London: Cassell, 1932), vol. 2, p. 12.

operas at Covent Garden and Drury Lane (where Chaliapin sang his first *Boris Godounov* in London in June 1913), and Russian actresses in London theaters. Admiration for Russian art had reached such a pitch that Russianness alone sometimes seemed a measure of value, as when a reviewer of *Petrouchka* rejoiced that "the whole thing is refreshingly new and refreshingly Russian, more Russian, in fact, than any ballet we have had."[49]

The vogue for Russianness is one of the most striking aspects of English taste in the pre-war years, but it must be seen as only one part of an increased British awareness of Europe. This awareness may have been born of political anxiety, but it took the form of a new, international attitude toward the arts. As a consequence, London saw more that was European during those years than it had in any Edwardian's memory. If one had wished to be entertained, for example, on June 29, 1914, there were the following in London to choose from: Lydia Yavorska in *La Dame aux Camélias*—a Russian actress playing a French play in English—at the Scala; Russian dancers and Will Rogers at the Empire; a French revue at the New Middlesex; Russian Ballet at Drury Lane; Sardou's *A Scrap of Paper* at the Criterion; and, from across the other Channel, the Irish Players in *Riders to the Sea* at the Royal Court and *Pygmalion* at His Majesty's. It was a rich international offering, only overshadowed in drama by the newspaper headlines of the day, which told of the assassination of the Archduke Francis Ferdinand at Sarajevo.

By the summer of 1914, the traditions in the arts that we think of as modern had entered England and had become established. English audiences applauded European artists, and English artists imitated them. The catastrophe that the Tories feared had happened, though not in the way that the Tories expected—England had been successfully invaded from the Continent.

[49] *Times*, Feb. 5, 1913, p. 8.

Chapter X

··

THE END OF THE PARTY

··

Virginia Woolf was right in observing that a radical change took place in England (if not exactly in human character) around the end of 1910. The first Post-Impressionist exhibition is a fair symbol of that change, since it forced upon the English consciousness ideas that were at once modern and foreign; but it is obviously no more than a symbol. The disturbance of English life that was then in progress was far more vast and complex in its implications than a change in painting style: it involved the disordering of social and political systems and a radical revision of England's relations to the thought and life of Europe.

If we take "on or about December 1910" to include a period from the beginning of 1910 to the end of 1911, we can indicate by means of a simple calendar the dimensions of the turmoil that stirred in England then.

1910

JANUARY. General Election (the first since 1906). Liberals win, but are dependent on Labour and Irish support for their majority.

FEBRUARY 19. Strauss' *Elektra* premiered at Covent Garden.

FEBRUARY 21. Opening of Galsworthy's *Justice*.

FEBRUARY 23. Opening of Shaw's *Misalliance*.

MARCH 9. Opening of Barker's *Madras House*.

APRIL 18. First public appearance of Pavlova in London.

MAY 6. Death of King Edward VII.

JULY. Beginning of negotiations with Germany to limit fleets.

SEPTEMBER. Miners' strike, South Wales.

NOVEMBER 8. "Manet and the Post-Impressionists" opens.

NOVEMBER. *Sex and Society*, sixth and last volume of Havelock Ellis' *Studies in the Psychology of Sex*, is published in Philadelphia. Reviewed in England, but not published there.

DECEMBER. Second General Election; results the same as in January.

DECEMBER 8. Strauss' *Salomé* premiered in England, in censored version.

1911

MAY. Negotiations with Germany on fleets broken off, without positive results.

MAY 29. Chekhov's *Cherry Orchard*, the first of his plays to be seen in London, is produced by the Stage Society.

MAY 31. National Council of Public Morals issues manifesto to "people of Great and Greater Britain."

JUNE 14. Seamen's strike.

JUNE 21. Diaghilev's Russian Ballet gives first performance in England, at Covent Garden.

JUNE 20, 27, 28. Dockers' strikes at Hull, Manchester, Liverpool.

JUNE 22. Coronation of King George V.

JULY. German government dispatches gunboat to seize Moroccan port of Agadir, nearly precipitating war with France.

AUGUST 1. Dockers' strike in London.

AUGUST 10. Parliament Bill passes House of Lords.

AUGUST 15. National railway strike.

SEPTEMBER 23. Sir Edward Carson reviews Ulster Unionists at Craigavon, defies Home Rule for Ireland.

OCTOBER 20. Henri Bergson delivers first lecture in London.

NOVEMBER 23. Cubist drawing by Picasso—the first Cubism

to be reproduced in England—appears in *New Age,* with admiring articles on Picasso's art.

NOVEMBER-DECEMBER. Suffragettes open campaign of window-breaking and arson.

In this calendar there are three categories of events: social and political conflicts at home, introductions of new European art, and political problems abroad. Of these, the first two represent that continuing conflict of liberation and control that defines the Edwardian period. As the flood of radically new ideas entered England from the Continent, the pressure for intellectual and artistic liberation increased. But at the same time the counter-pressure of conservative and reactionary elements also became greater, and more extreme and rigid in its expressions. As social unrest and political anxiety increased, so did the conservative will to suppress evident forces of change and to preserve by force majeure the stability of England. The result is that during these years the terms of liberation and control became more clearly defined, but as the terms of a sterile and debilitating stalemate.

If one adds to this internal stress the growing tensions in international affairs, one can begin to understand the mood of England at this time. In spite of the infusion of new ideas there was little expressed optimism, and little sense of anticipation evident in the nation. The dominant mood was rather a mixed one: nostalgia in those who looked backward, apprehension in those who looked toward the future. It was in some ways like the mood of England at the turn of the century, at the passing of Victoria and her age.[1]

This mood of anxious depression found its symbol in the death of the King. It is perhaps inevitable in a monarchy that the end of a reign should seem the end of an era—even so short a reign as Edward's; certainly the passing of King Edward seemed to Englishmen to mark the passing of a solid and

[1] For a more detailed account of the mood of England just before the First World War see George Dangerfield, *The Strange Death of Liberal England* (New York: H. Smith & R. Haas, 1935).

familiar world. He had stood in the popular mind for an *English* way of life that seemed in retrospect comfortable and good—better, surely, than the European darkness that threatened ahead. It may seem paradoxical that the death of a "good European" should strike his countrymen as the end of a kind of Englishness, but it was nevertheless true. Though the King had turned often to Europe, both in duty and in pleasure, he remained to his subjects archetypally themselves, a secure symbol of what was familiar and trustworthy in the English character. At the time of his death the *New Age* wrote:

> In the case of the late King it is not difficult to discern the romantic conception to which his personal qualities most easily lent themselves in the workshop of the Crown. For his qualities were in almost every sense the typical qualities of the average Englishman. No man among his subjects was ever indeed more typically English, and no king was ever made to appear more symbolic in the largest sense of his people. It has never been recorded that King Edward ever had a taste for doing anything that the average Englishman does not himself desire to do. Moreover, he had the courage to follow his bent in the certainty that it would never lead him beyond the pale of the average Englishman's private approval. His love of sport, his aversion to the aesthetic, his love of travelling and mixing with men of the world, his indifference to the scholar and student, his love of pleasure and his rigid practice of duty, were shared by him in common with the vast majority of his subjects. These qualities were understood and appreciated exactly because they were common; and in their magnified form they made of King Edward the most popular and representative king that has perhaps ever sat upon a modern throne.[2]

This image of the average Englishman—ordinary, philistine, independent, dutiful—is essentially a Victorian one,

[2] "Notes of the Week," *New Age*, vol. 7 (May 12, 1910), 25.

derived from an imperial age of solidity and confidence, and it has little relation to the changing political and social realities of Edward's reign. But there is no doubt that Edward did succeed in preserving the image during his reign by the sheer force of his personality. His death was therefore more than the end of a reign: it was the end of a conception of what it meant to be English. The *New Age*'s writer noted this at the time:

> The last genuine link with the Victorian age has been broken with the death of King Edward VII. Nobody who will reflect for a moment on the circumstances of the Queen's death and on the historic as well as family relationship in which the late King stood to the late Queen, will fail to realise at once that King Edward was spiritually the mere executor of Queen Victoria. The impulse of her epoch flowed over, as it were, and merged in his reign, begun actually before her death, colouring it with the peculiar tones of the Victorian era. King Edward VII was adored almost as much as the son and successor of his mother as for his own qualities and merits.
>
> This fact, indeed, puts the seal of difference on the two accessions to the throne which the last ten years have witnessed. The accession of Edward VII was neither felt to be, nor in fact was it, a leap in the dark or a plunge into a new period. Everything that the late King did on the throne had been anticipated and expected, both from the evidence of his own public life and from the impetus given to his times by the long reign that drew to a close in him. But the situation is strangely different at this moment, and all the surrounding circumstances mark it off as unique in English history for many a generation. For if it is felt, as it is clearly felt, that the era of Victoria is indeed and at last over, who is so bold as to dare forecast the nature of the epoch that is now opening?[3]

[3] *New Age*, vol. 7 (May 12, 1910), 26.

The uncertainty expressed here, in an editorial published in a Socialist weekly, suggests one reason for considering Edward's death as the end of Edwardian England and treating the years immediately following as a kind of epilogue. Like his mother, Edward had made his personality the spirit of his reign, and that spirit did not survive him.

The heir who succeeded King Edward was in almost every way unlike his father, and few of his subjects can have viewed his succession, in that time of stress, with complacency. The judgment of King George that Wilfrid Blunt wrote was a severe one, but it was just, and many Englishmen must have shared it. "King Edward's successor," Blunt wrote,

> whose life had been that of a sailor, knowing the world only as a sailor sees it at the seaport towns where his ship stops to coal—and seaport towns all the world over are alike—and being without any experience of politics, even those of his own country, was quite unable to supply the directing power his father had exerted at times so successfully. Consequently from this point onward, the year 1910, our English policy on the Continent exhibited a series of blunders of the most dangerous kind, leading by a logical sequence in four years' time to England's entanglement in a war, the result of which was not foreseen, and for which no preparation whatever had been made.[4]

Blunt's opinion of Edward's influence was perhaps somewhat extravagant—he believed, for instance, that if Edward had lived the war would not have happened—but the point he makes about George is nonetheless true. In the years from 1910 to 1914 the King played no visible part in the foreign affairs of his country.

No doubt this diminishing of the King's influence was

[4] Wilfrid Scawen Blunt, *My Diaries*, Part Two (New York: Knopf, 1921), p. 309. The passage was probably written in 1919.

one factor in the creation of the mood of helpless anxiety that one senses in the England of those pre-war years. Another factor, perhaps, was the struggle over the Parliament Bill. Edward had died in the midst of negotiations between the Houses—indeed some Tories said he had been killed by the crisis—and his successor inherited a situation in which the hereditary upper house seemed bent on destroying itself rather than accept democratic limitations. When, in August 1911, the Lords finally voted away their veto power, they not only removed an obstacle to efficient government, they also destroyed one source of traditional English feelings of security—the belief that a disinterested, benevolent legislative body existed, raised by the good fortune of birth above party pettiness, and dedicated to directing the destinies of England and the Empire. If this belief scarcely corresponded to reality, it nevertheless existed as an ideal, and conservative Englishmen must have felt themselves cut adrift from a secure mooring by the passage of the Parliament Bill. In place of that noble ideal, England was left with a new kind of class rancor, the upper classes' resentment of their middle-class rulers (one can see this at work, surely, in the Ulster Crisis of 1911-1914). At the same time, the unbending resistance of the "Die-hard" Lords to any change had further intensified the hostility that progressive-minded people felt for the Tories and thus had widened the breach between the two extremes of Edwardian society.

The national mood of undefined anxiety was given sharp focus in 1911 and 1912 by a sudden and violent outburst of strikes. The number and duration of strikes had remained fairly low during Edward's reign—an average of about 200,000 workers involved per year—though it had increased in 1908 and 1909. In 1910 the number rose to 514,000 men in 521 disputes, at a cost of nearly ten million work days lost. In 1911 the number of disputes increased to 872, the men involved totalled nearly a million, and the days lost were slightly more than ten million. The following year was even more troubled; there were fewer individual disputes (partly because unions were consolidating), but the total number of strikers increased to a million and a half, and the work days lost rose to forty million, more than ten times the number in any year before 1908.

These strikes were not only disruptive and expensive, they were also often violent. There were riots in the South Wales coal fields and on the Liverpool docks, where troops fired on the strikers and killed two men. This sudden explosion of existing tensions into open violence was echoed in other late-Edwardian conflicts. The suffrage movement began a campaign of destruction that included the burning of houses and public buildings and the mail in pillar boxes, window-breaking, and picture-slashing. In Ulster the Unionists armed themselves to defy their government's apparent intention of giving Home Rule to the Irish. In such circumstances of open and violent conflict, there was no hope of rational, moderate change; Edwardian England approached its end in a state of helpless rage. By the summer of 1914 the British Isles were an armed camp, armed for a war against the workers, a war against women, or a war against the Irish—for every war, in fact, except the one that was already begun on the far side of Europe.

In that last summer of the pre-war world, Edwardian England moved ignorantly toward its end, with all its aspirations and problems still intact. While on the Continent ultimatums were uttered and armies massed, in England the same Edwardian issues were debated; reading the press of that period, one feels not a sense of a new crisis, but the same old crises being hopefully turned over. Take the July issues of the *New Statesman* as an example. The issue of July 4 contains an attack on stage censorship, an article on the Russian Ballet, a review of a book on eugenics, and an article by Beatrice Webb on "Personal Right and the Women's Movement"; letters to the editor discuss women's right to motherhood, the crime of poverty, and the cost of divorce. In the issue of the following week there is an essay on the falling birth rate and an announcement of a forthcoming supplement on marriage and divorce. On the 18th an advertisement of the Fabian Summer School appeared, and on the 25th a piece about Russia and an editorial assurance that Germany "is entirely opposed to a military upheaval in Europe just now." The month's papers compose a catalogue of Socialist stands on the familiar issues and enthusiasms of the whole Edwardian period. Read in this way they suggest two conclusions about the period: that intelligent persons were astonishingly unaware of the disaster that was approaching; and that though such persons were conscious of domestic problems and liberating possibilities, they had made very little progress during the Edwardian years. Reading over those copies of the *Statesman* one hears the affirming voice of liberation, but one finds little evidence of achievement. A few advances had, to be sure, been made in those last weeks: *Ghosts* and *Monna Vanna* had been licensed for public performance, *Dubliners* had been published, and the Society for the Study of Sex Psychology had held its inaugural meeting. The instruments for liberation did exist—and in some cases had existed for some time; the Minority Report, the reports of the Divorce Commission, the Committee on Censorship, the Chantrey committee, the pamphlets of the Fabians were all there to be used. But no one used them, and the end came.

August 1914 began with a Bank Holiday weekend. For many well-to-do people it was a summer weekend much like any other; there were houseparties at country houses (though members of the government absented themselves), and at Cowes, on Southampton Water, gentleman sailors prepared for the Regatta and hoped that the crisis would not disturb their plans. Racing continued at Goodwood, though attendance was poor, and so did the flying displays at Hendon airport and the cricket at Canterbury. In London the official "season" was over, but fashionable people hovered restlessly around town, visited the Summer Exhibition at the Royal Academy, or went to the Kingsway Theatre to see Granville Barker and his wife in Arnold Bennett's *The Great Adventure*. For more plebeian taste there was a new display at Madame Tussaud's; the advertisements described it as

> The European Crisis. Lifelike Portrait Models of H.I.M. the Emperor of Austria, King Peter of Servia, and other reigning Sovereigns of Europe. The Home Rule Crisis. Sir Edward Carson, Mr. John Redmond, and other Celebrities. Naval and Military Tableaux. Delightful Music. Refreshments at Popular Prices.[5]

But for all the gestures of normality there was little doubt that by that weekend England was no longer capable of avoiding war. On Sunday, Labour and Socialist leaders staged a "War Against War" rally in Trafalgar Square, but the mood of the crowd was by this time so militant that the pacifist speakers were shouted down, and the rally ended in disorder. The leadership of England seemed to have passed from human hands.

> The chain of events we have to fear [the *Statesman* observed on August 1], the dragging first of one country and then of another into the conflict, until practically the whole white race in the Old World is involved, seems to have all the inevitableness of ancient tragedy, where persons and events are controlled not by reason, but by the spell of an ironic fate.[6]

Even in the Cabinet Room, where Asquith and his ministers met almost continuously during the weekend, the

[5] *Times*, Aug. 1, 1914, p. 1.
[6] "Comment," *New Statesman*, vol. 3 (Aug. 1, 1914), 513.

mood was one of helpless depression, as of men who watch the approach of some unavoidable natural calamity. Even Winston Churchill, a man who generally found war exhilarating, was pained by "the grief and horror of so many able colleagues."[7] Masterman, the junior member of that cabinet, recalled the spirit of their meetings as the time of peace ran out:

It was a company of tired men who for twelve hot summer nights, without rest or relaxation, had devoted their energies to avert this thing which had now come inevitably to pass. No one who has been through the experience of those twelve days will ever be quite the same again. It is difficult to find a right simile for that experience. It was like a company of observers watching a little cloud in the east, appearing out of a blue sky, seeing it grow, day by day, until all the brightness had vanished and the sun itself had become obscured. It was like the victim of the old mediaeval torture enclosed in a chamber in which the walls, moved by some unseen mechanism, steadily closed on him day by day, until at the end he was crushed to death. It was most like perhaps those persons who have walked on the solid ground and seen slight cracks and fissures appear, and these enlarge and run together and swell in size hour by hour until yawning apertures revealed the boiling up beneath them of the earth's central fires, destined to sweep away the forest and vineyards of its surface and all the kindly habitations of man.

And all this experience—the development of a situation heading straight to misery and ruin without precedent—was continued in the midst of a world where the happy, abundant life of the people flowed on uncon-

[7] Winston Churchill, *The World Crisis* (New York: Scribner's, 1928), vol. 1, p. 232.

cerned, and all thoughts were turned towards the approaching holidays and the glories of triumphant summer days.[8]

The life of the people was not, in fact, unconcerned on that last weekend. In London, as the crisis grew, crowds gathered at Buckingham Palace to sing "God Save the King" and to cheer the Royal Family, who appeared from time to time on a balcony, like the cast of a play taking curtain calls at the closing of a successful run. There were crowds in Bedford Square singing the "Marseillaise," and in Whitehall their triumphant cries drifted into the Cabinet Room; "War or anything that seems likely to lead to war is always popular with the London mob," Asquith observed bitterly.[9] The still undeclared war was, for the crowds of London, another kind of competition, a struggle of force as exciting as a Cup Final, and with no more historical meaning.

For thoughtful men, however, the historical meaning was clear: the cracks and fissures that Masterman imagined were cracks in the fabric of English society, and the tremor that was coming would shake that flawed structure to the ground. It was not only the beginning of a war, it was the end of a world, and men viewed it, whatever their expectations, with fear and apprehension. Wells acutely recognized that it would bring a new world in which everything would be different, and since he approved of new worlds he might have been expected to rejoice; but he viewed the approaching war as a vast catastrophe that threatened pure destruction.[10] And Rupert Brooke, who was to become the laureate

[8] Quoted in Lucy Masterman, *C. F. G. Masterman* (London: Nicholson and Watson, 1939), p. 266.

[9] Quoted in Roy Jenkins, *Asquith* (London: Collins, 1964), p. 328.

[10] Wells recorded his immediate reactions in *Mr. Britling Sees It Through* (New York: Macmillan, 1916); see especially Book I, Ch. 5: "The Coming of the Day."

of the war he never really saw, spent the first day of war in speechless depression.[11] In the presence of unimaginable disaster, there was nothing to say.

Among the writers who record their feelings on August 5, 1914, it was Henry James, one of the oldest and wisest of them, who saw its enormous meaning most clearly. That day he wrote to a friend in a mood of profound despair,

> The plunge of civilization into this abyss of blood and darkness by the wanton feat of those two infamous autocrats is a thing that so gives away the whole long age during which we have supposed the world to be, with whatever abatement, gradually bettering, that to have to take it all now for what the treacherous years were all the while really making for and *meaning* is too tragic for any words.[12]

James saw at once that the declaration of war was bitter not simply because it was a war, but because it was the logical and inevitable end of the years that had preceded it. By coming to pass—almost, as it seemed, accidentally—it contradicted and destroyed the benevolent assumptions of the Edwardian Age, denied liberalism and progress and the goodness of the human heart, and left men with no cause but war itself. The treacherous years would have to be read anew, and all their cracks and fissures understood as signs of the approaching destruction.

The Edwardian Age ended when peace ended. There remained only one task—the writing of the age's epitaph, and for that task what poet could be more appropriate than Kipling, the writer who had lost most from the age and was to lose his only son in the war? The epitaph that Kipling offered was written in passing, in the course of an incite-

[11] See Christopher Hassall, *Rupert Brooke* (New York: Harcourt, Brace & World, 1964), p. 457.
[12] In Percy Lubbock, ed., *Letters of Henry James*, vol. 2, p. 384.

ment to the fierce pursuit of bloodshed, and that too seems
appropriate.

> For all we have and are,
> For all our children's fate,
> Stand up and take the war.
> The Hun is at the gate!
> Our world has passed away
> In wantonness o'erthrown.
> There is nothing left today
> But steel and fire and stone![13]

[13] "For all we have and are," *Rudyard Kipling's Verse* (Garden
City, N.Y.: Doubleday, Page, 1922), p. 378. The poem was first published in the *Times*, Sept. 2, 1914, p. 9.

APPENDIX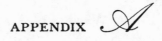

....

BIOGRAPHICAL SKETCHES

....

In a book like this that mentions a great many people, some names are bound to be strange to any reader. The notes that follow identify briefly some of the names that appear in the text and provide bibliographical references for further information. I have limited myself to Edwardians—to persons, that is, who were alive, adult, and resident in England between 1901 and 1914. Foreigners have been omitted, unless, like James, Sargent, and Whistler, they lived and worked in England; any other omission simply means that the subject eluded my researches.

My bibliographical suggestions are very selective and are focused on books that give most information about the Edwardian years.

ALEXANDER, Sir George (1858-1918). Actor-manager, St. James's Theatre. Produced and starred in *Lady Windermere's Fan* (1892), *Second Mrs. Tanqueray* (1893), *Importance of Being Earnest* (1895). Knighted 1911.

ALEXANDRA, Caroline Mary Charlotte Louise Julia (1844-1925), Queen, wife of Edward VII. Eldest daughter of Christian IX of Denmark, married Edward (then Prince of Wales) 1863. Three sons, three daughters.

AMERY, Leopold Stennett (1873-1955). Politician. Fabian in his youth. On staff of *Times* 1899-1909. Conservative M.P. 1911-1945; First Lord of Admiralty 1922; Colonial Secretary 1924-1929; Secretary of State for India and Burma 1940-1945. *My Political Life*, 3 vols. (1953-1955).

ANSON, Sir William (1843-1914). Jurist, author of standard works on English law. Warden of All Souls, Oxford, from 1881 and M.P. for Oxford University from 1899.

ARCHER, William (1856-1924). Dramatic critic, translator of Ibsen, champion of modernism and freedom in English theater. *Collected Works of Ibsen* (1906-1907). C. Archer, *William Archer, Life, Work and Friendships* (1931).

ASQUITH, Herbert (1852-1928), first Earl of Oxford and Asquith (1925). Statesman. M.P. 1886-1918, 1920-1924; Home Secretary 1892-1905; Chancellor of the Exchequer 1905-1908; Prime Minister 1908-1916. *Memories and Reflections* (1928). Jenkins, *Asquith* (1964).

AUSTIN, Alfred (1835-1913). Journalist and poet. Editor *National Review* 1883-1895; Poet Laureate 1896-1913. *Autobiography* (1911).

BADEN-POWELL, Agnes (1858-1945). Sister of Lord Baden-Powell; with him organized Girl Guides (1910).

BADEN-POWELL, Robert Stephenson Smyth (1857-1941), first Baron Baden-Powell (1929). Soldier, youth leader. Served in army in India and Africa; won fame as defender of Mafeking (1899-1900). Founder of Boy Scouts (1908) and with sister of Girl Guides (1910). *Scouting for Boys* (1908). Reynolds, *Baden-Powell*, 2nd ed. (1957).

BALFOUR, Arthur James (1848-1930), first Earl of Balfour (1922). Statesman and philosopher. Conservative M.P. 1874-1922; First Lord of the Treasury 1891-1892 and 1895-1902; Prime Minister 1902-1905 (succeeding his uncle, Lord Salisbury). *Defence of Philosophic Doubt* (1879); *Foundations of Belief* (1895); *Chapters of Autobiography*, ed. Dugdale (1930).

BALFOUR, Lady Frances (1858-1931). Churchwoman and suffragette, daughter of Duke of Argyll, wife of Arthur Balfour's brother Eustace.

BALFOUR, Gerald (1853-1945), second Earl Balfour. Politician. Younger brother of Arthur Balfour, whom he succeeded in title. Conservative M.P. 1885-1906; Chief Secretary for Ireland 1895-1900; and holder of various other offices. Active in psychic research.

BANCROFT, Sir Squire (1841-1926). Actor-manager. Knighted 1897.

BARING, Maurice (1874-1945). Diplomatist, journalist, author, traveller. Early admirer of Russian literature; wrote *Landmarks in Russian Literature* (1910), *An Outline of Russian Literature* (1914). *The Puppet Show of Memory* (1922).

BARKER, Harley Granville (1877-1946). Actor, manager, dramatist; Fabian and friend of Shaw. His management of Royal Court gave Edwardian London its best theater. Married to Lillah McCarthy, actress. Purdom, *Harley Granville Barker* (1955); *The Shaw-Barker Letters*, ed. Purdom (1956).

BARRIE, Sir James (1860-1937). Scottish playwright and novelist. His Edwardian plays include *The Admirable Crichton* (1902), *Peter Pan* (1904), and *What Every Woman Knows* (1908). Baronet 1913. *Letters*, ed. V. Meynell (1947); Darlington, *J. M. Barrie* (1938).

BEECHAM, Sir Thomas (1879-1961). Conductor and producer, son of millionaire manufacturer of bile pills. Introduced into England Russian Ballet, operas by Richard Strauss. Later conducted at Covent Garden and New York Metropolitan. *A Mingled Chime* (1944).

BEERBOHM, Sir Henry Maximilian (1872-1956). Essayist and caricaturist. Contributor to *Yellow Book* in 'nineties; drama critic for *Saturday Review* 1898-1910. Married and retired to Rapallo, Italy, 1910. *Christmas Garland* (1912); *Fifty Caricatures* (1913); *Zuleika Dobson* (1912); *Around Theatres* (1953). Cecil, *Max* (1964).

BELL, Vanessa (1879-1961). Painter. Daughter of Sir Leslie Stephen, Victorian editor and author, elder sister of Virginia Woolf. Married Clive Bell, art critic, 1907. Member Bloomsbury Group.

BENSON, Arthur Christopher (1862-1925). Man of letters,

Son of Archbishop of Canterbury. Taught at Eton 1885-1903; Master of Magdalene College, Cambridge, 1915-1925. Author of many volumes of essays, memoirs, fiction. Lubbock, ed., *Diary of Arthur Christopher Benson* (1926).

BENSON, Edward Frederic (1867-1940). Author, brother of Arthur; like him, a prolific but undistinguished writer. *As We Were* (1930); *As We Are* (1932).

BESANT, Annie (1847-1933). Woman of many causes—birth control in the 1870's, Fabian socialism in the 'eighties, theosophy in the 'nineties. Contributor to *Fabian Essays* (1889), quit socialism for Theosophy and Indian nationalism. President Theosophical Society 1907-1933. Nethercot, *Last Four Lives of Annie Besant* (1963).

BLAND, Hubert (1856-1914). Journalist. One of the founders of Fabian Society. Husband of E. Nesbit, children's writer, with whom he ran bohemian household. *Essays*, ed. E. Nesbit Bland (1914).

BLUNT, Wilfrid Scawen (1840-1922). Poet, diplomat, anti-imperialist. Diplomatic service 1859-1870. Supported Egyptian and Irish nationalism. *My Diaries*, 2 vols. (1921).

BROOKE, Rupert (1887-1915). Poet. Member of Cambridge Fabian Society. Died of natural causes en route to Gallipoli 1915. *Collected Poems*, with memoir by E. Marsh (1918); *Democracy and the Arts*, ed. Keynes (1946). Hassall, *Rupert Brooke* (1964).

BROOKFIELD, Charles H. E. (1857-1913). Actor and playwright. Wrote or adapted nearly 50 plays, mostly farces. Examiner of Plays in Lord Chamberlain's Office 1912. *Random Reminiscences* (1902).

BUCKMASTER, Stanley Owen (1861-1934), first Viscount Buckmaster (1933). Lawyer and jurist. Liberal M.P. 1906-1914; Solicitor-General 1913; Lord Chancellor 1915-1916.

BURNE-JONES, Philip (1861-1926). Painter. Son of the Victorian painter Edward Burne-Jones. Succeeded father as second baronet 1898.

BURNS, John (1858-1943). Trade union leader and politician. Working-class origins; leader of London dock strike 1889. M.P. 1892-1918; first of his class to become Cabinet Minister (Pres. Local Government Board 1905-1914.)

CAINE, Sir Thomas Henry Hall (1855-1931). Novelist. Many popular romantic novels, often with religious themes. *My Story* (1908).

CAMPBELL, Mrs. Patrick (1865-1940). Actress. Created title roles in *Second Mrs. Tanqueray* (1893) and *Notorious Mrs. Ebbsmith* (1895); Eliza Doolittle in *Pygmalion* (1914). Friend of Shaw. Dent, ed., *Bernard Shaw and Mrs. Patrick Campbell: Their Correspondence* (1952).

CAMPBELL-BANNERMAN, Sir Henry (1836-1908). Statesman. Liberal M.P. 1868-1908; leader of party in Commons from 1899; Prime Minister 1905-1908. Knighted 1895. Spender, *Life* (1923).

CARPENTER, Edward (1844-1929). Writer on social and psychological subjects, Socialist of an eccentric kind, poet and simple-lifer. First to write in defense of homosexual love. *Love's Coming of Age* (1896); *My Days and Dreams* (1916).

CARPENTER, W. Boyd (1841-1918). Clergyman. Bishop of Ripon 1884-1911; canon of Westminster 1911-1918. President of the Society for Psychical Research and of the National Council of Public Morals (both 1911). *Some Pages of my Life* (1911); *Further Pages* (1916).

CARSON, Sir Edward (1854-1935). Baron Carson (1921). Lawyer, leader of Ulster Unionists. Conservative M.P. 1892-1921; Solicitor-General 1900-1906; Attorney-General 1915-1916; First Lord of Admiralty 1916-1917. Leading opponent of Irish home rule. Marjoribanks and Colvin, *Life* (1932-1936).

CARTE, Mrs. Richard D'Oyly (d. 1913). Second wife of Gilbert and Sullivan impressario; managed company after his death in 1901.

CASSON, Sir Lewis (1875-   ). Actor, manager, and director. Acted in Royal Court productions under Barker-

Vedrenne; in Shaw's *Man and Superman*, Elizabeth Robins' *Votes for Women!*. Knighted 1945.

CHESTERTON, Cecil (1879-1918). Journalist. Brother of G. K. Chesterton. Member Fabian Executive 1906-1907; later abandoned socialism, attacked party system and liberal ideas. *Party and People* (1910) ; *The Party System* (with H. Belloc, 1911). Mrs. C. Chesterton, *The Chestertons* (1941).

CHESTERTON, Gilbert Keith (1874-1936). Essayist, novelist, poet. Roman Catholic convert (1922). A Liberal, and anti-imperialist. *Napoleon of Notting Hill* (1908) ; *Heretics* (1908) ; *Autobiography* (1936).

CHILDERS, Robert Erskine (1870-1922). Writer, soldier. Parliamentary clerk 1895-1910. Served in South African War and World War I; subsequently joined Irish Republican Army, captured and executed by Irish Free State. *Riddle of the Sands* (1903).

CHURCHILL, Sir Winston (1874-1965). Statesman. Entered Parliament as Tory 1900; crossed to Liberal side 1906; served in Asquith's Cabinet as President of Board of Trade 1908-1910; Home Secretary 1910-1911; First Lord of Admiralty 1911-1915. Rejoined Conservative party 1924. Prime Minister 1940-1945, 1951-1955. *The World Crisis*, 4 vols. (1923-1929). Randolph Churchill, *Winston S. Churchill* (first volume 1966; continuing).

CLIFFORD, Mrs. W. K. (d. 1929). Novelist and playwright. Wife of British mathematician William Kingdon Clifford (1842-1879).

CONRAD, Joseph (1857-1924). Novelist and mariner. Born in Poland, trained as a seaman, settled in England in 1894, began writing career. *A Personal Record* (1912). Jessie Conrad, *Joseph Conrad and His Circle* (1935) ; Baines, *Conrad* (1960).

DAVIDSON, John (1857-1909). Poet and novelist. After unsuccessful attempt at London career, committed suicide by drowning. *Fleet Street Eclogues* (1893) ; *Testaments* (1901-1908).

DAVIES, William Henry (1871-1940) . Poet and tramp. *Collected Poems* (1940) ; *Autobiography of a Super-Tramp* (1908).

DAWSON, Sir Douglas (1854-1933) . Soldier. Military attaché, Vienna-Bucharest-Belgrade, 1890-1895, Paris-Brussels-Berne, 1895-1901. Comptroller in Lord Chamberlain's department 1907-1920. *A Soldier Diplomat* (1927) .

DELL, Ethel May (1881-1939). Prolific writer of romantic novels; her first was *Way of an Eagle* (1912) .

DE MORGAN, William (1839-1917) . Artist and author. Pre-Raphaelite maker of stained glass and tiles. Began writing fiction when over 60; wrote seven novels between 1906 and 1914. Stirling, *Life* (1922) .

DESBOROUGH, William Henry Grenfell (1855-1945) . Baron Desborough (1905) . Athlete, sportsman, politician; Liberal M.P. 1880-1893; Conservative 1900-1905. His wife was a celebrated society hostess.

DESLYS, Gaby (1884-1920) . French singer and music-hall artist, more notable for her figure than for her talent. First appeared in London 1906.

DIBDIN, Sir Lewis (1852-1938) . Ecclesiastical lawyer. Dean of the Arches 1903-1934; member Royal Commission on Divorce and Matrimonial Causes 1909-1912.

DOUGLAS, Lord Alfred (1870-1945) . Poet and homosexual. Son of Marquess of Queensberry. His friendship with Oscar Wilde led to Wilde's trial and imprisonment in 1895. Editor of *Academy* 1907-1910. *Autobiography* (1929).

DOYLE, Sir Arthur Conan (1859-1930) . Author of Sherlock Holmes stories and of several historical romances. Spiritualist in later years. *Memories and Adventures* (1924) . Carr, *Life* (1949) .

DU MAURIER, Sir Gerald (1873-1934) . Actor-manager. Played in *Admirable Crichton* (1903) , *Peter Pan* (1904) ;

produced his brother's play, *An Englishman's Home* (1909). Knighted 1922. D. Du Maurier, *Gerald: A Portrait* (1934).

DU MAURIER, Guy (1865-1915). Soldier. Brother of Gerald. Served in South African War, awarded DSO. Author of *An Englishman's Home* (1909).

EDER, Montague David (1870?-1936). Psychoanalyst and Zionist. Read first paper on clinical psychology at British Medical Association meeting 1911; translated Freud and Jung. Socialist, member Fabian Society, and staff writer for *New Age* 1907-1915.

EDWARD VII (1841-1910). King of Great Britain and Ireland and of the British Dominions beyond the Seas, Emperor of India. Son of Queen Victoria and Prince Albert; succeeded his mother Jan. 22, 1901. Died May 6, 1910; succeeded by his second son, George. Magnus, *King Edward the Seventh* (1964).

ELCHO, Hugo Richard Wemyss Charteris, Lord Elcho (1857-1937), later 11th Earl of Wemyss. M.P. 1883-1885, 1886-1895. His wife was a leading society hostess.

ELIOT, Thomas Stearns (1888-1965). American-born poet and critic. Studied at Harvard (1906-1910, 1911-1914), at the Sorbonne (1910), and at Oxford (1915). Settled permanently in London 1915. Became British subject 1927. *Poems written in Early Youth* (1967).

ELLIS, Edith Mary Oldham Lees (1861-1916). Author; married Havelock Ellis 1891. *Three Modern Seers* (1910). Goldberg, *Havelock Ellis* (1926).

ELLIS, Henry Havelock (1859-1939). Scientist and man of letters. His great work, *Studies in the Psychology of Sex*, was begun in 1897, and the sixth volume published in 1910 (a seventh appeared in 1928). Also first editor of Mermaid series of Elizabethan and Jacobean dramatists, and prolific writer on social and literary subjects. *My Life* (1940); Peterson, *Havelock Ellis, Philosopher of Love* (1928).

EPSTEIN, Sir Jacob (1880-1959). American-born sculptor. Moved to London 1900; later became British subject. Principal works of Edwardian years are figures on British Medical Council Building, Strand (1907-1908), Wilde Memorial (1911), Rock Drill (1913-1914). Knighted 1954. *Let There be Sculpture* (1940); *Autobiography* (1955).

FORD, Ford Madox. *See* Hueffer.

FORSTER, Edward Morgan (1879-   ). Novelist. Of his five novels, four were written during the Edwardian years. Later writings critical and biographical. A friend of the Bloomsbury Group. *Abinger Harvest* (1936); *Two Cheers for Democracy* (1951). Stone, *The Cave and the Mountain* (1966).

FRY, Roger (1866-1934). Painter and critic. Organized first London exhibition of Post-Impressionists (1910). Member Bloomsbury Group. *Vision and Design* (1920). Virginia Woolf, *Roger Fry* (1940).

GALSWORTHY, John (1867-1933). Playwright and novelist, reformer. Nobel Prize 1932. H. V. Marrot, *Life and Letters of Galsworthy* (1935); Garnett, *Letters from Galsworthy* (1934).

GARNETT, Constance (1861-1946). Translator of Russian literature, including first complete English editions of Turgenev, Dostoevsky, and Gogol, virtually all of Chekhov. Wife of Edward Garnett. Heilbrun, *The Garnett Family* (1961).

GARNETT, Edward (1868-1937). Editor, publisher's reader, man of letters. Author of plays and stories, none successful. Friend and advisor to many writers, including Conrad and Galsworthy. Heilbrun, *The Garnett Family* (1961).

GEDDES, Sir Patrick (1854-1932). Biologist, sociologist, town planner. Co-author (with Sir J. A. Thomson) of *The Evolution of Sex* (1889) and *Problems of Sex* (1912). Professor, St. Andrews U., U. of Bombay. Knighted 1932.

GILBERT, Sir William Schwenk (1836-1911). Dramatist,

librettist, poet. Besides his collaborations with Sir Arthur Sullivan, Gilbert wrote serious plays and farces of his own. Knighted 1907. Dark and Grey, *W. S. Gilbert His Life and Letters* (1923).

GILL, Eric (1882-1940). Sculptor, engraver, and author. His sculpture was included in the Second Post-Impressionist Show (1912). *Autobiography* (1940).

GISSING, George (1857-1903). Realistic novelist. A. and E. Gissing, eds., *Letters of George Gissing* (1927); Korg, *George Gissing* (1963).

GLADSTONE, Herbert (1854-1930). First Viscount Gladstone (1910). Son of the Victorian Prime Minister. Chief Liberal Whip 1899-1906; Home Secretary 1906-1910; Governor-General of South Africa 1910-1914. *After Thirty Years* (1928).

GLYN, Elinor (1864-1943). Author of sensational novels of high society, of which the most famous was *Three Weeks* (1907). *Romantic Adventure* (1937). A. Glyn, *Elinor Glyn* (1955).

GORE, Spencer (1878-1914). Painter. Friend of Sickert and Pissarro; member New English Art Club. Rothenstein, *Modern English Painters, Sickert to Smith* (1952).

GORELL, John Gorell Barnes (1848-1913), first Baron Gorell (1909). Judge of Probate, Divorce and Admiralty Division, 1892, President 1905-1909. Chairman, Royal Commission on Divorce and Matrimonial Causes, 1909-1912.

GORST, Sir John Eldon (1835-1916). Lawyer and politician. M.P. for Cambridge University 1892-1906. Educational reformer; directed Education Act of 1902 through Parliament. *The Children of the Nation* (1907); *Education and Race-Regeneration* (1913).

GOSCHEN, George Joachim (1831-1907), first Viscount Goschen (1900). Statesman. M.P. 1863-1900. Held various cabinet posts, including First Lord of Admiralty (1871-1874 and 1895-1899), Chancellor of the Exchequer 1886-1892.

GOSSE, Edmund (1849-1928). Civil servant and man of letters. Librarian, House of Lords, 1904-1914. Author of many books of verse and criticism; first introduced Ibsen to English readers. Charteris, *Life and Letters* (1931).

GRAHAM, Robert Bontine Cunninghame (1852-1936). Author, socialist, traveller. A romantic, adventurous figure who rode with gauchos in Argentina, led political demonstrations in London. M.P. 1886-1892. Tschiffele, *Don Roberto* (1937).

GRANT, Duncan (1885-   ). Painter. Friend and associate of Roger Fry; exhibited in Second Post-Impressionist Show. Member Bloomsbury Group. Fry, *Duncan Grant* (1923); Mortimer, *Duncan Grant* (1947).

GREGORY, Lady Augusta (1852-1932). Irish playwright, patron of the arts. Founder of Abbey Theatre (1904); director 1904-1932. Friend of Yeats and Synge. Robinson, ed., *Lady Gregory's Journals* (1946); Coxhead, *J. M. Synge and Lady Gregory* (1962).

GREY, Edward (1862-1933), first Viscount Grey of Fallodon (1916). Liberal statesman. Foreign secretary in Asquith's cabinet 1905-1916. *Twenty-five Years* (1925).

GWENN, Edmund (1875-1959). Actor. In Royal Court company under Barker-Vedrenne; in many Shaw plays, including *Man and Superman, Major Barbara*, and in plays by Galsworthy and Barker.

HAGGARD, Sir Henry Rider (1856-1925). Novelist and agricultural writer. *King Solomon's Mines* (1885); *She* (1887). *The Days of My Life* (1926).

HALDANE, Richard Burdon (1856-1928), first Viscount Haldane of Cloan (1911). Liberal statesman, lawyer, philosopher. As Secretary of State for War (1905-1912) he remodelled the British Army. Lord Chancellor 1912-1915. *Autobiography* (1929).

HALSBURY, Hardinge Stanley Gifford (1823-1921), first Earl (1895). Lawyer; Lord Chancellor 1885-1886, 1886-1892,

1895-1905. Leader of "diehard" peers against Parliament Bill 1911.

HANKIN, St. John (1869-1909). Playwright. His most popular play was *The Cassilis Engagement* (1907). *Dramatic Works*, 3 vols. (1912).

HARCOURT, Lewis (1863-1922), first Viscount (1916). Son of the Victorian statesman Sir William Harcourt. Liberal M.P. 1904-1916; First Commissioner of Works 1905-1910; Secretary of State for Colonies 1910-1915.

HARCOURT, Robert (1878-?). Journalist and playwright; brother of Lewis. Liberal M.P. 1908-1918.

HARDY, Thomas (1840-1928). Novelist and poet. All of his novels were written before 1900; his principal Edwardian work was his epic-drama, *The Dynasts* (1903-1908). F. Hardy, *The Early Life of Thomas Hardy* (1928) and *The Later Years* (1930).

HARRADON, Beatrice (1864-1936). Novelist. Active in women's suffrage movement.

HARRISON, Frederick (1853-1926). Actor, manager of Haymarket Theatre, London, 1896-1905.

HAWKINS, Sir Anthony Hope (1863-1933). Novelist and playwright, under name of Anthony Hope: *The Prisoner of Zenda* (1894). *Memories and Notes* (1927). Mallet, *Anthony Hope and His Books* (1935).

HEWLETT, Maurice (1861-1923). Novelist, poet, essayist. His romantic novels were popular during the Edwardian period: *The Forest Lovers* (1898); *The Queen's Quair* (1904). Later gave up fiction for poetry. Binyon, ed., *Letters of Maurice Hewlett* (1926).

HOBHOUSE, Henry (1854-1937). Politician. Liberal Unionist M.P. 1886-1906; member Royal Commission on Secondary Education. Active in local government. Married to sister of Beatrice Webb.

HOLROYD, Sir Charles (1861-1917). Painter and etcher. First Keeper of Tate Gallery 1897-1906; Director of National Gallery 1906-1916. Knighted 1903.

HOPE, Anthony. *See* Hawkins.

HOUSMAN, Alfred Edward (1859-1936). Poet and classical scholar. Professor of Latin, University College, London, 1892-1911; Cambridge, 1911-1936. *A Shropshire Lad* (1896). Watson, *A. E. Housman* (1958).

HOUSMAN, Laurence (1867-1959). Novelist and playwright, brother of Alfred. Pacifist and supporter of suffrage movement; founder of British Society for Study of Sex Psychology (1914). *Unexpected Years* (1937).

HUDSON, William Henry (1841-1922). Naturalist and writer. Born in Argentina, wrote about nature there and in England; best known book *Green Mansions* (1904). Garnett, ed., *Letters from W. H. Hudson* (1923).

HUEFFER, Ford Madox (1873-1939). Novelist and poet. Collaborated with Conrad on two novels: *The Inheritors* (1901) and *Romance* (1903). Founder and editor of *English Review* 1908-1909. A lively, if untrustworthy memoirist. *Memories and Impressions* (1911); *Thus to Revisit* (1921); *Return to Yesterday* (1932). Ludwig, ed., *Letters* (1965).

HUNT, William Holman (1827-1910). Painter. One of the founders of Pre-Raphaelite Brotherhood (1848). *Pre-Raphaelitism and the Pre-Raphaelite Brotherhood*, 2 vols. (1905).

IRVING, Sir Henry (1838-1905). Actor-manager, known for extravagant Shakespearian productions. First actor knighted (1895). Craig, *Life* (1931).

ISAACS, Rufus (1860-1935), first Marquess of Reading (1926). Lawyer and politician. Attorney-general 1910-1913; involved in Marconi scandal 1912-1913, but acquitted. Lord Chief Justice 1913-1921.

JACKSON, Holbrook (1874-1948). Essayist and editor. Fabian; co-editor, with Orage, of *New Age* 1907-1908. *The Eighteen-Nineties* (1913).

JAMES, Henry (1843-1916). Novelist. During the Edwardian years he lived at Rye and wrote his last three novels there:

Wings of the Dove (1902) ; *Ambassadors* (1903) ; *Golden Bowl* (1904). Became British citizen 1915. Lubbock, ed., *Letters*, 2 vols. (1920) ; Edel, *Henry James*, 3 vols. and continuing (1953-   ).

JAMES, Montague Rhodes (1862-1936). Biblical scholar, antiquary, writer. Director of Fitzwilliam Museum 1893-1908; Provost, King's College, Cambridge, 1905-1918; Vice-Chancellor of Cambridge 1913-1915; Provost of Eton 1918-1936. Author of many popular ghost stories. *Eton and King's* (1926).

JAMES, William (1842-1910). Psychologist; brother of Henry. Interested in psychical research; member of Society for Psychical Research. *Letters*, 2 vols. (1926). Murphy, ed., *William James on Psychical Research* (1960).

JOHN, Augustus (1878-1961). Painter. Best known for his portraits and for his bohemian life. *Chiaroscuro* (1952) ; *Finishing Touches* (1964).

JONES, Henry Arthur (1851-1929). Playwright. His "realistic" plays had considerable success in the 'nineties. *Case of Rebellious Susan* (1894). *Life and Letters* (1930).

JOYCE, James (1882-1941). Irish writer. Lived in Trieste 1904-1914. *Dubliners* completed 1906, published 1914; *Portrait of the Artist as a Young Man* completed 1915, published 1916. Gilbert and Ellmann, eds., *Letters*, 3 vols. (1957-1967); Ellmann, *James Joyce* (1959).

KEYNES, John Maynard (1883-1946), first Baron (1942). Economist; lecturer in economics, Cambridge, 1908-1915. Member Bloomsbury Group. Harrod, *Life of Keynes* (1951).

KIPLING, Rudyard (1865-1936). Author. Born in India; worked as journalist there 1882-1889. In South Africa during Boer War. Became increasingly extreme in his imperialistic views, advocated force in Ulster (1914). Nobel Prize 1907. *Something of Myself* (1937).

LAMB, Henry (1883-   ). Painter and draughtsman. R.A. 1949.

LANE, Sir Hugh (1875-1915). Irish art dealer and critic. Director of Irish National Gallery 1914. Died in sinking of Lusitania. His collection of French Impressionists was claimed by both the Dublin Gallery and the Tate; the Tate won, but now shares the collection with Dublin. Lady Gregory, *Hugh Lane's Life and Achievements* (1921).

LANE, John (1854-1925). Publisher. His *Yellow Book* published works of many fin-de-siècle authors. Co-founder of Bodley Head press. May, *John Lane and the Nineties* (1936).

LANG, Andrew (1844-1912). Scottish poet and man of letters. His writings include folklore, history, novels, and children's books. President of Society for Psychical Research, 1911. Grein, *Andrew Lang* (1946).

LAWRENCE, David Herbert (1885-1930). Novelist and poet. Schoolmaster until 1911; first published writings, poems, appeared in *English Review* 1909. Early novels are *The White Peacock* (1911), *The Trespasser* (1912), *Sons and Lovers* (1913). Left England with Frieda von Richthofen Weekley 1912, returned during war years, left permanently 1918. Moore, ed., *Collected Letters* (1962); Nehls, ed., *D. H. Lawrence: a Composite Biography*, 3 vols. (1957-1959).

LEHMANN, Rudolph Chambers (1856-1929). Journalist. On staff of *Punch* 1890-1919; Liberal M.P. 1906-1910. Father of Beatrix, John, and Rosamond Lehmann.

LE QUEUX, William (1864-1927). Journalist and popular novelist. *The Invasion of 1910* (1906); *Things I Know About Kings, Celebrities, and Crooks* (1923). Sladen, *The Real Le Queux* (1938).

LEWIS, Percy Wyndham (1884-1957). Artist and author. One of first English Cubists; founder, with Ezra Pound, of *Blast* (1914). His portraits of T. S. Eliot and Edith

Sitwell are in the Tate. In later years his writings became increasingly reactionary. *Blasting and Bombardiering* (1937); *Rude Assignment* (1950). Rose, ed., *Letters* (1963).

LITTLE TICH (1868-1928). Stage name of Harry Relph, music-hall comedian.

LLOYD, Marie (1870-1922). Stage name of Matilda Wood, music-hall comedienne and singer.

LLOYD GEORGE, David (1863-1945), first Earl (1945). Welsh statesman. Entered Parliament 1890; President Board of Trade 1905-1908; Chancellor of Exchequer 1908-1915. His Old Age Pensions Act (1908) and "People's Budget" (1909-1910) led to the revolt of the House of Lords and the Parliament Bill. Prime Minister 1916-1922. *The People's Budget* (1909). Thomson, *David Lloyd George* (1948).

LODGE, Sir Oliver (1851-1940). Physicist. Principal of Birmingham University 1900-1919. Became deeply involved in psychical research after 1900. *Raymond* (1916); *Past Years* (1931).

LYTTELTON, Edward (1855-1942). Schoolmaster and clergyman. Headmaster of Eton 1905-1916. *Cause and Prevention of Immorality in Schools* (1887); *Training of the Young in Sex* (1900).

LYTTON, Victor Alexander George Robert Bulwer-Lytton (1876-1947), second Earl of Lytton. Political figure and patron of the arts. Grandson of the Victorian novelist, son of the first Earl, statesman. His idealistic support of unpopular issues (women's suffrage was one) kept him from political leadership.

MACCARTHY, Sir Desmond (1878-1952). Critic and editor. Drama critic for the *Speaker* (1904) and later for *New Statesman*. Knighted 1951. *The Court Theatre* (1907); *Memories* (1953).

McCARTHY, Lillah (1876- ?). Actress. First wife of Granville Barker. Starred in many Shaw plays, including *John Bull's Other Island* (1905), *Man and Superman* (1905),

The Doctor's Dilemma (1906). With Barker, produced a distinguished season of Shakespeare plays 1912. *Myself and My Friends* (1933).

MacColl, Dugald Sutherland (1859-1948). Art critic. Publicized Impressionism in England. Art editor of *Spectator* 1890-1896; *Saturday Review* 1896-1906. Keeper, Tate Gallery, 1906-1911; Keeper of Wallace Collection, 1911-1924. *Confessions of a Keeper* (1931).

MacDonald, James Ramsay (1866-1937). Statesman and labor leader. Secretary of Labour Representation Committee (later Labour Party) 1900-1912; M.P. 1906-1918, 1922-1937; first Labour Prime Minister 1924. *Socialism and Society* (1905); *Socialism* (1907). Elton, *Life* (1939).

McEvoy, Arthur Ambrose (1878-1927). Painter best known for portraits. Friend of Augustus John and Sickert, member New English Art Club. Rothenstein, *Modern English Painters, Sickert to Smith* (1952).

Machen, Arthur (1863-1947). Welsh author of fantastic tales; occultist. *Far Off Things* (1922); *Things Near and Far* (1923).

MacKenzie, Edward Montague Compton (1883-   ). Novelist and Scottish nationalist. His *Sinister Street* (1913-1914) was one of the most successful novels of the immediate pre-war period. Knighted 1952. *My Life and Times*, 4 vols. and continuing (1963-   ).

Mansfield, Richard (1857-1907). Actor, first in England and later in the United States. Played Bluntschli in *Arms and the Man* (1894) and Dick Dudgeon in *The Devil's Disciple* (1897). Winter, *Life and Art of Richard Mansfield* (1910).

Marchant, Rev. Sir James (1867-1956). Clergyman and reformer. At various times associated with Congregationalists, Presbyterians, Baptists, and Anglicans. Secretary of National Social Purity Crusade from 1901; Secretary of National Birth Rate Commission 1913-1934.

Marsh, Sir Edward (1872-1953). Civil servant and patron

of the arts. Private secretary to Winston Churchill 1905-1915. Founder and editor of *Georgian Poetry* (5 vols. between 1912 and 1922); editor of *Poems* of his friend Rupert Brooke. Knighted 1937. *A Number of People* (1939). Hassall, *Edward Marsh* (1959).

MASEFIELD, John (1878-1967). Poet, novelist, and playwright. Made reputation with *Everlasting Mercy* (1911). His play *The Tragedy of Nan* produced by Barker at Royal Court 1908. Poet Laureate 1930. *In the Mill* (1941); *So Long to Learn* (1952).

MASON, Alfred Edward Woodley (1865-1948). Actor, novelist, playwright. Liberal M.P. 1906-1910. *Four Feathers* (1902). Green, *A. E. W. Mason* (1952).

MASTERMAN, Charles Frederick Gurney (1873-1927). Politician, journalist, author. Liberal M.P. 1906-1914, Cabinet minister (Duchy of Lancaster) 1914. Lost his seat in Parliament 1914; never again prominent. *The Condition of England* (1909). L. Masterman, *C. F. G. Masterman* (1939).

MASTERMAN, Lucy (1884-   ). Wife of C. F. G., daughter of Sir Neville Lyttelton, chief of Army General Staff.

MAUGHAM, W. Somerset (1874-1965). Novelist, playwright, short-story writer. First novel *Liza of Lambeth* (1897). Principal Edwardian success was as playwright; four plays running simultaneously in London 1908 (*The Explorer, Lady Frederick, Mrs. Dot, Jack Straw*). *The Summing Up* (1938). R. Maugham, *Somerset and All the Maughams* (1966).

MAURICE, General Sir John Frederick (1841-1912). Professor of Military History at Staff College; author of works on military history and strategy.

MAXWELL, William Babington (d. 1938). Novelist. Son of "Miss Braddon," author of the Victorian best-seller *Lady Audley's Secret*. Wrote nearly 40 novels, including the controversial *Devil's Garden* (1913).

MEREDITH, George (1828-1909). Novelist and poet. By 1900

his productive career was over though his reputation continued to grow. *Letters* (1912) .

MIDDLEMORE, Sir John (1844-1925) . Politician and reformer. M.P. 1899-1918; active in social work with children. Baronet 1919.

MILNER, Alfred (1854-1925) , first Viscount Milner (1902) . Statesman, reformer, civil servant. High Commissioner for South Africa 1897-1905; Secretary of State for War 1918; Colonial Secretary 1918-1921. *Milner Papers 1897-99* (1931); *1899-1905* (1933) .

MONEY, Sir Lee George Chiozza (1870-1944) . Author and journalist; writer on economic and sociological subjects. Knighted 1915. *Riches and Poverty* (1905) .

MOORE, George (1852-1933) . Novelist and critic. By his own account he brought the French realistic novel to England, and he was instrumental in publicizing the Impressionist painters. Active in Irish literary revival from 1899. *Confessions of a Young Man* (1888) ; *Hail and Farewell,* 3 vols. (1911-1914) . Home, *Life* (1936) .

MOORE, Mary (1861-1931) . Actress; partner, co-star, and eventually wife of Sir Charles Wyndham; proprietor with him of three London theaters. Played Lady Susan in Jones' *Case of Rebellious Susan* (1894) .

MORRELL, Lady Ottoline (1873-1938) . Patroness, center of literary and artistic circle in Bloomsbury and at Garsington Manor, near Oxford. Half-sister of sixth Duke of Portland. Gathorne-Hardy, ed., *Ottoline* (1963) .

MUNRO, Hector Hugh (1870-1916) . [Saki.] Journalist and author. Wrote political satires (*Westminster Alice,* 1902) , short stories, two novels (*Unbearable Bassington,* 1912, and *When William Came,* 1914) , plays. A mordant Tory critic of Edwardian society. Killed in action, Western front.

MURRAY, George Gilbert Aimé (1866-1957) . Classical scholar, author. Professor of Greek at Oxford 1908. His translations of Greek tragedies were in the Royal Court repertoire. A Fabian and friend of Barker. *Unfinished Autobiography* (1960). Thomson, *Life* (1958).

MYERS, Frederick W. H. (1843-1901). Poet, school inspector, psychic researcher. Founder of Society for Psychical Research. 1882. *Human Personality*, 2 vols. (1903); *Fragments of Inner Life* (1961).

NEWBOLT, Sir Henry (1862-1938). Poet, editor, man of letters. Best known poem "Drake's Drum" (1896). Works express his faith in Christian virtues and the Empire. *My World as in My Time* (1931); *Later Life and Letters* (1942).

NEWTON, Thomas Wodehouse Legh (1857-1942), second Baron Newton (1898). Diplomat. Foreign service 1879-1886; Conservative M.P. 1886-1898. Member Joint Committee on Censorship (1909). *Retrospection* (1941).

NORTHCLIFFE, Alfred C. W. Harmsworth (1865-1922), first Viscount Northcliffe (1917). Newspaper magnate. Revolutionized British journalism with his popular *Daily Mail* (founded 1896). From 1908, proprietor of *Times*. Pound and Harmsworth, *Life* (1959); *History of the Times*, vol. IV, pt. 1 (1912-1920).

OPPENHEIM, E. Philips (1866-1946). Journalist and popular novelist of romance, adventure, and intrigue. *The Pool of Memory* (1941).

ORAGE, Alfred Richard (1873-1934). Editor. Theosophist in early years; became Fabian; editor of *New Age* 1907-1922. Later took up Social Credit, founded *New English Weekly* to publicize it. *Selected Essays* (1935). Mairet, *Orage* (1936).

ORPEN, Sir William (1878-1931). Painter, portraitist. Knighted 1918; R.A. 1919. Konody and Dark, *William Orpen: Artist and Man* (1932).

PANKHURST, Mrs. Emmeline (1858-1928). Suffragette. Leader of the militant wing of women's suffrage movement; founder, with her daughter, of Women's Social and Political Union 1903. *My Own Story* (1914). Fulford, *Votes for Women* (1957).

PARKER, Sir Gilbert (1862-1932). Novelist. M.P. 1900-1918. Knighted 1902; baronet 1915. Author of popular, sensational romances.

PATON, James (1843-1921). Superintendent of Museums and Art Galleries of the Corporation of Glasgow 1876-1910.

PEASE, Edward (1857-1955). A founder of the Fabian Society; General Secretary 1889-1914. *History of the Fabian Society* (1916).

PETHICK-LAWRENCE, Mrs. Emmeline (1867- ?). Suffrage leader. *My Part in a Changing World* (1938).

PHILLIPS, Sir Claude (1846-1924). Art critic. Keeper of Wallace Collection 1897-1911. Knighted 1911.

PHILLPOTTS, Eden (1862-1960). Novelist and playwright. Wrote more than 250 books; best known for his novels set on Dartmoor. Widecombe edition of Dartmoor novels (1927); *From the Angle of 88* (1951).

PINERO, Sir Arthur Wing (1855-1934). Playwright. Successful writer of "problem" plays: *Second Mrs. Tanqueray* (1893); *Mid-Channel* (1909). Knighted 1909. Dunkel, *Sir Arthur Pinero* (1941).

PLYMOUTH, Robert George Windsor-Clive (1857-1923), 14th Baron Windsor, first Earl of Plymouth (1905). First Commissioner of Works 1902-1905. Member Joint Committee on Censorship 1909.

POUND, Ezra Loomis (1885-). American poet. Travelled in Europe 1907-1908; settled in London 1908. Became leader of modernist poets, publicist of Imagism. Paige, ed., *Letters* (1950); Hutchins, *Ezra Pound in Kensington* (1965).

POYNTER, Sir Edward (1836-1919). Painter. Slade Professor of Fine Arts, University of London, 1871-1875; Director of National Gallery 1894-1904; President of Royal Academy 1896-1918. Knighted 1896; baronet 1902.

RALEIGH, Sir Walter (1861-1922). Professor and critic. Elected first Professor of English Literature, Oxford, 1904. Knighted 1911. *Letters* (1926).

RAYLEIGH, John William Strutt (1842-1919), third Baron.

Mathematician and physicist. Cavendish Professor of Experimental Physics, Cambridge, 1879-1884; Secretary of Royal Society 1885-1896; President of Society for Psychical Research 1901; Nobel Prize 1905. Married to sister of Arthur Balfour.

REDFORD, George Alexander (d. 1916). Bank manager; Examiner of Plays for Lord Chamberlain 1895-1911; film censor 1912-1916.

REEVES, William Pember (1857-1932). Administrator and educator. Member New Zealand Parliament 1887-1896; Minister of Education, Labour and Justice 1891-1896; Agent-general for New Zealand in London 1896-1905; High Commissioner 1905-1908. Director of London School of Economics 1908-1919. Member Fabian Society.

REYNOLDS, Stephen (1881-1919). Fisherman and writer on working class. Worked as fisherman, Devon, from 1903. Inspector of Fisheries 1914. *A Poor Man's House* (1908). Wright, ed., *Letters* (1923).

RIBBLESDALE, Thomas Lister (1854-1925), fourth Baron. Lord-in-Waiting 1880-1885; Master of the Queen's Buckhounds 1892-1895. Member Joint Committee on Censorship 1909.

RICHARDS, Grant (1872-1948). Publisher and author. Publisher of early works by Shaw and Joyce. *Author Hunting* (1934).

RICHMOND, Sir William (1842-1921). Portrait painter. Slade Professor of Fine Arts, Oxford, 1879-1883; R.A. 1895. Knighted 1897.

RICKETTS, Charles (1866-1931). Artist, designer of books and stage sets. In 'nineties, designed books by Oscar Wilde. R.A. 1928. Lewis, ed., *Self-Portrait* (1939).

ROBERTS, Frederick Sleigh (1832-1914), first Earl Roberts of Kandahar, Pretoria, and Waterford (1900). After distinguished military career in India and South Africa, he returned to England as Commander-in-Chief of British forces. Retired 1904; spent last years working for stronger national defenses. *Defence of the Empire* (1905). James, *Lord Roberts* (1954).

ROBINS, Elizabeth (1862-1952). American-born actress, playwright, novelist. One of the first to produce and act in Ibsen plays in England. *Votes for Women!* (1909); *Theater and Friendship* [her correspondence with Henry James] (1932).

Ross, Robert (1869-1918). Journalist and art critic. Director of Carfax Gallery 1900-1908; Trustee, National Gallery. Administrator of estate of his friend Oscar Wilde; edited Wilde's *Works* (1908). M. Ross, ed., *Robert Ross: Friend of Friends* (1952).

ROWNTREE, Benjamin Seebohm (1871-1954). Manufacturer, philanthropist, writer on social problems. *Poverty* (1901).

RUGGLES-BRISE, Sir Evelyn (1857-1935). Chairman of H. M. Prison Commission 1895-1921. Knighted 1902. *The English Prison System* (1921).

RUSSELL, Bertrand (1872-   ), third Earl Russell. Mathematician and philosopher. His work with Alfred North Whitehead produced one of the monuments of Edwardian thought, the *Principia Mathematica* (1910-1913). *Autobiography* (1967).

RUSSELL, John Francis (1865-1931), second Earl Russell. Elder brother of Bertrand. Electrical engineer. Of his three marriages, the first two unfortunately overlapped; he was tried by his peers for bigamy in 1901. A leader in the campaign to reform English divorce laws. *My Life and Adventures* (1923).

RUTHERFORD, Ernest (1871-1937), first Baron (1931). Physicist, pioneer in sub-atomic physics. Developed nuclear theory of atom 1906-1914. Cavendish Professor of Physics, Cambridge, 1919-1937. Nobel Prize 1908. *Radioactivity* (1904). Feather, *Lord Rutherford* (1940).

SAKI. *See* Munro, H. H.

SALEEBY, Dr. Caleb Williams (1878-1940). Physician and geneticist, reformer. Founder of Eugenics Society, writer and lecturer on eugenics. Divorce laws, alcoholism, and the birth rate were some of his other causes. *The Progress of Eugenics* (1914).

SALISBURY, Robert Arthur Talbot Gascoyne-Cecil (1830-1903), third Marquess of Salisbury. Three times Conservative Prime Minister: 1885-1886; 1886-1892; 1895-1902. Succeeded in that office by his nephew, Arthur Balfour. Kennedy, *Life* (1953).

SAMUEL, Herbert (1870-1963), first Viscount Samuel (1937). Liberal politician. Chancellor of the Duchy of Lancaster 1909; Postmaster-general 1910, 1915; Home Secretary 1916 and 1931-1932. *Memoirs* (1945).

SARGENT, John Singer (1856-1925). American painter, best known for his elegant portraits of the rich. Most of his work was done in England. Elected to Royal Academy 1897. Charteris, *John Sargent* (1927).

SHAW, Charlotte Payne-Townshend (1857-1943). Anglo-Irish heiress, married G. B. Shaw 1898. Like her husband, an active Fabian Socialist. Dunbar, *Mrs. G. B. S.* (1963).

SHAW, George Bernard (1856-1950). Playwright and Socialist, early leader of Fabians; edited *Fabian Essays* (1889). Laurence, ed., *Collected Letters* (1964 and continuing); Laurence, ed., *Platform and Pulpit* (1961).

SICKERT, Walter (1860-1942). Painter and critic. Best of the English Impressionists; founder of New English Art Club 1887. *A Free House* [selected writings] (1947). Emmons, *Life and Opinions of Walter Sickert* (1941).

SINCLAIR, May (1865?-1946). Novelist and suffragette. Her first successful novel was *The Divine Fire* (1904).

SMITH, C. Aubrey (1863-1948). Actor. Appeared in Shaw plays and in *Votes for Women!* (1907).

SMITH, William Frederick Danvers (1868-1928), second Viscount Hambleden (1913). Philanthropist, businessman; head of W. H. Smith & Son, booksellers, from 1891. Conservative M.P. 1891-1910.

SNOWDEN, Philip (1864-1937), first Viscount Snowden

(1931). Socialist, reformer; propagandist for Independent Labour Party 1895-1905. M.P. 1906-1918, 1922-1931. *Autobiography* (1934).

SPENCER, Sir Stanley (1891-1959). Painter, best known for religious subjects using Thames Valley scenes. R.A. 1950; knighted 1959. Collis, *Stanley Spencer* (1962).

STEER, Philip Wilson (1860-1942). Painter, impressionist in style; a founder of New English Art Club. MacColl, *Life* (1945).

STEPHEN, Sir Leslie (1832-1904). Critic, biographer, editor of *Cornhill Magazine, DNB.* Father of Virginia Woolf and Vanessa Bell. Agnostic. *An Agnostic's Apology* (1893). Annan, *Leslie Stephen* (1951).

STRACHEY, Giles Lytton (1880-1932). Critic and biographer. Member Bloomsbury Group. *Eminent Victorians* (1918); *Queen Victoria* (1921); *Virginia Woolf and Lytton Strachey Letters* (1956).

STRACHEY, John St. Loe (1860-1927). Journalist; editor of *Cornhill* 1896-1898, *Spectator* 1895-1925. *Adventure of Living* (1922). Holroyd, *Lytton Strachey* (1967).

SWINBURNE, Algernon Charles (1837-1909). Poet and radical. Spent last thirty years in retirement in Putney. *Letters,* 6 vols. (1959-1962).

SWINNERTON, Frank (1884-   ). Novelist and critic. First novel, *The Merry Heart* (1909). *The Georgian Literary Scene* (1932); *Swinnerton: an Autobiography* (1936); *Background with Chorus* (1956).

SYNGE, John Millington (1871-1909). Irish dramatist and poet. Active in Irish literary renaissance. Lady Gregory, *Our Irish Theatre* (1914); Price, ed., *Autobiography* (1965); Coxhead, *J. M. Synge and Lady Gregory* (1962).

TAYLOR, Sir William (1848-1917). Soldier-physician. Army Medical staff 1864-1904; Director-General Army Medical Service 1901-1904. Knighted 1902.

TENNANT, May Edith Abraham (1869-1946). Pioneer in social work. First woman Inspector of Factories. Married to Harold Tennant, Private Secretary to Herbert Asquith and brother of Asquith's wife, Margot.

THOMPSON, Francis (1859-1907). Poet and critic. Poverty and drug addiction led to early death. Best known poem "The Hound of Heaven" (1893). Reid, *Life* (1959).

THOMSON, Prof. Sir John Arthur (1861-1933). Biologist. Regius Professor of Natural History, Aberdeen, 1899-1930. Knighted 1930. *See* Geddes.

TREVELYAN, George Macaulay (1876-1962). Historian. Master of Trinity College, Cambridge, 1940-1951. *Autobiography* (1949).

UNWIN, Sir Stanley (1884-   ). Publisher. Founded firm of Allen & Unwin 1914. *The Truth About A Publisher* (1960).

UNWIN, Thomas Fisher (1848-1935). Publisher. Founded firm of Fisher Unwin; published Galsworthy, Conrad, Yeats.

VINCENT, Sir Edgar (1857-1941). Viscount D'Abernon (1926). Financier and diplomat. Governor, Imperial Ottoman Bank, 1889-1897; Conservative M.P. 1899-1906. Chairman Royal Commission on Imperial Trade 1912.

WALKLEY, Arthur Bingham (1855-1926). Critic. Drama critic of London *Times* 1900-1926. Shaw dedicated *Man and Superman* to him.

WALLACE, Alfred Russel (1823-1913). Naturalist, biologist. Independently discovered principle of natural selection (1858). Interested in spiritualism in later years. *My Life*, 2 vols. (1905).

WALLIS, Sir Whitworth (1855-1937). Art historian. Director Birmingham Art Gallery from 1885. Knighted 1912.

WARD, Mrs. Humphrey (1851-1920). Novelist and playwright; her most famous book was *Robert Elsmere* (1888). Leader of the anti-suffrage movement. *A Writer's Recollections* (1918).

WARWICK, Frances Evelyn Greville (1861-1935), Countess of Warwick; married fifth Earl 1881. Leader of late-

Victorian society, friend of Edward VII. Converted to socialism; devoted herself to charity and reform. *Life's Ebb and Flow* (1929). Blunden, *The Countess of Warwick* (1967).

WATTS, George Frederick (1817-1904). Painter and sculpter. His 800 pictures include many moral and allegorical subjects: "Sir Galahad," "Hope." R.A. 1867. *Life*, 3 vols. (1912).

WEBB, Beatrice Potter (1858-1943). Reformer. Daughter of a midlands industrialist. With her husband, one of the principal shapers of Fabian socialism. Co-author with him of many social and political studies: *History of Trade Unionism* (1894); *English Local Government* (1906-1929); *Minority Report of Poor Law Commission* (1909). *My Apprenticeship* (1926); *Our Partnership* (1945). M. Cole, *Life* (1949).

WEBB, Sidney (1859-1947), first Baron Passfield (1929). Economist and social reformer. London-born, lower-middle-class civil servant; married Beatrice 1892. Founder of London School of Economics (1895), *New Statesman* (1913). His wife declined to share his barony.

WEDGWOOD, Josiah (1872-1943), first Baron Wedgwood (1942). Politician and reformer; M.P. 1906-1942, first as Liberal, after 1919 as Labour.

WELLS, Herbert George (1866-1946), author. Of lower-class origins, trained as scientist. First literary success was with science fiction. Best works 1900-1914 were social novels, often comic: *Kipps* (1905), *Tono-Bungay* (1909), *Mr. Polly* (1910). Also wrote on social and political issues. *Experiment in Autobiography* (1934).

WHISTLER, James Abbott McNeill (1834-1903). American painter. Worked principally in London, where his radical style won both disciples and detractors. Founder and President, International Society of Sculptors, Painters, and Engravers, 1898-1903. E. & J. Pennell, *Life*, 2 vols. (1908).

WILLOUGHBY DE BROKE, Richard Greville Verney (1869-

1923), nineteenth Baron. A fox-hunting county peer; leader of "diehard" opposition to Parliament Bill.

WOOLF, Adeline Virginia Stephen (1882-1941). Novelist and critic. Sister of Vanessa Bell. Married Leonard Woolf 1912. First novel *The Voyage Out* (1915). *A Writer's Diary* (1953). See also her husband's autobiographical books.

WOOLF, Leonard (1880-   ). Journalist, writer on social questions, publisher. Husband of Virginia Woolf, and with her a leader of Bloomsbury Group. *Sowing* (1960); *Reaping* (1962); *Beginning Again* (1964); *Downhill All the Way* (1967).

WRIGHT, Sir Almroth (1861-1947). Bacteriologist. Introduced anti-typhoid inoculation; developed new uses of vaccines. Opponent of women's suffrage. Knighted 1906.

WYNDHAM, Sir Charles (1837-1919). Actor-manager. Co-proprietor (with Mrs. Mary Moore) of three London theaters. Produced plays of Henry Arthur Jones. Knighted 1902.

YEATS, William Butler (1865-1939). Irish poet and playwright. During the Edwardian years he was active in the administration of the Abbey Theatre, Dublin. Nobel Prize 1923. *Autobiographies* (1955); *Letters* (1955). Hone, *Life* (1942).

ZANGWILL, Israel (1864-1926). Jewish novelist and playwright; Zionist. *Children of the Ghetto* (1892).

THE LYTTELTON FAMILY:
AN "ESTABLISHMENT" GENEALOGY

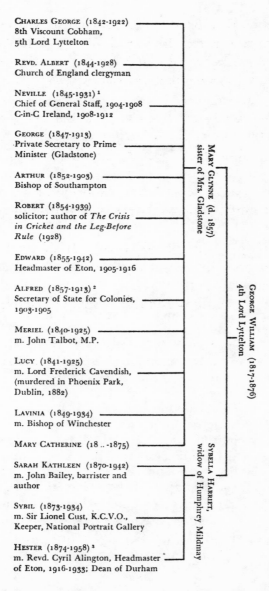

CHARLES GEORGE (1842-1922)
8th Viscount Cobham,
5th Lord Lyttelton

REVD. ALBERT (1844-1928)
Church of England clergyman

NEVILLE (1845-1931) [1]
Chief of General Staff, 1904-1908
C-in-C Ireland, 1908-1912

GEORGE (1847-1913)
Private Secretary to Prime
Minister (Gladstone)

ARTHUR (1852-1903)
Bishop of Southampton

ROBERT (1854-1939)
solicitor; author of *The Crisis
in Cricket and the Leg-Before
Rule* (1928)

EDWARD (1855-1942)
Headmaster of Eton, 1905-1916

ALFRED (1857-1913) [2]
Secretary of State for Colonies,
1903-1905

MERIEL (1840-1925)
m. John Talbot, M.P.

LUCY (1841-1925)
m. Lord Frederick Cavendish,
(murdered in Phoenix Park,
Dublin, 1882)

LAVINIA (1849-1934)
m. Bishop of Winchester

MARY CATHERINE (18 .. -1875)

SARAH KATHLEEN (1870-1942)
m. John Bailey, barrister and
author

SYBIL (1873-1934)
m. Sir Lionel Cust, K.C.V.O.,
Keeper, National Portrait Gallery

HESTER (1874-1958) [3]
m. Revd. Cyril Alington, Headmaster
of Eton, 1916-1933; Dean of Durham

MARY GLYNNE (d. 1857)
sister of Mrs. Gladstone

GEORGE WILLIAM (1817-1876)
4th Lord Lyttelton

SYBELLA HARRIET,
widow of Humphrey Mildmay

[1] Eldest daughter, Lucy, married C.F.G. Masterman, Liberal politician.

[2] Married Laura Tennant, sister of Margot, second wife of Herbert Asquith.

[3] Her daughter, Elizabeth Hester, married Sir Alec Douglas-Home.

APPENDIX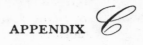

FAULTS OF THE FABIAN

[On Feb. 9th Mr. H. G. WELLS read a paper to a meeting confined strictly to members of the Fabian Society. It has been thought desirable to place it before the entire membership. The feeling will, however, be easily understood that the criticisms made by Mr. Wells, while perfectly legitimate in the intimacy of our society and its friends, are not of the sort that it is desirable to publish indiscriminately, amounting as they do in places to a very complete repudiation of courses to which the society as a whole has been committed. His comments are, it is considered, part of a private discussion of our policy and plans, conceived in a vein of frankness that the outsider might easily misunderstand. Particularly is any risk of press comment deprecated.]

MR. WELLS opened by declaring himself a socialist of long standing, but only recently a Fabian. "I came," he said, "into your society very curious to know what you were up to, I have made the acquaintance of a number of your members, and I have formed certain general conceptions of the range and possibilities of this association and of its difficulties, which I have embodied in this evening's paper. Let me state crudely the contrast that concerns me, my chief impression of you. I perceive on the one hand among more or less educated, more or less prosperous people of this country, a large number of socialists, partial socialists, people with socialistic sympathies, and undeveloped socialists, now quite urgently needing organization and a unifying propaganda; and on the other hand I see our society, with its seven hundred odd members, apparently under the impression that these seven hundred odd are the only thoughtful and authoritative socialists in existence in England, and that what does not occur in our meetings has nothing to do with socialism. . . .

I want to set myself to-night to correct this extraordinary mistake some of us make. So far from our being a little band of true believers in an individualistic or quite unenlightened and hostile world, we are, I hold, an extraordinarily inadequate and feeble organization in the midst of a world that teems with undeveloped possibilities of support and help for the cause we profess to further. That image of the little band of believers was perhaps true in the eighties, but we are twenty years from that. Everything almost in the world of thought has changed since those rebellious outcast years—unless it is our society. Our society, I feel, must go the way of all things now, and change also. I am here to-night to ask it to change. I have looked over my *Fabian News*, month by month, conversed with our members, attended many of our meetings, with an ever deepening discontent at the way in which things are done by this society, at its failure either to organize, develop, or represent the spirit of social reconstruction that is arising all about us, in its failure to use the prestige it has accumulated, to fulfil the promises it once made the world.

To begin with, let me ask what are the functions that the Fabian Society claims to discharge or does discharge or might discharge, in relation to the development of socialism at the present time. It seems to me that these are three in number. There is first of all the large amount of intellectual work that had to be done and which our society certainly has, sometimes with a certain lack of charm perhaps, with a certain diminishing enthusiasm and a certain increasing tendency to a hard practical tone, but with an undeniable persistence and vigour, managed to get done—in working out the first broad and crude propositions of socialism, and in bringing them into measurable relation with existing social institutions. In this direction the efficiency, not so much of the society as a whole, but of certain members of the society, has been very considerable, but they have carried this branch of work at last almost out of touch with any socialistic ideals at all. I believe it is not too much to claim the London School of Economics as an offspring, or at any rate a closely collateral development, of this side of our society's work. From among our members it drew capacity, energy, initiative, that we could ill spare. We gave to economic science much that might well, I think, have been kept for propaganda. But that, however, does not by any means detract from our claim to consideration upon this first score.

The second function of such a society as ours is of acting as a sort of official or representative mouthpiece for socialistic theory in England. In this direction I must confess I regard its performance with much more qualified admiration. I hope I shall not offend too deeply if I confess I think it has at times abused its authoritative claim. Time after time it has shown a disposition to intervene in contemporary political conflicts in which, I hold, socialistic principles were only remotely involved, in which indeed they scarcely apply. It spoke for socialism in relation to the Boer war, for example, it insisted upon doing this, I am told, in spite of the remonstrances of its executive; you will forgive me, I hope, for thinking it had no business to do so. It ought, I hold, to have left the war alone altogether. It was pretended that in some subtle manner Imperialism was sound socialism and nationalism wasn't—an absolutely gratuitous gloss. I have tried to make out how we were drawn into that particular indiscretion. I am inclined to think we did that because just then our genuine socialism stood at its lowest point. We were in a slack season, there was something very like a slump in socialism with the dawn of the new century, there was an extraordinary lull at that time in our faith in truly socialistic advance; we were doing nothing, and feeling dull and out of touch, and we—we became politicians. Our unnecessary, meddlesome intervention in that enormous emotional struggle, the three tailors of Tooley Street pronouncements we made, were made in sheer forgetfulness of our true concerns. They divided the forces of our society, they had a very detrimental effect upon the public estimate of socialism. Our interference in the squabble over the conditions of teaching in the popular schools was, I think, even more unfortunate. You must admit, if you think it over, that that conflict had very little to do with the essential principles of socialism. Excellent socialists were and are to be found on either side, and over these two affairs we tore ourselves asunder, lost members, disheartened members, gained in certain quarters the reputation of being an unaccountable and disingenuous political faction, in return for no good achieved whatever that I can see. These efforts were among our failures, and I recall them to you now only to remind you of the fact that we do profess to speak for socialism as a whole, and that therefore we are under a certain obligation to justify, by the quantity of our members and the quality of their efforts, this very extensive claim.

But neither the first of these functions, that of working out socialistic theory in an exhaustive manner, nor the second, that of giving a representation and official voice to socialistic theory, seems to me nearly so important as the third and most neglected of our possible functions, which is, I hold, to carry on a vigorous socialistic propaganda among all the more educated and intelligent sections of our population. I do not for one moment suggest that the Fabian may now aspire to a control of the general socialistic propaganda of this country; there are already pretty vigorous movements going on among the working classes in the direction of socialism. You have the S. D. F., for example, the I. L. P., you have such healthy developments as the Clarion organization, or the Guild of St. Matthew, covering a world of activity that seems to lie no longer within our sphere of influence. But there remains for us an enormous field still untouched in which we not only may work, but in which I hold we ought to be working most strenuously now, and that is the field of socialistic propaganda among the educated classes and the middle classes. I believe that we particularly could undertake that. We could be, we ought to be, pouring socialistic ideas into the student class, into the professional classes; every journalist ought to be a socialist, the clergy, the religious ministers, public officials, ought to be consciously saturated with our ideas; the whole generous multitude of the educated young. All this great mass needs educating for socialism, and then organizing for socialism, and we are doing scarcely anything, and except for isolated individual efforts, a book here, a word in season there, nobody seems to be doing anything in that direction. I thought this was an important enough duty before the last election, but now I think it a supremely important duty. In London particularly, under the peculiar conditions of London, the hope of socialism resides in the middle class, in that indeterminate class of which the poor doctor and the Board School teacher may perhaps be taken as the best types. Unlike the industrial regions of the Midlands and the North, in which socialism is now making such strides, *there is no homogeneous mass of London workers of sufficient relative magnitude to serve as a permanent basis for socialistic activity*. If London is to become socialistic, it will be through the middle classes receiving socialistic ideas. In London the general linking network of socialists *must* be middle class people, there is no other linking network possible, and it is in London particularly that you find educated people living under such conditions as to make them socialists.

It is to our neglect of this third and most urgent and important function of our society that particularly I wish to call your attention to-night.

And now, having told you of the duties I conceive we do or might perform, let me tell you quite frankly how our society strikes me in relation to the scope and magnitude of these duties.

In none of these three branches of its activity does it strike me as doing anything near what it might, and what therefore it ought, to be doing. In the first place, I will begin with what is perhaps my gravest charge: the society strikes me as being ridiculously small. It is small, not only in the matter of numbers. It has an air of arrested growth; it began its existence in the meetings of a limited number of people in each others' private houses, and to this day it strikes an impartial observer as being still half a drawing-room society, which by a wild, valiant effort took a central office in a cellar in Clement's Inn, and exhausted its courage in that enterprise. Small as our membership is, our staff strikes me as small even for that. We have one secretary, and he has one assistant. It carries out the tradition of your drawing-room days, and the social note that we must lose if we are to grow, that our secretary seems to know all our members by sight. Many years ago the Fabian Society got that secretary, long ago got the underground apartments in Clement's Inn, and it has become habituated to those dimensions of staff and office, just as it has become habituated to meeting in Clifford's Inn. I submit it has to grow out of that.

The first of the faults of the Fabian, then, is that it is small; the second that strikes me is that, even for its smallness, it is needlessly poor. You have it from Mr. Bernard Shaw that poverty is a crime, and if so, then by the evidence of your balance-sheet ours is a criminal organization. Small as our activities are, we barely pay our way. It is an open secret among us that the average subscription is not enough to carry things on; and if it were not for the very heavy subsidies of one or two generous members, the Fabian Society would long ago have had to sell its not very valuable office furniture and disperse. As it is, the society is always hard up and always in debt, and every proposal in the direction of enterprise encounters a financial difficulty. I will discuss the possibilities of remedying this later, and I will pass on now to the third in my list of faults, and that is, our collective inactivity.

That, I know, is not our general impression of ourselves. No doubt we number some very enthusiastic and active members, who are responsible for much dispersed and disjointed work for socialism; but collectively, what are we at? It is not only, for example, that we are small, but we are not growing and we are not attempting to grow. It is not only that our hands are tied by poverty, but we are not struggling to untie them. I am told of the extraordinary amount of work that the Fabian Society does insidiously through its tracts, in exchanging and disseminating information, and in all sorts of curious underground activities. Well, I think some of these claims, and particularly certain claims of personal influence, are justifiable. But this has very little to do with the average member and what the society does as a whole. It would go on just as well if there was no society at all. We circulate some book boxes, it is true, and a few useful things of that sort. Perhaps we have a fair show of that sort of thing for our size and means; but consider it in relation to the task we have to do. Here are some documents that were sent to me to show what the Fabian Society does and is doing. Here is the letter that goes out to all the new members, exhorting them to disperse themselves among borough and district councils, education committees and so forth, and talking in a vague and inconclusive way of lectures, of writing letters to the local papers, and such like things. Then there is an information department engaged in gathering scraps of information from members with sufficient leisure to answer sheets of questions. You are asked, for example, have you any means of influencing any tram, gas, water, or other joint stock company? I wonder how many members answered that, and what it all came to when they did. I wonder what dream of concerted action was in the head of our executive. . . . There is a long list of lecturers, who for the most part, I believe, don't lecture. There is one paper headed with a pencil note Local Census—"Dropped." There is an election results form, in which our members were bothered to give all sorts of exasperating information about electorates and votes; and so on. The effect of it all is of bright, impossible ideas taken up and abandoned, of wasted good intentions, and wasted time and energy,—some of it strikes me as wasted printing. It is almost as if we were being amused to keep us out of mischief. It is quite possible that in this matter I am being unjust; no doubt it would have served a useful purpose to ascertain exactly what percentage of our members could influence gas companies. But was that ever ascertained? Did we in some subtle way get the light of socialism mixed up in the gas flicker of any middle-class home? I don't believe we did. . . .

No doubt much of all this would have been worth doing if it had really been done, if it had been anything more than playing at politico-sociological research; but even if it had been done, do measure it against the task that everyone who confesses himself a militant socialist takes up with that confession. That task is nothing less than the alteration of the economic basis of society. Measure with your eye this little meeting, this little hall; look at that little stall of not very powerful tracts, think of the scattered members, one here, one there, who may or may not have responded to those printed enquiries. Then go out into the Strand. Note the size of the buildings and business places, note the glare of the advertisements, note the abundance of traffic and the multitude of people, take a casual estimate of the site-values as you go along. That is the world whose very foundations you are attempting to change. How does this little dribble of activities look then? That is what I want to keep before you in justification of these criticisms. You may say that to call attention to that contrast is pure materialism, you may say that the world has been changed by a smaller handful than those who meet here to-night, but they met under Pentecostal tongues of fire, and they adopted other methods than that of sending each other papers of questions, and saying in response to every proposal for action "The thing's been tried."

But let me get on with my catalogue of faults. The Fabian Society is small, it is shabbily poor, it is collectively inactive. What next? Well, I think that my next point must be that we are remarkably unbusinesslike, inadaptable, and uninventive in our ways. Our society grew out of a certain Fellowship of the New Life, of friends who met in one another's houses, and talked in a conversational manner. It spent its childhood in parlours and drawing-rooms, drawing-rooms that had at times a conscious touch of Bohemianism and the artistic temperament, and to this day, I hold, the traditions of those drawing-rooms cripple its procedure. To this day we do not like to entertain other socialists unless they have been properly introduced. Instead of trying to grow as large and rich and vigorous as we can, we still permit the most remarkable difficulties to be thrown in the way of the admission of new members. We don't advertise, thank you; it's not quite our style. We cry socialism as the reduced gentlewoman cried "oranges": "I do so hope nobody will hear me."

I have been making one or two new members lately, and my experience burns within me. In the first place the possible and potential Fabian has to discover our existence. Of this he may or may not learn, just accordingly as to whether he meets anybody who knows about us or not. Not only do we not advertise, but we make little or no use of the press in getting fresh members. . . . The possibility and advantages of becoming a member comes to anyone in the nature of a private and intimate tip, and then the business of documents begins. An application for membership has to be filled up, and on this the alleged basis of socialism is set forth, to which the aspirant must subscribe. This basis impresses me as being ill-written and old fashioned, harsh and bad in tone, assertive and unwise, and as likely to deter all sorts of wavering people who might otherwise come into the society and be converted into good socialists. . . . There are those who defend the rigid letter of the basis. They dread broad socialism, they smell heresy and sedition. In the old drawing-room days there seems to have been a great, and perhaps even reasonable, dread of some terrible individualist, someone wild and fierce like that Mr. Belloc who visited us before he became a member of Parliament, creating a dispute or breaking furniture, and perhaps even smuggling in a lot of friends until we found ourselves outvoted and passing resolutions in favour of the Liberty and Property Defence League. But is there any danger of that sort now, and does it matter if there is? . . . I must confess I would at any rate take the risk of demanding only a statement that the applicant is a socialist. If you do not think that sufficient, then anyhow let us define our socialism in compact, persuasive, untechnical phrases.

Well, having accepted this basis, the ambitious socialist must then declare he or she has attended two meetings of the society as a visitor, and must be proposed and seconded by two personal acquaintances, who can answer for his or her deportment; and both proposer and seconder must not only sign the nomination paper and send it about, but must write a letter to the secretary in praise of the candidate. Of course this is as much fuss and trouble as one takes to make a member of a London social club. The papers are sent in. The executive then debates the admission of the candidate. The amount of the subscription is left to the member, and this I presume in most cases means a holograph correspondence with our secretary. Then so soon as the member is elected he receives a letter of the most terrifying sort, from which he gathers, what is not correct, that he has pledged himself to take part, according to his abilities and opportunities, in the general work of the society. It is kept from his notice that the society does no general work at all practically. He is confronted by fantastic possibilities of having to lecture, write letters to his local paper, give away tracts, hold meetings, riot, rebel; and he is informed, or not, of the name of his local newspaper, the names of the various local organizations in his district, and all sorts of things of that kind, to just the extent Mr. Pease may or may not have the leisure and information needed to fill up the blanks provided. It is a most extraordinary document, that letter. Now all this is a tremendous waste of time and energy; a disastrous waste of office energy, when you remember that you are trying to change the industrial basis of civilization through the activity of one secretary and one assistant. It is a misdirection of the new enthusiasm that comes to us, it wastes the patience, it discourages no end of possible new helpers. Does it give us anything in return? Does it even secure orthodoxy? I do not want to start a heresy hunt in this society, or I would like to ask certain of our leading members by name whether they really are prepared to sign over again now the requirements of our basis. All this fumbling over the admission of new members must, I submit, be swept away if the Fabian Society is to do its proper work in the world. One first thing we shall have to do if our society is to embark upon a new career of usefulness, is to replace this obstacle race by a perfectly simple and easily opened door.

There are all sorts of other defects and little pettinesses come to us, I hold, from those old drawing-room days. . . .

Perhaps our worst pettiness, and the one most offensive and deterrent to the serious newcomer, is our little stock-in-trade of jokes, our little special style of joking. It is quite after the manner of the jokes one finds in a large, lax family. We play upon character overmuch. A little giggling excitement runs through all our meetings. I have a sort of idea—a theory—which I can assure you has no relation to any facts whatever, to anything that has ever happened, but which somehow will convey to you the quality of the particular fault I intend. I fable it that once upon a time two or three young persons were somehow roped in; they were shy, but they had a bright joy in observation, they did not understand, or want to understand, but to be startled, to be amused, and they were at that delightful age when the supreme joy of life is to giggle. They giggled at the socialistic idea. They giggled at every socialist who was at all out of the common. They giggled at the hair of this earnest socialist, and the hat of that. They went away giggling to describe socialism to their friends— the funniest thing in the world. I can assure you that constant flow of rather foolish laughter, of rather forced jesting, is no small defect in our work. It flows over and obscures all sorts of grave issues, it chills and kills enthusiasm. Its particular victim in this society is Mr. Bernard Shaw. It pursues him with unrelenting delight, simply because he is not like everybody else, as he rises, before he opens his mouth to speak it begins. Shaw has a habit of vivid statement, he has a habit, a brilliant habit, of seeking to arrest the attention by a startling, apparent irrelevance, and he has a natural inclination to paradox. Our accursed giggle lives on these things. Now Bernard Shaw is at bottom an intensely serious man, whatever momentary effect this instant dissolution of sober discussion into mirth may produce on him, he does in the long run, hate this pursuit of laughter. If you doubt that, go and hear Larry in *John Bull's Other Island* speaking Shaw's disgust.

"And all the while," said Larry, "there goes on a horrible, senseless, mischievous laughter . . . you chaff and sneer and taunt them for not doing the things you daren't do yourself; and all the time you laugh, laugh, laugh—eternal derision, eternal envy, eternal folly, eternal fouling and staining and degrading, until, when you come at last to a country where men take a question seriously and give a serious answer to it, you deride them for having no sense of humour, and plume yourself on your own worthlessness as if it were a superiority."

Well, I think that speaks clearly enough, and that you will not suppose that in attacking laughter I am assailing Bernard Shaw. But I do assail the strained attempts to play up to Shaw, the constant endeavour of members devoid of any natural wit or wildness to catch his manner, to ape his egotism, to fall in with an assumed pretence that this grave high business of Socialism, to which it would be a small offering for us to give all our lives, is an idiotic middle-class joke. . . .

In the old wild drawing-room days, of course, this jesting had a sort of excuse. Everything was fun then. There was so much freshness and intensity of conviction, and so much hard work afoot, and it was all so intimate and understood, that one could jest. But that is not the case with us now. Whether the society decides to renew its youth or enter upon its old age—the spring has gone out of its joking.

My list of the society's faults grows long. Our society is small; and in relation to its great mission small minded; it is poor; it is collectively, as a society, inactive; it is suspicious of help, and exclusive; it is afflicted with a giggle, and a deliberate and intended "sense of humour." And all these faults I have, I think, traced back to the conditions of its early origin. It met socially— to this day it meets socially. It has never yet gone out to attack the unknown public in a systematic and assimilatory manner. At a certain stage in its development its effort seemed to cease, it ceased to grow, ceased to dream, ceased to believe in any possible sort of triumph for socialism as socialism. It experienced just that arrest of growth one sees in a pot-bound plant.

Now, to cease to grow is to cease to believe in growth, to cease to fight is to abandon the thought of triumph, and to that in part I trace that underhand and indirect spirit that is so curiously present in your discussions. We have taken refuge from the fact that we are not openly winning over the world, by a queer pretence that we are, insidiously, and all the while that nothing seems to be happening—getting there. It is a queer pretence which is not altogether a pretence. So far as certain of us are concerned, things do get quietly done, and very good and considerable things too. Nevertheless, I have the temerity to think they do not compensate us for the effect upon our tone of these indirect methods. I find in our society, cropping up sometimes in a speech of this member, and sometimes in the speech of that, a curious conceit of cunning, something like a belief that the world may be manœuvred into socialism without knowing it; that by being very slim and lively and subtle we shall presently be able to confront the world with a delighted, "But you *are* socialists! We chalked it on your backs when you weren't looking." We in this society, I say this with doubtings and regret, have tended more and more to become the exponents of a masked socialism that I fear and dread, that in the end may, quite conceivably, not leave one shred of the true socialistic spirit alive in us. This society is to keep like it is, all existing institutions are to keep as they are, there is still to be a House of Lords, an established church, bishops—they'll not believe in Christianity, but still bishops—Tories—they won't believe in property in land, but they will still be Tories—and yet socialism will be soaking through it all, changing without a sign of change. It is a quite fantastic idea, this dream of an undisturbed surface, of an ostensibly stagnant order in the world, while really we are burrowing underground, burrowing feverishly underground—a quite novel way of getting there—to the New Jerusalem. . . .

You know this cryptic socialism is not a little reminiscent of the mouse that set out to kill the cat; violent methods were deprecated; an organization of all the available mice, and the old crude tactics of attack in multitude that extinguished Bishop Hatto, were especially discouraged. The mouse decided to adopt indirect and inconspicuous methods, not to complicate its proceedings by too many associates, to win over and attract the cat by friendly advances rather than frighten her by a sudden attack. It is believed that in the end the mouse did succeed in permeating the cat, but the cat is still living—and the mouse can't be found.

Then we are to invade municipal bodies, bring about the millennium by tempting the local builder on the town council with socialistic projects for the housing of the working classes, and by luring incompetent urban district boards administering impossible areas into the establishment of electric power stations they are about as well equipped to control as they are the destinies of this empire. Perhaps I go too far with this again. No doubt it is quite possible to achieve all sorts of good purposes through existing organizations and institutions, only—it isn't the way to socialism. Make socialists and you will achieve socialism; there is no other way. Democratic socialism is the only possible sane and living socialism. The only possible socialistic state is a state which is understood, upheld, willingly and cheerfully *lived*, by the great mass of its people. Even were it possible to achieve really socialistic institutions in our insidious way, what would it all amount to? We should have the body of socialism without its spirit, we should have won our Utopia with labour and stress—and behold it would be stillborn!

Anxious as I am to avoid controversial matter in this paper, I cannot conceal from myself that it is upon this point that the real practical conflict and division within our society is likely to arise; the division between dispersed, masked, and so-called "practical" activities on the one hand, and concentration upon propaganda upon the other, propaganda that will prepare the way for an open political campaign of socialists as socialists, in the coming years. You know this particular question is a question of the economy of energy, these minor activities, these little interferences, I contend, waste our energies and our resources, and are in the net result a loss. In the past it is quite possible that they have served a useful and educational purpose, but that time is over now. The time has come for us to attack.

It is possible that this Fabian indirectness is associated with the very name of our society. Quite early in that history, I am told, indeed in its very birth beginnings, it was decided that the time was not ripe for battle, that the electoral masses were unprepared for socialism, that fresh forces had to be accumulated, new methods and disciplines and plans worked out. Mr. Frank Podmore, one of our earliest members, discovered an analogy in the condition of Rome after Hannibal had defeated the Roman army at Lake Thrasymenus and when Fabius Maximus was made dictator. Fabius, you will remember, with such crude and insufficient forces as he had at his disposal, at once took to the hills and mountains, avoided battle on every occasion, sought petty advantages, sought opportunities of catching his enemy at a disadvantage. They were, *for the time*, the proper tactics to pursue. He did gather and husband strength for Rome. So Fabius became our godfather, and the waiting game our method. A quotation was invented to point the moral of this choice. You all know that quotation, of course; "For the right moment you must wait, as Fabius did most patiently when warring against Hannibal, though many censured his delays; but when the time comes you must strike hard, as Fabius did, or your waiting will be in vain, and fruitless." Now the interesting thing to remark is, not that this passage is a fabrication, but that it is untrue; when the time came, as you may see for yourself in Plutarch's Lives, Fabius did *not* strike hard. This waiting game, wise no doubt as its adoption was in the beginning, became at last an enervating habit of limited action.

I want you particularly to note that, to note how inactive methods react upon the soul. Fabius began by being a discreet general; he ended by being an impotent one. I am not sure that he did not come near being a disastrous one. If only Hannibal had not also had his touch of the Fabian quality, there seems little doubt that on three several occasions he might have taken Rome. But he, too, had caught the hovering habit. You will find the closing passages of Plutarch's account of Fabius Maximus melancholy but instructive reading. When the time came for action he led the party of paralysis. He opposed the counter attack that destroyed Carthage with extraordinary subtlety, persistence, and bitterness.

We read that Scipio "being appointed consul, and finding that the people expected something great and striking at his hands, considered it as an antiquated method and worthy only of the inactivity of an old man, to watch the motions of Hannibal in Italy; therefore determined to remove the seat of war from thence into Africa, to fill the enemy's country with his legions, to extend his ravages far and wide, and to attempt Carthage itself. With this view he exerted all his talents to bring the people into his design. But Fabius, on this occasion, filled the city with alarms, as if the commonwealth was going to be brought into the most extreme danger by a rash and indiscreet young man; in short, he scrupled not to do or say anything he thought likely to dissuade his countrymen from embracing the proposal. . . . He applied to Crassus, the colleague of Scipio, and endeavoured to persuade him not to yield to Scipio, but, if he thought it proper to conduct the war in that matter, to go himself against Carthage. Nay, he even hindered the raising of money for that expedition: so that Scipio was obliged to find the supplies as he could . . . Fabius therefore, took another method to traverse the design. He endeavoured to prevent the young men who offered to go as volunteers from giving in their names, and loudly declared both in the senate and forum, 'That Scipio did not only himself avoid Hannibal, but intended to carry away with him the remaining strength of Italy, persuading the young men to abandon their parents, their wives, and native municipality, whilst an unsubdued and potent enemy was still at their doors.'" . . .

The Romans destroyed Carthage, as you know, but poor old Fabius did not live to see the end. With Hannibal gone out of Italy, with the long habits of a lifetime broken and shattered, with nothing to wait for, nothing to hover round, he pined, and sickened, and died.

Well, you see how dangerous and paralysing the Fabian tradition can become. I don't suggest for a moment it has become so, to any extent, in this society. I offer this merely as a warning. Nothing has been more encouraging to me than the alacrity with which the enquiries, the suggestions I have made have been met. I am not in conflict with our executive, I am attacking no "Old Gang"—don't think I am. I believe much is wrong with our society, I have made a rather elaborate diagnosis to find out what can be done, I have had to criticise and blame, but so far as I have been able I have avoided personal conflict. I have met no Fabius among your executive practically. The readiness to help in this project of reconstruction has been very great, so great as almost to be embarrassing. Help comes in from every side, and the thing has been at times almost wrenched from my hands by eager and experienced co-operation. If we really do contrive to purge our faults and begin a new career, I am sure you will have your executive chiefly to thank.

Only a point or so of fault finding remains. But please do not run away with the impression that I have nothing but faults to find in the Fabian Society. I could, if I chose to praise, find much to outweigh all these faults, in our meetings, in our executive, in the activities I dealt with so lightly in my opening, in our staff. Praise is an agreeable exercise; it is sometimes very useful as a tonic. But that is not my business to-night; good as we are, we all know that. . . . I am playing the part of Devil's Advocate, I admit, but if I thought the Fabian Society was all wrong, should I be here to-night urging it to new enterprises? It is because I believe in our society, it is the result of much frank and intimate conversation with various members of your executive, and the firmest confidence that I shall not be misunderstood, it is in the conviction that we can rise to a searching of hearts and open confession without great stresses, that I have criticised our society so frankly.

And now, what do I propose we should do?

Obviously, my first proposal is that we should grow. We must get more members, more funds, a bigger staff, an altogether larger and more active organization. And first, as to getting new members. I think it is high time that we cut our last link with that temperately Bohemian drawing-room, sweep away all this complicated business about introductions and letters of recommendation, and simply require a declaration of general sympathy and agreement with socialism of the most elementary description, that, and the payment of a subscription from the new convert. And I propose also that we make our net still wider by getting in every possible person who is interested in socialism, or who disputes against socialism, or who wants to watch the proceedings of socialism, as a subscriber* to this society. Let us make this institution of subscribers a reality. Then having made our door as easy to open as it possibly can be, let us set all our members at once to the business of bringing in fresh members; let us at once set a snowball of personal propaganda going, particularly among the young.

Directly we get this under way, you will find a need for a new set of tracts. We want a special set that one can put in the hand of the possible convert, who doesn't quite see this, who wants to know that, who raises all the hackneyed old objections. Constantly I am being asked for some book or some tract of this sort, and it doesn't exist. Let us make it exist. Let us have some sort of special propaganda committee that can revise whatever tracts for the neophyte we do already publish; expand them, re-write them if necessary, add to them, and make a complete little gospeller's outfit. If I may make an unblushing proposal at this point I would say that you had better give a good piece of that job to me. I am pretty keen on it, and I am prepared—if you will give me a certain amount of freedom—to put in time and work at it. Well, then, when we have got this series of tracts, I propose we shall not only use them through our existing members in that snowball of propaganda, but also that we should publish them as widely as we possibly can.

From the very start, if we are to get this going, we shall want money, and we shall want all the secretarial assistance we can get.

* In the subsequent debate, Mr. T. B. Simmons made the excellent suggestion that we should imitate the Y.M.C.A., and have members (believers) and associates (not necessarily believers).

The real organ of growth in every society is the secretarial office. There may be convulsions of expansion, but there can be no steady growth without the sustained work of active, tactful, dexterous personalities—who will be constantly marking down, following up, trying at, new helpers, new fields of work, new resources of money, personality, enthusiasm. We want money, we want office organization, and secretarial assistance. At first I don't see any way of bringing in any of these things except by members *giving*. We must give. For this new start we shall want work given, time given, money given, thought given, zeal, and much mutual charity—the rarest of all gifts. Well, except for the last, I don't think there will be much difficulty about that part of the business. I believe you are prepared to give. I believe that if members understand they will get something like a show for what they give, they will give with extraordinary readiness. For some time they haven't had much of a show. That we have to change. I don't believe it would be really difficult to raise an initial fund of a thousand pounds or so, if we convince one another we mean business. So I think we could set the ball rolling.

But this giving will be done chiefly in the first enthusiasm of the new effort. It won't go on at the same pace. I have grave doubts of the wisdom of running a large and growing movement of this kind upon the chance of repeated gifts, and my next proposal is that we should try to increase the average subscription of our members. I propose to revive here a suggestion made some time ago by Webb, and which was not taken up at the time very encouragingly. Well—this is the second time of asking. Suppose then, instead of leaving the subscription to the choice of the new member—nobody knowing what the others give, and everyone feeling a little uncomfortable over the business—suppose we charged everyone at least five shillings as a minimum, and in addition invited them to tax themselves upon what they believed to be their incomes. Now, how much might we hope for, how much in the way of a tax can we ask for, and how much will members stand? Well, my suggestion is a graduated income tax. I propose that a quarter per cent. should be paid on an income under two hundred and fifty pounds a year and half per cent. on anything above that amount. I would go further and say one per cent. on a thousand pounds or over. I don't think that is an unreasonable demand to make from people sincerely anxious for a fundamental change in the economic basis of society, and I certainly think it would raise our average subscription from the half guinea at which it, roughly speaking, stands at present, to considerably over a pound. We ought to have this matter clearly settled before the society really begins to grow. The old system of voluntary assessments is really just another lingering trace of the drawing-room days, in which so-and-so would go to so-and-so and say, we're short this time again, and then ask someone to make it up.

Very well; so soon as you have got your tracts under way, your war chest filled, and the propaganda beginning, you will have to get into more convenient, more extensive, more attractive offices, you will have to have a thorough revision of your secretarial department, better accommodation for your ordinary meetings, and so on. Our offices at present are singularly unattractive; they give the new member no pride of proprietorship, to my eye they are aggressively, untidily, dingily "practical"—in the worst sense of the word. They miss entirely a social element we ought to have if we are to carry on a large movement. The young people we want to help us ought to come to our offices to talk, to be stimulated, to be helped, to be given work. They don't get anything of the sort. Our rooms ought to suggest a new and more pleasant way of living, they ought to be light and beautiful and hopeful, instead of being a dismal basement lit through a grating. The intruder ought to be dexterously handled—made the most of. Our secretary will probably say he has too much to do already and so on, that it isn't his speciality to convert the young and pacify the bores. He's quite justified in that. So we must get in a second secretary for that side of the business.

When first I drafted this plan I felt a twinge of compunction or so at the thought of how dreadfully all this will bother Mr. Pease. But I felt too that he had to be bothered; our cause was of more account even than that, and I know now much more clearly than I did how ready he is to face such botheration for the sake of our common ends. Of course, if we do anything at all, we shall have to pile assistance upon Mr. Pease from the very beginning—helpers, colleagues. How are we going to get them in the first instance? Perhaps in the beginning we may have to do with the services of volunteers, but for the regular persistent work which this project will involve, if it is not to shrivel and fade, we must have the whole time of specializing workers; we must have a large and increasingly numerous paid staff. I have very clearly in my eye the sort of helpers we want. We want energetic young men and young women whose ambition it is to push themselves into journalism, into political journalism, into affairs. That's the stuff we must look to. I believe if we were to offer mere maintenance allowances of seventy pounds to eighty pounds a year, we should get some extraordinarily good material. I believe there are, so far as our wants go, no end of young university men, of ambitious clerks, of board school teachers, of students, who would leap at such an opportunity, take the risks of it. I may be wrong, but that is my impression.

I suggest, therefore, that so soon as our propaganda gets under way, we should make a direct appeal to our younger members to come in as volunteer helpers and show their quality, and directly our finances permitted it, begin a salary for first one and then another of these. As I have said, I believe it is possible that we may get an average subscription from our members of about a pound a member. At that rate we should be able to run four or five new salaried propaganda secretaries for every thousand members.

So far the Fabian Society has never touched the figure of one thousand members, but unless I am the most unsubstantial of dreamers, such a propaganda as I am putting before you now, ought to carry our numbers up towards ten thousand within a year or so of its commencement. Long before that figure is reached, some process of decentralization must begin. The organization of local meetings must commence in each district as its population of Fabians thickens. I am disposed to attach great importance to the development of local and subordinate nuclei from the very beginning of the new movement. That brings me back to another and very difficult problem, which the Fabian has never, I think, really attempted to solve; and that is, the incorporation of the green members, the young members, the inexpert members, in the society's discussions. There is not only no attempt to get them in, but it seems to me there is even something like a disinclination to welcome them when they do get up. I am enormously impressed by the difficulty a new and untried member must encounter in speaking at these central meetings. The thought of that carries me back to the days when I used to hesitate, and long to bear my witness, in Morris's little meetings at Kelmscott House. It was much less formidable at that place, but I funked it always, and went silently away. Now here, about this platform, you have this sort of family pew of old and tested Fabians; we include some admirable debaters, and one or two of the most interesting and most entertaining speakers in the world. Well, the young member, who is after all the more important person here, sits in the background, keeps in the background—is never lured out of it, feels he isn't wanted out of it.

Nobody looks in his direction; your audience is looking for Webb, is looking for Shaw, it wants Bland, or Macrosty, or Pease, it is inclined to be just a little impatient, perhaps, with an inexpert new speaker; and so your new member comes, longing to take a part, and he really gets a most interesting display; and he goes away with a sense that he hasn't taken a part, that he isn't in it, that he isn't doing anything, that there is nothing he can do, and at last he drifts away. That, from the point of view of socialistic progress, is a grave loss. It is our essential failure, that failure. And if that is true of our members, still more is it true of our visitors. I wonder how many thousands of people have drifted through our meetings, have felt drawn to socialism, interested in socialism, actually converted to socialism, who might with a better constructed net, have been caught and retained in its service. Even so obvious an opportunity as the talk that goes on after a meeting is made nothing of. I have noticed after a paper is read here, people, new people, shy visitors, the people we want to get in, display a tendency to push up and talk. What do we do to encourage them? Usually we start turning out the lights.

I believe, too, that small subordinate local meetings, where inexpert speakers can find courage for discussion, little semi-social gatherings in private houses, in students' rooms, would be of enormous help in intercepting this leakage of possible socialists. I believe it would not pass the wit of man to organize and keep alive and healthy a great network of such local nuclei centring upon your office. I would like to see a students' Fabian Society branch in every college of the London University, and in these subordinate centres discussion would arise, papers would germinate, and come up prepared and tested to the central meetings here. All this is the most possible thing in the world given secretarial efficiency; all of it becomes hopeless, if things are to remain as they are in your central office. And to that I return as the vital and inevitable condition of any vigorous new development.

I will not go at any length into the question of the possibility of organizing the more religious aspect of socialistic propaganda—because, you know, socialism is religious, is to many people at any rate a sufficient religion; but I can see a very clear possibility of Sunday afternoon gatherings, for example, in which the emotional spirit of our propaganda should be kept alive and intensified. I believe that among other possibilities the propaganda I am proposing to would from the first fall into a sort of working alliance with a number of the ethical societies that are scattered about London. . . .

Finally, I will mention only in the most cursory way that it seems to me if we are not able to reconstruct the Fabian with a view to propaganda, then the alternative will be to set up a sort of propaganda wing, a daughter society, to do this work that we decline. None of us, I think, want a rival society, anyhow. . . .

Mr. Wells then proceeded to outline the committee he suggested should develop the scheme he had in this broad manner sketched.

CONTENTS OF THE FIRST AND
SECOND POST-IMPRESSIONIST SHOWS

(Titles are as given in the catalogues of the shows)

1. The First Show (Nov. 8, 1910–Jan. 15, 1911)

Oils and Water Colors

CÉZANNE, PAUL
Les Ondines
Nature morte
Paysage, St.-Cloud
L'Estaque
Nature morte
Portrait de l'artiste
Portrait de Mme. Cézanne
Les Pétunias
Dame au chapelet
La Toilette
Les Maisons
La Route
Baigneurs
Le grand pin
Petit chemin
Portrait d'homme à cravate bleue
La maison blanche
La Montagne Victoire
Maison à Auvers-sur-Oise
La maison du pendu
La Maison jaune

CROSS, HENRI-EDMOND
Coup de vent d'Est
Petites montagnes mauresques

DENIS, MAURICE
Orphée
Calypso
St. Georges
Nausicaa
Madone au jardin fleuri

DERAIN, ANDRÉ
Martigues
Eglise de Carrières
Le Parc de Carrières

FLANDRIN, JULES
La danse des vendanges
Scène champêtre

FRIESZ, OTHON
Anvers (Août)
Orage à Anvers
Croiseur pavoisé (Anvers)

GAUGUIN, PAUL
Adam et Eve
Fleurs au fond jaune
Étude de femme
Pont Aveu, 1888, Bretagne
Vue sur la Martinique: les cochons noirs
Nature morte: Tournesols

Bouquet de Fleurs
Femme sous les Palmiers
Martinique
Nature morte
Enfants
Portrait de M. X——
Nature morte
L'Appel
La Religieuse
La Montagne Sacrée
Négresses
L'Esprit veille
L'Esprit du Mal
Maternité
Les cochons noirs dans la
  prairie
Rêverie
Paysage Breton
Paysage bleu
Fleurs de soleil
Les Laveuses
Les Coiffes blanches
Le Christ au Jardin des
  Oliviers
Grandes Baigneuses
Paysage Bretonne
Two Breton Peasants
Pont Aveu
Tahitian Family
Groupe, de Bretonnes
Joseph and Potiphar's Wife
Oil painting (unfinished)

GIRIEUD, PIERRE
Paysage à Sienne
Rue à l'ombre
Paysage à Sienne
Paysage à Sienne
Paysage à Sienne

HERBIN, AUGUSTE
Vase de fleurs
Bruges
Maison au quai vert
Fruits

LAPRADE, PIERRE
Femme à l'éstampe
Nature morte aux Géraniums
Water Colour: Le Forum
Pinchio Rome

MANET, EDOUARD
Portrait d'enfant
Mademoiselle Lemonnier
L'Amazone
Un bar aux Folies-Bergère
Le femme aux souliers roses
Au Café
Baigneuses
La Promenade
Miss Campbell (pastel)

MANGUIN, HENRI
La Plaine de Cavalière
Nature morte
Paysage, Saint Tropez

MARQUET, ALBERT
Plage à Sainte Adresse
Notre Dame, Paris

MATISSE, HENRI
Paysage
Paysage
La femme aux yeux verts

PICASSO, PABLO
Nude girl with basket of
  flowers
Portrait de M. Sagot

PUY, JEAN
La Balançoire

REDON, ODILON
Vase de Fleurs
Le Christ
Femme d'Orient

ROUAULT, GEORGES
six untitled landscapes

SÉRUSIER, PAUL
  Les Vallons
  La Pluie
  Vallée, temps gris
  Paysage Convent
  Récolte du Sarrazin

SEURAT, GEORGES
  La plage
  Le Phare à Honfleur

SIGNAC, PAUL
  Bellevue
  Saint Tropez en fête
  Le Remorqueur

VALLOTTON, FELIX
  Femmes (Le Tub)
  La jetée de Honfleur
  Coup de vent à Dieppe,
    Juillet 14
  Marée Basse

VALTAT, LOUIS
  Paysage

VAN GOGH, VINCENT
  Orchard in Provence
  Garden of Daubigny in
    Auvers-sur-Oise
  Orchard in Provence
  Paysage

View near Arles
Iris
Le Postier
Jeune fille au bleuet (the
  mad girl in Zola's "Ger-
  minal")
Pont d'Asnières
Les Usines
Les blés d'or
Cornfield with Rooks
Les Soleils
Dr. Gachet
Pietà (after Delacroix)
Resurrection of Lazarus
  (after Rembrandt etching)
La Berceuse
Le gardeur d'oies
Arles
Cyprès
Evening Landscape
Tournesols

VLAMINCK, MAURICE DE
  Fleurs
  Le Remorqueur
  Le pont
  Le pont, Nantes
  La Voile
  La Garenne-Bezons
  Le Bougeoir
  Le Château

Drawings (nearly all untitled)

FLANDRIN—4.
FRIESZ—4.
GAUGUIN—10.
GIRIEUD—3.
LAPRADE—3.
MAILLOL—3.

MANGUIN—1.
MARQUET—3.
MATISSE—12.
PICASSO—7.
SIGNAC—2.

Sculpture

MAILLOL, ARISTIDE
  Femme aux bras levés

Femme sans bras
Femme avec un bras

Femme assise
Femme baissée

MATISSE, HENRI
Le Serf
Buste d'enfant
Fillette debout

Femme accroupie
Femme s'appuyant sur les
mains
Femme couchée
Torse
Buste de jeune fille

Faience pottery

DERAIN—2
FRIESZ—1
GIRIEUD—2

MATISSE—1
VLAMINCK—3

2. The Second Show (Oct. 5–Dec. 31, 1912)

The French Group

ASSELIN, MAURICE
Anticoli
Nature Morte
Parc Monceau
Usine à St. Denis
Notre Dame
Venus de Milo
water colors

BONNARD, PIERRE
La Salle à Manger
La Chasse
La Cascade

BRAQUE, GEORGES
Kubelik
La Forêt
La Calangue
Anvers

CAMIS, MAX
Batignoles

CÉZANNE, PAUL
Le Château Noir
La maison rouge dans les
arbres
Le Dauphin du Jas de
Bouffon

Les Moissonneurs
Gennevilliers
Maisons (aquarelle)
Village et la Montagne
Victoire (aquarelle)
La Maison sur la Colline
(aquarelle)
Nature Morte (aquarelle)
La Cahute (aquarelle)
La femme à la mante
(aquarelle)

CHABAUD, AUGUSTE
Chemin dans la Montagnette
Le troupeau sort après la
pluie
three untitled drawings

DERAIN, ANDRÉ
Le Rideau
La Forêt
La fenêtre sur le parc
Le Panier
L'Eglise
Le pot bleu

VAN DONGEN, KEES
Portrait de Madame Van
Dongen

La femme en blanc
Le doigt sur la joue
La fillette au bois

DOUCET, HENRI
Vauboyen
Le Repas
Jeune ouvrier
Route entres les murs
Les Moissonneuses

FLANDRIN, JULES
Porte de la Cuisine
Savoie
Canal à Venise
Paysage
Basilique Romaine
Pivoines

FRIESZ, OTHON
Composition
Nature Morte
Nature Morte
Paysage

GIRIEUD, PIERRE
Fleurs
Siena
Hommage à Gauguin
three untitled landscapes
Siena

HERBIN, AUGUSTE
Nature Morte
Le Pont Neuf (three
  versions)
Nature Morte (Livre et
  Corbeille)
Viaduc
five untitled landscapes

L'HOTE, ANDRÉ
Paysage à la vache
Tête de Nègre
Port de Bordeaux

Paysage d'Hiver
Paysage à la locomotive
Fortifications
La Rivière (watercolor)
La Banlieue (watercolor)
La vache (watercolor)
Sous les arbres (watercolor)
L'Embarcadère (watercolor)
La Lune (watercolor)

MARCHAND, JEAN-HIPPOLYTE
Nature Morte
Marly-le-Roi (two versions)
Vue de Ville

MARQUET, ALBERT
Femme au "Rocking Chair"
Le nu à contre-jour
St. Jean de Luz

MARVAL, MME. JACQUELINE-
MARIE
Les Lys
Esquisse pour une Com-
  position

MATISSE, HENRI
L'Enfant au cheval
La pose du nu
Les Capucines
Joaquina
Nu au bord de la mer
Nature Morte (Citrons)
La Coiffeuse
Cyclamens
Conversation
Les Poissons rouges
Portrait de Marguerite
Portrait au madras rouge
Le luxe
Les aubergines
Coucous sur le tapis bleu et
  rose
Le panneau rouge
Jeune Marin

Les Poissons
lithographs
sculptures:
Le Dos (plaster sketch)
L'Araignée (plaster)
Buste de Femme (plaster,
    1st state)
Buste de Femme (plaster,
    2nd state)
Buste de Femme (3rd state)
Buste de Femme (bronze)
Femme Accroupie (bronze)
Jaguar dévorant un Tigre
    (plaster; after Barye)

OTTMAN, HENRI
Route entre les arbres
Paysage

PICASSO, PABLO
Le Bouillon Kub
Composition
Nature Morte
Les Arbres
Nature Morte
Tête de Femme
Mademoiselle L. B.
Tête de Femme

Les Bananes
Tête d'homme
Livres et flacons
Buffalo Bill
La Femme au Pot de
    Moutarde
three untitled drawings

PUY, JEAN
La Baignade
Portrait de Madame Puy
Jeune fille à la Fenêtre

ROUSSEAU, HENRI
Scène de Forêt

VILETTE, CHARLES
Bois-Colombes
Nature Morte

VLAMINCK, MAURICE DE
Buzenval
Les Figues
Pontoise
Chapeau et gants
Rueil
L'Estuaire de la Seine
Rouen
Viaduc St. Germain

The English Group

ADENEY, BERNARD
The Barn
The Square
The Saw Mill
The Temple

BELL, VANESSA
Asheham
Nosegay
The Spanish Model
The Mantelpiece

ETCHELLS, FREDERICK
Landscape
Landscape

The Blue Thistle
The Dead Mole
Courtyard
On the Grass

ETCHELLS, JESSIE
Sussex Farm

FRY, ROGER
The Cascade
Newington House
Angles sur Langlin
The Terrace
Siena

GILL, ERIC (all sculpture)
  The Golden Calf
  Contortionist (Marble)
  Contortionist (Hopton-wood stone)
  The Poser (Hopton-wood Stone)
  Madonna and Child (Marble)
  St. Simeon Stylites
  A Garden Statue (Portland Stone)

GORE, F. SPENCER
  The Tree
  Letchworth Station

GRANT, DUNCAN
  The Seated Woman
  Henri Doucet

  The Queen of Sheba
  The Dancers
  The Countess
  Pamela

LAMB, HENRY
  Portrait of Lytton Strachey
  Composition

LEWIS, WYNDHAM
  Mother and Child
  Creation
  eight drawings from Timon of Athens series

SPENCER, STANLEY
  John Donne arriving in Heaven
  Composition
  Study for painting

The Russian Group

VON ANREP, BORIS
  L'Arbre sacré
  The desolation
  L'homme construisant un puits pour désaltérer le bétail
  Project for Mural Decoration
  Fisa playing on his Harp
  Allegorical composition

CHOURLIANIS
  The Knight
  The Mountain
  Rex

HASSENBERG, MME. RENA
  Mespoli
  Coin de Village
  Fuchsias

JOUKOFF, MLLE. VERA
  Portrait of an Old Woman

KOMAROVSKY, COUNT
  Gabriel
  The Virgin
  The Annunciation

LEWITZKA, MLLE. SOPHIE
  Nature morte (bouteille, mimosa)
  St. Nom

PETROFF-WODKINE, COSMA
  Les Gosses
  Site near the Volga

ROERICH, NICHOLAS
  Priests of Beyond
  Designs for Theatrical Costumes
  Night
  Village by night
  Ancient Russian Burgh
  The Goblin's Bower

The Sacred City
Gifts
The Battle of the Heavens

STELLETZKY, DMITRI
Four Decorative Panels
The Yard of the Kremlin in
the time of John the
Terrible

The Fox Hunt
The Tzaritza and her train
on a pilgrimage
The Stag Hunt
Le génie et la vie

ZAK, EUGÈNE
Le Berger
drawing

Index